A Feminist Companion to Mark

Feminist Companion to the New Testament
and Early Christian Writings, 2

A Feminist Companion to

Mark

edited by
Amy-Jill Levine
with Marianne Blickenstaff

Sheffield
Academic Press
www.SheffieldAcademicPress.com

Copyright © 2001 Sheffield Academic Press

Published by Sheffield Academic Press Ltd
Mansion House
19 Kingfield Road
Sheffield, S11 9AS
England

Printed on acid-free paper in Great Britain
by The Cromwell Press
Trowbridge, Wiltshire

British Library Cataloguing-in-Publication Data

A catalogue record for this book is available
from the British Library

ISBN 1 84127 194 2

CONTENTS

PREFACE

A Feminist Companion to Mark is the second volume in a new series with excellent precedent. These volumes on the texts and history of Christian Origins adopt the model established by Athalya Brenner, editor of the enormously successful Feminist Companion to the Bible. This sister to FCB marks an important new dimension in Sheffield Academic Press's list of titles in the areas of feminist hermeneutics and theology, and its content will underline the extent to which feminist critique is established as a core discipline of biblical, historical and theological research.

The new series, like FCB, contains contributions by new as well as established scholars; it presents both previously published work (primarily from sources either out of print or difficult to find) and new essays. In some cases, scholars have been invited to re-visit their earlier work to examine the extent to which their arguments and approaches have changed; in others, they have sought to apply their earlier insights to new texts.

We wish to thank both Marianne Blickenstaff for her numerous organizational contributions as well as her discerning insights, and the Kathy Williams for her help with proofreading. We also wish to thank the Carpenter Program in Religion, Gender and Sexuality at Vanderbilt Divinity School for financial and technical support.

This series seeks international representation; to this end, gratitude is due, as well, to Vanderbilt Divinity School, which has provided funding for translating into English both previously published work and new articles.

It is our hope that this new series will quickly establish itself as a standard work of reference to scholars, students and also to others interested in the New Testament and Christian Origins.

Amy-Jill Levine, Vanderbilt Divinity School
Philip R. Davies, Sheffield Academic Press

ACKNOWLEDGMENTS

The editors and publisher are grateful to the following for permission to reproduce copyright material: *Catholic Biblical Quarterly* for 'The Poor Widow in Mark and Her Poor Rich Readers', by Elizabeth Struthers Malbon, from *CBQ* 53; and Orbis Books for *Women and Jesus in Mark: A Japanese Feminist Perspective* (1991).

ABBREVIATIONS

ARA	*Annual Review of Anthropology*
ATR	*Anglican Theological Review*
BA	*Biblical Archaeologist*
BAGD	Walter Bauer, William F. Arndt, F. William Gingrich and Frederick W. Danker, *A Greek–English Lexicon of the New Testament and Other Early Christian Literature* (Chicago: University of Chicago Press, 2nd edn, 1958)
BETL	Bibliotheca ephemeridum theologicarum lovaniensium
BibInt	*Biblical Interpretation: A Journal of Contemporary Approaches*
BJS	Brown Judaic Studies
BNTC	Black's New Testament Commentaries
BR	*Bible Review*
BTB	*Biblical Theology Bulletin*
BZNW	Beihefte zur ZNW
CBQ	*Catholic Biblical Quarterly*
CQ	*Church Quarterly*
ETR	*Études théologiques et religieuses*
EvT	*Evangelische Theologie*
HDB	James Hastings (ed.), *A Dictionary of the Bible* (5 vols.; New York: Charles Scribner's Sons, 1898–1904)
HeyJ	*Heythrop Journal*
HTR	*Harvard Theological Review*
HUCA	*Hebrew Union College Annual*
IEJ	*Israel Exploration Journal*
Int	*Interpretation*
ISBE	Geoffrey Bromiley (ed.), *The International Standard Bible Encyclopedia* (4 vols.; Grand Rapids: Eerdmans, rev. edn, 1979–88)
JAOS	*Journal of the American Oriental Society*
JBL	*Journal of Biblical Literature*
JFSR	*Journal of Feminist Studies in Religion*
JHS	*Journal of Hellenic Studies*
JJS	*Journal of Jewish Studies*
JQR	*Jewish Quarterly Review*
JR	*Journal of Religion*

JRH	*Journal of Religious History*
JSNT	*Journal for the Study of the New Testament*
JSNTSup	*Journal for the Study of the New Testament*, Supplement Series
LCL	Loeb Classical Library
LIMC	John Boardman, *et al.* (eds.), *Lexicon Iconographicum Mythologiae Classicae* (8 vols.; Zürich: Artemis Verlag, 1981–97)
LSJ	H.G. Liddell, Robert Scott and H. Stuart Jones, *Greek–English Lexicon* (Oxford: Clarendon Press, 9th edn, 1968)
NA	Nestle-Aland, *Novum Testamentum Graece*
NIB	*New Interpreter's Bible*
NovT	*Novum Testamentum*
NRSV	New Revised Standard Version
NTS	*New Testament Studies*
PEQ	*Palestine Exploration Quarterly*
RSN	*Religious Studies News*
RSV	Revised Standard Version
SBLDS	SBL Dissertation Series
SNTSMS	Society for New Testament Studies Monograph Series
TDNT	Gerhard Kittel and Gerhard Friedrich (eds.), *Theological Dictionary of the New Testament* (trans. Geoffrey W. Bromiley; 10 vols.; Grand Rapids: Eerdmans, 1964–)
UBS	United Bible Society, *The Greek New Testament*
VT	*Vetus Testamentum*
VTSup	*Vetus Testamentum*, Supplements
WBC	Word Biblical Commentary
ZNW	*Zeitschrift für die neutestamentliche Wissenschaft*

LIST OF CONTRIBUTORS

Kathleen Corley, Department of Religious Studies and Anthropology, University of Wisconsin, Oshkosh, WI, USA

Wendy J. Cotter, CSJ, Department of Theology Loyola University of Chicago, Chicago, IL, USA

Joanna Dewey, Episcopal Divinity School, Cambridge, MA, USA

Hisako Kinukawa, International Christian University, Tokyo Women's Christian University Tokyo, Japan

Deborah Krause, Eden Theological Seminary, St Louis, MO, USA

Dennis R. MacDonald, Claremont School of Theology, Claremont, CA, USA

Elizabeth Struthers Malbon, Religious Studies Program Center for Interdisciplinary Studies, Virginia Polytechnic Institute and State University, Blacksburg, VA, USA

Victoria Phillips, West Virginia Wesleyan College, Buckhannon, WV, USA

Ranjini Wickramaratne Rebera, Consultant: Gender and Communication, Ngunnawal, Australia

Sharon H. Ringe, Wesley Theological Seminary, Washington, DC, USA

Marianne Sawicki, Department of Philosophy and Religious Studies, Morgan State University, Baltimore, MD, USA

INTRODUCTION

Amy-Jill Levine

It is appropriate that these essays on the Gospel of Mark begin with a contribution from Joanna Dewey, who was among the first of the contemporary feminist readers of the Gospels. Dewey offers both a history of modern feminist biblical study and an example of how its rigorous attention to history and language can lead to liberatory exegesis. As Dewey relates, those first feminist strides were taken with enthusiasm and idealism. She and her early colleagues (including Sharon Ringe, who contributes a similarly reflective essay to this collection) both named and decried patriarchal texts and interpretations even as they located positive images of women and so recovered the Bible for many alienated from text and tradition. On the other hand, they projected onto their readings an essentialist view of women typical of much 1970s feminist thought, and they used rabbinic texts uncritically in order to show how Jesus or Paul offered something better than Judaism as was typical of much 1970s biblical studies. Overcoming the mistakes and oppressions of past scriptural interpretation in one sector, they reinscribed them in others.

Informed by both the benefits and drawbacks of these early steps, Dewey here turns her attention to Mk 8.34, Jesus' assertion that those who choose to follow him should 'renounce themselves and take up their cross', a verse that has been understood as a glorification of suffering and an encouragement to victimization. (This very focus belies a common misconception about feminist biblical interpretation: it does not address only texts that mention women.) Dewey's analytical focus begins with theology, a frequently neglected area in feminist biblical analysis, for it is theological interpretation, especially a particular interpretation of the cross, that has led to problematic conclusions. She then reveals how this focus on victimization results from the verse's detachment from its literary and historical contexts and the concomitant projecting onto it of modern understandings of the self. From Mark's text, Dewey observes an insistence on the alleviation, not the promotion, of suffering; from its first-century context, she determines the very limited referent to 'taking up one's cross', the different notion of 'self'-denial especially in terms of kinship groups, and the effects on interpretation of an apocalyptic worldview no longer held by most interpreters. By conjoining literary- and historical-criticism with attention to theology and contemporary need, Dewey demonstrates how the Bible itself, when approached critically and with the goal of liberation, can be used to undo the damage certain interpretations of it have caused.

Deborah Krause, although of a younger academic 'generation' than Dewey, holds the same commitment to reading texts toward the goal of liberation and narrates as effectively and as bravely as Dewey her personal experiences—in the academy and the church—that prompt and influence her study. Attending to the frequently overlooked (one exception is an excursus by Hisako Kinukawa contained in this volume) account of the service provided to Jesus and a few of his male followers by Simon Peter's mother-in-law (Mk 1.29-31), Krause demonstrates how feminist readers particularly within the academy (e.g. Schüssler Fiorenza, Schottroff and Tolbert) find in this brief narrative a 'utopian moment': Peter's mother-in-law represents women's discipleship if not diaconate. Yet she also observes that women in her Bible study groups, although appreciative of their canon, are much more suspicious of its glorification of domestic service.

The recognition of this distinction between the academy and the church, between 'professional' and 'naïve' readers, between those who study and those who clean (Mary and Martha come to mind) as well as of the need for crossing these boundaries and so facilitating discussion and critique, is at the forefront of much contemporary feminist thought. It is through these tensions between liberation and constraint, gender-determined servitude and egalitarian discipleship, that Krause finds a potentially more integrative interpretation of the passage. Her recognition of a both/and rather than either/or model may be one of feminism's major contributions to biblical studies: cognizant of the projection the earlier generation made of their own value-laden categories and informed by the critiques that readers outside North Atlantic, Caucasian, middle class (etc.) contexts brought to the implicit definitions of what is normative or 'good for' women, feminist critics today appreciate that there is more than one way to read a text, and that what is 'good news' for some may be the same old oppressive story for others.

Krause does not find a heroine, a life-transforming interpretation, or a happy ending. She may, however, have found something better: a site for reflection upon the ambiguities in the mother-in-law's portrait, and in our own lives.

Unlike Dewey and Krause, whose personal experiences explicitly prompt their exegesis, Wendy Cotter brings her expertise in Classics to seek the sources of Mk 5.21-43, the intertwined accounts of the woman with the hemorrhage and Jairus's daughter. Her meticulous analysis first reveals the extraordinary attention the evangelist gives to the woman—the only woman who seeks from Jesus a miracle for herself—even as it highlights the narrator's nervousness about her story. Moving next to address Mark's Greco-Roman context, Cotter details the anomaly of a woman who, unaccompanied, deliberately touches a strange man in public; no wonder Mark is anxious.

Turning then to the ruler's daughter, Cotter demonstrates the parallels not only with the often-cited accounts of Elijah and Elisha (including their depiction by Josephus), but also with less frequently evoked stories including those of Asclepius, Heracles, Apollonius of Tyana and Isis. She is then able to demonstrate the implications of the parallels for Markan Christology, a subject not always developed in relation to a narrative concerning women.

Cotter's interests in source-criticism and in Greco-Roman literature demonstrate other approaches not generally used or even sufficiently understood by many contemporary students of the Bible, including feminist readers. As the academy recognizes the importance of competence in various methods beyond traditional text- and source-critical concerns, and as biblical studies branches out into such fields as literary studies, sociology and anthropology, detailed attention to history, and especially to early Christianity's Greco-Roman and Jewish contexts, have become in some quarters of increasingly less importance. Reclaiming—since in some settings they need reclamation—the value of Classics and of traditional methods and applying them to stories about women, Cotter makes evident the contributions of older forms of analysis, now themselves utilized with greater awareness of their limitations as well as their benefits, offer to an understanding of textual representations of women.

From Simon's mother-in-law to the stories of Jairus's daughter and the hemorrhaging woman, we move from less to more popular sites for feminist exegesis. Among the most interrogated texts is the next Markan pericope, the meeting of Jesus and the Syrophoenician woman (Mk 7.24-31a). Sharon Ringe here revisits her earlier, highly influential 1985 study of this account to see how changes in her own competencies and perspectives, including additional considerations of class, ethnicity, education, age and health, prompt changes in her reading. Courageously and self-critically, she reads Mark's story again.

Like Krause, Ringe displays a greater comfort with ambiguity, both in her own agenda and in her necessarily interested reading: she finds both consolation and disturbance in the text, and in her own reactions to it. Her diverse impressions then serve as the catalyst through which she is prompted to understand more about Mark's social context, the literary devices at work in the narrative, and the theological implications of how the story affects present-day readers. Ringe's application of postcolonial reading strategies (an intrepid move, given her explicitly noted western and privileged location) facilitates her rereading of Mark's constructions of insider and outsider, gender and ethnicity, and instucts her assessments of her own positions of power and marginalization.

Attentive to the pericope's structure, geographical references, personal identifications, and dialogue as well as its cultural setting, Ringe no longer assumes the Syrophoenician woman to be an impoverished widow or the embodiment of the outcast and oppressed. The woman's crucial identification is now, for Ringe, that of a desperate mother who will do whatever is necessary to save her daughter.

Her reading of Jesus' refusal of aid complements this shift in her perception of the Syrophoenician. Jesus' refusal to heal the woman's demon-possessed daughter is now seen in terms of the disproportionate share of the Galilee's resources upon which Tyre and Sidon capitalize. Jesus' power in this interpretation may also be considered a limited resource, and one dedicated to 'those who always wait at the end of the line', his own people. Thus the feminist reading moves from a concentration on stereotypical attributions to a more subtle consideration of the characters' multiple identities.

Turning in her conclusion to studies of Mark published subsequent to the original article, Ringe places herself in dialogue with an expanded reading community ranging from Nicaraguan peasants to Asian, Australian and Hispanic academics. Given their various readings, Ringe can only confirm that the passage continues to perplex and elude her. Her earlier happier reading, in which a woman functions as a positive role model and Jesus evolves from sexist to 'teachable', is no longer befitting, but her impressions about the importance of reading in as diverse a community as possible and of sharing accountability, create surely healthier, necessarily tentative, and possibly even happier consequences.

Ranjini Wickramaratne Rebera, who writes from a postcolonial, South Asian perspective, confirms the import of Ringe's observations.

By addressing the categories of clean and unclean which she finds in Mark 7, the encounter of monotheism with polytheism, and the question of women's voice and marginalization, she demonstrates how the story reflects the experiences of some South Asian Christian women and inspires them to fight for change.

Describing how notions of purity can disempower women, Wickramaratne Rebera opens with a personal reflection on the condemnation she received from a 'good Christian' for accepting a gift from a Hindu friend. For Wickramaratne Rebera, the dialogue between Jewish man and Syrophoenician woman serves as a corrective to such a limited (at best) reaction. She presents the encounter on the border of Tyre and Sidon as a model for sustaining multi-religious and intercultural respect, especially in a pluralistic setting such as Sri Lanka. The woman claims her inclusion within Jesus' circle without losing her distinct racial and ethnic identity. Simultaneously, the woman becomes an icon for women of South Asia who resist discrimination where rituals, customs and attitudes treat them as unclean and therefore dirty or dangerous.

Wickramaratne Rebera then turns to the Syrophoenician woman's tenacity, her continual calling out to Jesus as she seeks a healing for her daughter. By reading the woman's persistent voice as an ongoing echo of women's vocal participation in political rallies, this essay demonstrates 'the power of shouting as a means for confrontation and resolution'. With this step coupled with her observations on the marginalizing of women in her social location, Wickramaratne Rebera compellingly explores the alternatives the pericope presents not merely to inter-faith relations or the silencing of women's voices, but also to cultures in which female children are aborted or killed. She thereby recognizes the power of women's voices even as she underscores the deadly ways in which they have been and continue to be silenced.

Elizabeth Struthers Malbon's 'The Poor Widow in Mark and Her Poor Rich Readers', originally published in the *Catholic Biblical Quarterly* (1991), accentuates how differing approaches create an embarrassment of riches: for some pericopae, there is too much to be said. Opening with an analysis of interpretations ranging from Swete (1898) to A. Wright (1982), Malbon explores the multiple contexts accorded the story of 'the widow's mite' within the larger Gospel narrative and so demonstrates that '*the* context does not exist'. Understanding the account requires not only multiple contextual readings but, in most cases, multiple contextual readers.

Malbon does not stop with the observation of difference; she rather offers several means by which readers can avoid sinking under the weight of singular, hegemonic claims or finding themselves floating off into space without an anchor of critical prudence. From the field of law, she locates a partial exemplar in the practice of advocacy. Although not a perfect model given its adversarial component, the advocacy approach has its benefits: different cases require different consultants, just as the differing interests readers import require information from different secondary sources. Perhaps an even better rubric may be one Malbon borrows from the historian of religions Jonathan Z. Smith: the view that the historian's task is to complicate, not clarify. The result is an appreciation not only for diverse contexts but also for various and even competing conclusions.

From the Markan widow and her multiple narrative contexts, we move to the 'woman who anointed Jesus' and one specific context: the field of Classics. Dennis R. MacDonald contests the common scholarly view that the account of the anointing (Mk 14.3-9) derives from an actual event in Jesus' life by detailing its parallels with the washing of Odysseus's feet by his old nurse, Eurycleia. The juxtaposition of Mark's Gospel and Homer's *Odyssey* for MacDonald reveals previously unobserved aspects of the evangelist's agenda: the desire that readers not only note the parallels in the single story but also view the anointing woman's recognition of Jesus' forthcoming passion, a recognition based on no external sign or word, as more perspicacious than the nurse's recognition of her former charge.

Although this approach is similar to Cotter's in its appeal to Classical parallels, for some readers it will be more threatening. MacDonald poses to those in search of history—not only those seeking women's presence but also those seeking 'the historical Jesus'—the question: what if a major scene, particularly one featuring an exceptionally positive depiction of a woman, is only that, a scene, and not an historical 'fact'? As some feminist readers today turn their attention from the search for 'real women' to the question of how gender is and can be constructed, MacDonald's approach provides some encouragement by demonstrating that an event need not be 'real' in order for it to be inspirational, if not liberatory.

Not all scholars are ready to dismiss the search for 'real women', or even the reality of Mark's anointing woman, as Marianne Sawicki demonstrates. Like MacDonald, Sawicki begins with Mk 14.3-9, the 'grooming of the messiah' as she describes it, and like MacDonald, she seeks earlier texts including those from the Greco-Roman corpus that might serve to enhance understanding of the pericope. She too is interested in conventional scenes, and she too casts doubt on the historicity of Mark's account. But her methods and her conclusions concerning women's roles and representations are dramatically different.

Informed by feminist anthropological work, Sawicki begins by dismissing the constructs of a unified Mediterranean cultural region, the categories of public and private, and the honor/shame model as unhelpful for understanding Mk 14.3-9. She then turns to Greek cultural comparisons and finds Mark may have adapted at least four components: tableaux involving a glass bottle containing perfumed balm, dining customs, the practice of a matron showering sweets and the discourse of tombs and mourning. The cultural tour (*de force*) that follows incorporates plays, vase art, philosophical texts, domestic architecture, and epitaphs in order to describe, *inter alia*, ancient uses of perfume, the function of 'belief', the relation of persuasion to seduction, practices of cooking and serving, girls' choirs and dancing schools, marriage customs, civic rituals and religious festivals. The tour concludes with possibly illuminating connections for Mark's account in the Septuagint, the Mishnah and Babylonian Talmud, and even cultural practices retained by elderly Jewish women in today's Jerusalem.

This interdisciplinary approach leads Sawicki to adduce several moments in the history behind Mark's narrative: a very early stage of women's recounting the death of a beloved man; the passing of this women's story to men; and their adding such traditions as male dining, the distribution of flesh and vicarious atonement. Although Sawicki has located a history for Mark's text, it is not a history that confirms the reality of the scene, or of Jesus' encounter with an anointing woman. Readers may tell the story 'in memory of her', but in doing so they may want to reconsider what has been remembered, by whom, and why. Through rigorous scholarly investigation, and through informed recreation, they may also consider what and who may have been forgotten.

The next two essays, by Hisako Kinukawa and Kathleen Corley, offer differing approaches to Mark's Passion Narrative. Kinukawa, contributing a revision of a chapter in her 1994 *Women and Jesus in Mark: A Japanese Feminist Perspective*, begins by declaring the impact of Elisabeth Schüssler Fiorenza's *In Memory of Her* on her feminist perspective and historical study. At the same time, she applies a hermeneutics of suspicion to the now-classic volume as she asks whether a 'discipleship of equals' was ever realized in Jesus' time. Her suspicion is prompted by Mark's usual separation of characters by gender coupled with her own experiences with what she describes as a patriarchal society, that of Japan.

Through a close reading of select events in the Markan Passion, Kinukawa demonstrates how the women disciples, and for her they are 'disciples', challenge not only patriarchal privilege but also those who refuse to join the struggle against it. In her reading, the women's discipleship of 'following and serving' is not a secondary mode de-signed to keep them in subordinate positions but a means by which a true community of faith, consisting of both women and men, may be (re)generated.

Proceeding from the same set of texts and employing an historical perspective, Kathleen Corley begins her investigation of gender and social class in Mark's Gospel. Her scrupulous research leads her to conclude that Jesus' women followers were perhaps hired servants or slaves and not the wealthier donors Lk. 8.1-3 suggests. Nor were they 'prostitutes', a group with whom Jesus is accused of consorting. Instead, Corley intriguingly posits that they were married but not in the company of their husbands, a possibility hinted at by Luke's refer-ence to Joanna the wife of Chuza the steward. Drawing on her earlier research on dining practices in Greco-Roman and early Jewish settings, she conjectures that women were likely present with Jesus at meals and that they likely traveled with him. Although Mark does not note their presence until the account of the crucifixion, Corley provides one reconstruction of their ongoing relationship with Jesus.

Corley then indicates how Mark incorporates, nervously (cf. Cotter), the authentic tradition of some female followers. Complementing Sawicki's argument but using different methods and sources, she too concludes that the all-male Last Supper narrative is a later literary creation, following Greco-Roman literary conventions. Thus, Jesus appears, at least in Mark's telling, as one who conforms to contempo-rary standards of social propriety and who by no means would dine with lower-class women or female servants. Only at the cross, a scandalous event in itself, does Mark finally acknowledge the women's presence, and that 'from afar'.

The final essay, by Victoria Phillips, moves from the cross to the tomb as it poses a question that has long perplexed readers, feminist or not: why do the women flee, silently, and in fear? Noting popular feminist readings—that the three women's failure mirrors the failure of the three sleepy men in Gesthemane and so presents a teaching about discipleship; that both men and women are faithful as well as flawed disciples—Phillips reveals the problems of comparison. The men's failing their teacher after promising loyalty is not equivalent to the women's failing to deliver a message; failing to obey Jesus is not equivalent to accepting an order from a strange man who has no claim on one's obedience. Failing Jesus at his moment of personal agony after he had detailed information about his fate is not equivalent to being silent: whereas the male disciples had been told that Jesus would meet them in Galilee (14.28), the women in this Gospel received no such explicit teaching.

Phillips does not seek to exonerate the women at the tomb; for her the earlier feminist concern with redeeming characters gives way to an attempt to understand them. Her analysis, based on a refined use of gender as a tool of categorization, leads first to one possible interpretation in which there is lack on all sides: Jesus failed to consider how his restricting certain teachings to men would affect the women; the man at the tomb failed to give the women any reason to trust him; the women failed to confront the young man as well as to follow his instructions. But the essay, and so this volume, refuses to end with this distressing conclusion. Phillips brings her study into the present by adducing other occasions that prompt women's silence—abuse, poverty, ridicule—and then offers her own response: one of compassion, even in cases where women fail one another.

The texts investigated, methods employed, and conclusions reached by these eleven essays represent only a small measure of the contributions feminist scholars have made to the study of Mark's Gospel. As the bibliography in this volume reveals, many others have explored this narrative to understand its depiction of gender, its potential for fostering interpretations that abuse and disenfranchise, and that comfort and encourage. Many more will continue to explore, and new routes will be charted even as some old ones broadened or perhaps abandoned. Feminist-critical analysis may thus summarized as the response to an exorcism (of interpretations that ignore, sustain, and promote silencing), 'What is this? A new teaching—with authority!' (Mk 1.27).

'LET THEM RENOUNCE THEMSELVES AND TAKE UP
THEIR CROSS': A FEMINIST READING OF MARK 8.34
IN MARK'S SOCIAL AND NARRATIVE WORLD

Joanna Dewey

In Mk 8.34, the Markan Jesus invites everyone to become disciples: 'If
any want to follow after me, let them renounce themselves and take
up their cross and follow me'.[1] If read out of context and with modern
Western understandings, the invitation can be understood as a glorification of suffering and an encouragement to become a victim: one is
to deny oneself, sacrifice oneself, wipe out any sense of self, and to
embrace the cross, that is, suffering in general. On the basis of this
verse, discipleship is portrayed as 'suffer now', presumably for reward
later in the age to come. Many a woman has failed to develop her own
identity and strengths and has embraced or endured suffering that
could be alleviated because she has come to believe that such a way of
life is pleasing to God and an imitation of Christ.

I believe this is a fundamental misreading of the Gospel of Mark. Mark
does not glorify either self-sacrifice or suffering. Indeed, the Markan
Jesus inaugurates the rule of God; he alleviates much suffering and
empowers others to do the same. Mark does, however, indicate that
one particular cause of suffering—namely, persecution by the powers-
that-be—is a part of discipleship as long as this age continues, until
God's rule comes in the fullness of power. In the first-century cultural
context, to renounce or deny oneself did *not* mean self-sacrifice as we
understand it today, and taking up one's cross referred *only* to one
specific type of suffering. The inbreaking of God's rule meant joy,
healing, feasting, the overcoming of much suffering. Before I develop
this argument, however, I want to place this study in the context of
feminist work on Mark of the last 25 years.[2]

---

1. The translation used in this article is from David Rhoads, Joanna Dewey
and Donald Michie, *Mark as Story: An Introduction to the Narrative of a Gospel*
(Philadelphia: Fortress Press, 2nd edn, 1999).
2. On the history of feminist biblical work and women in the academy in

1. *Feminist Markan Scholarship*

✓ I well remember my exhilaration 25 years ago as the second wave of feminism began to impact biblical studies. In those days, there were few women clergy, very few women seminary professors and not many women seminary students. In 1974, Letty Russell gathered together Elisabeth Schüssler Fiorenza, Sharon Ringe and myself in her living room in New York City. We brainstormed about feminism and the Bible and then wrote *The Liberating Word: A Guide to Nonsexist Interpretation of the Bible*, a useful and—for many—an exciting and liberating book.[3] We investigated biblical authority and interpretation in general, interpreting patriarchal traditions, images of women and changing language. I wrote the chapter on positive images of women, using, among other passages, two Markan stories: the one describing Jesus' true relatives as those (male and female) who do the will of God and the one about the Syro-Phoenician woman convincing Jesus to heal her daughter (Mk 3.31-35; 7.24-30). We were in the process of discovering that there really were a lot more positive images for women than our upbringings in various churches or our academic doctoral training had led us to believe.[4]

Looking back from today's perspectives, the book seems naïve in some respects. We were all Euro-American middle-class Christian women. While we were certainly aware of issues of race and class, we nonetheless treated 'woman' as a largely essentialist category, as was customary in the feminism of the 1970s. We were just beginning to deal with methodological issues. We had not fully sorted out what were men's views of women and what were women's own views and actions. We had not made a clear distinction between prescriptive and descriptive statements. (A prescriptive statement gives someone's [usually an elite male's] opinion of what someone else should do, and thus indicates that the opposite behavior is occurring. One does not need to instruct, 'women should be silent in the churches. For they are

the United States, see Carolyn DeSwarte Gifford, 'American Women and the Bible: The Nature of Woman as a Hermeneutical Issue', in Adela Yarbro Collins (ed.), *Feminist Perspectives on Biblical Scholarship* (Chico, CA: Scholars Press, 1985), pp. 11-33.

3.   Letty Russell *et al.* (eds.), *The Liberating Word: A Guide to Nonsexist Interpretation of the Bible* (Philadelphia: Westminster Press, 1976).

4.   For Schüssler Fiorenza's reflections on that time, see her *Sharing Her Word: Feminist Biblical Interpretation in Context* (Boston, MA: Beacon Press, 1998), pp. 1-9.

not permitted to speak' [1 Cor. 14.34] unless women *are* speaking in church. A descriptive statement tells us someone's view of what women did — for instance, discovered the empty tomb.) For example, I contrasted prescriptive statements of a few misogynist rabbis with descriptions of Jesus' interaction with women, instead of with the similar misogynist statements in the Pastoral Epistles or some church fathers. Thus, we engaged in the long-standing and still troublesome practice of making Jesus and early Christians look better (in this case, pro-women) by making the Judaism of the time look worse (very anti-women and patriarchal), as if Jesus were not a Jew.[5] Unfortunately we reinforced Christian anti-Semitism, now with a feminist twist. Finally, we tended to focus on specific passages of the Bible as troublesome or helpful, rather than grappling with the Bible or individual biblical writings as a whole.

Nonetheless, *The Liberating Word* was a good solid beginning. Feminist New Testament scholarship progressed rapidly in both methodological sophistication and knowledge. The year 1983 saw the publication of both Elisabeth Schüssler Fiorenza's *In Memory of Her: A Feminist Theological Reconstruction of Christian Origins*[6] and *The Bible and Feminist Hermeneutics*, edited by Mary Ann Tolbert.[7] Schüssler Fiorenza provided a fundamental revisioning of the history and theology of early Christianity, including women as both agents and victims. Tolbert's *Semeia* volume began to address literary-critical issues of women as readers of androcentric narratives. Increasingly, women entered the profession of biblical scholarship, and by the 1990s there were enough academically trained women to produce major feminist biblical anthologies: *The Women's Bible Commentary* (1992),[8] *Searching the Scriptures* (1993, 1994),[9] and The Feminist Companion to the Bible series from Sheffield Academic Press. In addition, anthologies representing the voices of women who were not white middle-class westerners are

---

5. On Jewish culture, Jesus and women, see Amy-Jill Levine, 'Second Temple Judaism, Jesus, and Women: Yeast of Eden', *BibInt* 2 (1994), pp. 8-33.

6. Elisabeth Schüssler Fiorenza, *In Memory of Her: A Feminist Theological Reconstruction of Christian Origins* (New York: Crossroad, 1983). See pp. 316-23 on Mark.

7. Mary Ann Tolbert (ed.), *The Bible and Feminist Hermeneutics* (Semeia, 28; Atlanta: Scholars Press, 1983).

8. Carol A. Newsom and Sharon H. Ringe (eds.), *The Women's Bible Commentary* (Philadelphia: Westminster Press, 1992).

9. Elisabeth Schüssler Fiorenza (ed.), *Searching the Scriptures: A Feminist Introduction* (2 vols.; New York: Crossroad, 1993, 1994).

increasingly available.[10] The Gospel of Mark specifically has received a variety of feminist treatments.[11]

What, then, have these 25 years accomplished? On the positive side, the academic climate has drastically changed. Women in the biblical text are no longer invisible to scholarship. The 'women at the empty tomb' stories are no longer ignored. At the 1976 Society of Biblical Literature Annual Meeting, Norman Perrin referred to the women at the end of Mark's Gospel as 'surrogate disciples'—the first time they had been granted even so much dignity. Today it is not uncommon to find scholars referring to that group of women as disciples, without even feeling the need to argue for it. Some of this information has begun to filter down into the churches and contemporary preaching. In 1997, teaching New Testament in a liberal seminary in the Northeast, I assigned a portion of *In Memory of Her* to supplement the still inadequate introductory text. A first-year seminary student actually asked me if the book had been all that seminal, since the information seemed to be mostly old hat to her. This is progress indeed!

As feminist scholars continue to work on the Bible, however, it has become increasingly clear to us how problematic biblical texts are for women (and Jews and often other non-dominant groups as well). Turning specifically to the Gospel of Mark, we do indeed find positive pictures of women in the stories of the woman with the flow of blood, the Syro-Phoenician woman whose daughter is healed, the woman who anoints Jesus on the head at Bethany, and the women at the cross, burial and empty tomb. However, these stories—the very same stories that provide us with positive images and give us a glimpse of the important roles of women around Jesus—are generally used not to portray significant women in relation to Jesus, but to teach men.[12]

---

10. As well as some articles in the above-mentioned volumes, see Fernando F. Segovia and Mary Ann Tolbert (eds.), *Reading from This Place: Social Location and Biblical Interpretation in the United States* (2 vols.; Philadelphia: Fortress Press, 1995); Katharine Doob Sakenfeld and Sharon H. Ringe (eds.), *Reading the Bible as Women: Perspectives from Africa, Asia, and Latin America* (Semeia, 78; Atlanta: Scholars Press, 1997).

11. Elizabeth Struthers Malbon, 'Fallible Followers: Women and Men in the Gospel of Mark', *Semeia* 28 (1983), pp. 29-48; Rita Nakashima Brock, *Journeys by Heart: A Christology of Erotic Power* (New York: Crossroad, 1988), pp. 71-104; Mary Ann Tolbert, 'Mark', in Newsom and Ringe (eds.), *Women's Bible Commentary*, pp. 263-67; Joanna Dewey, 'Gospel of Mark', in E.S. Fiorenza (ed.), *Searching the Scriptures*, II, pp. 470-509; Hisako Kinukawa, *Women and Jesus in Mark: A Japanese Feminist Perspective* (Maryknoll, NY: Orbis Books, 1994).

12. Joanna Dewey, 'Women in the Synoptic Gospels: Seen but not Heard?', *BTB* 27 (1997), pp. 53-60; Lone Fatum, 'Gender Hermeneutics: The Effective History of

Even in its positive portrayals of women, then, Mark tends to serve the interests and aims of males. Furthermore, since in an androcentric narrative the implied author and reader are basically constructed as male, to read a text such as Mark forces a woman either to read 'as male' or to exclude herself from the intended audience of the narrative.[13] In the last 25 years we have *both* rediscovered the women of the Bible and reconstructed their significant role in early Christian history, *and* learned how problematic for women the Bible is.

As far as the Gospel of Mark is concerned, I believe the basic feminist work has now been done on the portrayal of women in the narrative. We recognize both the positive images for modern women to be found in Mark and the continued dangers for women in reading such an androcentric narrative where women are invisible, relegated to minor roles and/or used for the instruction of men. Scholars will continue to give feminist interpretations of Mark. The application of new methodologies, both feminist and otherwise, will provide new insights. Work in greater depth on particular passages will increase our knowledge and understanding.[14] New readers will give new interpretations; work from women from different social locations in different parts of the world will enrich our understandings greatly. Readings will vary in how positively or negatively they view the narrative overall.[15] Such views will depend not only on how we interpret Mark, but also on how Mark's world compares to our own various experiences of the role of women. I venture to guess, however, that the basic picture of

Consciousness and the Use of Social Gender in the Gospels', in F.F. Segovia and M.A. Tolbert (eds.), *Reading from This Place*, II, pp. 157-68.

13. See Judith Fetterley, *The Resisting Reader: A Feminist Approach to American Fiction* (Bloomington: Indiana University Press, 1978); Janice Capel Anderson, 'Matthew: Gender and Reading', *Semeia* 28 (1983), pp. 3-27. Reprinted in A.-J. Levine (with Marianne Blickenstaff) (eds.), *A Feminist Companion to the Gospel of Matthew* (Sheffield: Sheffield Academic Press, 2001), pp. 25-51.

14. See in particular the explosion of work on the hemorrhaging woman (Mk 5.25-34): Malika Sibeko and Beverley Haddad, 'Reading the Bible "with" Women in Poor and Marginalized Communities in South Africa (Mark 5.21–6.1)', *Semeia* 78 (1997), pp. 83-92; Marie-Eloise Rosenblatt, 'Mark 5', in Ingrid Rosa Kitzberger (ed.), *Transformative Encounters: Jesus and Women Re-Viewed* (Leiden: E.J. Brill, 2000), pp. 137-61; Mary Rose D'Angelo, 'Gender and Power in the Gospel of Mark: The Daughter of Jairus and the Woman with the Flow of Blood', in John C. Cavadini (ed.), *Miracles in Ancient Jewish and Christian Antiquity* (Notre Dame, IN: University of Notre Dame Press, 1999), pp. 83-109.

15. For an entirely negative view, attempting to integrate race and class as well as gender, see Tat-siong Benny Liew, *Politics of Parousia: Reading Mark Inter(con)textually* (Political Interpretation; Leiden: E.J. Brill, 1999), ch. 6.

the Markan narrative as fostering both some positive women models and the overall marginalization of women will remain.

Much less work from a feminist perspective has been done on the *theology* of Mark. Quite apart from the roles of women in a narrative, the theology or ideology advocated can empower and/or oppress women and other non-dominant groups. As Elisabeth Schüssler Fiorenza writes,

> It is true that Christian theology *overtly* condemns oppressive forms of exploitation and victimization of wo/men… Nevertheless, the Christian proclamation of the kyriarchal politics of submission and its attendant virtues of self-sacrifice, docility, subservience, obedience, suffering, unconditional forgiveness, male authority, and unquestioning surrender to 'G*d's will' covertly promotes, in the name of G*d and love, such patriarchal-kyriarchal practices of victimization as Christian virtues.[16]

Feminist theologians have done major work criticizing traditional atonement theology for its exalting of self-sacrifice and suffering, and the issues they raise are beginning to be addressed in 'malestream' theology.[17] Feminist New Testament scholars, however, have done much less work on the theologies of particular writings.[18] And this is needed. For women, insofar as they submit to the narrative world created by a Gospel, absorb not only that world's ideas about the proper role for women, but also its values.[19] And if what Christian women readers absorb from reading Mark is a glorification of victimage, then no matter how powerful positive female role models in Mark may be, the Gospel is indeed harmful to women as they strive to lead Christian lives today.

16. Fiorenza, *Sharing Her Word*, p. 147. Emphasis is author's.

17. See the classic article by Joanne Carlson Brown and Rebecca Parker, 'For God So Loved the World?', in Joanne Carlson Brown and Carole R. Bohn (eds.), *Christianity, Patriarchy, and Abuse* (New York: Pilgrim Press, 1989), pp. 1-30; Delores S. Williams, 'Black Women's Surrogacy Experience and the Christian Notion of Redemption', in Paula M. Cooey *et al.* (eds.), *After Patriarchy: Feminist Transformations of the World Religions* (Maryknoll, NY: Orbis Books, 1991), pp. 1-14; Joanna Dewey, 'A Rejection of Sacrifice', *The Centerpoint* 1: *Voices* (May 1997), pp. 1-4; Darby Kathleen Ray, *Deceiving the Devil: Atonement, Abuse, and Ransom* (Cleveland, OH: Pilgrim Press, 1998). The term 'malestream' derives from Elisabeth Schüssler Fiorenza. For mainstream attempts to deal with the feminist critique, see, for example, *Atonement and the Church* (*Int* 53 [1999]).

18. Again, the work of Elisabeth Schüssler Fiorenza has been ground-breaking here. See, in particular, *Jesus: Miriam's Child, Sophia's Prophet* (New York: Continuum, 1994), pp. 97-128; *Sharing Her Word,* pp. 137-59. On the Gospel of Mark, see Brock, *Journeys by Heart*, pp. 71-104.

19. See Rhoads, Dewey and Michie, *Mark as Story,* pp. 39-46.

2. *Mark 8.34 in its Social and Narrative Context*

The question I am asking about Mk 8.34, Does Mark encourage victimage and suffering?, comes out of the feminist theological and
biblical work I have described above. My argument that Mark does
not encourage suffering and victimage depends on literary and sociological analysis of the Gospel. Not only has feminist criticism arisen in
the last 25 years, but the methodologies of literary criticism and sociological approaches to the Gospels have become major avenues of
research in New Testament studies as a whole.[20] It is these new tools
that enable me to read Mk 8.34 in the contexts of both the Markan
narrative and first-century culture. A full analysis of the Markan
views on suffering and victimage would include study of the interpretation of Jesus' execution, the understanding of service (who serves
whom), and of forgiveness, but this would be far beyond the scope of
one article. This article is a beginning, limited to Mk 8.34.[21]

To understand Mk 8.34, I shall begin by looking briefly at first-
century views of suffering. Then I shall turn to the Gospel of Mark,
the Markan understanding of the inauguration of God's rule and its
impact on suffering. Next I shall focus directly on Mk 8.34, first looking at the cross as one particular type of suffering occasioned by
discipleship and then looking at the first-century understanding of
'self' to determine that 'to renounce self' does not carry its modern
connotations, since the ancient concept of self was quite different.

The first century viewed suffering quite differently than we do
in the post-industrial West today. We reject suffering as a normal,
everyday part of life. We think pain should go away, preferably
immediately. Television advertises instant cures for almost anything
that might ail us. If a person seems unhappy, we are likely to

20. For literary approaches, see Janice Capel Anderson and Stephen D. Moore
(eds.), *Mark and Method: New Approaches in Biblical Studies* (Philadelphia: Fortress
Press, 1992). For the approach used in this article, see Rhoads, Dewey and Michie
(eds.), *Mark as Story*, and Elizabeth Struthers Malbon, 'Narrative Criticism: How
Does the Story Mean?', in Anderson and Moore (eds.), *Mark and Method*, pp. 23-49.
For sociological approaches, see Jerome H. Neyrey (ed.), *The Social World of Luke–
Acts* (Peabody, MA: Hendrickson, 1991); Bruce Malina and Richard Rohrbaugh,
Social Science Commentary on the Synoptic Gospels (Philadelphia: Fortress Press,
1992); Richard Rohrbaugh (ed.), *The Social Sciences and New Testament Interpretation*
(Peabody, MA: Hendrickson, 1996).

21. For brief interpretations of these views which support the general conclusions reached here, see Dewey, 'Gospel of Mark'; and Rhoads, Dewey and Michie
(eds.), *Mark as Story*.

recommend therapy. We view suffering as an exception or disruption of life, something to be changed or overcome as soon as possible, or — when that is impossible — drugged out of human consciousness. At the same time, Christian values, which often encourage suffering as a Christian virtue — especially for women — are also part of contemporary American culture.

Ancients viewed suffering as a normal if unpleasant part of life rather than as an interruption to normal human existence.[22] Since they understood themselves to have little control over their lives, they did not expect to have the power to make suffering go away.[23] Therefore, their task was to be able to endure it. For most people in antiquity, suffering indeed was much less avoidable than it is for middle-class westerners. At least 90 per cent of the population lived at subsistence level or below, with hunger and disease as common experiences. The high taxation levied by Roman imperial control meant that even subsistence existence was always threatened, and families were often in danger of losing their land to cover their debt.[24] In varying degrees, then, suffering was an ever-present reality. So, in antiquity, parents trained their children to be able to endure suffering, for this was a survival skill.[25] However, suffering was not considered good or redemptive; it was just the human lot.

Mark uses the words 'to suffer, suffering' only three times, always in the construction 'to endure many things' (Mk 5.26; 8.31; 9.12). Most English translations obscure the parallelism of the Greek.[26] These uses are a clue to the understanding of suffering in the Markan narrative world. The term occurs once in reference to the woman with the hemorrhage and twice in relation to the son of humanity's[27] coming passion. The sickness of the woman is to be cured, while the lot of Jesus is to endure many things, that is, to be persecuted by the powers-that-be. For Mark does not lump all forms of suffering together. The

---

22. John J. Pilch, 'Understanding Healing in the Social World of Early Christianity', *BTB* 22 (1992), pp. 26-33.

23. Bruce Malina, 'Understanding New Testament Persons', in Rohrbaugh (ed.), *Social Sciences and New Testament Interpretation*, pp. 47-48.

24. William R. Herzog II, *Parables as Subversive Speech: Jesus as Pedagogue of the Oppressed* (Louisville, KY: Westminster/John Knox Press, 1994), pp. 53-73.

25. John L. Pilch, ' "Beat His Ribs While He Is Young" (Sir. 30.12): A Window on the Mediterranean World', *BTB* 23 (1993), pp. 101-13.

26. 'Many things' (πολλά) followed by some form of the verb 'to endure, suffer' (πάσχω).

27. Άνθρωπος, the inclusive word for humanity, is used in the phrase 'son of man'. Therefore I use the phrase 'son of humanity'.

narrative sharply distinguishes between general human suffering, which is to be cured or alleviated with Jesus' inauguration of God's rule, and persecution, which is the lot of those who persevere in following the way of God as long as this age endures.

For an apocalyptic view of time undergirds Mark's narrative world. The present age is under the control of Satan; God will act soon to bring about the new age of the rule of God. With the beginning of his public ministry, the Markan Jesus inaugurates God's rule (Mk 1.14-15) and with it the blessings of that rule: healings, feedings, and new community. In Mark, the present is a time of the overlapping of ages. The new age or rule of God has indeed begun, and Jesus' power over sickness and nature reveals its present reality. However, the powers of the old age are not yet fully defeated, and until that age ends its adherents will struggle to defeat those who participate in the new age. Mark expects the end of this age and the arrival of the rule of God in full power soon, within a generation (Mk 9.1).

This double sense of time, of God's rule having truly begun but the old age still struggling to maintain its grasp, provides the context for the Markan understanding of suffering. In Mark, chs. 1–8 portray the arrival of God's rule. Jesus is shown repeatedly alleviating suffering, exorcizing demons, healing illnesses, feeding people in the desert, stilling storms. Furthermore, not only Jesus but others who join God's realm also have this power over suffering. Jesus sends out the disciples to preach, heal and exorcize, and they do so successfully (6.7-13). Jesus also expects the disciples to trust God's power over nature available to humans: he expects them to trust that the storm will not destroy them and to be able to feed thousands with little food (4.35-41; 6.35-44; 8.1-10). Once, someone not even known to Jesus or the disciples is able to exorcize in Jesus' name (9.38-39). In the Markan narrative world, the marvelous new reality of God's rule has indeed begun.

While the inbreaking of God's rule on earth gives Jesus and his followers power over sickness and nature—the power to end suffering and wrest health, life and safety for humans—it does not give them the power to dominate or control other human beings or to use force against them. During the overlap of the ages, human freedom is maintained. Humans are free to reject the rule of God and oppose its agents, and most of those who hold power in the old age do reject God's rule. They correctly perceive the rule of God as a threat to their own rule and set out to destroy it. In Mark 1–8 the narrator shows the Markan audience both the present real blessings and the two ways people respond to them: those who follow enthusiastically (disciples and crowd) and those who reject and oppose Jesus (scribes, Pharisees, Herodians). And, unlike those who belong to God's rule, those who reject it have no hesitation in using force. As early as Mark 3.6, the Pharisees plot with the Herodians how to destroy Jesus. In Mark 6, Herod has John the Baptizer beheaded. Later in the narrative, the Roman governor Pilate will have Jesus crucified (15.1-47), and Jesus prophesies that the disciples will also face persecution, even execution (13.9-13). This persecution by the powers-that-be who reject God's rule will only end when God's rule comes in full power and the present evil age ends.

Thus, it is only after the good news of God's rule is clearly established in the Markan narrative, along with the two responses to it, that the cost of following Jesus is made explicit. In Mk 8.34, the Markan Jesus issues a general invitation to discipleship to the crowd: 'If any want to follow after me, let them renounce themselves and take up their cross and follow me'. Along with the good news, there comes persecution from those who adhere to the old age. Following Jesus is both blessing—the ending of much human suffering—and incurring new suffering at the hands of those who will do their best to destroy Jesus' followers. The Markan narrative does not lump all suffering together in this time of the overlap of the ages: some is decisively ended while new dangers are incurred because of the new situation.

Mark 8.34 introduces the new danger in strong terms, 'take up their cross'. The cross, after all, is an instrument of execution. Crucifixion was a cruel, shameful and legal means of execution reserved by Roman imperial authorities primarily for slaves and rebels or troublemakers. Anyone questioning Roman authority—as someone living the life of the new age necessarily did—was from their perspective a potential or actual troublemaker, and political authorities believed in pre-emptive action against possible threats. To take up your cross is specifically to pick up the crossbeam, to carry it out to the place of execution, where you will be nailed or tied to it and then hoisted up on the upright pole. It is like instructing someone today to 'take up your electric chair'.

No ancient audience could miss the reference to execution or think of the cross as a general reference to all human suffering. This persecution caused by adherence to God's rule will not be overcome until the new age is fully here. Yet, unlike human suffering in general, it is easily avoidable. All one has to do is renounce Jesus—renounce the new age. It is only because one persists in following Jesus, in embracing the new age, that one is persecuted. In Mk 8.34 and following, the narrative attempts to prepare the disciples—and the gospel's audiences—for this persecution and to encourage faithfulness in face of it. The emphasis on the inevitability of persecution, however, in no way negates the blessings of God's rule; both are true, and both are the experience of Jesus' followers.[28]

The first demand in Mk 8.34, 'let them renounce themselves', certainly sounds to modern ears like a call to self-sacrifice. Today many do tend to read it as denial of the individual self, a call to give up one's will, always to put oneself last. I suggest that this is not what it would have conveyed to a first-century audience. First, their sense of self was different; they had little idea of any individual identity. Second, the demand is in parallel with taking up one's cross and is to be interpreted in the context of persecution.

In modern Western post-Enlightenment societies the basic unit of society is understood to be the individual self. In such a culture, to renounce oneself comes to mean to renounce one's very individuality. In antiquity, however, and indeed in much of the world still today, the basic unit of society is not the individual person but the multi-generational kinship group.[29] The group is responsible for the actions of its individual members, and within the group it is the chief member, usually the male head of household, who determines appropriate behavior. Malina writes, 'There is always the dominant male or his surrogate'.[30] Adult sons continue to owe obedience to their fathers as long as their fathers live; daughters are transferred from the authority of their fathers to that of their husbands upon marriage. 'People are not expected to have personal opinions, much less voice

28. Some scholars argue that Mark wants to replace miracle-based power (the blessings of God's rule) with suffering. See, for example, Theodore J. Weeden, *Mark: Traditions in Conflict* (Philadelphia: Fortress Press, 1971); Werner H. Kelber, *The Oral and the Written Gospel: The Hermeneutics of Speaking and Writing in the Synoptic Tradition, Mark, Paul, and Q* (Philadelphia: Fortress Press, 1983). I believe such views are a misreading, for (a) they do not pay sufficient attention to the nature of 'cross' as a specific image of execution, and (b) they read Mark as if it were a modern linear print narrative rather than an aural/oral both/and type of narrative characteristic of manuscript cultures with high residual orality. See Joanna Dewey, 'The Gospel of Mark as Oral/Aural Event: Implications for Interpretation', in Elizabeth Struthers Malbon and Edgar V. McKnight (eds.), *New Literary Criticism and the New Testament* (JSNTSup, 109; Sheffield: Sheffield Academic Press, 1994), pp. 145-63.

29. Malina, 'Understanding New Testament Persons', pp. 41-61; Bruce J. Malina, ' "Let Him Deny Himself" (Mark 8.34 and par): A Social Psychological Model of Self-Denial', *BTB* 24 (1994), pp. 106-19. This section is strongly indebted to Malina.

30. Malina, 'New Testament Persons', p. 48.

their opinions... Social behavior derives from relative status where hierarchy is the essence of social order'.[31] In such a society, to deny self means, in effect, to renounce the kinship unit. Today, modern westerners live in a culture in which we routinely do exactly what ancient society understood as renouncing self: we move out from under parental authority and establish independent households upon reaching adulthood. To do so in antiquity was not normal at all.

The kinship group was not only a unit of consumption, as the family is today, but also the basic unit of production, whether of subsistence farming or a small household industry. It was also the basic political unit that composed the empire. The household was the state in miniature; the empire the household writ large, each hierarchically structured. To step outside of one's kinship unit, then, was not only a rejection of one's parents but also quite likely a loss of one's means of earning a living. It also put one outside of the accepted social-political order. It was a radical act indeed to renounce kin. If one did so, and if one had any voice, power or following at all, one would be perceived as a threat to the social order of the empire.

That renouncing self in Mk 8.34 means, in effect, renouncing one's kinship group is confirmed in two ways. First, in similar sayings in Q and the *Gospel of Thomas*, the denial of kin is explicit. Luke's rendition of Q reads, 'Whoever comes to me and does not hate father and mother, wife and children, brothers and sisters, yes, and even life itself, cannot be my disciple. Whoever does not carry the cross and follow me cannot be my disciple' (Lk. 14.26-27; see also Mt. 10.35-38). The *Gospel of Thomas* reads, 'Jesus said: "He who does not hate his father and his mother will not be able to be my disciple; and (he who does not) hate his brothers and his sisters and (does not) bear his cross as I have, will not be worthy of me"' (*Gos. Thom.* 55; see also 101). All connect rejection of kin with carrying one's cross. In the place of 'renounce self' in Mk 8.34, these statements with parallel structure and content spell out that kin is what is to be rejected.

In Mark, to become a disciple is to renounce one's kinship group and to join those following Jesus, that is, to join the new community or fictive kinship group around Jesus. The Markan Jesus says, '"Who are my mother and my brothers?" And looking around at those seated about him in a circle, he said, "Look, here are my mother and my brothers! For those who do the will of God, *they* are my brother and sister and mother"' (Mk 3.33-35). Later, in response to Peter's question about what the disciples get for following, Jesus spells out the riches

31. Malina, 'Deny Himself', p. 113.

and cost of rejecting kin: 'There is no one who has left a house or brothers or sisters or a mother or a father or children or fields for me and for the good news who does not receive a hundred times as many now, in this time, houses and brothers and sisters and mothers and children and fields—with persecutions—and in the coming age life eternal' (10.29-30). In addition, the only other uses of 'renounce' (ἀπαρνέομαι) in Mark are found in the prediction and relating of Peter's renunciation of Jesus (14.30, 31, 72). In renouncing Jesus, Peter is renouncing his new fictive kinship group. To deny self, then, is to deny one's kin.

Since to reject kin is to reject the basic social-political-economic structure of ancient society, it is not surprising that rejection of kin and persecution should occur together. Societies do not tend to support those who break their rules. The parallels cited above from Q and the *Gospel of Thomas* suggest the close connection between denying kin and persecution. The chiastic pattern (that is, the crossing or abb'a' pattern) of Mk 8.34 also suggests a close parallel.[32] The structure of the verse may be laid out as follows:

A   If any want to follow after me,
    B   let them renounce themselves [that is, deny kin]
    B′   and take up their cross [that is, risk persecution]
A′   and follow me.

The parallelism between A and A′ (to follow Jesus) suggests that B and B′ are similar to each other in meaning as well. To follow Jesus is to join the new community of God's rule, the fictive kinship group gathered around Jesus. In order to do this, one must renounce kin and be prepared to face persecution—take up one's cross—from those in authority in the larger society. Bas van Iersel writes:

> Today's readers must be careful not to see this passage as being unrelated to a possible situation of persecution, and interpret it, for instance, as a call for an ascetic way of life that is characterized by self-renunciation or even self-contempt... The sayings are not about anything so vague as general lifestyle, but about a person's willingness to give his or her life for the sake of Jesus when this ultimate sacrifice is demanded.[33]

In summary then, when read in the context of the first-century cultural world and the larger narrative of Mark, Mk 8.34 is not an exhortation to suffering and victimage in general. It is an exhortation

---

32. Malina, 'Deny Himself', p. 107.
33. Bas van Iersel, *Mark: A Reader-Response Commentary* (trans. W.H. Bisscheroux; JSNTSup, 164; Sheffield: Sheffield Academic Press, 1998), p. 291.

to remain faithful to Jesus and the rule of God in face of persecution, even execution, by political authorities. While the end of much human suffering is realized by the breaking of the rule of God into history in Jesus' ministry, persecution for following Jesus is a real possibility as long as this age lasts. Any reading of this passage as encouraging individual suffering is a misreading of the text.

3. *Postscript: Reading Mark Today*

Thus Mk 8.34 does not encourage suffering or self-sacrifice, as we often interpret this verse today. However, modern readers are still likely to read such meanings into the text. We all come to the Bible with our assumptions informed by our contemporary societies. Most of us are not educated about the massive differences between our time and the first century; it is indeed a foreign culture to us. Furthermore, we tend to read the Bible in snippets, in lessons at church or daily readings, and thus never experience Mark as a complete narrative whose parts find their meaning only in context of the whole. Thus, we read and abstract messages the evangelist never envisioned.

The problems that arise from reading Mk 8.34 with modern assumptions serve as an instance of the larger problems that arise from continuing to use the New Testament as sacred scripture for Christians today. While the New Testament contains much obvious good, it remains an androcentric and patriarchal text. A naive reading enculturates androcentric and patriarchal values. Every person who continues to read the Bible will either be caught in such constructions of reality or will have to go through the work of deconstruction and reconstruction for a more liberative and liberating faith. Translations and paraphrases can certainly help, but they cannot eradicate the problem. I believe the problem is too fundamental.

But as long as Christianity remains a viable religion—and I as a feminist still count myself a Christian—we will need to grapple with these issues. The Gospel of Mark may offer us some resources in this struggle. Mark's view of the new age working to ameliorate most suffering, while exhorting faithfulness in the face of persecution from the powers that be, may serve as a resource against some other portions of the New Testament and much of later Christian theology that has tended to valorize suffering as redemptive. As Mary Ann Tolbert writes, 'One must defeat the Bible as patriarchal authority by using the Bible as liberator'.[34]

34. Mary Ann Tolbert, 'Defining the Problem: The Bible and Feminist Hermeneutics', *Semeia* 28 (1983), p. 120.

SIMON PETER'S MOTHER-IN-LAW – DISCIPLE OR DOMESTIC SERVANT? FEMINIST BIBLICAL HERMENEUTICS AND THE INTERPRETATION OF MARK 1.29-31

Deborah Krause

Just as the woman in the parable sweeps the whole house in search of her lost coin, so feminist critical interpretation searches for the lost traditions and visions of liberation among its inheritance of androcentric biblical texts and their interpretations.[1]

Sometimes you can want to believe something so badly – you end up looking too hard.[2]

1. *Introduction*

What are feminist critics of the canonical Gospels looking for? Much of feminist New Testament critical discourse has been fairly agreed upon in its goal, namely, the liberation of women and other 'non persons' from patriarchal oppression.[3] Given the clear patriarchal

1.   Elisabeth Schüssler Fiorenza, *Bread Not Stone: The Challenge of Feminist Biblical Interpretation* (Boston, MA: Beacon Press, 1984), p. 16.

2.   FBI Special Agent Dana Scully in Chris Carter, 'The Beginning', *The X-Files* (dir. Kim Manners; Episode 6X01; 8 November 1998).

3.   The phrase derives from Elisabeth Schüssler Fiorenza's works, *In Memory of Her: A Feminist Theological Reconstruction of Christian Origins* (New York: Crossroad, 1983), and *Bread Not Stone*. Certainly a single definition of feminism in its practices and goals is impossible. Moreover, the single definition of feminist biblical criticism is impossible. The liberationist goals articulated by Schüssler Fiorenza, however, have had a significant influence on the work of feminist critics of Christian Scriptures. On the varieties of feminist practice and purpose in biblical critical scholarship see The Bible and Culture Collective, 'Feminist and Womanist Criticism', in *The Postmodern Bible* (New Haven: Yale University Press, 1995), pp. 225-70. According to Claudia Camp, Schüssler Fiorenza's work has represented the cutting edge of the liberationist feminist approach in that she has critically engaged the more 'neo-orthodox' approaches of such feminist interpreters as Letty Russell and Rosemary Radford Ruether regarding the authority of Scripture.

ideological bias of both the Gospels and their interpretation, however, how are feminist interpreters best able to read these texts toward the goal of liberation? In this sense, feminist critics of the Gospels have variously engaged reconstructive and deconstructive stances toward these texts and their history of interpretation. Such projects have read the Gospel narratives both to reclaim the lost voices and models of women's roles within the traditions, and to critique their androcentric bias. The whole enterprise requires careful navigation between the shoals of positivistic idealism on the one hand, and nihilistic dismissal on the other. Such are the vagaries of a political endeavor chartered by and engaged in the interpretation of such a diffusely androcentric and yet powerfully liberative tradition as the Bible.

Over the past 20 years feminist biblical critics have focused on a little considered tradition in the Gospel of Mark: the service of Simon Peter's mother-in-law to Jesus, Simon, Andrew and John (with parallels in Mt. 8.14 and Lk. 4.38). What most previous biblical interpreters had understood as a quick demonstration of Jesus' powers as healer at the beginning of the Galilean ministry has been explored by feminist interpreters as evidence for the role of women in the Jesus movement and combed for its clues to Mark's disposition toward the issue of women in ministry. The tradition of this nameless woman (identified by her legal bond to Simon Peter), her healing and her activity of service present a rich field within which to discern how feminist critics have looked for both the androcentric bias and liberative potential of the Gospel.

2. *Reading Mark 1.29-31 in My Context*

> And immediately he left the synagogue and went into Simon and Andrew's house with James and John. And Simon's mother-in-law lay sick with a fever, and immediately they told him about her. And he came to her and took her by the hand and lifted her up, and the fever left her, and she served them (Mk 1.29-31).

When I teach the Gospel of Mark in seminary classes and lead Bible studies in Presbyterian (USA), United Church of Christ, Disciples of Christ, United Methodist, Lutheran (ELCA) and Episcopal churches, I often find that in reading the tradition about Jesus' healing Simon Peter's mother-in-law many women snort under their breath at the

See her 'Feminist Theological Hermeneutics: Canon and Christian Identity', in E.S. Fiorenza (ed.), *Searching the Scriptures: A Feminist Introduction and Commentary* (2 vols.; New York: Crossroad, 1993), I, pp. 154-71 (158-59).

detail in Mk 1.31 about her 'serving them'.[4] With the most minor amount of encouragement (such as the quip 'Healed her just in time for supper!') many women laugh and nod with recognition. This is their tradition, their good news, their story about their savior, Jesus. Yet they can laugh at how it retains vestiges of unquestioned patriarchy. They can appreciate the complexity of a tradition that at once bears life-giving good news about healing for a woman, and bears the unexamined oppression of feminine domestic servitude. Such, nearly two thousand years later, is the reality of their faith and their lives.

As a teacher I find such moments to be a gift. They embody a complex feminist hermeneutic of politically charged suspicion about the tradition and deep personal piety within it. I could never *teach* this posture. With their laughing the women achieve a critical distance from the tradition, and yet their faith is not threatened. There is more to the Gospel than simply the words on the page. There is more to Jesus than the Gospel of Mark. Yet within the words on the page, the narrative, they find an affirmation of their experience of tension in the church and in their everyday lives. Healed just in time for supper, indeed!

3. *Toward Discerning the Biblical Hermeneutic of My Context*

In reflecting critically on the above-described reaction to Mk 1.29-31, I am impressed by how it embodies a now-standard feminist hermeneutical posture 'of suspicion'. As Elisabeth Schüssler Fiorenza has defined this approach, it 'does not presuppose the feminist authority and truth of the Bible, but takes as its starting point the assumption that biblical texts and their interpretations are androcentric and serve patriarchal functions'.[5] In the case of many of the women I teach, the tradition about Simon Peter's mother-in-law illustrates the androcentric nature of the Bible and its potential to serve patriarchal functions, specifically functions of women's domestic servitude.

Beyond the hermeneutical posture, the method these students of the Bible employ in reading Mk 1.29-31 is exemplified in the social-

---

4.   The seminary in which I teach is United Church of Christ with its heritage in the German Evangelical tradition. The churches in which I teach are middle and upper-middle class, predominantly white, Anglo-American congregations that range from having large educational programs and staffs to one adult Sunday school class and solo pastors. I teach with some regularity in urban, suburban and rural settings of the church.

5.   Fiorenza, *Bread Not Stone*, p. 15.

historical work of Luise Schottroff.[6] Schottroff employs many of the tools of traditional historical criticism, but she applies these tools to the text by asking different questions and assessing different data to attain an understanding of women in early Christianity.[7] In particular, Schottroff examines the everyday life of women in the New Testament. Rather than dross covering some larger theological claim, she sees the details of women's lives, their work (both paid and unpaid), families, homes and villages to be a site for historical and theological investigation.[8] In this vein, the traditions of the New Testament document patriarchal constriction for women as well as good news about their liberation. As such, they are tense and complex discourses that describe the struggle of women for liberation.

> A new understanding of canon is needed: it is a document of a history of contempt for human beings, of a history burdened with guilt. And yet, at one and the same time it is the gospel. The life-giving gospel will surely not suffer damage when Christian women and men face up to the history of Christianity, tainted as it is with contempt for women, colonialism, persecution of Jews and Judaism, and its traffic in patriarchy.[9]

Schottroff's claims about the Christian canon reflect a posture that is comfortable with ambiguity and tension. It seems to me that the women with whom I do Bible study are (at least with regard to Mk 1.29-31) situated in her 'new understanding of the canon'. They enjoy the apparent contradictions in Simon's mother-in-law's healing and service. They connect these conditions to their own material and social reality. They find within them a place of connection for reflecting on their own lives. They do not seek to apologize or defend the tradition

6. Luise Schottroff, *Let the Oppressed Go Free: Feminist Perspectives on the New Testament* (Louisville, KY: Westminster/John Knox Press, 1993), and *Lydia's Impatient Sisters: A Feminist Social History of Early Christianity* (trans. B. and M. Rumscheidt; Louisville, KY: Westminster/John Knox Press, 1995).

7. This approach, of course, can also be attributed to Fiorenza in her groundbreaking *In Memory of Her*.

8. Note Schottroff's criticism of traditional historical-critical practice (particularly that of Rudolph Bultmann) for its disregard of women's particularity as a site for theological reflection: 'In [Bultmann's] view the narratives from everyday life (parables in the stricter sense) and those about interesting, individual events in the world of humans and animals (similitudes) do not seek to communicate anything about everyday life and the world'. Feminist practice, however, is different: 'The parables speak of social reality, including so-called parables of nature. The parables describe and then turn upside down the world of owners, large estates and farms, of female and male daily-wage earners, tenants, and slaves' (*Lydia's Impatient Sisters*, p. 52).

9. Schottroff, *Lydia's Impatient Sisters*, p. 78.

or Jesus over and against her. They do not have to account, it seems, for every bit of data within the Gospel of Mark and make it all out to be 'good news' for them. Yet in sum it remains their gospel.

Mary Ann Tolbert, in her reflections on Protestant feminist biblical hermeneutics, describes the tense situation within which these students of the Bible find themselves:

> How is it that texts that negate the experience of women and define them as 'other' are also texts that women continue to wish to claim as their own—and not out of ignorance but out of the realization that they have actually experienced these 'negative' texts as liberating?[10]

In her conclusion, Tolbert quotes the feminist literary theorist, Patrocinio Schweichart, who characterizes the posture of feminist biblical interpreters to the androcentric tradition of the Bible as dual: 'Male texts merit a dual hermeneutic: a negative hermeneutic that discloses their complicity with patriarchal ideology and a positive hermeneutic that recuperates the utopian moment'.[11] The case of Simon Peter's mother-in-law offers the feminist students in my context the opportunity to struggle with the Bible in the midst of this dual hermeneutic. In their reading, it is both a text that reveals the patriarchal ideology of Mark's Gospel and early Christianity, and a text that offers insight into the 'utopian moment' of a Jesus tending to a woman's need for healing.

Imagine my surprise, however, upon finding the majority of feminist critical commentary on Mk 1.29-31 thoroughly at odds with the above-described interpretation. The interpretations of Mk 1.29-31 offered by Schüssler Fiorenza, Schottroff, Tolbert and others find the text to be wholly an example of 'the utopian moment'. They argue that Simon Peter's mother-in-law's service to Jesus and the disciples is part of a comprehensive narrative message from Mark about the importance of women as models of faith, or as part of a historical tradition that bears witness to the centrality of women disciples within the service (διακονέω) of the Jesus movement and the early church. Simon Peter's mother-in-law is thus heralded as the 'woman who *ministers* to Jesus',[12] and as an example of an early disciple.[13]

---

10. Mary Ann Tolbert, 'Protestant Feminist Hermeneutics and the Bible: On the Horns of a Dilemma', in Alice Bach (ed.), *The Pleasure of Her Text: Feminist Readings of Biblical and Historical Texts* (Valley Forge, PA: Trinity Press International, 1990), p. 15.

11. Tolbert, 'Protestant Feminist Hermeneutics', p. 19.

12. E.g., Tolbert, 'Mark', in C.A. Newsom and S.H. Ringe (eds.), *The Women's Bible Commentary* (Louisville, KY: Westminster/John Knox Press, 1992), pp. 263-74 (267).

In what follows I am not seeking to dismantle the gains made by feminist New Testament critical scholarship toward reclaiming the roles of women within the Gospel narratives and early Christianity. To me, however, these particular readings of Mk 1.29-31 represent a positivistic exaggeration of women's discipleship in the Gospel tradition at the expense of critically examining the context and object of Simon's mother-in-law's service. Moreover, they seem dangerously close to reifying the patriarchal value for traditional gender roles of feminine domestic servitude.[14] Here I seek to examine this mode of feminist critical interpretation of Mk 1.29-31, and to venture a different critical engagement of the tradition that resonates with the experience of the women with whom I teach and learn.

4. *Feminist Critical Scholarship on Mark 1.29-31*

Traditional historical-critical scholarship asserts that the detail of Mk 1.31c is merely a proof of Simon Peter's mother-in-law's healing. Simply put, the tradition portrays how, after Jesus' healing, things got back to normal. Jesus touches her, the fever leaves her, and she serves them (διηκόνει αὐτοῖς).[15] Simon's mother-in-law's 'service' to the men

---

13. See, e.g. Schottroff, 'Women as Disciples of Jesus in New Testament Times', in her *Let the Oppressed Go Free*, pp. 80-118.

14. While not within the category of self-consciously feminist interpretation, Pheme Perkins's reflections on this text are illustrative of the potential for reifying the value of patriarchally prescribed gender roles. Important for this investigation is Perkins's refutation of the reading my students and I have explored. In the face of such readings she defends Mark's text and portrays the healing of Simon's mother-in-law for service as her restoration to a position of honor within her home: 'Peter's mother-in-law is wracked with fever. She cannot fulfill the role of preparing and serving a meal to the guests, which would have fallen to her as the senior woman within the household. Many women today react negatively to the picture of a woman getting up after a severe illness to serve male guests. That sentiment hardly seems appropriate to the complex gender and social roles involved in the household. Certainly, Peter's wife or a female servant may have prepared the food. The privilege of showing hospitality to important guests falls to Peter's mother-in-law as a manner of honor, not servitude. We even exhibit similar behavior. When special guests are expected for dinner, no one gets near the kitchen without clearance from the person who has the privilege of preparing the food' ('Mark', *The New Interpreter's Bible*, VIII [Nashville: Abingdon Press, 1995], p. 543).

15. R. Bultmann, *The History of the Synoptic Tradition* (trans. John Marsh; Oxford: Basil Blackwell, 1963), p. 212.

is an example of her everyday domestic work. The tradition merely reveals that, fever free, she is able to return to her regular duties.[16]

In response to this interpretation, feminist critical interpreters of Mark have engaged the tradition about Simon's mother-in-law and her service in order to explore the role of women within both the Gospel of Mark and the Jesus movement. In terms of Mark, feminist critics working within a redaction- and narrative-critical mode have taken up the detail of Simon's mother-in-law's 'service' (διακονέω) and placed it alongside other uses of the verb in the Gospel (Mk 1.13; 10.45; 15.41). Throughout the Hellenistic literary milieu the verb and its word family (διακονία and διάκονος) have a range of meanings from table service and the domestic work of women and slaves to the service of a citizen to the state.[17] Specifically within the early church the verb also has a wide variety of uses, from table and domestic service of women and slaves to the particular activity of discipleship to and ministry with Jesus.[18] The contexts of the subject and the object of the verb, therefore, are important in assessing the meaning of its activity. Within many feminist redaction- and narrative-critical readings of Mark, however, the verb is translated to imply 'discipleship' or 'ministry' in every case.

In her article in *The Women's Bible Commentary*, Mary Ann Tolbert notes that English translations of Mark (such as the RSV)—which render διακονέω as 'serve' in the case of Simon's mother-in-law and 'minister' in the case of the angels who tend to Jesus in Mk 1.13—reveal a double standard with an androcentric bias. Championing Simon's mother-in-law in the cause of equal treatment for women in Mark, Tolbert argues for consistency in the translation of the verb:

> Translating the same Greek word as 'minister' when the angels are the subject but 'serve' when a woman is the subject downplays her action. The author of Mark, by using the same word for the action of the angels and the action of the healed woman, obviously equated their level of

16. E.g. E.P. Gould, *The Gospel According to St. Mark* (Edinburgh: T. & T. Clark, 1896), p. 26: 'διηκόνει αὐτοῖς. She served or waited on them. This is added to show the reality and completeness of her recovery'. See also V. Taylor, *The Gospel According to St. Mark* (London: Macmillan, 1955), p. 180: 'The serving at the evening meal is mentioned as a sign of the cure'.

17. Hermann W. Beyer, 'διακονέω, διακονία, διάκονος', *TDNT*, II, pp. 81-93.

18. Most specifically, the 12 disciples are described in Mk 3.14-15 as those whom Jesus called for the purposes of being with him (ὦσιν μετ᾽ αὐτοῦ) and who are being sent to preach and to cast out demons (ἀποστέλλη αὐτοὺς κηρύσσειν καὶ ἔχειν ἐξουσίαν ἐκβάλλειν τὰ δαιμόνια).

service to Jesus. What the angels were able to do for Jesus in the wilderness, the woman whose fever has fled now does for him in her home.[19]

Tolbert is right. The verb should be translated consistently in each case. The angels tend to Jesus' needs in the wilderness. The woman tends to the needs of Jesus and his disciples. Tolbert's presumption, however, that the woman's work is somehow redeemed to the level of 'ministry' by the same work of the angels is fanciful and has problematic implications for a feminist challenge to patriarchy.

Rather than 'minister' as Tolbert implies, the verb is best rendered as 'serve' with regard to the angels and the woman. This becomes clear upon a careful examination of the dynamics between the subjects and objects of serving in both contexts. With regard to the service of the angels to Jesus in the wilderness, the introduction to Mark's Gospel states that Jesus is the Christ, the Son of God (Mk 1.1). In the baptism scene the heavenly voice confirms this with an allusion to a formula of adoption from a Royal Psalm (Ps. 2.7): 'You are my beloved son, in whom I am well pleased' (Mk 1.11).[20] In this context, the angels' service to Jesus represents the service to a king within the royal court. The angels, in Mark's theological and cosmological perspective, are subservient beings to Jesus. Likewise, Simon's mother-in-law is subservient within the context of the household of Simon and Andrew.

In her interpretation of the context of Simon and Andrew's household, Tolbert's commentary further masks the woman's true social location with the phrase 'in her home'. The introduction of the pericope has already established the legal parameters of the woman's existence. Indeed, this is not her home. It is Simon and Andrew's home (τὴν οἰκίαν Σίμωνος καὶ Ἀνδρέου) and she (without a proper name in the narrative) is described only by her bond to Simon as his mother-in-law (ἡ πενθερὰ Σίμωνος).[21]

Through her method Tolbert intends to redeem Simon's mother-in-

---

19. Tolbert, 'Mark', p. 267.

20. Hans Joachin Kraus, *Psalms 1–59* (trans. Hilton C. Oswald; Minneapolis: Augsburg, 1988), pp. 129-32.

21. In her monograph *Sowing The Gospel: Mark's World in Literary-Historical Perspective* (Philadelphia: Fortress Press, 1989), Mary Ann Tolbert classifies Simon's mother-in-law as a character in Mark's narrative who displays attributes of 'good earth'. In particular, Tolbert claims that Simon's mother-in-law responds to her healing by 'gladly serving the needs of others' (p. 226). Clearly Mark describes her service to others, but from an exegetical point of view there is no evidence as to her state of mind (i.e. gladly) in performing this service.

law from years of androcentric interpretation as a 'real' character in Mark's story. This is perhaps a noble aim. She does so, however, by disregarding the context of this particular woman's service to men. Moreover, through the connection to the angels, Tolbert runs the risk of legitimizing the woman's subjugation to men in her social context as divinely inspired.

Feminist redaction critic Marla Selvidge has also argued for the larger narrative role of Simon's mother-in-law in Mark's Gospel.[22] In addition to a connection to the service of the angels (Mk 1.13), Selvidge connects the woman's service with Jesus' saying to the Twelve in Mk 10.45, 'For even the Son of Man did not come to be served [διακονηθῆναι] but to serve [διακονῆσαι], and to give his life as a ransom for many'.[23] For Selvidge, such a connection establishes the fact that Mark intends to portray Simon's mother-in-law as a model, even Christ-like character in the Gospel:

> If we compare the word διακονέω, 'to serve', with its remaining usages in the Markan story, we find that is indeed central to the mission of Jesus and to those who claim to be followers of Jesus. The word διακονέω is never used of the Twelve and is only employed in a context with women and Jesus (other than angels). In this story the mother-in-law is carrying out the same mandate that Jesus requires of all followers. It does not necessarily have to be menial tasks.[24]

Like Tolbert, Selvidge seeks to establish Simon's mother-in-law as an important character in Mark. Her example of service is equated with Jesus' claim about the Son of Man's service in Mk 10.45.[25] She neglects, however, the different contexts of Jesus' teaching about service in Mk 10.45 and the woman's service to the men within Simon and Andrew's home. In Mk 10.45 Jesus teaches the Twelve (all men) about serving others on the way to Jerusalem (an itinerant mission). The context that inspires the teaching is the disciples' reaction to James and John's request for 'chief seats' in Jesus' glory. These followers are 'lording' it over one another, like the Gentiles. Jesus corrects them. Such is not the character of those who follow him. If they are to be great, if they are to be first, he instructs, they must be (ἔσται) servant (διάκονος) and slave of all. In other words, they must become something they are not. They must elect to change.

22. Marla Selvidge, 'And Those Who Followed Feared (Mark 10:32)', *CBQ* 45 (1983), pp. 396-400.
23. Selvidge, 'And Those Who Followed Feared', p. 397.
24. Selvidge, 'And Those Who Followed Feared', p. 398.
25. Also on this point see Monika Fander, 'Frauen in der Nachfolge Jesu: die Rolle der Frau im Markusevangelium', *EvT* 52 (1992), pp. 417-18.

In Mk 1.29-31, the narrative presents a detail about Simon's mother-in-law's service to men within Simon and Andrew's house. Unlike the male disciples, however, her service is not voluntary. She has not left home and family to follow Jesus. Indeed, she serves within her family's home. Finally, unlike the disciples in Mk 10.44-45, her role as servant is a previously existing condition. She is not in the process of becoming something new in her service. Indeed, her service seems more reflective of the static order Jesus describes in Mk 10.44-45 of 'lording it over' (and being lorded over) as held 'among the Gentiles'. Were Mark so intent on connecting these notions of service, why would he not portray Jesus stopping the woman in Mk 1.31 as she comes to serve them: 'The Son of Man came not to be served but to serve...?' Conversely, if Mark does intend to connect these uses of διακονέω, he presents Jesus' acceptance of Simon's mother-in-law's service as a direct contradiction to his saying in Mk 10.45. Finally, what of the disparaging reference to Martha's domestic service in Lk. 10.38-42? Here Jesus is portrayed characterizing Martha's service (διακονία) as being distracted with 'many things' (πολλά), in contrast with Mary's choice of 'the better part' (τὴν ἀγαθὴν μερίδα). Such a reference seems to suggest that the synoptic tradition does not uniformly affirm the value of the term.[26]

From the perspective of Christian origins, other feminist scholars argue that Mark's use of the term διακονέω in 1.31 is intended as a technical term for Christian ministry. This argument seeks to establish a connection between Mk 1.31 and 15.40-41. The women who watch the crucifixion in Mk 15.40-41 are described as both following and serving Jesus in the Galilee (ἠκολούθουν αὐτῷ καὶ διηκόνουν αὐτῷ). As such, they represent ancient evidence that women were disciples of Jesus. So too, it is argued, Simon's mother-in-law's service (διηκόνει αὐτοῖς) denotes her role as an early disciple.[27] Her service to Jesus, as Elisabeth Schüssler Fiorenza has argued, is a part of a larger early Christian concept of διακονία that captures the whole sense of Jesus' ministry, epitomized by one 'who does not subordinate and enslave others in the manner of Gentile rulers [10.42], but is the suffering servant who liberates and elevates them from servitude'.[28] Likewise, Luise Schottroff, on the basis of Mk 10.42-45, argues that:

26. Kathleen Corley, *Private Women, Public Meals: Social Conflict in the Synoptic Tradition* (Peabody, MA: Hendrickson, 1993), pp. 133-44.

27. Elizabeth Meier Tetlow, *Women and Ministry in the New Testament: Called to Serve* (Lanham, MD: University Press of America, 1985), p. 97.

28. Fiorenza, *In Memory of Her*, pp. 320-21.

free men did serve slaves and free women in terms of domestic work...
That is why usages of 'to serve' in the context of women's discipleship
(Mk 1.31 and par.; Mk 15.41 and par.) are to be understood as denoting
discipleship, and not a hierarchical gender division of labor in which
women do all the work of looking after other people's needs.[29]

As in the cases of Tolbert and Selvidge, these readings of διακονέω
are uncharacteristically (for both Schüssler Fiorenza and Schottroff)
disconnected from their contexts. In Mk 15.40-41 the women are
described as 'followers' of Jesus, a term intimately connected to the
discipleship of the Twelve (e.g. Mk 1.16-20; 2.13-14). Moreover, like
the Twelve, they are itinerant, having left the context of home to
follow Jesus around Galilee and to Jerusalem. In Mk 1.29-31 Simon's
mother-in-law is not described as a 'follower' of Jesus, and she serves,
as noted earlier, within the context of Simon and Andrew's house. In
addition, the object of the women's service is different. In Mk 15.41
the women are described as serving Jesus specifically (διηκόνουν
αὐτῷ), whereas in Mk 1.31 Simon's mother-in-law serves a general
group of people consisting of her son-in-law Simon, Andrew, James,
John, and Jesus (διηκόνει αὐτοῖς).[30] Is it not possible that on the one
hand Mk 10.42-43 indicates that free men served slaves and free
women within Jesus' ministry and the early church, while on the
other hand Mk 1.29-31 reveals that free men, slaves and free women
continued to relate within traditionally prescribed roles, with some
women continuing to serve within the domestic realm and tend to the
needs of others?

The champions of Simon's mother-in-law's discipleship, as described
above, all attend to the verb of her service (διακονέω); however, their
research is entirely silent on her given title, in other words, her being
(ἡ πενθερὰ Σίμωνος). While they focus on the ecclesialogical significance of her action, they do not ask what the role of mother-in-law
might have meant for her within a Hellenistic Jewish household.
What was expected of a mother-in-law in such settings? What were

29. Fiorenza, *In Memory of Her*, p. 214.

30. Matthew's version of the tradition changes the Markan plural object of
service (αὐτοῖς) meaning Jesus, James, John, Simon and Andrew, to a specific
singular object (αὐτῷ), meaning Jesus alone. Mark provides a general reference to
service that Matthew, true to form, piously emends. On this point see Taylor,
Gospel According to St. Mark, p. 180: 'Matthew replaces αὐτοῖς with αὐτῷ, thus
representing the act of service to all as an act of gratitude to Jesus.' In arguing that
Simon's mother-in-law's service implies her discipleship, Selvidge notes that mss.
W and 529 replace αὐτοῖς with αὐτῷ ('And Those Who Followed Feared', p. 398).
It is clear, however, that these versions follow Matthew.

her duties? What would the codes of honor and shame have held for her in such a place? Would the mere term 'mother-in-law' conjure for Mark's audience similar caricatures of dreary obligation as in many North American popular cultural expressions? Such questions attend not merely to the activity of this woman as it gets taken up into some Christian ideal, but also with the reality of her daily existence.[31]

While the overwhelming weight of feminist critical commentary on Mk 1.29-31 has focused on the equal discipleship of Simon's mother-in-law, there are notable exceptions that take into account the object and context of her service. In a 1982 article entitled 'Women Disciples in Mark?', Winsome Munro engages all of the texts that refer to women's service within the Gospel.[32] She begins her article with the problem of a discrepancy in Mark's presentation of women characters:

> That women are present in Mark's Gospel is not an issue. They clearly are, in no less than sixteen contexts. What is problematic is that prior to 15.40 they are visible among all categories of people in the narrative (apart from obvious ones such as scribes, Pharisees, elders, priests, guards, and soldiers) except the inner circle of Jesus' disciples. Yet at

31. Although the primary texts of a thoroughgoing patriarchal culture might make the straightforward research of such questions very difficult, there is a growing number of excellent resources for the study of women's daily lives in the Hellenistic context. In terms of the Greco-Roman milieu, e.g., Eva Canterella's *Pandora's Daughters: The Role and Status of Women in Greek and Roman Antiquity* (trans. Maureen B. Fant; Baltimore: The Johns Hopkins University Press, 1987); Sarah B. Pomeroy's 'Selected Bibliography on Women in Antiquity', in John Peradotto and J.P. Sulivan (eds.), *Women in the Ancient World: the Arethusa Papers* (Albany, NY: State of New York University Press, 1984), pp. 315-72; Mary R. Lefkowitz and Maureen B. Fant (eds.), *Women's Life in Greece and Rome: A Sourcebook in Translation* (Baltimore: The Johns Hopkins University Press, 1982). In terms of the early Jewish and Christian milieu, Bernadette Brooten's 'Jewish Women's History in the Roman Period: A Task for Christian Theology', *HTR* 79 (1986), pp. 22-30; and *Women Leaders in the Ancient Synagogue: Inscriptional Evidence and Background Issues* (BJS, 36; Chico, CA: Scholars Press, 1982). In early Christianity, the above-cited work of Kathleen Corley, *Private Women, Public Meals*, offers an excellent analysis of the Greco-Roman social context of women's domestic lives as expressed in Mark, Luke and Matthew. Carolyn Osiek and David L. Balch, *Families in the New Testament World: Households and House Churches* (Louisville, KY: Westminster/John Knox Press, 1997) review different elements of family life, and thereby the roles of women in early Christianity.

32. Winsome Munro, 'Women Disciples in Mark?' *CBQ* 44 (1982), pp. 225-41. Munro's article provided the impetus for Selvidge's 'And Those Who Followed Feared'. See Munro's response to Selvidge and Fiorenza in her 'Women Disciples: Light from Secret Mark', *JFSR* 8 (1992), pp. 49-51.

15.40-41 they suddenly appear, unheralded, as among those who habitually followed Jesus from the time of his ministry in Galilee onward and are prominent from that point till the end of the Gospel in 16.8. How is this to be explained?[33]

Munro claims that Mark's use of διακονέω varies according to its context. Her purpose in delineating the different contexts of 'service' is to argue against androcentric interpretations that dismiss the service of the women described in Mk 15.40-41 as merely providing food and doing menial tasks.[34] She argues that Simon's mother-in-law does indeed provide table service and hospitality for Jesus, Andrew, James and John, while the service of the women named in Mk 15.40-41 is more probably in accordance with discipleship (i.e. following Jesus in his itinerant ministry).[35]

In Munro's interpretation, Mark presents women in a variety of settings of service: from traditional, patriarchally prescribed roles of domestic servitude to more non-traditional, egalitarian roles of discipleship.[36] Such an appreciation for the varied contexts of women's service in the Gospel of Mark yields a feminist hermeneutic that critiques the androcentric bias of Mark's text, and the androcentric nature of its history of interpretation. At the same time, however, Munro's reading embraces a glimpse of the utopian moment in the gospel tradition, most probably unappreciated by Mark, regarding the presence of women as disciples within the Jesus movement:

33. Munro, 'Women Disciples in Mark?', p. 225.

34. For example, Munro, 'Women Disciples in Mark?', p. 232 n. 12, challenges the interpretation of E. Schweizer, *The Good News According to Mark* (trans. D.H. Madvig; Atlanta: John Knox Press, 1970), pp. 359-60, who heads his commentary on Mk 15.40-41 'The Women Who Were Disciples of Jesus', and yet adds 'but see "waiting" in 1.31'.

35. Munro, 'Women Disciples in Mark?', pp. 232-33. With regard to Mk 15.40-41 she argues, 'It is true that serving at table is the primary sense of διακονέω, but that Mark has something different in mind seems evident from the use, twice over (as if for emphasis) of αὐτῷ after ἠκολούθουν and διηκόνουν. It seems that following and serving would not be so pointedly related to Jesus unless it involved more than the performance of menial tasks' (p. 232). But with regard to Mk 1.31 she notes, 'For Mark διακονέω does not characteristically have to do with table service, for its sense varies according to context. The passage in which it is most likely to bear this sense is 1.31, where Simon's mother-in-law, on being healed, "served them." In the setting of the home it can be expected that she had recovered sufficiently to play the part of hostess' (p. 233).

36. Munro's assessment of Mark's references to women's service is affirmed by Corley in *Private Women, Public Meals*, pp. 83-107.

> Despite the overall invisibility of women in the Second Gospel, and
> even because of this tendency, it can be concluded that Mark testifies,
> albeit evasively, to the continuing presence of considerable numbers of
> women, both among Jesus' close disciples and a larger following... The
> evidence is limited, yet Mark points to the possibility of a strong female
> constituency and power base for the ministry of Jesus and for the
> church after his death'.[37]

More recently Joanna Dewey, in her commentary on Mark in *Searching the Scriptures* (edited by Schüssler Fiorenza) notes the difference
between the service of Simon's mother-in-law and that of the women
described at the cross in Mk 15.40-41. Interestingly, Dewey seems to
have come full circle in appreciating the old androcentric claim that
her service is merely a demonstration of Jesus' healing. Finally, however, she suggests that Mark ultimately may have more in store for
Simon's mother-in-law than merely making dinner.

> To demonstrate that the healing has occurred, Mark relates that she rose
> 'and served them.' *Diakonia* (service) often refers to waiting on table. It
> is an important word, here describing women's or (slaves') activities but
> later describing Mark's ideal of discipleship—which in retrospect may
> apply here as well.[38]

Dewey's final claim poignantly expresses the deep wish at work in
the history of feminist critical engagement of Mk 1.29-31. The origin of
this wish resides within the liberative drive of the endeavor: namely,
that not one sister be left behind. Through the connection of Simon's
mother-in-law's service in Mk 1.29-31 with Jesus' teaching in Mk 10.45
and the description of the women who have followed and served
Jesus in Mk 15.40-41, feminist interpreters have carried Simon's
mother-in-law forward through the Gospel and the history of early
Christianity and championed her as an example of true discipleship.
In the various methodological executions of this project, however,
Simon's mother-in-law's redemption as a disciple of Jesus has come at
the cost of discounting her context and idealizing her service.

Is it not possible, and more compelling, that Mark's Gospel
preserves traditions that reveal women in traditionally bound roles of
domestic servitude, while at the same time preserving traditions that
reveal women in liberated roles of equal discipleship? Is it not possible that the Gospel traditions bear witness to the fact that women were

---

37. Corley, *Private Women, Public Meals*, p. 241.

38. Joanna Dewey, 'Mark', in E.S. Fiorenza (ed.), *Searching the Scriptures*, II,
pp. 470-509 (476).

active participants within the Jesus movement, as well as to the fact that women lived within patriarchally organized gender roles in the movement and that within those roles they were subject to the practice of unpaid domestic labor?

I contend that the political struggle to liberate women and other 'non persons' from patriarchal oppression requires a clear appreciation for, and challenge to, Simon's mother-in-law's context of service. Rather than a mascot in the parade of egalitarian discipleship, such work yields an appreciation for the various inequities among subjects, objects, and contexts of 'service' at work in the Gospel traditions. Indeed, such insights might correspond to a renewed awareness for such inequities in the world today and the conviction to work to change them.

5. *Conclusion*

This review of feminist critical scholarship on Mk 1.29-31 reveals a strategy for reading Simon Peter's mother-in-law's service as a witness to the discipleship of women in the Gospel and early Christianity. Ironically, the attempt to redeem her work has led to the disregard of the particularities of her service (i.e. its context and its object). The quest to establish a larger claim about women and service in the Gospel and early Christianity subordinates the particularities, ambiguities, and tensions of the individual traditions and the individuals described within the traditions. Such a quest runs the risk of idealizing Simon's mother-in-law's work at the expense of attending to her person. Furthermore, it misses the opportunity to reflect upon her work, its specific context and object, as a site for critique and challenge in the political goal of feminist biblical scholarship to work toward the liberation of women and other 'non persons' from patriarchal oppression.

In this investigation I have found myself in the peculiar position of reading against the grain of feminist biblical critical discourse that has sought to establish the Gospel of Mark as a witness to the equal discipleship of women and men in early Christianity. No doubt such claims about the service of women in the Jesus movement and early church have had a great deal to do with popularizing the acceptance of women in leadership roles within the church today. Perhaps such an overstatement of the case was necessary for a time to correct the androcentric bias against women's discipleship in Mk 15.40-41. The time has come, however, to hear Winsome Munro's case again.[39] The references to διακονέω in Mk 1.31 and 15.41 are different. The implications of this claim leave us with a narrative that is far from a feminist charter, and a Jesus movement that is far from a pristine origin of equality between the sexes. Such an interpretive practice does not read Mark's Gospel as a linear, coherent story, but as a site of competing and conflicting power relations—a discourse—in which 'the good news' is not arrived at in a utopian conclusion, but rather is glimpsed repeatedly in the struggle of women and other 'non persons' for liberation from oppression.[40]

Such a reading of this pericope does not present a moral of the story in which Jesus is constructed into a feminist hero who 'frees' women to the service of God through invisible domestic labor. It does not find transforming, life-giving good news in the slim hope that Jesus had women disciples, even though they continued to function within their socially inscribed roles of cook, cleaner and servant. In this reading there is no 'happy' ending for Simon's mother-in-law, no ultimate transformation. The reading, however, does see in the text a witness to Jesus' attention to Simon's mother-in-law's particular situation, to her healing, as well as to her service. As such, the tradition offers a site to view the ambiguity of her context, and our own. Larger constructs of subjugation and domination can be read for evidence of healing. So too, larger utopian visions such as liberation and equality

---

39. Such a rehearing of her case must, unfortunately, be posthumous. Professor Munro died in her native South Africa in 1994. She had returned there for a visit after living and teaching in exile in the United States for 19 years. In 1965 South African police raided her apartment for her anti-apartheid activities. Since that time and until her death she worked as a Presbyterian minister, a professor of religion, and a church educator in the United States. While academically accomplished and well published, Professor Munro never held an academic position above that of assistant professor. In light of the struggle of her own national context and professional situation, I would guess that she had a great deal to say about the ambiguities and complexities of liberation and servitude. For a full review of her life and accomplishments see Michael Cooper, 'Winsome Munro—1925-1994', *RSN* 9.3 (September 1994), p. 24.

40. Munro, in her article 'Women Disciples: Light from Secret Mark', p. 48, articulates a similar sentiment about feminist-critical scholarship's stance toward the androcentric nature of the Bible: 'There should, moreover, be no presumption that feminist rereadings of texts will, or ought to, yield good news for and about women, or accord with modern feminist values. They may or may not. Both outcomes are to be accepted as bringing to light the history and experience of women. "Mirror reading," or reading backwards from an antagonistic text can possibly help recover the submerged history of assertive women.'

can be discerned for their own inconsistencies and injustices. The insight that such contradictions, and the struggles they evidence, are in Mark's Gospel—and in our own everyday lives (if we read them closely)—might just be the best news for Simon's mother-in-law, and for us.

MARK'S HERO OF THE TWELFTH-YEAR MIRACLES:
THE HEALING OF THE WOMAN WITH THE HEMORRHAGE
AND THE RAISING OF JAIRUS'S DAUGHTER (MARK 5.21-43)

Wendy Cotter CSJ

Markan scholarship has recognized for almost a century that just as surely as this Gospel shows that it is not the historical memoirs of St Peter, neither is it the free composition of the evangelist we call Mark. Wrede illustrated the evidence that it was Mark who deliberately shaped the Gospel,[1] but Dibelius and Bultmann uncovered the basic forms, the earlier sources upon which he was dependent.[2] Redaction criticism is only sharpened when one identifies those pre-Gospel forms, for then the patterns of the evangelist are all the more clear, while the positioning of the material further illuminates his purpose. Mark's redaction of his sources, both by editing the forms themselves and by the way he organized their presentation allow his particular Christology to shine out as distinctly his own.

It was all of 25 years ago that Etienne Trocmé critiqued Markan studies for a lack of attention to these important distinctions in strata and their significance to Markan exegesis.

> No sensible person would dream to-day of going back to a non-christological interpretation of this fascinating little book [Mark's Gospel]. But it may be doubted whether enough thought has been given to the relationship between the evangelist's own Christology and that...of the various layers of tradition used by him.[3]

Certainly this applies to the pre-Markan miracle stories employed by Mark in his Gospel. It is commonplace to notice that Mark wants the power (δύναμις) of Jesus to underline his identity as Son of God,

---

1. Wilhelm Wrede, *Das Messiasgeheimnis in den Evangelien* (Göttingen, 1901).

2. Martin Dibelius, *Die Formgeschichtedes Evangeliums* (Leipzig, 1919); Rudolf Bultmann, *Die Geschte der synoptischen Tradition* (Leipzig, 1921).

3. Étienne Trocmé, 'Is There a Markan Christology?', in Barnabas Lindars and Stephen S. Smalley (eds.), *Christ and the Spirit in the New Testament: Festschrift for Charles Francis Digby Moule* (Cambridge: Cambridge University Press, 1973), pp. 3-13 (3).

as he wants the disciples' blindness to that identity to be shown up in their obtuse responses to those miracles. Both of these themes serve the 'Messianic Secret', a secret that is only uncovered when, at the death of Jesus, the curtain in the Temple is ripped from top to bottom (Mk 15.38), and the centurion mysteriously calls out, 'Truly, this man was the son of God' (Mk 15.39). But Mark's Christology should be explored beyond the Messianic Secret themes, when there are grounds for doing so. To begin with, if Mark has accepted pre-Markan traditions and uses them, surely this means that he endorses the claims they make. That too deserves to be noticed and factored into any reconstruction of Markan Christology. One of the best examples of Mark's incorporation of pre-Markan material is found in his use of the two 'twelfth-year miracles', the healing of the woman with the hemorrhage and the raising of Jairus' daughter (Mk 5.21-43).

With respect to Markan interventions, the evidence would suggest only two additions: Mk 5.37, where the disciples are included in the story of Jairus (as they are not in the first account), and Mk 5.43a, 'and he gave orders that no one should know this', an obvious example of the 'Messianic Secret' theme. Aside from these, the stories themselves do not hold any particular Markan theme that could support the conclusion that it was he who created them.

What does Mark gain by presenting these two pre-Markan stories? The answer to this question involves the deeper probe into the function of these miracle stories rather than quickly assigning them to the service only of the Messianic Secret.

First of all, was it Mark who joined these stories as is his habit elsewhere in the Gospel?[4] Or in this case, were the miracles linked already at the pre-Markan stratum? For Dibelius the number of linkages between the stories is so dense that it would seem that they were indeed joined prior to Mark's own work. Besides the fact that the stories link two females in need of Jesus' miracles, there is: (a) the theme of 'twelve' in the length of illness of the woman (5.25) and the age of the girl (5.42); (b) the element of 'daughter' found in Jesus' address to the woman (5.34) and the relation of the sick girl to Jairus (5.23); (c) the contrast of public and private, in Jesus' public exposure of the woman cured (5.32-33), and the Jesus' privacy for the raising of the girl (5.40-41); (d) the contrast of the woman needing to touch Jesus for her healing (5.27-28) and Jesus touching the girl to bring her back to life (5.41-42).[5]

---

4. Mk 3.21-31; 6.7-6.30; 9.2-14; 11.12-20.
5. Dibelius, *Die Formgeschichte des Evangeliums*, p. 219; Bultmann, *The History*

These special internal connections stand apart from the usual Markan 'sandwiches', where the purpose is usually only to establish a sense of time lapse. We just do not find such close narrative comparisons and contrasts in the linked stories themselves. In my view, the evidence better supports Dibelius's judgment that the stories were linked prior to Mark.

The reason for the joining of the miracles at the pre-Markan stage is still an open question, but perhaps the most frequent assumption is that the mention of Jairus as 'a leader of the synagogue' is to introduce a theme of 'Jesus versus Jewish religious custom/Law'. Whether this can be substantiated, and the article of A.-J. Levine has persuasively challenged any such interpretation,[6] the fact is that Mark himself shows that he is quite ignorant of Jewish scripture and customs. As we know, his Gospel opens with an erroneous identification of Mk 1.2 as from Isaiah when it is a conflation of Exod. 23.20 and Mal. 3.1! But if Mark knows little of the scripture he knows even less of Pharisaic prescriptions as his awkward and inadequate comment in Mk 7.3-4 makes so clear. Therefore, a linkage of the stories to introduce a conflict over Torah is not coherent with this evangelist.

To understand how Mark uses the miracle stories to his advantage we have to understand their nature. The definition of the character of miracle stories has been heavily influenced by Dibelius and Bultmann. One example is their agreement that there is no 'portraiture' in miracle stories. Rather, the miracles focus on power with 'automatic functioning' which 'is particularly clear in the story of the woman with an issue of blood: Jesus feels, when the woman touches him, that a power (δύναμις) has gone out of him'.[7] 'It is consistent with this to observe that what is as good as no notice at all is taken of the inner disposition of the person healed.'[8]

Here Bultmann appeals to Dibelius when he denies 'portraiture' to

---

of the Synoptic Tradition, pp. 214-15; E. Lohmeyer, *Das Evangelium des Markus* (Göttingen: Vandenhoeck & Ruprecht, 1963), pp. 104-110; P.J. Achtemeier, 'Towards the Isolation of the Pre-Markan Miracle Catenae', *JBL* (1970), pp. 276-79; L. Schenke, *Die Wundererzählungen des Markus evangeliums* (Stuttgart: Katholisches Bibelwerk, 1974), p. 199.

6.   Amy-Jill Levine, 'Discharging Responsibility: Matthean Jesus, Biblical Law, and Hemorrhaging Woman', in David R. Bauer and M.A. Powell (eds.), *Treasures New and Old: Contributions to Matthean Studies* (Atlanta: Scholars Press, 1996), pp. 379-97. Reprinted in A.-J. Levine (with Marianne Blickenstaff) (ed.), *A Feminist Companion to the Gospel of Matthew* (Sheffield: Sheffield Academic Press, 2001), pp. 70-87.

7.   Bultmann, *History of the Synoptic Tradition*, p. 219.

8.   Bultmann, *History of the Synoptic Tradition*, p. 219.

miracle stories: 'The style of the miracle story is related to that of the apophthegm to this extent—the "absence of portraiture" (Dibelius) and all that it involves is characteristic of both'.[9]

It is certainly true that the 'inner disposition' of the woman, and the father of the dead girl, are not described. But may we say that neither they nor Jesus have been given any portrait at all? In this paper, I want to explore the richness that each of these two pre-Markan stories brings to the portrait of the Markan Jesus on his way to the cross. In order to do that, I will first treat each miracle story in turn, for, despite their interconnectedness, they do not actually need each other to communicate their particular significance to the portrait of Jesus. Then, the paper will conclude with an observation about how the placement of these miracles assists the evangelist in his christological statement.

The Healing of the Woman with the Hemorrhage: Mark 5.25-34[10]

In what way does Mark's Christology take on more light by the inclusion of this pre-Markan story? An examination of its basic form shows that extraordinary attention is given to the woman's situation. In all, six items of information are supplied about her flow of blood: (1) she had suffered for 12 years (5.25); (2) she had suffered under many physicians (5.26); (3) she had spent all her money (5.26); (4) she was no better but rather was growing worse (5.26); (5) she heard about Jesus (5.27); and (6) she decided to come up behind him and touch his garments (5.27) because she said, 'If I touch even his garments, I shall be made well' (5. 28). In reality, only the detail of her having a flow of blood is necessary to fulfill the first part of the basic miracle story (i.e. the identification of the problem) (vv. 25-28). The lengthy and detailed introduction seems almost defensive, an excuse for unfitting behavior, an explanation of innocence on the question of why she would touch Jesus. This surely is the action that has caused nervousness in the narrator, as we see from the corroborating evidence of the woman's fear when Jesus demands to see the person who received a healing. 'But the woman, knowing what had been done to her, came in fear and trembling and fell down before him, and told him the whole truth' (5.33). Why, however, should the narrator treat the woman's behavior as if he thinks it requires an excuse, and why should the woman

---

9.   Bultmann, *History of the Synoptic Tradition*, p. 220.

10.   That this miracle story was originally independent and has its own message and function, see Bultmann, *The History of the Synoptic Tradition*, pp. 214-15; E. Lohmeyer, *Das Evangeliums des Markus*, p. 104.

behave in such a fearful way? Notice how the story builds tension between the woman who wants to remain hidden and the healer insistent on discovering the healed. Jesus will not move and demands an encounter with the person healed.

Although some scholars suggest that the woman must be ashamed that she has violated Torah by entering a crowd, and touching another when she has an emission, we have to ask if such an allusion was at all available to the Gentile Mark and his Gentile community? Moreover, there is no mention of Torah by anyone in the story, including Jesus. Thus the explanation of the shyness of the woman, and her fearfulness before Jesus must be seen as it would have been understood in the context of the general world of Greco-Roman antiquity.

The ideal woman was expected to be found at home, surrounded by her family, shy, modest and quiet.[11] A few examples help to clarify these expectations. Valerius Maximus, the first-century historian, provides a discussion of 'Severity' in which he includes examples of the punishment of wives for indiscretion. Among them we read about these two examples:

> Rugged too was the marital brow of C. Sulpicius Galus. He divorced his wife because he learned that she had walked abroad with head uncovered. The sentence was abrupt, but there was a reason behind it. 'To have your good looks approved,' says he, 'the law limits you to my eyes only. For them assemble the tools of beauty, for them look your best, trust to *their* closer familiarity. Any further sight of you, summoned by needless incitement, has to be mired in suspicion and crimination.'
> Nor did Q. Antitius Vetus feel otherwise. He divorced his wife because he had seen her in public talking tête-à-tête with a certain common freedwoman.[12]

While Valerius notes the severity of the punishment, we note that he does not contradict the values directed towards these wives.

We see the same values in the praise Pliny the Younger awards to the Emperor Trajan on the virtue of his wife Plotina, 'How modest she [Plotina] is in her attire, how moderate in the number of her attendants, how unassuming when she walks abroad!'[13] Tertullian only

---

11. For the general ideals of the upright woman, see Bruce Malina, 'Honor and Shame: Pivotal Values of the First-Century Mediterranean World', *The New Testament World: Insights from Cultural Anthropology* (Louisville, KY: Westminster/John Knox Press, rev. edn, 1993), pp. 28-62, especially pp. 48-52.

12. Valerius Maximus (translated by D.R. Shckleton Bailey; 3 vols; London, England and Cambridge, Massachusetts, 2000), pp. 2, 6, 10, 11.

13. Pliny the Younger, *Panegyricus* (trans. Betty Radice; 2 vols; London: Heinemann, 1969), pp. 2, 83.

echoes this when he says, 'A female would rather see than be seen.'[14]

Whether or not this is true, Tertullian clearly *thought* it was for the modest woman. As a matter of fact, there is no story in the New Testament where any woman asks Jesus for a miracle for herself. Rather, others ask for her, as in the case of Peter's mother in law (Mk 1.29-31), or Jesus himself notices the woman, as in the case of Luke's woman bent for 18 years (Lk. 13.10-17). We have a case of one woman asking for a miracle for someone else, and this is the Syro-Phoenician woman whose daughter is possessed (Mk 7.24-30), yet notice that her portrait is that of a pest. And Matthew furthers the image (Mt. 15.21-28) by including the element that the disciples 'came and begged him, saying, "Send her away, for she is crying after us"' (Mt. 15.23).

This would help explain the copious excuses for the woman, who violates the modesty of women and deliberately touches a strange man in the streets. As the story unfolds and Jesus demands to see who in the crowd has touched him, how is he to suppose that it is a woman? When the woman does come forward she exposes her identity in public and tells Jesus 'the whole truth'. Here, I suggest, the response of Jesus is very important to the Christian audience: 'Daughter, your faith has made you well; go in peace and be healed of your disease' (Mk 5.34). The choice of 'Daughter' is a very sensitive one. Given the intimate nature of the woman's ailment, it allows a tenderness of address and at the same time maintains the most non-erotic, protective character for Jesus' relationship to her. Second, Jesus attributes the healing to her faith. Thus whatever might have been deemed bold or unseemly is affirmed by Jesus as motivated by piety.

It is clear that the command 'go and be healed of your disease' is a secondary inclusion, since the story already tells us that the woman feels her healing (5.29) and that Jesus could feel the healing power that went out of him (5.30). Thus, the command to be healed is completely redundant.

Seen through the lens of the Greco-Roman world, what does this story reveal about the hero? In this miracle story, the expectations of sexual roles in the dynamic of honor–shame are surprised. Despite the fact that Jesus is so sure that power has gone out from him, so sure that he insists on an encounter with the person who touched him, he disclaims public honor for the healing of the woman when she presents herself. With the woman physically at his feet, feeling ashamed

---

14. Tertullian, 'On the Veiling of Virgins', in *The Ante-Nicene Fathers*, IV (New York: Charles Scribner's Sons, 1905), p. 17.

of her boldness, Jesus calls her 'Daughter', protecting her honor by giving to their encounter the safest relationship for her touch.

Second, Jesus grants the honor of the cure to her, by virtue of her 'faith', the decision she took to touch him. Yet, it is clear to the listener that the power that flowed from Jesus and created the instant cure in the woman and indeed is the reason for the miracle. Jesus protects the woman's honor by affirming her bold action as an expression of deep faith. This removes her shame and accords her respect. In my view, this story functions to signal the reader that the hero around whom the community is gathered is astonishingly free from the need for public honors, and also from the need to dominate women. Moreover, Jesus' identification of the woman's act as one of 'faith' illustrates his *humanitas*, his attention to the human heart over the rigid norms of society's codes. There is a theme of liberation from strictures that penetrates the entire story. The uncontrollable flow of power from Jesus stops the sickly flow of blood from the woman. Her decision to touch him means that his power can touch her and set her free not only from her illness but from the strictures of her fear.

The Raising of Jairus's Daughter[15]

It is important first of all to state that the claim that a hero could actually bring someone back from the dead is very rare in antiquity.[16] We can only understand the significance intended by the Jesus story if we know the set of Gods and Heroes, and their legends, already known by the first Christians.

Gods Who Have Raised the Dead

Only three deities have legends that include such power: Asclepius, Heracles and Isis. A brief review of these deities' legends so familiar to the audience is in order here, since they form one sort of religious backdrop for the significance of Jesus' miracle.

Isis belongs to the Egyptian pantheon, of course, but she should be

15. Dibelius, *Die Formgeschichte des Evangeliums*, p. 219; Bultmann, *The History of the Synoptic Tradition*, pp. 214-15; E. Lohmeyer, *Das Evangelium des Markus* (Göttingen: Vandenhoeck & Ruprecht, 1963), pp. 104-110; P.J. Achtemeier, 'Towards the Isolation of the Pre-Markan Miracle Catenae', *JBL* (1970), pp. 276-79; L. Schenke, *Die Wundererzählungen des Markus evangeliums* (Stuttgart: Katholisches Bibelwerk, 1974), p. 199.

16. Wendy Cotter, *Miracles in Greco-Roman Antiquity: A Sourcebook for the Study of New Testament Miracle Stories* (London: Routledge, 1999), pp. 12-15, 24-26, 33-34, 45-47, 48, 52-53.

included here since by the Hellenistic period her devotion was spreading throughout the Mediterranean world. In the Imperial period, a shrine to her was erected in the Roman Pomerium by Gaius Caligula.[17] Isis discovered the drug that gives immortality, but the only person on whom she used it was her son Horus.[18]

As for Heracles and Asclepius, both began their life as mortals and won divinity through their heroism on behalf of humankind. It is their compassion that leads them to perform this most perfect of all 'healings'. In the case of Asclepius, the price of his compassion is his own death.

Asclepius/Aesculapius (Homeric Period). Asclepius was slain by Zeus for bringing the dead back to life. Several versions of the story exist. One of the popular versions of the story is connected to the myth of Hippolytus. When Theseus's son, Hippolytus, discovered that his step-mother desired him, he violently upbraided her. As a result she committed suicide, but she left a note falsely accusing Hippolytus of raping her. Theseus exiled Hippolytus and, while the young man drove away in his chariot by the sea, a monster appeared above the water, frightening the horses. As they reared up, Hippolytus was thrown from the chariot and killed. Then Artemis, who had a special love for Hippolytus, inspired Asclepius to bring him back to life. But this drew Zeus's outrage, and he killed Asclepius with a thunderbolt.

In another version, this one told by Diodorus Siculus (c. 60–30 BCE),[19] the god Hades comes to the throne of Zeus to bring charges against Asclepius that through his interference Hades' kingdom is being denied its proper population. As punishment, Zeus takes a thunderbolt fashioned by the Cyclopes and kills Asclepius.

Apollodorus (c. 146 BCE) contributes the names of six men Asclepius raised from the dead. He explains that Zeus's execution of Asclepius was due to his fear that humans would eventually 'come to the rescue of each other', that is, be independent of Zeus's power to threaten their lives.[20]

---

17. See, for example, her treatment by Plutarch, 'Isis and Osiris', *Moralia*, V (trans. Frank Cole Babbitt; London: Heinemann, 1936), pp. 41ff.
18. Diodorus Siculus 1.25.6.
19. Diodorus Siculus 4.71.1-3.
20. Apollodorus 3.10.3. The popularity of the legend is clear from its representation in Philodemus (c. 110–40 BCE), *De Pietate* 52; Virgil, *Aeneid* (first century BCE), 7.765-773; Pliny the Elder (first century CE), *Natural History* 29.1.3; Pausanias (c. 150 CE), 'Corinth', *Description of Greece* 26.4-5; Sextus Empiricus (c. 200 CE), *Against the Professors* 260-62.

I found some who are reported to have been raised by him, to wit, Capaneus and Lycurgus, as Stesichorus [645–555 BCE] says in the *Eriphyle*; Hippolytus, as the author of the *Naupatica* [sixth century BCE] reports; Tyndareus, as Panyassis [c. 500 BCE] says; Hymenaeus, as the Orphics report; and Glaucus, son of Minos, as Melasagoras [fifth century BCE] relates. But Zeus, fearing that men might acquire the healing art from him and so come to the rescue of each other smote him with a thunderbolt.

In the Roman period the statue of Asclepius was placed in the temple of Apollo, now said to be his father. Apuleius' text shows us that Asclepius' worship was 'everywhere':

Of these [good daimones] they deem gods only those who, having guided the chariots of their lives wisely and justly and having been endowed afterward by men as divinities with shrines and religious ceremonies are commonly worshipped as Amphiaraus in Boeotia Mopsus in Africa, Osiris in Egypt, one in part of the world and another in another part, Asclepius everywhere.[21]

Finally we should mention Artemidorus's five-volume work of collected dream interpretations, which records the most common associations concerning dreams of Asclepius, which serve to prove his pre-eminence as the god of healing and 'help in time of need':

If Asclepius is set up in a temple and stands upon a pedestal, if he is seen and adored, it means good luck for all. But if he moves and approaches or goes into a house, it prophesies sickness and famine. For then especially do men need this god. But for those who are already sick, it signifies recovery. For the god is called Paean (the Healer). Asclepius always indicates those who help in time of need and those who manage the house of the dreamer. [22]

In this dream interpretation we can see that Asclepius's powers to heal and to raise the dead have resulted in his being regarded as 'judge' of life:

A young wrestler who was anxious about the preliminary examination dreamt that Asclepius was the judge and that, as he marched in review along with the other boys, the god eliminated him from the competition. In real life, he died before the start of the match. For the god was responsible for his leaving not the contest but rather life itself, of which he is considered to be the judge.[23]

---

21. Apuleius, *De Deo Socratis* 14.153; *Asclepius*, 1.254.
22. Artemidorus, *Oneirocritica* 2.37.
23. Artemidorus, *Oneirocritica* 5.13.

These many references to Asclepius and his various legends, his devotions and his popularity as a god of compassion 'everywhere', help us see that for the Christians to make a similar claim for Jesus is to place him on an equal ground with the greatest god of healing known to the Greco-Roman world.

Heracles/Hercules (Legendary). Heracles is said to have fought with Hades for the life of Alcestis. According to the legend as told by Apollodorus, Admetus longed to marry Pelias's daughter, Alcestis, but Pelias demanded that Admetus was to first harness a lion to a chariot. Apollo stepped in and did this for Admetus so that it looked as if Admetus would be able to marry Alcestis. However, at the marriage ceremony, Admetus committed grave offense against the goddess Artemis by forgetting to sacrifice to her. Furious at his insult, Artemis demanded his life. Apollo cajoled Artemis to accept a substitute for Admetus, but on the day that Admetus was to die, no one including his parents, was willing to die for him. Finally, Admetus's bride, Alcestis, offered herself, and cowardly Admetus allowed her to die. It is at this point that Heracles appears on the scene. Some legends say that he went down to the underworld and fought Hades for Alcestis's life. 'But the maiden [Artemis] sent her up again, or as some say, Hercules fought with Hades and brought her up to him'.[24]

Euripides (485–406 BCE) immortalized the legend of Alcestis in his play of the same name. In the following dialogue, Heracles explains that he ambushed Hades at the tomb:[25]

Admetus:	O scion nobly-born of Zeus most high,
	Blessings on thee! The Father who begat thee
	Keep thee! Thou only has restored my fortunes.
	How didst thou bring her from shades to light?
Hercules:	I closed in conflict with the Lord of the Spirits.
Admetus:	Where, say'st thou, didst thou fight this fight with Death?
Hercules:	From ambush by the tomb mine hands ensnared him.

(Heracles now explains that Alcestis must wait until the third day to be unconsecrated to the Underworld)

Admetus:	Now wherefore speechless standeth thus my wife?
Heracles:	Tis not vouchsafed thee yet to hear her voice,
	Ere to the Powers beneath the earth she be
	Unconsecrated, and the third day come.
	But lead her in, and, just man as thou art,

24. Apollodorus 1.9.15.
25. Euripides, *Alcestis* 4.1136-63.

Henceforth, Admetus, reverence still the guest.
Farewell. But I must go, and work the work
Set by the king, the son of Sthenelaus.

(Finally, Heracles leaves and Admetus promises sacrifices of praise and rejoicing)

Admetus: Abide with us, a sharer of our hearth
Heracles: Hereafter this. Now must I hasten on.
Admetus: O prosper thou, and come again in peace!
[exit Heracles]
Through all my realm, I publish to my folk
That, for these blessings, dances they array,
And that atonement-fumes from altars rise.
For now happier days that those o'erpast
Have we attained. I own me blest indeed.
Chorus: O the works of the Gods — in manifold forms they reveal them.
Manifold things unhoped — for the Gods to accomplishment to bring.
And the things that we looked for, the Gods deign not to fulfill them;
And the paths undiscerned of our eyes, the Gods unseal them.
So fell this marvelous thing.

Significant for our study is the testimony of Aelius Aristides (c. 129–181 CE) to the ongoing devotion to Heracles throughout the Greco-Roman world:[26]

> But why should we speak of ancient history? For the activity of the god is still now manifest. On the one hand, as we hear, he does marvelous deeds at Gadira and is believed to be second to none of all the gods. And on the other hand, in Messene in Sicily he frees men from all diseases, and those who have escaped danger on the sea attribute the benefaction equally to Poseidon and Heracles. One could list many other places sacred to the god, and other manifestations of his power.

As we see, both Asclepius and Heracles are associated with healings and raisings from the dead, but are very different in character. Lucian spoofs this contrast in his 'Dialogues of the Gods. Zeus, Asclepius and Heracles'. His satirical humor rests on the conventionally pious devotions known and accepted in his own day. In this scene below, the two gods are fighting and Zeus must intervene to stop their quarrel:[27]

26. P. Aelius Aristides, *Heracles* 40.12.
27. Lucian, *Dialogues of the Gods* 7.15.

Zeus:	Stop quarreling, you two; you're just like a couple of men. It's quite improper and out of place at the table of the gods.
Heracles:	But, Zeus, do you really mean this medicine man to have a place above me?
Asclepius:	He does, by Zeus, for I'm your better.
Heracles:	How, you crackbrain? Because Zeus blasted you with his thunderbolt for your impious doings, [here the reference is clearly to his raising people from the dead], and now you've received immortality because he relented and pitied you?
Asclepius:	You must have forgotten, Heracles, how you too were scorched to death on Oeta,[28] that you taunt me with getting burned.
Heracles:	That doesn't mean our lives were the same. I'm the son of Zeus, and performed all those labors cleaning up the world, by overcoming monsters, and punishing men of violence; but you're just a herb-chopper and quack, useful perhaps among suffering humanity for administering potions, but without one manly deed to show.
Asclepius:	Have you nothing to say of how I healed your burns when you came up half-scorched the other day? Between the tunic and the fire after it, your body was in a fine mess. Besides, if nothing else, I was never a slave like you, carding wool in Lydia, wearing purple, and being beaten with Omphale's golden sandal.[29] What is more, I never killed my wife and children in a fit of spleen.
Heracles:	If you don't stop insulting me, you'll pretty soon find out that your immortality won't help you much. I'll pick you up and throw you head first out of heaven, so that you'll crack your skull, and not even Apollo the Healer will be able to do anything for you.
Zeus:	Stop it, I say; don't disturb our dinner-party, or I'll send you both from the table. But it's only reasonable, Heracles, that Asclepius should have a place above you, as he died before you.

In particular, the insults here act as cultural instruction on the ways in which certain features of these heroes leave them open to censure. Asclepius' work with herbs and medicines opens him to charges of quackery, and he is derided for his lack of manly acts of bravery. Heracles is a son of god, and brave, but the other side of his bravery is his violence.

Despite the wit of Lucian, in fact, by observing it, we see how thoroughly these gods were loved and admired. Their death and

28. Heracles is said to have committed suicide by fire.
29. A reference, as we know, to Heracles having to be Queen Omphale of Lydia's slave for three years.

eternal life are seen by people as directly connected to acts of compassion for others.

The Jewish Deity and his Prophets Elijah and Elisha

For the millions of Jews in the Greco-Roman world, stories of raising a dead child easily bring to mind the miracles of their God in response to the prayers of the two great prophets Elijah and Elisha. First, Elijah's prayer is answered so that a pagan woman's dead son is brought back to life.

> After this the son of the woman, the mistress of the house, became ill; his illness was so severe that there was no breath left in him. She then said to Elijah, 'What have you against me, O man of God? You have come to me to bring my sin to remembrance, and to cause the death of my son!' But he said to her, 'Give me your son'. He took him from her bosom, carried him up into the upper chamber where he was lodging, and laid him on his own bed. He cried out to the Lord, 'O Lord my God, have you brought calamity even upon the widow with whom I am staying, by killing her son?' Then he stretched himself upon the child three times, and cried out to the Lord, 'O Lord my God, let this child's life come into him again'. The Lord listened to the voice of Elijah; the life of the child came into him again. Elijah took the child, brought him down from the upper chamber into the house, and gave him to his mother; then Elijah said, 'See, your son is alive'. So the woman said to Elijah, 'Now I know that you are a man of God, and that the word of the Lord in your mouth is truth (1 Kgs. 17.17-24 NRSV).

It is easy to see how the Elisha story is dependent on the Elijah account, but it is much more elaborate. Here is how Elisha's prayer wins the life of the woman's dead son:

> When the child was older, he went out one day to his father among the reapers. He complained to his father, 'Oh my head, my head!' The father said to his servant, 'Carry him to his mother'. He carried him and brought him to his mother; the child sat in her lap until noon, and he died. She went up and laid him on the bed of the man of God, closed the door on him, and left. Then she called to her husband, and said, 'Send me one of the servants and one of the donkeys, so that I may quickly go to the man of God and come back again'. He said, 'Why go to him today? It is neither new moon nor Sabbath'. She said, 'It will be alright'. Then she saddled the donkey and said to her servant, 'Urge the animal on; do not hold back for me unless I tell you'. So she set out, and came to the man of God at Mount Carmel. When the man of God saw her coming, he said to Gehazi his servant, 'Look, there is the Shunammite woman; run at once to meet her, and say to her, 'Are you all right? Is your husband all right? Is the child all right?' She answered, 'It is all right'. When she came to the man of God at the mountain, she caught hold of his feet. Gehazi approached to push her away. But the man of

God said, 'Let her alone, for she is in bitter distress; the Lord has hidden it from me and has not told me'. Then she said, 'Did I ask my Lord for a son? Did I not say, 'Do not mislead me?' He said to Gehazi, 'Gird up your loins, and take my staff in your hand and go. If you meet anyone, give no greeting and if anyone greets you, do not answer; and lay my staff on the face of the child'. Then the mother of the child said, 'As the Lord lives, and as you yourself live, I will not leave without you'. So he rose up and followed her. Gehazi went on ahead and laid the staff on the face of the child, but there was no sound or sign of life. He came back to meet him and told him, 'The child has not awakened'. When Elisha came into the house, he saw the child lying dead on his bed. So he went in and closed the door on the two of them, and prayed to the Lord. Then he got up on the bed and lay upon the child, putting his mouth upon his mouth, his eyes upon his eyes, and his hands upon his hands; and while he lay bent over him, the flesh of the child became warm. He got down, walked once to and fro in the room, then got up again and bent over him; the child sneezed seven times, and the child opened his eyes. Elisha summoned Gehazi and said, 'Call the Shunammite woman'. So he called her. When she came to him, he said, 'Take your son'. She came and fell at his feet, bowing to the ground; then she took her son and left (2 Kgs 4.18-37 NRSV).

How such stories were understood or interpreted by Jews in the first century CE cannot be answered with just one example. But since Josephus offers us his own retelling of the Elijah account we are able at least to view the elements he modifies according to his own perception and first-century sensibilities:

Now the woman of whom we spoke [the widow of Sareptha], who gave food to the prophet—her son fell ill so seriously that he ceased to breathe and seemed to be dead, whereupon she wept bitterly, injuring herself with her hands and uttering such cries as her grief prompted; and she reproached the prophet for having come to her to convict her of sin and on that account causing the death of her son. But he urged her to take heart and give her son over to him, for he would, he said, restore him to her alive. So she gave him over, and he carried him into the chamber in which he himself lived, and placed him on the bed; then he cried aloud to God, saying that He would ill requite the woman who had received him and nourished him, if He took her son from her, and he prayed God to send the breath into the child again and give him life. Thereupon God, because He took pity on the mother and also because He wished graciously to spare the prophet from seeming to have come to her for the purpose of harming her, beyond all expectation brought the child back to life. Then the mother thanked the prophet and said that now she clearly realized that the Deity spoke with him (*Ant.* 8.325-27).[30]

---

30. Josephus, *Ant.* 5.

Josephus has added three elements that bring greater emotion to the rather laconic presentation of the situation in 1 Kgs 17.8-16. He introduces the woman's cries of grief, the prophet's consoling words and promise to restore the child to life, and he has articulated reasons for God's granting the prophet's prayer. At the same time he has removed two elements from the story.

First, he changes the roughness of the prophet's behavior from taking the child from his mother without an explanation. Second, he has avoided the description of the prophet's prostration on the child. Josephus thus places the emphasis on the mercy and compassion of Elijah and the power of his petition to God for the life of the child.

Heroes Who Have Raised the Dead

Apollonius of Tyana (first century CE). The only human hero known to the first-century Greco-Roman world for his raising the dead is Apollonius of Tyana. Since his miracles postdate the time of Jesus, his tradition could not have influenced pre-Markan material. We should present this story, however, because it allows us to see the way a miracle of this type would be/could be interpreted and the dangers associated with it.

The Life of Apollonius of Tyana was written by the Neo-Pythagorean philosopher, Philostratus (b. 170) as a favor to the empress, Domna Julia, a great devotee of Apollonius. Philostratus was to show that the holy man was in no way a magician. We sense his discomfort with this traditional story about him in his readiness to concede that the young woman described below might well have been still alive. After all, the claims of such miraculous deeds were something of an embarrassment to Neo-Pythagoreans. In the following story Apollonius raises a young bride from the dead. Notice the appeal to Hercules' rescue of Alcestis, which proves how popularly that legend was known, and how easily it came to mind.

> Here too is a miracle which Apollonius worked. A girl had died just in the hour of her marriage, and the bridegroom was following her bier lamenting as was natural[,] his marriage left unfulfilled, and the whole of Rome was mourning with him, for the maiden belonged to a consular family. Apollonius then witnessing their grief, said: 'Put down the bier, for I will stay the tears that you are shedding for this maiden'. And withal he asked what was her name. The crowd accordingly thought that he was about to deliver such an oration as is commonly delivered as much to grace the funeral as to stir up lamentation; but he did nothing of the kind, but merely touching her and whispering in secret some spell over her, at once woke up the maiden from her seeming death; and

the girl spoke out loud, and returned to her father's house, just as Alcestis did when she was brought back to life by Hercules. And the relations of the maiden wanted to present him with the sum of 150,000 sesterces, but he said that he would freely present the money to the young lady by way of a dowry. Now, whether he detected some spark of life in her, which those who were nursing her had not noticed, for it is said that although it was raining at the time, a vapor went up from her face—or whether life was really extinct, and he restored it by the warmth of his touch, is a mysterious problem which neither I myself nor those who were present could decide.[31]

Although Philostratus is writing to defend Apollonius from charges that he was a magician, he still reported the whispering of a spell in the girl's ear. This element must have been such a well-known part of the story that it could not be omitted. It is clear that Philostratus had no intention of copying from a Jesus story. The embarrassment he expresses in the claims that Apollonius raised the dead shows us that he is not impressed by such tales.

As for Apollonius himself, he prefers to associate his miracles with Asclepius. In a letter arguing with his denouncers, he makes a parallel between himself and Asclepius on the basis that both 'ease the flesh of its agonies and allays suffering':

[Your denunciation is:] 'He practices divination'. Yes for many are the things we know not, and there is no other way of foreseeing anything that is going to happen. 'But such practices are not consonant with philosophy'. Nevertheless they befit the deity. 'And moreover he eases the flesh of its agonies and allays suffering'. You might equally bring charges against Asclepius...'[32]

It is important to see the world-wide devotion given to a god/hero whose miracles display this tender compassion in the face of suffering. If Apollonius was remembered and honored for this mercy more than his philosophy it helps us better to appreciate the weight of a hero's miraculous healings and his raising of the dead in the Greco-Roman Mediterranean world. It is not only the sign of deity but a testimony to the hero's respectful and compassionate care for the length and quality of human life here and now.

The subsequent attacks of St Eusebius only serve to show us the enormous credibility associated with this hero. Notice how he uses Philostratus' doubt to advantage:

---

31. Philostratus, *The Life of Apollonius of Tyana* 4.45.
32. Philostratus, *The Epistles of Apollonius of Tyana* 8.

> You must then, as I said, regard the whole series of miracles wrought by him [Apollonius] as having been accomplished through a ministry of demons; for the resuscitation of the girl must be divested of any miraculous character, if she was really alive all the time and bore in herself a vital spark, as the author says, and if a vapor rose over her face. For it is impossible, as I said before, that such a miracle should have been passed over in silence in Rome itself, if it happened when the sovereign was close by.[33]

The possibility that the girl might have been sleeping or in some kind of coma has also been suggested for the Jesus story as we shall discuss below. In this case the hero can be said to 'rescue someone from the grave'. Such rescues were considered super-human and prophetic.

In the first century CE two heroes would have been known to have saved a living person from the grave, Empedocles the Pythagorean, and the first-century CE physician to Caesar Augustus, Asclepiades. What is important for us in these stories is to note how their deeds were interpreted since they are proof of associations available to ordinary persons of the Greco-Roman world.

Heroes Who Revive Persons Thought to Be Dead
Empedocles (fifth century BCE). Empedocles was a disciple of Pythagoras and a healer in his own right. In the two stories below that relate his resuscitations, notice that whereas Hermippus simply reports Empedocles's cure of Panthea, Heraclides interprets his rescue of the woman as proof that Empedocles is 'not merely a physician but a diviner as well'.

Both accounts are recorded by Diogenes Laertius (early third century CE). In the first case, Empedocles saves a woman who had been given up by physicians:

> Hermippus [third century BCE] tells us that Empedocles cured Panthea, a woman of Agrigentum, who had been given up by the physicians, and this was why he was offering sacrifice, and that those invited were about eighty in number.[34]

In a second case, Empedocles maintained the life of a woman in a trance for some 30 days, even though she neither breathed nor had a pulse.

33. Eusebius, *Treatise of St Eusebius* 31.
34. Diogenes Laertius, *On Empedocles* 8.69.

Heraclides (75 BCE) in his book *On Diseases* says that he [Empedocles] furnished Pausanias with the facts about the woman in a trance. This Pausanias, according to Aristippus and Satyrus, was his [Empedocles] bosom-friend, to whom he dedicated his poem, 'On Nature...' At all events, Heraclides testifies that the case of the woman in a trance was such that for thirty days he [Empedocles] kept her body without pulsation though she never breathed; and for that reason Heraclides called him not merely a physician but a diviner as well...[35]

Thus, for Heraclides, Empedocles' rescue showed that he was a 'prophet' of sorts.

Asclepiades the Physician (first century BCE)
Asclepiades rose to fame during the Augustan administration. The following story about his saving a man from being buried alive is related by the first-century author Celsus (not to be confused with the apologist against Christianity) who wrote a compendium on diseases and their appropriate medical treatment. It is also known to Apuleius. Notice that Celsus is more worried that such a story will contribute to the popular ridicule of medicine as quackery. Apuleius on the other hand praises the physician because he 'rescued him [the sick man] ...as it were from the very mouth of hell, and straightaway revived the spirit within him'. First the version by Celsus:

> Asclepiades, when he met a funeral procession, recognized that a man who was being carried out to burial was alive; and it is not primarily the fault of the art if there is a fault on the part of its professor. But I shall more modestly suggest that the art of medicine is conjectural, and such is the characteristic of a conjecture, that though it answers more frequently, yet it sometimes deceives. A sign therefore is not to be rejected if it is deceptive in scarcely one out of a thousand cases, since it holds good in countless patients. I state this, not merely in connection with noxious signs, but to salutary as well; seeing that hope is disappointed now and again, and that the patient dies whom the practitioner at first deemed safe; and further that measures proper for curing now and again make a change into something worse. Nor, in the face of such a variety of temperaments, can human frailty avoid this. Nevertheless the medical art is to be relied upon, which more often, and in by far the greater number of patients, benefits the sick. It should not be ignored, however, that it is rather in acute diseases that signs, whether of recovery or death, may be fallacious.[36]

35. Diogenes Laertius, *On Empedocles* 8.60-61.
36. Celsus, *De Medicina* 2.6.16-18.

Now Apuleius (c. 180 CE) rejoices in the drama of Asclepiades's salvation of the man. Notice the theatrical dismissal of the people by the physician and their ridicule of his judgment, which elevate the grandeur of the resuscitation:

> The famous Asclepiades, who ranks among the greatest of doctors, indeed, if you except Hippocrates, as the very greatest, was the first to discover the use of wine as a remedy. It requires, however, to be administered at the proper moment, and it was in the discovery of the right moment that he showed special skill, noting most carefully the slightest symptom of disorder or undue rapidity of pulse. It chanced that once, when he was returning to town from his country house, he observed an enormous funeral procession in the suburbs of the city. A huge multitude of men who had come out to perform the last honors stood round about the bier, all of them plunged deep in sorrow and wearing worn and ragged apparel. He asked whom they were burying, but no one replied; so he went nearer to satisfy his curiosity and to see who it might be that was dead, or, it may be in the hope to make some discovery in the interests of his profession. Be this as it may, he certainly snatched the man from the jaws of death, as he lay there on the verge of burial. The poor fellow's limbs were already covered with spices, his mouth filled with sweet-smelling unguent. He had been anointed and was all ready for the pyre. But Asclepiades looked upon him, took careful note of certain signs; handled his body again and again, and perceived that life was still in him, though scarcely to be detected. Straightaway he cried out, 'He lives! Throw down your torches, take away your fire, demolish the pyre, take back the funeral feast and spread it on his board at home'. While he spoke, a murmur arose. some said that they must take the doctor's word, others mocked at the physician's skill. At last, in spite of the opposition offered even by his relations, perhaps because they had already entered into possession of the dead man's property, perhaps because they did not yet believe his words, Asclepiades persuaded them to put off the burial for a brief space. Having thus rescued him from the hands of the undertaker, he carried the man home, as it were from the very mouth of hell, and straightaway revived the spirit within him, and by means of certain drugs called forth the life that still lay hidden in the secret places of his body.[37]

Implications for Mk 5.35-43

What is it that the Christian listeners were expected to understand about the nature of Jesus' miracle? C.H. Turner holds that Jesus does not raise her from the dead, but rather saves a living girl from a burial.[38] However, Vincent Taylor astutely notes that Jesus tells the

37. Apuleius, *Florida* in *Apologia and Florida*.
38. C.H. Turner, *The Gospel according to St. Mark* (reprinted from, *A New*

mourners that the girl is sleeping *even before* he sees her.[39] To this Ernst Haenchen answers that the point of the miracle is still not to claim that Jesus brings the girl back from the dead, but rather that he has foreknowledge that the girl is only sleeping.[40] That is, Haenchen understands the story to show Jesus as 'prophet', like Heraclides pronouncing Empedocles, a 'diviner'. It would have been a great attribution to Jesus for persons in the first century world, albeit not as great as the claim that he raised the girl from the dead! Max Wilcox supports Haenchen's proposal and notes that v. 43b, in which Jesus orders that the risen girl be given something to eat, supports a situation of coma brought on by hypoglycemic shock.[41] And long ago, Bultmann stated that it would not be unusual for the hero to suggest that food be given as a proof that the patient is well.[42] But on the question of Jesus acting like a physician, treating a coma, Taylor argued 'His [Jesus'] words are not a diagnosis, and it is foreign to His manner to speak as a physician'.[43] To be fair to Wilcox, however his argument is not that Jesus is presented as a *physician*, but rather that the account illustrates Jesus' powers of prophecy. Nevertheless, the arguments of Wilcox and Haenchen are not convincing. If the author intended to highlight Jesus' prophecy, why wouldn't Jesus demonstrate that power to the girl's father as soon as he is told the girl is dead, and so save him his terrible grief all the way to the house? Is Jesus so in need of a houseful of witnesses to his power of prophecy that he would conceal it from the grieving parent, saying, 'Do not fear, only believe' (v. 36)? Rather such a counsel is more appropriate if he intends to turn the event around. After Jesus arrives at the house, his statement to the mourners that the girl is only sleeping highlights for the listener Jesus' intention to raise her, but hide the magnitude of the miracle on the pretext that she has not really died. Further ensuring privacy, he sends the crowds away and goes into the room with only the parents and his own three disciples. It is there in that room that the divine power of Jesus is revealed. Note that Jesus does

Commentary on Holy Scripture, edited by C. Gore, H.L. Goudge, and A. Guillaume; London, 1928), p. 30.

39. See this discussion in Vincent Taylor, *The Gospel According to St. Mark* (London: Macmillan; New York: St Martin's Press, 1966), p. 295.

40. Ernst Haenchen, *Der Weg Jesu: Eine Erklärung des Markusevangeliums und der kanonischen Parallelen* (Berlin: Alfred Töpelmann, 1968), p. 209.

41. Max Wilcox, 'Talitha Koum(i)' in Mark 5,41', in Joël Delobel (ed.), *Logia* (BETL, 59; Leuven: Leuven University Press, 1982), pp. 470-76, esp. p. 476.

42. Bultmann, *History*, p. 215.

43. Taylor, *Gospel of Mark* (1966), p. 295.

not say, 'Little girl, I say to you awaken', which would communicate the idea of a girl asleep in a coma, but rather, 'Little girl, I say to you, *arise*', ἔγειρε a verb that belongs to the set of Christian metaphors relating to life after death (e.g. Mk 16.6).

This story makes it plain that Jesus' greatness is not found by aligning him with heroes like Asclepiades or Empedocles, but with deities. Jesus has power over life which for the ordinary person of Greco-Roman antiquity, would invite a comparison of Jesus' power with that of Heracles or Asclepius. Of these two deities, it would be Asclepius, the Helper and Healer of all humankind everywhere who would surely be the most appropriate parallel. But what of the Jewish precedents to Jesus' miracle? What associations with Jewish scriptures are invited in a direct way by this account?

Elijah, Elisha, and Jesus

With respect to the echoes between the Elijah and Elisha stories and Jesus' raising of the dead girl, we see that the narrative element particular to all three accounts is the private place for the miracle. Two dramatic differences, however, separate the Jesus story and these two miracle stories of the great Jewish prophets. First, notice that Jesus does not pray to God as both Elijah and Elisha do. Even in Josephus' retelling of the Elijah miracle, an explicit prayer is offered.

Second, the 'method' of the heroes is distinct. Jesus has only to take the girl's hand. So, aside from the identity of Jesus as Jewish (known to the listener), it is only the private bedroom location in all three stories that is similar. It is difficult to find evidence that the Christian formulator of this story either knew the Elijah and Elisha stories or intended them to stand as a backdrop to the Jesus account. But what is clear to me is that even if any such comparison was intended, and I see no internal evidence of that intention, Jesus far surpasses both of these Jewish heroes. For unlike Elijah and Elisha, who must explicitly call on God to perform the miracle, Jesus shows that he has received a heavenly empowerment, a heavenly authorization that neither of these prophets were given. Jesus commands 'ταλιθα κουμ'. John Hull claims that Matthew removes this foreign language because it has a 'controversial nature' and might sound as though Jesus were pronouncing a magic spell.[44] Luke also omits it, as he does all foreign-sounding words. But in the case of Apollonius of Tyana, Philostratus,

---

44. John M. Hull, *Hellenistic Magic and the Synoptic Tradition* (London: SCM Press, 1974), p. 137.

who belongs to the world of philosophy, does not seem to find anything alarming about stating that Apollonius used a spell! And this is all the more telling when we recall that the purpose of Philostratus's biography of Apollonius was to defend him from charges of wizardry. Thus the view that the pronouncing of a spell automatically separates a holy man from a wizard is too simple. It may well be however that Mark or the pre-Markan formulator of the miracle provided a translation of Jesus' words into Greek precisely *to avoid* any conclusion that Jesus used a spell. Nevertheless, since a syncretistic spirit flourished in the Greco-Roman world, it seems out of keeping with that world to expect that Jesus' command was never described as a 'magical' spell by any community, or that the idea of a 'magical' spell was abhorrent to every Christian, including the original formulators. This certainly would not discount his identity as divine or as God's Son!

It is more important to allow the dynamic of the story to perform its job of presenting the circumstances in which Jesus used divine power and for whom. Jesus is indeed cosmically powerful, but that power is at the service of ordinary people, and in situations of frank human vulnerability, the crushing finality of death, and in particular the pathos of the dead child. Second, in this enormous miracle Jesus has created confusion over the real situation in order to avoid public acclaim over his miracle. His simple taking of the girl's hand makes no dramatic performance. Finally, in the actual miracle itself, as the girl is up and walking, it is Jesus who thinks to give her something to eat. And here the hero shows his own focus, which is not himself but the good of the girl.

The details of the narration, then, promise to the faithful that Jesus can be counted on to be compassionate, to use his enormous power to serve those vulnerable in their humanity. Put another way, the elements of the narration teach the community about the character of the cosmic power of Jesus, the character of Jesus himself. This *humanitas* of Jesus defines his use of power. The miracle story says that Jesus is not focused on his own rule after death, as some commentators' eschatological interpretations would lead us to conclude, but rather the miracle shows Jesus' incapability to deny the request of those in need of him. The miracles affirm the respect and commitment to humankind, right here and now. I suggest that this presentation of the hero/god instructs the members of the community to think about Jesus as he presents himself to Jairus, grieving and distraught with the horrible truth of his daughter's death. The miracle story tells the listener to turn to the great Jesus and listen to his counsel not to fear but only believe. He will turn death around to life.

This miracle story is of extreme importance because it elevates him to the stratum of a god like Asclepius. It is not only Jesus' power to bring life to a dead child that has been featured here, but his 'character'. The story affirms that this power is completely governed by true compassion, deepest *humanitas*.

Mark's Use of the Two Twelfth-Year Miracles

What do these two miracles grant to Mark's Gospel? Many important studies have addressed the question. Some scholars have concluded that the issue Mark wants to underline is faith. For example, Eduard Schweizer holds.

> The point is clearly made that faith comes to fulfillment only in a personal encounter with Jesus, in dialogue with him. Without this there is no value in the experience of miracles which stagger the imagination, although such experience may help us to reach a proper understanding.[45]

Faith is certainly a theme in these miracles but is it Mark's intent to teach his Greco-Roman audience that if they do not 'dialogue' with Jesus there is 'no value in the experience of miracles?'

Indeed the dialogue in the miracle of the woman with the hemorrhage comes after her cure, while the dialogue with Jairus' father is minimal, and we do not know of he had faith that Jesus would be able to raise the dead! But the real question here is whether miracle stories were inserted to teach rules about how we attract Jesus' attention. Surely if anything, the miracles demonstrate a free-flowing compassion of this Jesus who has such power. They seem designed to raise our admiration and love of the hero, and to feel confident about our approaching him.

A second suggestion of Schweizer that is extremely popular is that Mark wants to symbolize the world to come:

> This power [to raise the dead] appears in the story in a symbolic manner. The believer can learn through Jesus to take the reality of God who raises the dead more seriously than the apparent reality of death. Then, by the side of the casket or on his own deathbed he will be able to

[handwritten margin note: No need for dialogue]

---

45. Schweizer, *Good News*, p. 120. See also Morna Hooker, *A Commentary on the Gospel According to St. Mark* (BNTC; London: A. & C. Black, 1991), p. 151. See the full treatment of faith by Gerd Theissen, *The Miracle Stories of the Christian Tradition* (trans. Francis McDonagh; Philadelphia: Fortress Press, 1983), pp. 133-37.

believe in life which is more concrete and real than anything on earth which is called personal life.[46]

It is true that these miracles can be used to inspire confidence in the raising of the dead in the world to come. It is interesting that no such statement is to be found in the miracle stories themselves. Is it our own dissatisfaction with the miracle stories that causes us to search for their merit as teachings about the resurrection, or the eschaton? As they stand, both miracle stories point out the fact that Jesus greatly respects our earthly life, so as to heal illness and to bring back a child to her family. That is, both stories affirm Jesus as divine, powerful and benevolent like Asclepius, and therefore someone who can be trusted to care about our health and the life of our children, right now. That is often overlooked.

In the overall Gospel organization, the two miracles of Mk 5.21-43 conclude a section of great miracles (Mk 4.35–5.43), after which Jesus returns to Nazareth where he will be rejected (Mk 6.1-5). That section begins with the demonstration of Jesus' astonishing cosmic empowerment as he stills a storm to console his disciples (Mk 4.35-41) and then exorcizes a man so possessed with powerful demons that he is now completely isolated from everyone and given up as hopeless by his neighbors. After Jesus has expelled the demons and urged the man to go and tell everyone what the Lord has done for him, Jesus crosses the Sea of Galilee once more, to Jewish lands. It is there that the leader of the synagogue approaches him and asks him to lay hands on his dying daughter.

In my view, the miracle of the woman with the hemorrhage could have been placed anywhere in the Gospel design, but linked as it is with the raising of Jairus's daughter its placement contributes to an important emphasis on Jesus' conduct in sensitive situations with women. This is the first time that the Gospel shows Jesus and a woman conversing, one to one. We have already seen Jesus' kindness to Peter's mother-in-law, in Mk 1.29-31, but it is small, swift, and holds no dialogue. In this miracle story, however, the world of women is more directly engaged and it is that world that is exposed to Jesus, much to his surprise, as the result of his insistence on meeting the person who had experienced power coming out of him.

These miracles are important to Mark for the credibility they give not only to Jesus' divine power, but because they illustrate the *character* of Jesus' power, the way Jesus uses it, the way he seems unable to

---

46. Schweizer, *Good News*, p. 121.

refuse anyone who calls on it, incapable of denying its salvific transformations.

We know that for Mark Jesus is the unique Son of God, and that
there is no question but that Jesus far surpasses Asclepius or Heracles.
As Mark places Jesus' raising Jairus's daughter at the conclusion of
his first major miracle section, he seems to create a climax in which he
makes it clear that Jesus is preeminent in his authorization from
heaven. But, especially in these last two miracles of the set, he emphasizes Jesus' moving *humanitas* to women, one a woman suffering
without recourse, the other a girl dead at the threshold of her
womanhood.

Conclusion

The two concluding miracles about these women balance the big
cosmic miracles of the Stilling of the Storm and the wild and frightening, fascinating exorcism of the Gerasene demoniac by showing a
more 'Asclepian' Jesus in his intense kindness to these women, his
sensitivity, and his unfailing benevolence. For Mark, they function to
augment the pathos of the Gospel as Jesus goes to his cross. These
miracles align Jesus with the ordinary person, and particularly forgotten women, as a contrast to the powerful political and spiritual
leaders who never show any interest in the ordinary person's troubles.

Mark's community claims for themselves Jesus' concern for the
rejected and forgotten 'little people'. These stories affirm that Jesus
the Son of God has power and compassion that is available to any
who call on him, and these stories encourage the community to call
on him for miracles and signs of his ongoing benevolence, even as
they await his coming on the clouds of heaven.

A GENTILE WOMAN'S STORY, REVISITED:
REREADING MARK 7.24-31_A*

Sharon H. Ringe

Introduction

When Amy-Jill Levine invited me to revise my earlier article[1] for inclusion in this volume, I was both honored to be invited and eager to do so. I was aware of having learned much since the early 1980s, especially about cultures and customs in first-century Palestine and in the early church, and about the experiences of women in those contexts. Then as now, such factors as class, ethnicity, demographic context, education, health, age and family circumstances made for a richly textured fabric of experiences whose variations needed to be examined closely. I had not done that, being largely captive to the fiction of being able to analyze biblical texts from a unitary perspective of gender. I was also unaware then of how my Christian concern led me to try to 'rehabilitate' the Jesus portrayed in this story to a form more acceptable to my confessional commitment to Jesus as the Christ. I acknowledged my purpose of seeking a reading of the text more appreciative of the role of women in the early Christian movement than had been the readings of European and North American male commentators on the text, who were my principal conversation partners. I was, however, unaware of how my reading was shaped by my professional commitment to reclaim the traditional tools of biblical criticism to support that goal.

I do not pretend to have overcome all of these blinders that have narrowed my field of vision, but I have at least become aware of

---

* I dedicate this article to the memory of Leslie Carol Montgomery, my neighbor and friend who lost her battle with leukemia on 22 January 1998, while I was working on this passage. Leslie was a woman of wit and grace and a tireless intercessor on behalf of healing for others—an apt companion for the woman in this story.

1. 'A Gentile Woman's Story', in Letty M. Russell (ed.), *Feminist Interpretation of the Bible* (Philadelphia: Westminster Press, 1985), pp. 65-72.

enough of them to recognize that I could not simply tinker with my original work to correct a few details. I had to start over. The approach I use now is described in *Biblical Interpretation: A Road Map*, which I co-authored with Frederick C. Tiffany.[2] I begin with an identification of my reading context and the concerns it generates for me about the text. While the work I have previously done on the text is part of my previous experience with the text, it does not constitute an authoritative reading that I feel I must refute or support. After identifying initial questions and issues for study related to my context and my previous encounters with the text, I examine the structure and literary context of the narrative and explore the intersection of the narrative with what can be reconstructed about the social contexts of early first-century Palestine and of the gospel communities. While this study focuses on the Markan account, the Matthean parallel (Mt. 15.21-28) and several other gospel healing stories provide points of intersection that illuminate our text. Several published interpretations of this narrative in both Gospel versions by interpreters outside the dominant cultures of Western Europe and North America expand my reading community and set the stage for my concluding comments on my engagement with and by this story.[3]

Encountering the Reader Encountering the Text

I come to this interpretive task as a member of the dominant culture of the United States who is by confession a clergywoman in the United Church of Christ, and by profession a biblical scholar and a professor in a United Methodist seminary. Several aspects of that identity shape the questions prompted by this text.

First, as a woman I am fascinated by the prominence of the woman in the narrative. The fascination is one of repulsion, then attraction. I am offended by the response to the woman attributed to Jesus (Mk 7.27). With the very next sentence (7.28), I find myself cheering the wit of her response to the rejection and satisfied by her success in reversing the denial of her request and obtaining healing for her daughter (7.29-30). My ambivalent experience of the text leads me to want to

---

2.　Nashville: Abingdon Press, 1996.

3.　Students in my classes have been important reading partners who have shaped my present encounter with this narrative. Their comments in class have opened many questions and avenues of inquiry for me. Unfortunately these gifts are impossible to document adequately. In this vein, I am especially indebted to a seminar paper on this passage presented by Patricia D. Barth in a course I taught at Wesley Theological Seminary on the Gospel of Mark in the Fall semester of 1997.

understand more about the social data underlying the author's interpretation of the woman and about the literary devices at work in her
petition, Jesus' response, and her retort.

As a Christian I am troubled by the picture this passage paints of
Jesus. His response to the woman's plea for help is, at best, ungracious
—far from the picture of Jesus as a compassionate healer who is
committed to persons in need, and who (I say by faith) has called me
to a similar ministry. What is accomplished by such a portrait of Jesus?
How does it figure in the larger Gospel narrative? To what agenda of
Mark's church (or its predecessors) is this story transparent, and how
do those concerns intersect the life of its present-day heirs? Such
theological questions need to be addressed in the course of the reading.

The final issue of my identity that intersects the story is my professional interest in postcolonial reading strategies, which is shaped by
my existential concern with the issue of dominance and subordination
as that is affected by both gender and ethnicity. The woman and Jesus
differ on both counts: they are in that sense 'outsiders' to each other.
The narrative does not present such a neutral, balanced view, however, because the encompassing Gospel narrative makes Jesus the
norm, and she inhabits the margins of the page. Despite the woman's
prominence in the story, it is told as part of the Gospel of which he is
the focus, and not as her story. Similarly, while the setting of the story
suggests that she is a member of the dominant group in that place, the
Gospel narrative makes Jesus the insider and her the one whose
inclusion is contested. As a reader, I find myself resonating with the
woman on the question of gender, but with Jesus on the question of
ethnicity. As a woman, I have experienced the co-optation of my story
and perspective by male history and interpretation that determine the
'real' meaning and importance of events. 'My' story becomes instru-
mental to a male meta-narrative. On the other hand, as a member of
the dominant culture of the United States, I find that I identify with
the evaluations of importance and meaning often imposed on others
even in their home territory by the political, economic, and cultural
power that resides with 'us'. Similarly, as a Christian, I find myself
often unaware of the ways the alliance of that religion with other
categories of power has allowed its confessional assumptions to set
the terms even of scholarly interpretation of biblical texts. This reading thus must probe the ways relative power comes to expression in
and through this account, and what is thus conveyed about the agenda
of the Gospel writers, the circumstances of Jesus' context, and the interpretive projects of modern readers.

Questions of religion and ethnicity intersect in the interpretation of this passage most familiar to me in my religious community. First of all, the assumption has gone unquestioned that the reference in the passage to 'dogs' introduced a pejorative term generally used by Jews about Gentiles. Furthermore, the interpretation continues by perpetuating the assumption that gender roles in first-century Palestine (presumably for all social classes and religious and ethnic groups) dictated that no woman should have approached a man not of her family, and especially not of her own ethnic group. Thus it is assumed that Jesus was giving the response that both such a Gentile woman and any Jewish hearers would have expected to this interruption of an important Jewish man by a Gentile woman. The explanation is either that the human Jesus had absorbed the racism and sexism assumed to be inherent in his context, or else that the 'perfect' Jesus Christ of faith of course did not really mean to insult the woman, but rather he was only joking with her or testing the sincerity of her request for help. Even a cursory rereading of the text makes me suspicious of such conclusions imported in their entirety to the narrative. More important than mere questions of accuracy in representing the social world of the first century, the blatant anti-Jewishness undergirding that reading needs to be confronted.

A Close Reading of the Text

Mark encloses this pericope between comments about Jesus' arrival in and departure from 'the region of Tyre' (Mk 7.24, 31). The geographical frame defines this as a discrete unit of text whose structure can be sketched as follows:

    a. Jesus' arrival near Tyre and effort to escape notice (24)
      b. The woman approaches (25)
        (parenthetical note on the woman's ethnicity [26a])
        c. The woman's petition (26b)
          d. Jesus' response (27)
            e. The woman's retort (28)
          d'. Jesus' second response (29a)
        c'. The woman's petition is granted (29b)
      b'. The woman returns home and finds her daughter healed (30)
    a'. Jesus' return from the region of Tyre (31a)

Two observations can be made about the meaning carried by that structure. First, one can note the obvious chiastic structure, in which the woman's comment—her only line of dialogue[4]—forms the hinge

---

    4.   Note how different Matthew's account is at this point. The woman is given

or focal point. The centrality of her comment is confirmed also by the second structural observation evoked by the passage, namely that the initial hostile question, an answering and correcting question or comment, and an acknowledgment of the effectiveness of the challenge (steps c through c') mirror the form of the stories of Jesus' conflicts with various authority figures or other opponents elsewhere in the Synoptic Gospels (see, for example, Mk 2.7-11, 18-20, 24-27). Here, however, Jesus takes what is usually his opponents' role by asking the hostile question, for which the woman provides the retort that Jesus acknowledges as effective. She triumphs in the conflict, and her 'word' (λόγος) is credited for changing Jesus' mind and, implicitly, for the departure of the demon from her child (Mk 7.29-30).[5]

Contextual Readings of the Text

Though it is clear from this analysis of the structure of the narrative that the woman's retort is the focal point of the story, our gaze reaches that comment only by making its way through the framing steps, beginning with the setting itself. In order to be understood adequately, both that setting and the stages of the woman's interaction with Jesus must be examined in their first-century contexts, both that

two additional lines of dialogue in which her own voice, instead of the narrator's observation, gives her reason for approaching Jesus (Mt. 15.22, 25). Despite that apparently larger role, however, her comment is not credited with the power that it has in Mark. Instead, her 'faith' is praised (which appears here to be equated either with her persistence in the face of the disciples' and Jesus' opposition to her, or with her recognition of Jesus' identity as 'Lord' and 'Son of David'), and Jesus' decree effects the healing (Mt. 15.28). See Joanna Dewey, 'Women in the Synoptic Gospels: Seen but Not Heard?' *BTB* 27 (1997), pp. 53-60 [56-57]. See also Gail R. O'Day, 'Surprised by Faith: Jesus and the Canaanite Woman', *Listening: Journal of Religion and Culture* 24 (1989), pp. 290-301 [294-98] for a discussion of the resemblance between Matthew's account, with its emphasis on the woman's 'faith', and the lament psalms of the Hebrew Bible. Reprinted in A.-J. Levine (with Marianne Blinkenstaff (eds.), *A Feminist Companion to Matthew* (Sheffield: Sheffield Academic Press, 2001), pp. 114-25.

5. Jim Perkinson makes a similar observation in 'A Canaanitic Word in the Logos of Christ; or the Difference the Syro-Phoenician Woman Makes to Jesus', *Semeia* 75 (1996), pp. 61-85. He analyzes the rhetoric of the woman's retort as a counter-voice to the dominant christological definition assumed by the passage as part of his study of this passage through the lens of postcolonial theory. I should note that my study was completed before I saw his article (which appeared only in 1998, despite the alleged date of publication of the journal). Although many of our conclusions are similar, his beginning point in postcolonial and feminist theory differs from my more inductive exegetical approach.

of Jesus' day and that of Mark's community. The pericope must also be read as part of the author's literary project expressed through the surrounding Gospel narrative.

Up to this point in the narrative, Jesus' ministry has been set in various parts of Galilee, with one foray into 'the country of the Gerasenes' (5.1).[6] The prominence of Capernaum as a setting for his early work (1.21–2.12) and mention of Bethsaida (6.45) and Gennesaret (6.53) locate him principally in northern Galilee. When Mark reports the extent of Jesus' renown, the area where his fame has spread includes not only the territory in the south toward Jerusalem, but also the northern 'region around Tyre and Sidon' (3.8). Thus, while in Mark's narrative our passage is Jesus' first journey into the region, he is portrayed as already known there.

A key question, however, is what is meant by this geographical cue. The city of Tyre is located on a small island off the coast of modern-day southern Lebanon. As the leading city of Phoenicia during much of the first millennium BCE, it was a center of trade and metallurgy as well as of political influence.[7] Its 'region' or 'environs' (τὰ ὅρια) included not only that city, but also the farmlands and villages located near the border of Galilee that were essential to the agricultural production needed to feed the population of the urban center.

Typical of most borderlands, this area was ethnically mixed. Though Tyre itself was populated principally by Gentiles, the surrounding territory included Jews as well.[8] The result was an often uncomfortable collision of ethnic, religious and cultural differences, with resulting suspicions and prejudices, between city dwellers and residents of the villages. This ethnically mixed region was also the site of economic tension, principally between the wealthier urban trading centers and the poorer farming communities that were captive to the needs and desires of the city dwellers, such that in times of poor harvests,

6.   The actual location is unknown, but the narrative location is in hilly terrain near the 'sea' (5.13) but on its opposite shore. The presence of the herd of swine (5.11) identifies it as an area with a substantial Gentile population.

7.   Thomas L. McClellan, 'Tyre', *HDB*, pp. 1101-1102.

8.   Not only would that ethnic distribution have prevailed in the time of Jesus, but it continued into the middle third of the first century, when these 'regions' provided some of the most ferocious opposition to the Roman presence in Palestine, and even leading instigators of the revolt that began in 66 CE (Josephus, *War* 2.588; *Life* 372). For an extended discussion of the economic and social reality of this region, see Gerd Theissen, *The Gospels in Context: Social and Political History in the Synoptic Tradition* (trans. Linda M. Maloney; Philadelphia: Fortress Press, 1991), pp. 65-77.

when food was scarce everywhere, the requirement to supply the needs of the city dwellers meant that the farmers themselves would go hungry. The urban–rural tension with its economic factors combined with the cultural, ethnic, and religious tensions to make the region a miniature version of the larger context of Roman-occupied Palestine.

That Jesus may actually have made his way into these borderlands is both reasonable to imagine and impossible to document. Nothing in the narrative itself suggests that Mark viewed Jesus' 'going away' (ἀπέρχομαι) to this region as a foray into Gentile territory.[9] In fact, since nothing is said about the occupants of the house into which he has gone as being Gentiles or in any other way remarkable, it would be appropriate to conclude that Mark takes it to be one of the Jewish homes in the 'region'.[10] It is likely that Mark would have known enough about the demographics of the region to allow him to make such an assumption, if indeed this was the location of the Markan community.[11] That community itself appears to have been a mixed community in which Jews and Gentiles may still have lived in their traditional rural and urban areas, respectively. If this was Mark's own home territory, he would naturally treat this region as a safe and hospitable place of refuge for Jesus (7.24b), in contrast to the place of his encounter with 'the Pharisees and some scribes' in the preceding pericope (7.1-23).

9.   O'Day ('Surprised by Faith', p. 291) draws attention to the reading in all but a minority of manuscripts that distinguishes the setting of this pericope from the later leg of the journey, not just in the 'region of Tyre', but through the city of Sidon itself. We should note, however, that Mark describes the continuation of that journey as taking Jesus into the 'region' (also the word τὰ ὅρια) of the Decapolis, which may also have been an ethnically mixed area, and not the Gentile territory that is generally assumed.

10.   Given the narrative setting, she and not Jesus is portrayed as having crossed the social, political, economic, and symbolic boundaries between them in order to approach Jesus. This is contrary to the point made by M. Eugene Boring (*The Gospel of Matthew* [NIB, 8; Nashville: Abingdon Press, 1995], p. 336), who understands this as a Gentile house, which Matthew has Jesus avoid entering by changing the setting of the story. Amy-Jill Levine ('Matthew', in Carol A. Newsom and Sharon H. Ringe [eds.], *The Women's Bible Commentary* [Louisville, KY: Westminster/John Knox Press, 1992], pp. 252-62 [259]) reads her 'coming out' in Mt. 15.22 as indicating that the woman has physically left her 'native land' to meet Jesus, and Levine sees this as a difference between Matthew and Mark. I think rather that it is the case in both accounts that she is implied to have crossed into his 'space' in order to obtain healing for her daughter.

11.   Ched Myers, *Binding the Strong Man: A Political Reading of Mark's Story of Jesus* (Maryknoll, NY: Orbis Books, 1988), p. 41.

Within that context, the woman in the story is introduced by both her ethnicity (Greek, Ἑλληνίς) and her provenance (Syrophoenician by birth, Συροφοινίκισσα τῷ γένει). Mark's parenthetical introduction of these details of her identity interrupts the flow of the story (7.26), and by its literary awkwardness calls attention to itself. Its importance on the Jesus-level of the story and for Mark's community may have been similar. Such a formulation of her identity would mark her not just as a Gentile (see Gal. 3.28), but as one of the city dwellers separated from Jesus not only by religion and ethnicity, but also by economic loyalty. She is portrayed as part of the group in that region whose policies and lifestyle would have been a source of suffering for her mostly poorer, rural, Jewish neighbors. Insofar as that is true, she would have been among those frequently targeted by Jesus' parables and teachings that proclaimed 'good news to the poor'.[12]

In addition to the social and political dimensions of the woman's identity that would have been salient factors on the Jesus and Markan levels of the story, several details in the Markan story suggest that he was already wrestling with the way the different ethnic identities of Jesus and the woman were refracted through the lens of Jewish and Gentile participation in the Jesus movement and eventually in the church. This issue would become more explicit—even the focal point —in Matthew's version, as well as in the church's and scholars' inter-pretations of Mark's account. As geographical and eventually tem-poral distance obscured the political and economic implications of the woman's identity, what appears to have been portrayed as the prin-cipal issue is that she was a Gentile to whom Jesus' healing ministry extended, albeit reluctantly, and at a distance.[13] The reluctance is puzzling, for it does not figure in such other stories as the healing in Gerasa (Mk 5.1-20).[14] The reluctance here might be explained by the

12. For a discussion of some of those passages, see Sharon H. Ringe, *Jesus, Liberation, and the Biblical Jubilee: Images for Ethics and Christology* (Philadelphia: Fortress Press, 1985), pp. 33-64.

13. Note that in the Matthean account it is not clear whether we are to see the daughter as present (although not an active character in the story), whereas in Mark she is said to be at home lying on her 'bed' (ἡ κλίνη). This word indicates a piece of furniture and not a portable 'pallet' (ὁ κράβατον) like that on which the paralyzed man was carried (Mk 2.4, 9, 11). That glimpse into the household of the woman and her daughter suggests additional confirmation that she should be seen as among the economically privileged.

14. Elizabeth Struthers Malbon ('Fallible Followers: Women and Men in the Gospel of Mark', *Semeia* 28 [1983], pp. 29-48) interprets the woman's story as part of a male-female pair with the healing of the man that follows (7.31-37), in the

reference to 'bread', which is incongruous in a reply to a request for healing, and which in surrounding pericopes seems to refer to Jesus' complete ministry—teaching and 'feeding' as well as healing (Mk 6.30-44, 45-52; 8.1-10, 14-21). Thus, Mark's portrayal of Jesus' reluctance to heal the woman's daughter could reflect his recognition that the Gentile mission as a whole, though grounded in Jesus' ministry of healing that did extend outside of the Jewish community, was in fact the task of the church, while Jesus focused his attention on 'the lost sheep of the house of Israel' (Mt. 15.24), the 'children' (τὰ τέκνα) who are to be 'fed first' (Mk 7.27).[15]

The geographical setting and information about the woman's identity set the scene for the action of the story. The healing of the daughter frames the verbal exchange between Jesus and the woman. The little girl[16] herself is off-stage through the entire narrative, and she is represented by her mother. Her illness is attributed to possession by 'an unclean spirit', and hence the healing is in fact an exorcism. That makes the healing at a distance the more striking, since other exorcisms are marked by Jesus' confrontation of the demon, and often a verbal exchange with it, to establish his dominance over it (see, e.g., 1.21-28; 5.1-20; 9.14-29). In this narrative, however, the act of healing itself fades into the background. The narrator's voice conveys the necessary information about it: both that it is the object of her quest and that the quest is successful (7.25-26, 30). Direct speech, however, draws the reader's attention to the exchange between Jesus and the woman.

At the very least, Jesus' initial words to the woman convey a refusal to heal her daughter. Christological biases aside, it is not the response that would be anticipated from any practitioner of healing when confronted with a situation of need. The narrative itself provides few clues to account for the vehemence of Jesus' initial rejection of her. Assuming that the woman's use of κύριε in 7.28 should be understood as the polite 'Sir!', and not the confessional 'Lord!', she parallels other recipients of healing whose prior relationship to or confession of Jesus

context of Mark's emphasis on discipleship. Her analysis is persuasive, but it does not preclude also comparing this narrative and other healings of Gentiles.

15. It is interesting to note that Matthew omits the saying about the children's temporal priority. That omission has the effect of breaking the initial denial of help only when the woman's 'faith' is recognized (Mt. 15.28), and not on the basis of any ethnic criteria or picture of a sequential extending of salvation, first to the Jews and only later to Gentiles.

16. τὸ θυγάτριον is a diminutive form, suggesting that she is a child rather than an adult daughter.

is not clear.[17] The fact that the woman's approach to Jesus—falling at his feet—parallels the deferential request of Jairus on behalf of his daughter (Mk 5.22), to which Jesus responds positively, suggests that either her ethnicity or her gender might be at the root of the response. Both of these criteria, however, are challenged by other texts in Mark. As noted above, according to Mark's larger Gospel narrative, Jesus' healing ministry has already been extended to Gentiles. Further, other women are said to approach Jesus in a similar fashion (Lk. 7.38) or even (at least initially) less deferentially (Mk 5.25-33), so it would be inappropriate to conclude that she is being punished for dishonoring Jesus simply because she is a woman who approaches him.[18]

My own interest in the woman's role as a female character in the narrative, coupled with the assumptions often made by interpreters of the passage about the significance of the woman's gender, lead me to look more closely at gender-related issues implicit in the passage. In fact, despite assumptions and generalizations often made by interpreters about 'rabbinic rules' or 'Jewish customs', nothing in the Synoptic Gospels suggests that a rigid separation of women and men (outside or even within the family structure) was the norm in the culture and communities in which the stories are set.[19] Cross-cultural studies suggest that even where there is such a norm in some parts of a society (among the well-to-do, for example, or for persons in religious leadership), among the rural and urban poor, where much of the Gospel narrative unfolds, the demands of survival require the full participation of all members of the society in economic life and other dimensions of household management. The woman's transgression also cannot be that she makes her request herself instead of waiting for the help of a male relative.[20] To suggest that Mark as narrator and

17. Note that the Matthean parallel uses κύριε and υἱὸς Δαυίδ in the woman's initial address to Jesus, making this parallel to his account of the healing of the two blind men (Mt. 20.29-34; see Mk 10.46-52). Those christological titles corroborate Matthew's attribution of Jesus' change of mind to the woman's πίστις. Mary Ann Tolbert (*Sowing the Gospel: Mark's World in Literary-Historical Perspective* [Philadelphia: Fortress Press, 1989], p. 185) concludes that in the Markan narrative κύριε should be seen as a confessional title, and hence as revealing the woman's faith.

18. Myers (*Binding*, p. 204) draws this conclusion.

19. What is curious is that such standards are assumed (without supporting evidence or documentation) in many scholarly studies and most Christian preaching about the passage.

20. Mary Ann Tolbert ('Mark', in C.A. Newsom and S.H. Ringe [eds.], *The Women's Bible Commentary* [Louiseville, KY: Westminster/John Knox Press], pp. 263-74 [269]) makes that suggestion when she observes that though the woman approaches Jesus inside a house, which would have been an appropriate venue for

the community to which he addressed the story would accept the legitimacy of such a warrant for the rejection flies in the face of even basic human sense! The narrative suggests that she is a woman on her own (though in fact nothing is said about her family or marital status other than that she has a sick daughter), but that also cannot be her offense, since most of the women with whom Jesus is said to interact appear on the margins of the traditional patriarchal family structure (see, for example, Mk 5.25-34; 12.41-44; 14.3-9; Lk. 7.11-17, 36-50; 10.38-42; 13.10-17; the stories of the healing of Jairus's daughter [Mk 5.22-24, 35-43, and parallels] and of Peter's mother-in-law [Mk 1.29-31 and parallels] are noteworthy exceptions).

If, then, her behavior is portrayed as appropriate to the occasion, and if her gender and ethnicity by themselves (or even, presumably, taken together) appear not to account for the response attributed to Jesus, we are left with the need to look behind the overt details of the narrative to understand the verbal exchange. The conclusions drawn above about the woman's likely identity as part of an elite economic class related to the 'region' where the story is set commend themselves for further examination as an explanation of the saying in Mk 7.24.

The saying itself is harsh. To compare the woman and her daughter to dogs is insulting in the extreme. Sayings about 'dogs' in the Hebrew Bible portray them as contemptible scavengers who lick human blood, and the term is a metaphor for Israel's enemies (see 1 Sam. 17.43; Ps. 22.11; Prov. 26.11; Isa. 56.10-11). There is no evidence that it was a term used by Jews to refer to Gentiles in general, but rather to groups overtly hostile to God's people or to God's law.[21] The wealthy Gentile city dwellers of Tyre certainly fit the description of 'enemies' relative to the poorer Jewish residents of the surrounding region in a context of chronic scarcity (limited 'bread'), and their exploitative behavior would have counted as hostility to the divine mandates of justice that

a woman, she is rejected for taking on an intercessory role appropriate to a male relative.

21. I am not persuaded that one ought also to see the word 'dog', or, more precisely, 'little dog', as a derogatory term referring to the woman as a 'little Cynic' (in the literal sense of the movement of wandering urban philosophers referred to that way because of their flouting of social convention) because of her unconventional behavior. (See Tolbert, *Sowing the Gospel*, p. 185 n. 15; 'Mark', p. 269; F. Gerald Downing, 'The Women from Syrophoenicia', in George J. Brooke (ed.), *Women in the Biblical Tradition* [Lewiston, NY: Edwin Mellen Press, 1992], pp. 129-49 [145 and Appendix 1].) It is clear that the Cynic movement existed in Jesus' day, but whether he would have encountered them is unclear. Similarly unclear is how effective such a reference would have been to communicate to Mark's community.

Jesus' ministry and Jewish law alike affirmed. The response attributed to Jesus, then, rejects her request as an inappropriate one to make in light of the disproportionate share of the region's resources her people had been exploiting. The saying implies that Jesus' power to heal is also a limited resource (see also 5.30), and *this* time, priority would go to those who always wait at the end of the line.

If the story ended here, it would be a simple echo of Jesus' insistence on what liberation theologians have called 'God's preferential option for the poor'. The contextualized saying in 7.27 would function as a *chreia*[22] that in its simplest form might read, 'Jesus, when asked by a Gentile woman to heal her daughter, said: 'Let the children be fed first, for it is not fair to take the children's food and throw it to the dogs'.[23] That *chreia* would stand as paradigmatic of the teacher's—in this case Jesus'—wisdom and point of view. In fact, however, the woman's reply turns the story into a double *chreia*, with the punch line in the second half. That half would read, 'But the woman, when accused of being a dog, said: "Sir, even the dogs under the table eat the children's crumbs."'[24] Her retort wins the day. Her point of view prevails in the story and is eventually adopted by Jesus (7.29). Hers is the defining wisdom of the story.

The result is a puzzling, even a shocking, story in the context of the Gospel narrative, for Jesus, the character whose point of view Mark endorses throughout the Gospel, is portrayed as reversing his initial decision. Furthermore, what otherwise might be seen as a posture consistent with Jesus' gospel agenda on behalf of the poor ends up being reversed by her 'word' or reasoning (λόγος). Two things seem to have happened. First, in the rhetoric of the passage, the woman demonstrates how to avoid being trapped by another's characterization as enemy. Her tactic is the verbal form of the strategy in martial arts of meeting the opponent's attack by using its own force against

22. A *chreia* is a saying that conveys an example of the wit and wisdom of a philosopher or other famous person. It was a common form in Greek rhetoric and was often used as a teaching device in rhetorical schools.

23. I am indebted to the study of Patricia Barth mentioned in note 3 above for pointing me to the study of the *chreia* form by Ronald F. Hock and Edward N. O'Neil (eds.), *The Chreia in Ancient Rhetoric*, I [Atlanta: Scholars Press, 1986]).

24. The double *chreia* form can be seen in the following example: 'Diogenes, as he was washing off some edible greens, mocked Aristippus as he was passing by, saying: "If you had learned to eat these greens, you would not be a flatterer at the courts of tyrants." But Aristippus said: "If you knew how to associate with men, you would not be washing those greens"' (Hock and O'Neil, *Chreia in Ancient Rhetoric*, p. 41).

the perpetrator. Instead of confronting the insult, she turns the offensive label into a harmless one, and uses it to her advantage. 'Dog' moves from a label of contempt to a character in a domestic scene so familiar and so obvious that the logic cannot be refuted: children are always dropping food, and pets gobble it up almost before it hits the ground. Likewise, she and her daughter will get what they need from the bits and pieces that fall from the table on which Jesus' 'food' is intentionally served. Her witty 'word' turns his rejection into assent to her request.

The second consequence of her retort focuses on the historical level of the story. She confronts the assumptions about the meaning of her identity that appear to undergird Jesus' saying. His words label her as contemptible, a 'dog', apparently (in this analysis) because she is part of the class of exploiters in the region. Instead of presenting a list of credentials to argue that the label is unfair (either in principle or in her individual case)[25], her reply relinquishes the place of privilege his response attributes to her, and her 'word' moves her into the place of receiving only what is left over — the place where the poor of the region have always been. The correct facts about her social and economic status are not the issue. She may be an impoverished widow (as my earlier study of this passage assumed) or a wealthy dowager from the social and economic elite.[26] Regardless, the crucial factor is the crisis in which she finds herself, and her resulting readiness to do whatever is necessary to see it resolved. The urgency of her daughter's illness

25. In my earlier study of this passage, I ignored the hints in the passage to the woman's membership in such an elite *class*, to focus on a reconstruction of her own *personal* situation. I concluded that she is portrayed by implication as in financial straits, both as a woman alone, and also because she is said to approach this itinerant healer instead of taking her daughter to a more established healing center. (See Gerd Theissen, *The Miracle Stories of the Early Christian Tradition*, [trans. Francis McDonagh; Philadelphia: Fortress Press, 1983], pp. 249-53.) I thus attributed the feistiness of her 'word' to Mark's portrait of her recognition that she was at the bottom of the social order already, and thus that she had nothing more to lose. I then attributed Jesus' change of heart to the church's memory of a puzzling episode when Jesus himself learned about the radical implications of being messiah to the outcast from one of the most outcast, a poor Gentile woman on her own.

26. In the ancient as in the modern world, the fact that there is no male family member in evidence does not always mean impoverishment, though it often does. (See the discussions in Bonnie Bowman Thurston, *The Widows: A Women's Ministry in the Early Church* [Philadelphia: Fortress Press, 1989], pp. 10-17; and Elisabeth Schussler Fiorenza, *In Memory of Her: A Feminist Theological Reconstruction of Christian Origins* [New York: Crossroad, 1983], pp. 160-84.)

determines her posture toward the one with a reputation as an itinerant healer, and her articulation of that posture with wit and common sense sets free his response to her and to her daughter's need as well.

Engaging the Text in an Expanded Reading Community

This reading is moving away from the common attempts by interpreters to make the passage in Mark address in some way the legitimization of the church's mission to the Gentiles. That salvation-historical reading may be supported a bit more by Matthew's version, but its survival in Mark hangs only on the word 'first' in Mk 7.27. This reading also moves away from attempts (my own included) to see the Gentile woman as the embodiment of all categories of the outcast and oppressed persons to whom the Gospels suggest much of Jesus' ministry was directed. It also does not explain away Jesus' initial rejection of her as a momentary lapse before he is brought back to his mission by the woman's wit. It is a harsh saying contextually congruent with analyses of the social and economic reality of the region in which the story is set. This reading also presents Jesus' initially harsh response to the woman as congruent with the emphasis of the meta-narrative of Mark's Gospel on the poor and outcast as the particular beneficiaries of Jesus' ministry (although it is incongruent with pictures dear to Christian piety of 'gentle Jesus, meek and mild').

Having resolved those problems, the reading being proposed introduces others. While the reading offers a hint of how the prosperous and the non-poor can participate in Jesus' ministry, the means to do so involves accepting an insult before deflecting it to less violent ends. The fact that the desperate circumstances of her daughter are portrayed as the key to the woman's approach, witty retort and eventual positive reception by Jesus leads to the question of whether the privileged must be brought low by such a personal crisis, if not by social revolution, before Jesus' ministry extends to them. Finally, this reading has so far not addressed the fact that the character treated so harshly, and who must defend herself from insults, is a woman. Does it therefore not risk supporting the notion that suffering and abuse is the natural—even appropriate—lot of women, and that only their witty parrying of insults can save the day?

The purpose of this section is to bring those preliminary insights and the emerging problems into dialogue with perspectives on the passage from readers in contexts markedly different from my own. Their insights confront and nuance my own emerging responses and set the stage for my concluding reflections on and engagement with the story.

Theissen's insights (referred to above) into the economic and cultural realities of the region where the story is set are intuitively echoed in the reflections on the Matthean version of this passage by the Nicaraguan peasants and their companions recorded in *The Gospel in Solentiname*.[27] 'She must have been a rich old woman', they say. 'She must have been an oppressor'. They reach this negative assessment of her solely on the basis of Jesus' harsh response to her, and their assumption that he would treat only oppressors in so harsh a way. Their popular (unschooled in the formal sense) reading struggles with the ethnic exclusivism they encounter in the Matthean account, but their experience of oppression leads them to appreciate the picture of her need to humble herself to get help in her daughter's illness. The fact that all of the identified speakers are men may account for the fact that issues of gender are not raised. Their instinctive appreciation of the embittering effects of economic domination on those forced into the subordinate role, however, gives affective support to the importance of the data about the relationship between the people of Tyre and those of the surrounding 'region'.

The Japanese feminist, Hisako Kinukawa,[28] focuses on the consequences of the woman's otherness in both gender and ethnicity relative to Jesus according to the Markan version of the story. Her principal lens is the effect of Jesus' rejection of what she views as Jewish preoccupation with purity and ethnic exclusivism — attitudes to which she encounters parallels in her own culture. Her assessment of the woman is sympathetic, viewing her speech and actions as the desperate acts of a woman oppressed and maligned for the double factors of her ethnic identity and her gender. Jesus' initially harsh response to her is attributed to the honor–shame culture in which he lives, and his ultimate granting of her request to his becoming 'fully himself' as a breaker of boundaries.[29] In this case, she says that he 'challenges the barrier-building between the pure and the unclean and negates an artificially warranted cultic purity',[30] though she does not provide evidence from primary sources to support the secondary sources she cites.

27. Ernesto Cardenal, *The Gospel in Solentiname*, II (trans. Donald D. Walsh; Maryknoll, NY: Orbis Books, 1978), pp. 210-15.

28. Hisako Kinukawa, *Women and Jesus in Mark: A Japanes Feminist Perspective* (Maryknoll, NY: Orbis Books, 1994), pp. 51-65.

29. Kinukawa, *Women and Jesus in Mark*, p. 60.

30. Kinukawa, *Women and Jesus in Mark*, p. 52.

Her harshly anti-Jewish reading of the text, and her assumptions about Jesus' distinction from his cultural and religious context, lead her nonetheless to significant challenges to the Christian church in Japan in the matter of attitudes and policies affecting the 'inside others' of that society, namely Koreans living in Japan.[31] The challenge of her reading for my study is its recognition of the significance of the role of 'inside others' in the story—those seen as foreigners in their own land, for my own reading context contains many such groups of (apparently) permanent outsiders according to the ethnic and racial norms of the dominant culture. It seems to me that one could recover that challenge in the story without importing the anti-Jewish assumptions on which much of Kinukawa's argument is grounded.

Elaine Wainwright, an Australian woman from a dominant culture who is also a Christian and a feminist, was prompted by her encounters with the divergent experiences of aboriginal women and others from outside the dominant culture to reconsider her previous work on Matthew's version of this story.[32] Her purpose in the re-examination is to nuance the reading from the perspective of gender by uncovering the interlocking ideologies of oppression based on gender, class, ethnicity and religious affiliation that are at work in the narrative itself and in various reading communities. According to her analysis of the story, it shows Jesus moving from the center in his own culture and in a male world to the periphery where he encounters an important dimension of the '*basileia* vision', namely that a foreign woman comes to voice. She analyzes Matthew's use of literary and rhetorical devices of voice to make this her story, in the literary context of Jesus' story as the meta-narrative. The woman's angle of vision as one who has entered the story from the outside reveals aspects of its meaning that are not visible from the static insider's perspective held by the narrator. Wainwright's conclusion[33] inscribes that perspective as a permanent wrinkle in the fabric of the story, as the specificity of this foreign woman's voice is preserved and ultimately redefines the larger whole. The literary devices Wainwright

31. Kinukawa, *Women and Jesus in Mark*, p. 62.

32. Elaine M. Wainwright, 'A Voice from the Margin: Reading Matthew 15.21-28 in an Australian Feminist Key', in Fernando F. Segovia and Mary Ann Tolbert (eds.), *Reading from this Place: Social Location and Biblical Interpretation in Global Perspective*, II (Philadelphia: Fortress Press, 1995), pp. 132-53. Her previous study of this passage is in her doctoral dissertation, published as *Towards a Feminist Critical Reading of the Gospel according to Matthew* (Berlin: W. de Gruyter, 1991), pp. 96-118, 217-51.

33. Wainwright, 'Voice from the Margin', pp. 150-53.

has identified apply to the Matthean version of the story, but are absent from the Markan one, where the narrator's voice controls all but the central verbal exchange between Jesus and the woman.

Leticia Guardiola-Saenz reads the Matthean version of this story 'with a spirit of dispossession' and from her 'socio-historical condition of dispossessed neighbor born and bred in the borderlands of the U.S. empire', a condition she assumes she shares with the woman in the story.[34] Her own experience allows her to understand the complex dynamics of insider and outsider in border regions where cultures collide and contest. She recognizes that the context of the one inter-preting such dynamics often determines the governing assumptions embedded in the narrative concerning the appropriate behavior of the various parties. In particular, she is sensitive to assumptions about the roles and behaviors of women among the 'dispossessed' groups that color various interpretations of this story. Her analysis is particularly helpful in unmasking the romantic and fundamentally harmful view of the Other (and especially the female Other) as winning favor by submissive behavior in the presence of a male from the dominant group. Her study has adopted the perspective of the meta-narrative, and not of a historical reconstruction of the situation in the region where the story is set, to assess categories of dominance and dispos-session. Thus, in her analysis, Jesus defines dominance in the story, and the woman as Gentile is looked upon as outsider or Other. The clarity and persuasiveness of her reading leads me to reflect on the process by which original relationships (in which the urban Gentile population was likely the dominant group) are inverted in the retelling of the story. The political and economic dominance has been replaced by an apparently even stronger narrative dominance to define desirable and unacceptable behavior, who is 'in' and who is 'out'.

Kwok Pui-lan frames her study of this passage[35] explicitly through concerns of postcolonial hermeneutics. She examines how this woman as a foreigner—whom Kwok sees as 'colonized'—is inscribed in the 'master discourse' of the gospel story, and how the speech attributed to her functions in the rhetorical project of the author. Kwok is search-ing for an interpretation of the story that will further the liberation of Third World women, and that will support a rereading of the story to enhance respect for one another as persons of different gender, race,

34. Leticia A. Guardiola-Saenz, 'Borderless Women and Borderless Texts: A Cultural Reading of Matthew 15.21-28', *Semeia* 78 (1997), pp. 69-81.

35. Kwok Pui-lan, *Discovering the Bible in the Non-Biblical World* (Maryknoll, NY: Orbis Books, 1995), pp. 71-83.

religion and social origin. Using a narratological model of analysis, she examines the dynamic of subject and object in the text by noting how the focalizing role of the narrator overpowers the woman's limited voice and action to make her the model of 'Otherness'. Because the woman has been written into the story in that way, Kwok concludes that this story has been ripe for appropriation to support projects of sexism, colonialism and anti-Judaism, and also (especially by Asian women) to counter such projects. That principal reading perspective appears to have predisposed Kwok to see the woman in a sympathetic light, defined by the author as bearer of the multiple oppressions shared also by the women of Kwok's principal reading community. While she takes into account Theissen's study of the economic and ethnic dynamics of the 'region' where the story is set, and of the woman's likely membership in a privileged group, Kwok concludes only that 'Other' is not a unitary category, either of experience or of interpretive lens, but rather one that includes 'the Other within the Other'.[36]

Concluding Reflections

At the conclusion of this study, the passage continues to elude me and to leave me perplexed. I still am both challenged and repelled by what I find here, but now for different reasons than at the beginning. The passage requires careful discernment of layers and agenda in the single dynamic of dominance and subordination to which it is transparent. Given my own ambivalent position as dominant by some criteria (race, economics, nationality and — in some situations — profession) and subordinate by others (notably gender), it is probably not surprising that this is my focus, and a source of both positive and negative reactions.

Clearly the most difficult task in interpreting this passage is addressing it as a literary creation and not as a window into a real encounter. So vivid is the scene that the author has crafted, with the focus of both structure and content on the dialogue between Jesus and the woman, that the temptation for many interpreters — myself included — is to 'psychologize', that is, to attribute motives, feelings, and assumptions to both characters, and to identify with their interaction as that of real people. It is of course not impossible that Jesus did have such an encounter once-upon-a-time with a Gentile woman needing help for her sick daughter, but historicity is not the point.

36. Kwok, *Discovering the Bible*, p. 82.

Rather, the author has crafted the woman with specific attributes—her ethnicity, her provenance, the urgency of her need, her wit—highlighted for our perception and reaction. Some are universal in their appeal: who could fail to sympathize with the urgency of her desire to find help for her daughter? Others—her ethnicity or her gender—change in meaning and importance depending on where the reader stands, and what the reader understands about the context of the author. Therein lies the shifting terrain of dominance and subordination that affects my response to the story.

Thus, on the Jesus-level or that of the Markan church (as I have reconstructed the social history of those two communities), the woman's privileged place relative to the poorer Jewish peasants of the region around her city earns her a label of contempt ('dog') in light of Jesus' agenda elsewhere in Mark's Gospel of bringing 'good news to the poor', to whom she represents bad news in the extreme. The harshness of the language attributed to Jesus still offends me as a would-be follower of Jesus, but I understand how fervent political commitment (Mark's as well as, apparently, Jesus') un-tempers the tongue. As one of the world's 'non-poor', I am uncomfortable with the picture of the privileged woman's acceptance of the subordinate posture 'under the table' as the price of her participation in the blessings Jesus offers, but that discomfort with the costliness of discipleship is appropriate.

I remain troubled, however, by the harshness of the language attributed to Jesus, regardless of its political comprehensibility. The power dynamics in this story are determined not only by her social setting. The crisis of her daughter's illness that is posited as the specific occasion of this encounter establishes the woman's absolute need, and it moves her into a subordinate position relative to Jesus, whom she perceives as having the healing power she needs for her daughter. Consequently, I am brought up short by her humiliation. No one, regardless of other attributes of their lives, deserves such treatment at a time like that! I am at a loss to understand what Mark is up to in crafting the story in this way, where it presents not general principles of social critique, but a specific individual case.

Two details in Mark already introduce a layer of reading of this passage that will come to dominate the passage, beginning in Matthew's redaction of it, and continuing in Christian interpretation, both ecclesial and academic. That new layer relates to the relationship between Jews and Gentiles in Jesus' ministry and subsequently in the church. The details by which that agenda is already introduced are the indication, not of exclusion, but of priority ('first') in the 'feeding' that is to happen, and the larger narrative context of the episode. In that context, 'food' sounds a metaphorical echo that invokes the entirety of Jesus' ministry, and not just the immediate healing. Also, the episode is situated in a section of the Gospel (Mk 4.35–8.26) in which Jesus' ministry moves through the regions around the Sea of Galilee, touching women as well as men, Gentiles as well as Jews, opponents of his movement as well as supporters. Incorporating both feeding stories (6.30-44; 8.1-10)[37] and the two stories on the 'sea' itself (4.35-41; 6.45-52), which I understand to be resurrection appearance stories inserted into the account of Jesus' earthly ministry, this section seems to represent the life of Mark's church as well as its traditions about Jesus.

In Matthew's version of the story, the churchly level seems more clearly in view, given the emphasis on the woman's 'faith' in prompting both Jesus' change of mind and the healing action that is effected by his decree (Mt. 15.28) rather than by her 'word' (Mk 7.29). The explicit affirmation in Jesus' initial word to the woman that he was sent 'only to the lost sheep of the house of Israel' implies that the incorporation of the Gentiles into the movement that became the church—though not their eligibility to be recipients of Jesus' healing ministry—was part of the (chronologically later) post-Easter mission. The emphasis on the contrast between Jews and Gentiles makes the woman clearly the ethnic and religious Other to the norm held by Jesus, and thus inverts the power dynamic between her people and Jesus' in the early socio-economic context: she is the marginalized outsider trying to gain a hearing from someone of greater power.

In the religious imperialism and implicit (or even explicit) supercessionist reading of subsequent Christian interpreters, the roles shift again, with Jesus now still holding the normative position, 'the Jews' being portrayed as the exclusivist opponents of the Gentile Christians as the new Chosen People, and the woman relegated to the position of 'pagan'—a sassy one at that—to whom Jesus' ministry is graciously extended. Kinukawa and Guardiola-Saenz have written eloquently of the toll this picture of the woman has taken on women who occupy similar social positions as 'pagans' and ethnic outsiders to a dominant

---

37. The first of these stories has such 'Jewish' details as the numbers (5 and 12), the type of basket (κόφινος)—the lunch basket Jews would carry tied to their waist if their journeys were to take them away from a certain supply of proper food—and the 'blessing' before the meal. The second has 'Gentile' details, such as the 'perfect' numbers 4 and 7, a different word for basket (more like a large laundry basket) and 'giving thanks' before the meal.

culture. Equally harmful have been the readers who elaborate on the picture of the 'exclusivist' Jews to label the word 'dogs' as a racial epithet assumed to be in general use by them about Gentiles. Such caricatures, in addition to being inaccurate, become part of a larger hermeneutic project of Christian anti-Judaism.

Through all of these shifting dynamics of dominance and subordination in the passage, the one that remains constant is that of gender. In this story the one who feels the sting of Jesus' harsh words is a woman. The privileged one who takes her place under the table is a woman. If the story does not represent a remembered incident, but rather if the saying was the core around which the story took shape, was it simply more believable that such an insult would be parried by a woman rather than a man of the powerful class (whose response might have been more direct or even violent)? Did early hearers consider such treatment of a woman acceptable in general, or only if she is an Other, an enemy? (The gender-specific torture and humiliation of women in contexts of war comes inevitably to mind: it is acceptable because they are enemies and therefore non-persons.) Are we really supposed to excuse the behavior attributed to Jesus as an illustration of the way he is gracious despite her sassiness? Should he be praised for at least allowing himself to be corrected—even changed —by a (mere) woman? Read in its canonical context as Scripture of the church, does this passage sanction the humiliation and verbal (as well as physical) abuse of women as a legitimate test of their faith? Should I as a woman celebrate the picture of this woman's loyalty to her beloved daughter, and the woman's wit and quick tongue that change Jesus' mind? I do. Or should I read it with lament or even rage at the picture of the treatment she receives at the hand—or, more accurately, the mouth—of the one I confess as Emmanuel? I do that, too. And I am left perplexed.

My earlier struggles with this text had a happier outcome. I was able to find in the woman of the story a positive role model, and in the portrait of Jesus an initially sexist, but finally teachable man, one able to learn about the meaning of his messiahship from this woman (whom I took to be among the most marginalized of the society). This time I find the pictures of her and of him more ambiguous. More importantly, I am struck by the resourcefulness of the tellers and the interpreters of this tale to use it to reinforce our places of privilege or pride. I am reminded once again of the importance of reading in as diverse a community as possible, so that our various perspectives can uncover what none of us can see alone, and so that we can hold one another accountable for what we cannot face alone.

This reading, then, claims no definitive answers, but only a place in a conversation that must continue. I have talked long enough: who will take the floor?

THE SYROPHOENICIAN WOMAN:
A SOUTH ASIAN FEMINIST PERSPECTIVE

Ranjini Wickramaratne Rebera

The story of the Syrophoenician woman, as she is referred to in the Gospel of Mark (7.24-29) and the Canaanite woman, as she is called in the Gospel of Matthew (15.21-28), makes interpretation an uneasy task since it relates an uncomfortable incident in Jesus' ministry. It is an incident that places Jesus on the defensive. Yet it was sufficiently significant to both writers for it to be included in the two Gospels. It is interesting that Luke, who records a great deal about women and their interaction with Jesus, does not mention this encounter. However in Mark and Matthew this triple outsider is identified through her cultural, religious, and ethnic identity.[1] Scholars are in agreement that both tellings refer to the same incident and the same woman as the similarities in detail are indisputable.

For Christian women in South Asia this pericope has many resonances. Though its primary purpose was to address the issue of purity, it also focuses on identity, difference, power, inter-religious dialogue, and Christology as experienced within a pluralistic society. It challenges us to look beyond the needs of the writers of the two Gospels who have used this encounter to strengthen Jesus' messianic role. For most Christians in Asia Jesus transcends his Jewish identity. The Indian theologian S.J. Samartha captures this focus when he claims that 'within the New Testament there is one Jesus but several christologies'.[2] The establishing of an Asian Christian identity tends to focus more on Christology than on a historical ethnic identity of Jesus.

---

1. Elisabeth Schüssler Fiorenza writes: 'Whereas Matthew calls her by the antiquated Scriptural name Canaanite (race), Mark elaborately characterizes the woman as a Greek (indicates religious affiliation), who was a Syro-Phoenician (ethnicity) by birth'. See Elisabeth Schüssler Fiorenza, *But She Said* (Boston, MA: Beacon Press, 1992), p. 12.

2. S.J. Samartha, *One Christ, Many Religions: Toward a Revised Christology* (Maryknoll, NY: Orbis Books, 1991), pp. 115-20. His theory of a 'helicopter

In both Gospels the incident is placed immediately following Jesus' response to questions regarding traditions of Jewish elders pertaining to what is clean and unclean. The positioning of his encounter with a woman who is identified by her racial and ethnic identity leads the reader to assume that the choice was a deliberate one. It raises the question of the category to which she belongs: clean or unclean. She is a woman, she belongs to an outside race, and being Greek, she may have worshipped Greek gods and goddesses. She also has a daughter who is unclean according to the culture of that time because she is possessed by a demon (Mk 7.26). In South Asian cultures demon possession is an acceptable phenomenon. Women who display signs of demon possession are considered to be either evil or unclean. Many rituals are used even today to exorcize the demon and cleanse the woman before she is accepted back into the family and community as a 'normal' person. The search for healing is therefore also a search for cleansing. This woman's encounter with Jesus culminates in his casting 'an unclean spirit out of an unclean female who is not even present'.[3] It is unlike the rituals in South Asia that are performed by exorcists in the presence of the person who is demon possessed and unclean.

Mark perhaps needed to use this encounter at this particular juncture in the discourse to address issues that were becoming important in the early church as more Gentile Christians received baptism into the church community. It would be safe to assume that among these converts there were many women.

Matthew's focus in including this story seems to slant more towards addressing the rejection of Jesus by the elders and others in authority within his community. Mark seems to be the source for Matthew's expanded version of the encounter which probably originated as a miraculous healing story and was later used to address the issue of purity and rejection.

Impurity and rejection are issues of significance for all South Asian women irrespective of religious beliefs. As in other cultures, the South Asian world views menstruation as one of the main reasons for the subordination of women. Despite scientific and medical information and education on the subject, assumptions of impurity still surround this bodily function. It is not unusual to see women with severe

---

Christology' versus a 'bullock-cart Christology' for a postcolonial faith in a religiously plural society pushes his viewpoint further.

3.   Joanna Dewey, 'The Gospel of Mark', in E.S. Fiorenza (ed.), *Searching the Scriptures*, II (New York: Crossroad, 1994), p. 484.

menstrual dysfunction being labeled as demon possessed or unclean. Anjali Bagwe, researching attitudes towards gender in rural India, cites the example of how a young woman named Kaki learned about menstruation from the behavior and attitudes of her mother. The mother, who 'acted strangely on certain days', claimed that 'she was polluted because a crow touched her'. While menstruating, the mother would not touch any utensils, especially in the kitchen. She would sit and sleep 'in the backroom that had a separate entrance, for fear of defiling the household with her pollution'.[4] The association of impurity with women, as in the case of the woman with a hemorrhage (Mk 5.24-34; Mt. 9.20-22; Lk. 8.43-48), seems similar to the association of impurity and rejection of the Syrophoenician woman based on her race and ethnicity. She and her daughter are portrayed as being unclean. Both Gospels record the words used by Jesus to reject her request for healing. It is the only episode in Jesus' ministry where he begins by refusing to meet a human need. 'The very strangeness and the offensiveness of the story's portrayal of Jesus may suggest that the core of the story was indeed remembered as an incident in Jesus' life when even he was caught with his compassion down'.[5]

Many scholars, theologians and preachers attempt to minimize the impact of Jesus' response to her, since the image of Jesus one sees in this incident does not fit the inherited image we have of him as 'the kind, understanding, ever-helpful savior'.[6] However, his claims that he came to the 'lost sheep of the house of Israel' (Mt. 15.24), that 'the children need to be fed first' (Mk 7.27), that 'it is not fair to take the children's food and throw it to the dogs' (Mk 7.27) reflect both the criticism he is facing from Jewish authority as well as his awareness of his own racial identity. The use of the term 'dog' as a put-down in his response to the woman reads as a rejection of both the woman and her need. She, however, refuses to accept his position in the argument. The refusal of modern women to accept rejection on the grounds of impurity resonates within this woman's refusal. Many women refuse to accept gender-based attitudes and customs that persist in isolating them as outsiders to the human race.

4.   Anjali Bagwe, *Of Woman Caste: The Experience of Gender in Rural India* (Atlantic Highlands, NJ: Zed Books, 1995), pp. 89-90.

5.   Sharon Ringe, 'A Gentile Woman's Story', in L. Russell (ed.), *Feminist Interpretation of the Bible* (Philadelphia: Westminster Press, 1984), pp. 65-72 (69).

6.   Kathleen Corley, *Private Women, Public Meals: Social Conflict in the Synoptic Gospels* (Peabody, MA: Hendrickson, 1993), pp. 95-96.

Identity and Naming

Naming racial and ethnic identity is not the only way in which recognition of identity is given within South Asian culture. In many Asian cultures a name is more than a label that assists others to refer to a person. It carries with it the identity of one's family and place of origin; in some parts of South Asia it also indicates one's community or caste. An often-asked question when one is introduced to another is 'What is your family name (or father's name)?' This is not an intrusive inquiry but rather a desire to know the other's total identity. The family name is much more central to the roots of a person's identity. It denotes heritage, kinship and one's location within a particular community. The Syrophoenician woman's right to a name has been minimized because of the writers' desire to focus on the issue of purity and Jesus' ministry to the Gentile people. By omitting the woman's name in this story, the writers have used her while denying her an essential part of her identity.

Within postcolonial societies of South Asia, the issue of clean and unclean practices is still a significant one. For Christians the teachings of the early missionaries enhanced these issues as converts from Hinduism and Buddhism joined the church. Some of these attitudes still persist. For example, a Hindu friend invited me to a celebration meal in her home during one of her religious festivals. On arrival I was deeply touched when she offered me the gift of an exquisite length of embroidered silk. Not long after that I was chastised by a friend who considered herself to be a 'good Christian' for accepting the invitation to the meal and even more for accepting a gift that was obviously an item used in my friend's *pooja* (worship ritual) during the festival. The honor I felt in the gesture of my friend was lost in the Christian attitudes to contamination. Such attitudes do little for inter-religious tolerance or understanding. They make religious dialogue almost impossible.

Voice as Power

Both Gospels give this woman voice. While many women in the biblical narrative are talked about or referred to within their relationship to a male, this woman does her own talking. In Matthew's Gospel she is the first woman to speak. Matthew says she was shouting to be heard (Mt.15.2), and this led the disciples to request Jesus to send her away. For a woman to shout in public is still considered an 'unwomanly' act in Asian society. Our socialization includes sayings such as

'Girls should be seen and not heard'. Therefore, a woman who speaks loudly or shouts is stereotyped as ill-behaved, hysterical or excessively aggressive. All of these adjectives are used to put women down.

However, there are times when raised voices of women are powerful. I have witnessed women shouting publicly during the many religious processions that take place in Sri Lanka. I have vivid memories of standing on sidewalks with my mother and watching the annual Hindu processions wind their way along the streets as women and men shouted out to the priests for their blessings. Some mothers would carry their babies, push through the crowds and shout to gain the attention of the priests. Such actions are acceptable for gaining attention in the circumstances. The shouting of this woman to gain the attention of the healer and miracle worker is in a similar category, despite the impression raised by the disciples that she is a nuisance. How could it be otherwise? Her choice is to shout or to be silent and lose the possibility of healing for her daughter. Which mother would remain silent, given such an option? She claims her right to be heard, and she is heard.

Women's political rallies in South Asia are good examples of the power of shouting as a means for confrontation and resolution. Society may have formulated the voiceless role for women. Yet governments in Asia are known to use women's protest marches to their advantage. In Sri Lanka the shouts and curses of mothers after the disappearance of their children during periods of political unrest and government-instigated atrocities were used by the government to divert attention from its actions. The government sought to underscore the freedom granted to women which includes the right to demonstrate in this manner! However, when finally the focus shifted from the shouting of the mothers to the actions of the government, the politicians used force to control the organization named 'Mothers' Front'. Undeterred by these sanctions, the shouting of the demonstrators continued. Each time the Mothers' Front met with police resistance, there was 'loud chanting of "*Sadhu! Sadhu!*" [Holy! Holy!] that rent the air [and] all gates were hastily opened by a chagrined Senior police officer'.[7]

By placing the Syrophoenician woman's encounter with Jesus within the purity debate both Gospel writers have downplayed the

---

7. Malathi de Alwis, 'Motherhood as Space Protest: Women's Political Participation in Contemporary Sri Lanka', in Patricia Jeffrey and Amrita Basu (eds.), *Appropriating Gender: Women's Activism and Politicized Religion in South Asia* (London: Routledge, 1998), pp. 185-201 (190).

humanity of this nameless mother. As a possible single mother with a continuously sick daughter who is solely dependent on her, her situation is familiar to countless mothers across the world. To continue to live with a child who has no hope for a cure is an unimaginably painful experience. The pain of mothers whose children have been killed in ethnic and racial war, permanently wounded through the effects of militarism, of drugs, of substance abuse and of AIDS and HIV-related illnesses, is reflected in the pain of this mother. She seems to have no husband or family, as none is mentioned in the text. She seems to be alone with only her sick girl-child through whom she sees an extension of herself and her right to a future.

This woman is different than the other women who encountered Jesus as the healer. The woman with a hemorrhage (Mt. 5.25-34), Peter's mother-in-law (Mt. 8.14-15) and the crippled woman (Lk. 13.10-17) receive healing in their own bodies and experience Jesus as healer as well as messiah for themselves. The Syrophoenician woman does not experience healing for herself but for another: her girl-child whom she had carried within her body and whom she had nursed with no hope of a cure. Her rejoicing is twofold: for her daughter and for herself.

In cultures where the girl-child is aborted, killed at birth, or discriminated against, the tenacity of this mother to heal her girl-child stands out as a role model for us. In South Asia the stigma attached to the birth of a girl-child colors her identity into her adult life. It contributes to the low self-esteem of women, particularly those who are forced into the sex trade as the only avenue for economic survival. For a girl-child to be a victim of an illness that carries the stigma of 'unclean' would be an incredible burden for both mother and daughter. However, the burden of a prolonged illness does not confine the girl-child in this story to obscurity. The woman sees her girl-child as a mirror image of herself. In the giving of unconditional love to her girl-child, she loves herself. In the healing of her girl-child, she is also healed. Her healing is validated by the tenacious faith of her mother: that the healer can heal!

The Syrophoenician woman meets the power of the rabbi Jesus with the knowledge of her own sense of power. Her power is rooted in her protective strengths, her capacity to care, and her commitment to the task she had set herself. She is an icon to women in today's church who are prevented from claiming the right to own their power and to use it for others, as this woman did. She does not hesitate to acknowledge Jesus' own power when she addresses him as 'Lord, son of David' (Mt. 15.22) and when she kneels before him to plead her case. But she retains her own power to challenge him and confront him with the legitimacy of her request. She does not attempt to influence him, as women sometimes do when confronted with a stubborn male. She does not try to avoid creating conflict by permitting him to win the argument. She feels he is wrong to claim exclusivity for his healing ministry, and she uses her strong feelings as the source of her power to initiate a change of attitude in him. She meets Jesus as an equal in her tenacity to be true to her mission, as much as he feels the need to be true to his mission to the covenant community. Because of her tenacity, her commitment to her daughter's healing, and her ability to use the 'power of the weak'[8] in a positive and life-giving manner, she also becomes the catalyst for moving Jesus to acknowledge his ministry to the Gentile people.

Faith and Inter-religious Dialogue

The pericope concludes with the healing of the daughter, as Jesus vindicates this mother's faith in his ability to cure: 'Woman, great is your faith! Let it be done as you wish' (Mt. 15.28). There is no doubt that this encounter portrays a woman who was different from many of the other women who met Jesus during his lifetime. The Samaritan woman at the well and the Syrophoenician woman are both Gentile outsiders. However, the Samaritan woman returns to her village after her encounter with Jesus and becomes the catalyst for people from her village to follow Jesus. The Syrophoenician woman returns to her home and her cured daughter. There is no evidence of her becoming a follower of Jesus or a Gentile Christian in the early church. It is possible that she continued in her own faith practices. Her 'faith' as is recorded in the two Gospels points more to a faith in Jesus as a healer and miracle worker than as messiah. It is her faith that makes her unique in her ministry to Jesus.

8.   Rosine Perelberg develops a convincing argument for the power of the weak in 'Equality, Asymmetry, and Diversity: On Conceptualization of Gender', in Rosine Josef Perelberg and Ann C. Miller (eds.), *Gender and Power and Families* (London: Routledge, 1990), pp. 43-45. I have applied this concept to the use of personal power by women in my 'Women's Identity in Leadership', in Ranjini Rebera (ed.), *Affirming Difference, Celebrating Wholeness: A Partnership of Equals* (Hong Kong: CCA, 1995), pp. 77-95, and at the collective level in 'Power in a Discipleship of Equals', in Musimbi Kanyoro (ed.), *In Search of a Round Table: Gender, Theology and Church Leadership* (Geneva: WCC Publications, 1997), pp. 82-90 (88-89).

The encounter reveals the ability to enter into inter-religious dialogue without coercion from either side. Conversion to be a follower of Jesus does not seem to have been the result of the woman's achieving her goal. The different implications of purity were named and resolved. A human need was addressed because the woman's faith transcended the racial and ethnic differences that divided her and the healer. Similarly, for the majority of South Asian Christians, Jesus' ethnic and racial identity is not the focus for being a Christian. It is the centrality of faith in God as revealed in Jesus, the Christ, that is the core of Christian identity. As the effects of living in a global culture begin to find expression in daily lives, the need to balance historical realities of a transplanted Christianity and the recognition of Christianity as one of the many great religions in Asia have become more than theoretical exercises. This need and recognition are reflected in the current struggle to interpret Christianity as it is lived with our neighbors from other faiths and not as a confrontation with the beliefs of people from other religions.

The Syrophoenician woman and Jesus were from different cultures, religious beliefs, genders and racial origins. They encounter each other for a brief moment; if each had claimed the right to use his or her identity and difference as power over the other, this encounter may have had a different ending. Although each of them challenged the other, the challenge was done with intentions of trying to establish understanding of each other's positions. It was not for the purpose of controlling the other. The outcome to the encounter was positive because both were able to place their different identities side by side and not as opposing forces. They worked towards the goal of being able to relate to each other rather than to dominate each other. They experienced power with each other.[9] The woman gave Jesus the power to recognize his ministry to the Gentile people. Jesus gave her the power of life by healing her daughter. There is a mutual ministry in this encounter that is often lost in its focus on what is clean and what is unclean.

For those of us who belong to countries that are experiencing violence based on claims of ethnic, racial or religious superiority and

9.   For a more detailed discussion of power, especially 'power-with', see my 'Women's Identity in Leadership'. I have developed the concept further as 'life-centered power' in 'Recognizing and Naming Power', *In God's Image: Journal of Asian Women's Resource Centre for Culture and Theology* 17.1 (1998), pp. 38-42, and 'Understanding Power: Intellectual Elitism or Catalyst to Change', *In God's Image: Journal of Asian Women's Resource Centre for Culture and Theology* 17.3 (1998), pp. 2-4.

arrogance, the encounter between this woman and Jesus has a powerful message. Japanese feminist theologian Hisako Kinukawa explores the implication of racial purity within the context of her own race as she analyzes this encounter. She writes:

> The Israelites kept their ethnic identity and national integrity through holding to the laws and cultic traditions. It was very important, especially for men, to keep their family lineage pure. So they excluded foreigners from their ethnic borders in order to retain their purity of blood... Japan as a country is also known for its ethnic exclusivism, though the causes are different from those of the Israelites... Ethnically there has been a myth, which is actually an illusion that the Japanese people are a homogenous race. This myth has given rise to the belief that it is important to maintain the purity of Japanese blood... Ethnic homogeneity has been identified with superiority, connected with the religious concept of purity, and used by the authorities to exploit other peoples.[10]

The concern for purity of heritage and bloodline is evident in the anger and displeasure of parents when children enter into cross-cultural and inter-religious marriages. In South Asia children have been disinherited or declared as 'dead' when they have married outside their caste, ethnic or racial group. In Sri Lanka the long-running ethnic war reflects the same concepts of arrogance and chauvinism. Unfortunately the church does not claim a prophetic role in the struggle. Despite its many attempts at being a voice for the advocacy of peace, its practice and action often contradict this position. Preoccupation with religiosity and the preservation of racial and ethnic purity are present underneath outward attempts to bring resolution to a war-torn island.

Who Is Clean?

Reinterpreting the encounter of the Syrophoenician woman and Jesus from a South Asian feminist perspective reveals many icons for women caught between understandings of purity and impurity. As the incidents in this article demonstrate, the definition of cleanliness still forms one basis for discriminating against and isolating women. The designation of what is clean and what is unclean is not a clinical diagnosis of one's surroundings. It is still embedded in cultural structures that determine who is clean and who is unclean.

10. Hisako Kinukawa, *Women and Jesus in Mark: A Japanese Feminist Perspective* (Maryknoll, NY: Orbis Books, 1994), p. 61.

The ability of the Syrophoenician woman to rise above discrimina-
tory practices to claim her right to inclusion within the circle of those
whose lives touched Jesus, is a significant one. She claims inclusion
without losing her identity as a person from a different racial and
ethnic group. She claims inclusion through her faith in herself to find
healing for her girl-child and her faith in the healing power of the
person she addressed as 'Lord, son of David'. For Christian women in
South Asia she stands tall as the sister who refused to take 'No' as the
answer and who held her own until she achieved her goal. She is one
more role model for courage and tenacity when we are confronted by
put-downs and derogatory remarks. She will continue to be the icon
for challenging discrimination wherever rituals, traditional customs
and cultural practices continue to define women as being unclean. She
challenges both church and society to re-examine their attitudes
toward difference and to relearn the need to see difference as the basis
for mutual ministry and not for polarization. She invites us to find
new and inclusive ways to dialogue as people of a multi-religious,
intercultural South Asia.

THE POOR WIDOW IN MARK AND HER POOR RICH READERS*

Elizabeth Struthers Malbon

And sitting opposite the treasury, he was observing how the crowd cast money into the treasury. And many of the rich cast in much. And one poor widow, coming, cast in two *lepta*, which is [in value] a *quadrans*. And calling his disciples, he said to them, 'Amen, I say to you, the poor widow herself cast in more than all of those casting into the treasury. For all (of them) cast in from their surplus, but she from her need cast in all of whatever she had, her whole life' (Mk 12.41-44).[1]

Reviewing and adding to the varying interpretations of this small story in Mark's Gospel offer a way of raising an important methodological issue in the larger story of New Testament or, more broadly, biblical interpretation. Here examination of the interpretations presented in three representative commentaries—historical-critical (Swete), form-critical (Taylor), redaction-critical (Nineham)—and one intriguing article (by Addison Wright) preludes my reading of the story of the poor widow in six Markan narrative contexts. These multiple interpreta- ✓ tions provide a basis for reflection on the methodological issue of dealing with differences in interpretation. There are a wealth of readings of the poor widow's story, yet one must sometimes wonder whether our embarrassment of riches as readers is not akin to poverty: both can be paralyzing.

I. *Three Commentaries*

The Markan commentary of Henry Barclay Swete was first published in London in 1898.[2] Swete is especially interested, in his comments

*   Originally published in *CBQ* 53.4 (1991), pp. 589-604. Reprinted by permission.

1.   Author's (fairly literal) translation. The translation of *bios* as 'life' rather than as 'means of living', both of which are legitimate, is based on the narrative contexts of the passage, as will become clear below.

2.   Henry Barclay Swete, *Commentary on Mark* (repr. 3rd edn; Grand Rapids, MI: Kregel, 1977 [1913]).

here and elsewhere, to clarify matters of the Greek text and the ancient historical background. The 'treasury' referred to in this passage, he tells us, would have been the colonnade in the Temple's Court of the Women under which 13 chests of trumpetlike shape, and thus known as *Shopharoth* (trumpets), were placed.[3] The two coins involved were Greek λεπτά, which, as Mk explains for the benefit of his Roman readers were each worth half a Roman *quadrans,* and which, as Swete explains for the presumed benefit of his English readers, were the eighth part of an *as* or the one one-hundredtwenty-eighth part of a *denarius* or the seventh part of a *chalkous'*.[4]

But Swete also expands the details of the minimal Markan story in colorful ways. 'Passover was at hand', he notes, 'and wealthy worshippers were numerous and liberal'.[5] 'The Lord's attention is attracted by the rattling of the [widow's] coin[s] down the throats of the Shopharoth. He looks up…from the floor of the Court [of the Women] on which his eyes had been resting, and fixes them on the spectacle…'[6] Delightful as these imagined sights and sounds may be, more striking are Swete's observations of verbal and narrative contrasts. 'The widow stands out on the canvas, solitary and alone', he notes, 'in strong contrast to the πολλοὶ πλούσιοι [the many rich], and is detected by the Lord's eye in the midst of the surrounding ὄχλος [crowd]'.[7] 'The rich cast in…πολλά [much], the widow πάντα [all]'.[8]

For Swete the point of the story is the lesson 'the Lord' would teach the disciples about giving. 'The lesson is taught, as usual,' he notes, 'by an example—in the concrete, not in the abstract'.[9] The difficulty and yet importance of the lesson are indicated by 'the use of the solemn formula ἀμὴν λέγω ὑμῖν [Amen, I say to you]'.[10]

The magisterial Markan commentary of Vincent Taylor, published in England in 1952, 54 years after Swete's, also seeks to explain the intricacies of the Greek text and (to a lesser extent) to fill in details about the historical background. Taylor's focus, however, is on both the *Sitz im Leben Jesu,* the 'situation in life' of Jesus, and the *Sitz im Leben* of the early church reflected in the oral tradition behind the

---

3. Swete, *Commentary on Mark,* p. 292.
4. Swete, *Commentary on Mark,* p. 293.
5. Swete, *Commentary on Mark,* p. 293.
6. Swete, *Commentary on Mark,* p. 292.
7. Swete, *Commentary on Mark,* p. 293.
8. Swete, *Commentary on Mark,* p. 294.
9. Swete, *Commentary on Mark,* p. 294.
10. Swete, *Commentary on Mark,* p. 294.

Markan text.[11] According to Taylor, the 'narrative is a Pronouncement-story', that is, the 'story is told, not for its own sake, but because it leads to a significant saying of Jesus about almsgiving'.[12] Taylor also reports other form-critical opinions: Bultmann 'classifies it as a Biographical Apothegm'; Redich as 'an Apothegm-story'; Dibelius 'prefers to regard it as a narrative constructed by Mark on the basis of a saying of Jesus, and especially a parable'.[13] 'The position of the narrative', Taylor observes, 'is due to topical reasons. The reference to widows in xii.40 and its connexion with the Temple account for its place in the Markan outline'.[14]

In terms of historical backgrounds, Taylor's references to trumpet-shaped chests and the λεπτά and *quadrans* are much briefer than Swete's, but Taylor discusses in addition the historical literary parallels to the story in other religious traditions: Jewish, Indian, and Buddhist. Particularly he cites (following Lohmeyer) 'the Jewish story [from *Leviticus Rabbah*] of a priest who rejected the offering of a handful of meal from a poor woman, and was commanded in a dream during the night: "Despise her not; it is as if she offered her life."'[15] Taylor understands such parallels to challenge 'the genuineness of the story', that is, the probability of its historical occurrence. The genuineness can also be questioned, he admits, because 'we do not know' how Jesus knew so completely the widow's economic circumstances. But neither of these points, he argues, is 'a valid objection to the historical value of the narrative'.[16] On the one hand, 'The story is not so distinctive that similar incidents, with differences, could not happen in the case of other teachers,'[17] and, on the other hand, the Markan narrative simply 'betrays no interest in the question' of the *how* of Jesus' knowledge.[18]

For Taylor, as for Swete, the point of the story is the widow's exemplary giving of all that she had. The phrase ὅλον τὸν βίον αὐτῆς, Taylor translates as 'even her whole living', and, he comments on the phrase, it 'is in accordance with Mark's style, and effectively describes

11. Vincent Taylor, *The Gospel According to St Mark* (repr. Grand Rapids: Baker Book House, 2nd edn, 1981 [1966]).

12. Taylor, *St Mark*, p. 496.

13. Taylor, *St Mark*, p. 496.

14. Taylor, *St Mark*, p. 496.

15. Taylor, *St Mark*, p. 496.

16. Taylor, *St Mark*, p. 498.

17. Taylor, *St Mark*, p. 496.

18. Taylor, *St Mark*, p. 498.

the measure of the widow's generosity'.[19] The use of the phrase 'Amen, I say to you' 'indicates the earnestness with which Jesus spoke'.[20] Furthermore, Taylor asserts, 'the story is in harmony with [Jesus'] teaching elsewhere',[21] citing Mk 9.41, 'Amen, I say to you, whoever gives you a cup of water to drink because you bear the name of Christ, will by no means lose his reward', and Lk. 12.15, 'Take heed, and beware of all covetousness; for a man's life does not consist in the abundance of his possessions' (RSV).

Dennis E. Nineham's commentary on Mark was first published in England in 1963, just 11 years after Taylor's, but it reflects a significant development in New Testament scholarship in general: Taylor's orientation is form-critical, Nineham's is redaction-critical; Taylor asks about the history and tradition before Mark, Nineham asks about what Mark does with that tradition.[22] Nineham is skeptical about the by now traditional comments on the historical background of this passage. He does point out that λεπτόν means literally 'a tiny thing' and 'was used for the smallest coin in circulation'.[23] But, following Cadbury, he cautions that it is 'unsafe to deduce any conclusions about the Gospel's place of origin' from Mark's explanatory transliteration of the Latin word *quadrans* into Greek.[24] Nineham also mentions the traditional interpretation of 'what is meant by *the treasury*' (the 13 trumpet-shaped receptacles described in the Mishnah), but he notes as well that the Greek word used here, γαζοφυλακίον, elsewhere is used for 'the rooms or cells in which the temple valuables or deposits were stored'.[25] Nineham concludes that 'it is probably simplest to suppose that a story related *by* Jesus (on the basis of a current Jewish parable) has been transformed into a story about him', in which case 'St Mark himself may have had no very clear idea what *treasury* was intended'.[26]

Nineham considers the 'number of quite close parallels [that] are known from both pagan and Jewish sources' (he quotes the one from *Lev R.* 3.5) as evidence in favor of understanding the story as an enacted parable, 'a Jewish parable which Jesus took over in his

19. Taylor, *St Mark*, p. 498.
20. Taylor, *St Mark*, p. 497.
21. Taylor, *St Mark*, p. 496.
22. D.E. Nineham, *The Gospel of St Mark* (Pelican New Testament Commentaries; Baltimore, MD: Penguin Books, 1963).
23. Nineham, *St Mark*, p. 335.
24. Nineham, *St Mark*, p. 335.
25. Nineham, *St Mark*, p. 335.
26. Nineham, *St Mark*, p. 335.

teaching and which was later transformed into an incident in his life'.[27] Nineham, as a redaction critic, is particularly interested in the context of this parabolic story in Mark's Gospel:

> The present setting of the story may in part be due simply to the catchword *widow* (vv. 40 and 42), but a more apt position for it could hardly be imagined. Not only does it form a fitting contrast to the previous section ('In contrast to the bad scribes, who "eat" widows' property, we now have the tale of the good widow and her sacrifice' [Montefiore]), but with its teaching that the true gift is to give 'everything we have' (v. 44) it sums up what has gone before in the Gospel and makes a superb transition to the story of how Jesus 'gave everything' for men'.[28]

This brief statement is Nineham's full comment on this idea, an idea that moves away from a focus on the poor widow's gift as exemplary *financial* stewardship to an openness to the poor widow's giving as paradigmatic service or self-sacrifice; it is an idea I will develop further below.

2. *An Intriguing Article*

Most of the interpretive work on the story of the poor widow in Mark has been done in commentaries, such as those by Swete, Taylor, and Nineham, rather than in journal articles. An intriguing exception is an article by Addison Wright that appeared in the *Catholic Biblical Quarterly* in 1982.[29] This article will serve as my fourth and final example. Wright's essay is entitled 'The Widow's Mites: Praise or Lament? — A Matter of Context', and his thesis cuts against the grain of all those interpretations — the vast majority, including Swete's and Taylor's — that focus on the exemplary financial generosity of the poor widow. To a large extent I agree with Wright's diagnosis of the common interpretive disease, but I differ with him on the appropriate prescription for a cure. Yet I concur completely in finding the issue 'A Matter of Context'.

Wright opens his study with a tabular survey of the few articles and many commentaries that offer information relevant to or interpretations of the story of the poor widow. Most of the articles deal with some aspect of the coins, and most of the commentaries conclude

---

27. Nineham, *St Mark*, p. 334.
28. Nineham, *St Mark*, pp. 334-35.
29. Addison G. Wright, SS, 'The Widow's Mites: Praise or Lament? — A Matter of Context', *CBQ* 44 (1982), pp. 256-65.

that the point of the story is the extraordinary and exemplary financial generosity of the poor widow, a model contributor. Wright's chief
complaint about these interpretations is as follows. Many commentators recognize, explicitly or implicitly,

> that Jesus' observation [about giving] is a commonplace, and that
> indeed it is not a specifically Christian idea but a universal and human
> one. Thus they conclude that there must be some further depth to the
> saying and they supply that further depth by relating Jesus' remark to
> some element from the larger context of his preaching (blessed are the
> poor, a cup of cold water in his name, do not be anxious about what you
> shall eat or wear, you cannot serve God and Mammon, you shall love
> the Lord your God, etc.). This procedure of attempting to read in con-
> text is laudable, but the writer would maintain that the proper context
> has not been rightly identified in any of the commentaries...[30]

In fact, Wright suggests, the interpretive context has usually been
imported into the text for external religious reasons. He writes,

> Critical exegesis is supposed to inform preaching, piety, and church
> thinking, but one wonders to what extent preaching, piety, and church
> interests have affected critical exegesis in the history of the interpretation
> of this text.[31]

According to Wright, 'The context is immediately at hand'[32] in the
three immediately preceding verses (12.38-40):

> And in his teaching he said, 'Beware of the scribes, who like to go about
> in long robes, and to have salutations in the market places and the best
> seats in the synagogues and the places of honor at feasts, who devour
> widows' houses and for a pretense make long prayers. They will receive
> the greater condemnation' (RSV).

'If, indeed, Jesus is opposed to the devouring of widows' houses',
Wright asks, 'how could he possibly be pleased with what he
sees here?'[33] Wright argues that Jesus could not, that the story of the
poor widow, 'if viewed as an approbation, does not cohere any better
with the immediately preceding widow-saying, than it does with the
Corban-statement',[34] in which the truly 'religious values are human
values'.[35]

30. Wright, 'The Widow's Mites', p. 259.
31. Wright, 'The Widow's Mites', p. 265.
32. Wright, 'The Widow's Mites', p. 261.
33. Wright, 'The Widow's Mites', p. 262.
34. Wright, 'The Widow's Mites', p. 262.
35. Wright, 'The Widow's Mites', p. 261.

Wright asserts that we must

> see Jesus' attitude to the widow's gift as a downright disapproval and
> not as an approbation. The story does not provide a pious contrast to
> the conduct of the scribes in the preceding section (as is the customary
> view); rather it provides a further illustration of the ills of official
> devotion. Jesus' saying is not a penetrating insight on the measuring of
> gifts; it is a lament, 'Amen, I tell you, she gave more than all the
> others'... She had been taught and encouraged by religious leaders to
> donate as she does, and Jesus condemns the value system that moti-
> vates her action, and he condemns the people who conditioned her to
> do it.[36]

'If one seeks further context', Wright adds, 'the lines that follow the story should not be neglected'[37] — in fact the next two verses are all one needs. Mark 13.1-2 reads:

> And as he came out of the temple, one of his disciples said to him,
> 'Look, Teacher, what wonderful stones and what wonderful buildings!'
> And Jesus said to him, 'Do you see these great buildings? There will not
> be left here one stone upon another, that will not be thrown down'
> (RSV).

Wright comments: 'It is hard to see how anyone at that point could feel happy about the widow. Her contribution was totally misguided, thanks to the encouragement of official religion, but the final irony of it all was that it was also a waste'.[38] 'Instead of reaching ahead one chapter to connect the story with Jesus' self-offering in the passion narrative, as a few commentators [including Nineham] do', Wright proposes, 'let us simply be content with the lines that immediately follow both in Mark and in Luke.'[39] Thus for Wright the proper inter-pretation of 12.41-44 is 'a matter of context', and the proper context is 12.38-40 and 13.1-2, no less and no more.

But why should we be content to consider only the preceding three verses and the succeeding two verses *the* context of the poor widow's story? Does *the* context or *the proper* context of a passage even exist? Is it a sensible notion? It would seem more appropriate to consider a

36. Wright, 'The Widow's Mites', p. 262.

37. Wright, 'The Widow's Mites', p. 263.

38. Wright, 'The Widow's Mites', p. 263.

39. Wright, 'The Widow's Mites', p. 263. Strangely enough, the moralizing (and unconvincing) interpretation of 12.41-44 offered by Ernest Best *(Following Jesus: Discipleship in the Gospel of* Mark [JSNTSup, 4; Sheffield: JSOT Press, 1981], pp. 155-56, while the very type of thing against which Wright argues, is based not on a link back to 12.40 (widows' houses) but on 'a better link forwards' to 13.2 (and ch. 13 as a whole), the very thing for which Wright argues.

number of overlapping *contexts* in which the story of the poor widow can be read. I am especially interested in the multiple *narrative* contexts in which this little story functions in the larger narrative of Mark's Gospel.

3. *Six Narrative Contexts*

Wright is correct in calling attention to the three immediately preceding verses (about the typical behavior of scribes) as an important narrative context. I would, however, interpret the significance of this (first) context along the lines of what Wright complains of as 'the customary view'. [40] The poor widow who gives all, her whole means of living, is in striking contrast to the scribes who take all, who 'devour widows' houses' (12.40), that is, their means of living. The scribes who seek to call attention to themselves by means of wearing their long robes about and soliciting salutations in the market places as well as claiming the best seats in the synagogues and at feasts are in striking contrast with the poor widow who is so unobtrusive that only Jesus notices her; it is he who calls her action to the attention of the disciples. From beginning to end, Jesus' ministry itself is in striking contrast to the scribes' activities and attitudes. Many citations could be given, of which the first, Mk 1.22, is perhaps emblematic: 'And they were astonished at his teaching, for he taught them as one who had authority, and not as the scribes' (RSV).[41] Thus Jesus is unlike the self-centered scribes and like the self-denying widow in being one who gives.

Wright's argument to the contrary seems more ingenious than convincing. Of course the widow's gift of 'her whole life' is not reasonable, but that is the same complaint that Peter makes (in 8.31-33) of Jesus' willingness 'to give his life as a ransom for the many' (10.45). Wright's narrow contextual focus results in an unfortunate, if not unusual, case of 'blaming the victim'. Perhaps we *are* to assume that the poor widow has been victimized by scribes who devour widows' houses and by the authority of traditional religious teaching;[42] surely

40. Wright, 'The Widow's Mites', p. 262.

41. See also 2.6, 16; 3.22; 7.1, 5; 8.31; 9.11, 14; 10.33; 11.18, 27 (12.28, 32 refer to the exceptional scribe); 12.35, 38; 14.1, 43, 53; 15.1, 31.

42. Swete observes: 'It may have been the intention of the two Synoptists to compare her simple piety with the folly of the rich widows who wasted their substance on the Scribes (Victor), or she may once have been one of the latter class, and reduced to destitution by Pharisaic rapacity; at least it is worthy of notice that Mt., who does not mention this feature in the character of the Scribes, omits also

the Markan Jesus is victimized by the chief priests, scribes and elders, those who traditionally hold authority in the Temple and in the broader religious tradition. At an important transitional point in the Markan narrative, Jesus calls attention to the poor widow's action; the focus seems to be on giving, but not just of money. The *last* words of the passage are those left echoing in our ears: ὅλον τὸν βίον αὐτῆς, 'her whole life'.[43]

Wright also appropriately calls attention to the succeeding two verses, Jesus' prediction of the destruction of the Temple, as an important (second) context for the story of the poor widow. He argues that the foretold destruction of the Temple indicates the absurdity of the poor widow's gift. I would argue, rather, that the *overall* Temple context of the poor widow's story adds to the impressive *irony* of the Markan passion narrative. Jesus' summoning his disciples to observe the poor widow's action and to consider its significance is his final act in the Temple. The Markan Jesus' initial act in the Temple was the driving out of those who bought and sold there (11.15-19). This passage, as several of us have argued, is to be understood as a symbolic closing down of the Temple, not a cleansing of it.[44] The account of

the incident of the mites, whilst Mc. and Lc. have both, and in the same order of juxtaposition' (*Commentary on Mark*, p. 293).

43. See Joseph A. Grassi, *The Hidden Heroes of the Gospels: Female Counterparts of Jesus* (Collegeville, MN: Liturgical Press, 1989), pp. 22, 35-39. See also Bonnie Bowman Thurston's discussion of the recurrent early Christian imagery of the widow as 'altar': 'An individual's obedience to God is a form of sacrifice offered to God in imitation of Christ's sacrifice... It is in this sense that the widow as altar becomes an effective agent; she too is a living sacrifice. The key New Testament texts on widows (Mark 12:41-44; Luke 2:36-38; 4:25-26; 7:11-17; 18:1-8; Acts 6:1-7; 16:11-15; 1 Tim. 5:3-16) do not explicitly connect widows with sacrifice. If, however, love of God, love of neighbor more than self, and prayer are Christian sacrifices, then the widows embody Christian sacrifice. Anna worships "with fasting and prayer night and day" (Luke 2:37). The widow who makes an offering at the treasury exhibits love of God and care for neighbor above self, especially since the offering is her "whole living" ([Mark] 12:41-44). It is noteworthy that both these widows are placed within the temple environs, near the altars... In the words of Saint Basil, the altar is for the purpose of the holy remembrance of Christ in which Christ comes near himself as a sacrifice. Christ provides the atonement through his sacrifice; the altar [i.e., metaphorically the widow] reminds Christians of his sacrifice (Heb. 13:10)' (*The Widows: A Woman's Ministry in the Early Church* [Minneapolis: Fortress Press, 1989], p. 111).

44. Elizabeth Struthers Malbon, *Narrative Space and Mythic Meaning in Mark* (San Francisco: Harper & Row, 1986), pp. 120-26, 131-36; Werner H. Kelber, *The Kingdom in Mark* (Philadelphia: Fortress Press, 1974), pp. 97-102. But see also Craig A. Evans, 'Jesus' Action in the Temple: Cleansing or Portent of Destruction?', *CBQ*

Jesus' conflict with the buyers and sellers in the Temple is intercalated with the account of the cursing and withering of the fig tree (11.12-14, 20-26), which is generally recognized as a parabolic pointing to the destruction of the unfruitful Temple whose time or moment (καιρός, 11.13) has passed. The episode of the poor widow's gift of her all might well be understood as an enacted parable parallel to the fig tree incident (as L. Simon has argued[45]) or parallel to the intercalated fig tree/Temple incident as a whole. The fig tree episode introduces a series of controversies between Jesus and Jewish religious authorities in the Temple; the account of the poor widow's action closes the series.

As the withering of the fig tree alludes to the destruction of the Temple itself, which is made explicit in Jesus' prediction in 13.2, so the widow's gift of 'her whole life' alludes to Jesus' gift of his life, which is enacted in chs. 14–15. Furthermore, Jesus' death is related to the Temple's downfall, not in the sense in which the false witnesses accuse Jesus of claiming to be the *agent* of the Temple's destruction (14.57-59; see also 15.29-30), but in the sense in which the καιρός of the temple (alias fig tree) is surpassed by the καιρός of the kingdom and of the Messiah who proclaims, 'The καιρός is fulfilled, and the kingdom of God is at hand...' (1.15a). Thus Jesus' first action in the Temple, the driving out of the buyers and sellers, points to the Temple's end; and Jesus' final action in the Temple, or rather his reaction to the poor widow's action, points to his own end. And, most importantly, the Temple's end and Jesus' end are carefully interrelated in the Markan Gospel, not only in the juxtaposition of Jesus' death on the cross (15.37) and the tearing of the Temple curtain (15.38), but also in the intercalation (admittedly in the broadest sense) of the accounts of the passion of Jesus (chs. 11–12 and 14–15) and the passion of the

51 (1989), pp. 237-70, esp. 238-42, where Evans argues against E.P. Sanders that the Gospel writers, especially Mark, manifest an antitemple theme and thus would *not* be likely to change accounts of Jesus' historical Temple action as a portent of destruction (affirmed by Sanders) to narratives of a Temple cleansing; thus the Temple cleansing idea must be in the Gospels, including Mark, because of its historical authenticity. Evans's focus is 'the historical Jesus', not the Gospel of Mark, and he concludes 'that the cleansing idea is too firmly entrenched in the tradition to be so easily set aside. Since the cleansing idea, if properly understood (i.e., not as an attack against the sacrificial system itself), coheres well with what we know of Jesus and the background against which we must interpret him, it is appropriate that we let it stand [as authentic history]' (p. 269). I do not find Evans's arguments concerning 'Jesus' or Mark convincing.

45. L. Simon, 'Le sou de la veuve: Marc 12/41-44', *ETR* 44 (1969), pp. 115-26.

community (ch. 13).[46] The crises the community of Jesus' future followers will face—being delivered up to councils, being beaten in synagogues and standing before governors and kings (13.9), for example—are to be interpreted, and coped with, in the light of the crises Jesus does face in Jerusalem.[47]

This brings us to a third narrative context of the poor widow's story: beyond its immediate juxtaposition with the scribes who devour widows' houses and its closing out Jesus' activities in the Temple, the story of the poor widow's gift of her last two coins serves with the story of the unnamed woman's anointing of Jesus as a frame around ch. 13. Chapter 13, the eschatological discourse, is intrusive within the larger story of Jesus' passion in Jerusalem, which begins in chs. 11–12 and culminates in chs. 14–15. Even though the frame and middle of this large-scale intercalation are to be interpreted together, one can skip from the end of ch. 12 to the beginning of ch. 14 with no noticeable gap in the story line. The central discourse is framed by two stories about exemplary women in contrast with villainous men. Jesus' condemnation of the scribes' typical actions and his commendation of the poor widow's exceptional action immediately precede ch. 13; the accounts of the chief priests' and scribes' plot against Jesus and the woman's anointing of Jesus immediately succeed ch. 13.[48] One

46. The phrase 'the passion of Jesus and the passion of the community' comes from John Donahue (lectures given at Vanderbilt Divinity School, Fall 1977). But see Norman Perrin, *The New Testament: An Introduction* (New York: Harcourt, Brace, Jovanovich, 1974), pp. 148, 159. The positions of Perrin and Donahue represent developments, based on more detailed literary analysis, of the more historically oriented positions of Etienne Trocmé and Rudolf Pesch. My designation of chs. 11–12, 13 and 14–16 as an intercalation is in line with the literary analysis of Perrin and Donahue and does not judge the issue of the historical creation of the Gospel of Mark. Frank Kermode also recognizes ch. 13 as 'the largest of his [Mark's] intercalations', but in Kermode's view the insertion is not between chs. 11–12 and 14–16 but between 1–12, Jesus' ministry, and 14–16, Jesus' passion *(The Genesis of Secrecy* [Cambridge, MA: Harvard University Press, 1979], pp. 127-28).

47. See also Robert Tannehill, 'The Disciples in Mark: The Function of a Narrative Role', *JR* 57 (1977), p. 404, and R.H. Lightfoot, *The Gospel Message of St. Mark* (Oxford: Clarendon Press, 1950), pp. 48-59. Kermode's further expansion of the concept of intercalation is well taken: 'Should we think of the whole gospel as an intercalated story?... It stands at the moment of transition between the main body of history and the end of history; and what it says has a powerful effect on both' *(The Genesis of Secrecy*, pp. 133-34).

48. Interestingly enough, if the three criteria John Donahue established for a Markan insertion *(Are You the Christ?* [SBLDS, 10; Missoula, MT: Scholars Press, 1973], p. 241) were to be expanded from the level of the phrase to the narrative level, at least two of the three would be met in the case of chs. 11–12, 13 and 14–16.

woman gives what little she has, two copper coins; the other gives a great deal, ointment of pure nard worth 300 *denarii*; but each gift represents <u>self-denial</u>.

It is, of course, ironic that the poor widow's gift occurs in the doomed Temple; and it is ironic that the anointing of Jesus Christ, Jesus Messiah, Jesus the anointed one, takes place not in the Temple but in a leper's house (14.3), and not at the hands of the high priest but at the hands of an unnamed woman. A further irony is manifest in the juxtaposition of the unnamed woman, who gives up money for Jesus and enters the house to honor him (14.3-9), and Judas, the man who gives up Jesus for money and leaves the house to betray him (14.10-11).

As a fourth narrative context of the story of the poor widow, the character, her action, and its significance may be read in the context of all the women characters of Mark's Gospel. As I have tried to work this out elsewhere, I will not repeat myself here.[49] I will simply point out that the poor widow, along with three other important women characters (the hemorrhaging woman, the Syrophoenician woman, and the anointing woman), takes decisive action to which Jesus makes a significant *r*eaction. The hemorrhaging woman touches Jesus' garment and is immediately healed; Jesus reacts in admiration of her faith (5.24-34). The Syrophoenician woman argues with Jesus in his own metaphorical terms about bread for children and for dogs; Jesus reacts to her 'word' by healing her daughter at a distance, in spite of his initial refusal to do so (7.24-30). The poor widow gives for others

---

First, 'close verbal agreement' would become 'close narrative agreement' and would be satisfied by the two stories about self-denying women, each following a reference to devious and self-centered men in official religious positions. Second, 'synoptic alteration' at the narrative level is clear: both Matthew and Luke parallel Mk 13, but Matthew drops the preceding account of the poor widow, and Luke drops (or moves and significantly alters) the succeeding account of the anointing woman.

Grassi suggests that 'the whole tone for Jesus' final testament in ch. 13 is set by a deliberate "inclusion", a literary device that links the beginning and end of a section by means of repetition. In dramatic presentation, this device focuses audience attention on their own response to Jesus' example. At the beginning we find the story of the poor widow... At the end of Jesus' last discourse, just before Judas' betrayal of Jesus, we have the story of the...woman...at Bethany who anointed Jesus' head with oil as he sat at table (14.3-9)' (*Hidden Heroes of the Gospels*, p. 35). Grassi presents 'the significant parallels' of the two stories in parallel columns (p. 36).

49. Elizabeth Struthers Malbon, 'Fallible Followers': Women and Men in the Gospel of Mark', *Semeia* 28 (1983), pp. 29-48, esp. pp. 37-40, 43.

her last two coins, 'her whole life'; Jesus summons his disciples to attend to her action. The anointing woman anoints Jesus' head with expensive ointment; Jesus reacts by proclaiming that the story of her anointing him 'beforehand for burying' will be told in memory of her wherever the gospel is preached (14.3-9). Perhaps the historical reality of women's lower status and the historical reality of women's disci-pleship together support in Mark's Gospel the surprising narrative reality of women characters who exemplify the demands of follower-ship, from bold faith in Jesus' life-giving power to self-giving in parallel to, or in recognition of, his self-denying death. Perhaps women characters are especially appropriate for the role of illuminating fol-lowership, because in the Markan community women were in a position to bear most poignantly the message that among followers the 'first will be last, and the last first' (10.31).[50]

A fifth narrative context of the story of the poor widow is the context of Jesus as teacher. Several verbal clues in Mk 12.41-44 underline Jesus' words about the poor widow as a significant teach-ing. The pericope opens by noting that Jesus was 'sitting'. Sitting was the authoritative position of the rabbis while teaching. Jesus is sitting in the boat on the sea (4.1) as he speaks to the crowd in parables in ch. 4, an extended teaching discourse with interesting parallels to ch. 13, where Jesus is sitting on the Mount of Olives (13.3) as he speaks to four of the disciples about the eschaton. Jesus called his disciples (προσκαλέω) to himself in the Temple treasury as he had earlier called them from the Sea of Galilee (1.16-20) and on the mountain where he appointed the Twelve (3.13-19) and in preparation for sending them out (6.7) and for feeding the 5000 (8.1).

The three references to Jesus' calling his disciples immediately prior to the reference at 12.43 are especially revealing in their juxtaposition of calling, saying to them, on one occasion sitting, and teaching about self-giving service. Verse 8.34 reads: 'And calling the crowd with his disciples, he said to them, "If any one intends to follow after me, let that one renounce himself or herself and take up his or her cross and follow me"'. Verse 9.35 reads: 'And sitting, he called the Twelve, and he said to them, "If any one intends to be first, that one will be last of all and servant of all"'. And 10.42-45 reads:

50. In reference to *actual* widows (i.e., not characters in stories) in the early church (from the time of Jesus to 325 CE), Bowman Thurston notes: 'The widow was an effective agent in a spiritual transaction within the Christian community. First, she interceded for the community. Her prayers perhaps sanctified the gifts brought to her. Second, the example of her life of sacrifice provided the community with a living reminder of their Lord's sacrifice' (*The Widows*, p. 111).

And Jesus, calling them, said to them, 'You know that those supposed to govern the peoples lord it over them, and the great among them domineer them. But it is not so among you; but whoever would wish to become great among you will be your servant, and whoever would wish to be first among you will be slave of all. For the Son of humanity also came not to be served but to serve, and to give his life as a ransom for the many'.[51]

Finally, Jesus prefaces his statement about the widow's gift of her all with 'Amen' (RSV, 'Truly'), as he does also on a dozen other significant occasions, including 'Amen, I say to you, whoever gives you a cup of water...will by no means lose his reward' (9.41), and 'Amen, I say to you, there is no one who has left house or brothers or sisters ...who will not receive a hundredfold...' (10.29). The Jesus who sits and calls and says 'Amen, I say to you' is Jesus the teacher, and the moment so portrayed is a solemn proclamation about the kingdom — its coming now and in the future, its Messiah, and the demands and rewards that fall to the followers of such a Messiah of such a kingdom. Giving one's 'whole life' is required of this Messiah, and it may also be required of his followers.

A sixth and final narrative context of the poor widow's story to which I wish to draw attention is the overall pattern of Markan characterization. As I have suggested elsewhere, the author of Mark wishes to show who Jesus is and who Jesus' followers are. To do this he schematizes the characters of his story; he paints extreme cases of enemies and exemplars as the background against which the trials and joys of followers may stand out more boldly.[52] The enemies and exemplars are similar in their 'flat', one-sided characterization;[53] they differ in their negative or positive value as models for the reader. The unclean spirits and demons, as well as most of the Jewish leaders, are 'flat' and 'bad'. The minor characters, or 'little people',[54] tend to be 'flat' and 'good'. The 12 disciples, however, are 'round', or multisided

---

51. Although a parallel between 10.45 and 12.44 is clear from the larger narrative contexts, the words for 'life' differ: at 10.45 it is ψυχή, 'life' or 'animating principle', and at 12.44 it is βίος, 'life' or 'means of living'.

52. Elizabeth Struthers Malbon, 'The Jewish Leaders in the Gospel of Mark: A Literary Study of Markan Characterization', *JBL* 108 (1989), pp. 259-81, esp. 279 and 275-81.

53. 'The terms 'flat' and 'round' are associated with E.M. Forster, *Aspects of the Novel* (repr. New York: Harcourt, Brace & World, 1954 [1927]), pp. 103-18.

54. The phrase is employed by David Rhoads and Donald Michie, *Mark as Story: An Introduction to the Narrative of a Gospel* (Philadelphia: Fortress Press, 1982), pp. 129-35.

in their characterization, and also multivalent as models: they present both positive *and* negative models for the reader to follow or avoid. It would be inappropriate to focus on the 'goodness' of the poor widow in opposition to the 'badness' of the 12 disciples without also observing her 'flatness' in contrast to their 'roundness'. All the Markan characters work together for the sake of the Markan story, its teller, and its hearers. Thus the little story of the poor widow who gives 'her whole life' is thoroughly integrated into the larger Markan story of who Jesus is and what it means to be his follower.

4. *Multiple Readings*

There may well be other narrative contexts that would contribute significantly to our understanding of the story of the poor widow in Mark, but these six are more than enough to illustrate my methodological point. The three commentaries I have surveyed here (Swete, Taylor, Nineham) represent three different foci in New Testament studies: the historical Jesus, the oral tradition of the early church, and the redactional (or editorial) activities of the evangelists. Each makes some contribution to our understanding of the poor widow's story. It helps in a basic sort of way to know of the existence of *Shopharoth* and the value of λεπτά, but it does not take us far in the task of interpretation. It is most interesting to know of a quite parallel Jewish story, but looking elsewhere for parallel teachings of Jesus may have led us astray as *interpreters of this text*. It is enlightening to consider the widow's story in its broader context of Mark's telling of Jesus' story. Wright's article represents a literary approach seeking to be free of prior theological presuppositions, and for that I offer praise, not a lament. Yet my own brief analysis moves beyond Wright's in calling attention to six literary or narrative contexts and especially in leaving open the possibility of additional relevant contexts, seeking neither *the* proper context nor *the* final interpretation.

All of the readers mentioned here have read the Markan text, 12.41-44, in context—some context, but a contextual reading in itself provides no guarantee of the adequacy of a textual interpretation. *The context does not exist, and a text's multiple contexts seem to raise as many interpretive questions as they answer.* Yet to understand the text we must have contextual readings and multiple contextual readings, and, in most cases, multiple contextual *readers*. The critical question is how to interrelate the multiple readings of a single text that result from multiple interpreters focusing on multiple contexts. How do we listen to and talk with each other about our different or

differing observations? Does our wealth of scholarly readings over-
whelm other readers? Are we rich in diverse readings and poor in our
overall understanding of the situation of reading itself?

James Kincaid, writing in *Critical Inquiry*, has observed that 'Readers
proceed with the assumption that there must be a single dominant
structuring principle and that it is absurd to imagine more than one
such dominant principle'.[55] But texts themselves resist such 'coher-
ence', as he calls it: 'most texts, at least, are, in fact, demonstrably
incoherent, presenting us not only with multiple organizing patterns
but with organizing patterns that are competing, logically inconsistent'
—with 'a structure of mutually competing coherences'.[56] The story of
the poor widow in its Markan contexts seems not quite so extreme,
but Kincaid's general observation applies nevertheless. As he argues
against the text's single determinant meaning, Kincaid is not arguing
for the text's indeterminacy.[57] These seem to him, and to me as well,
false alternatives. We are not free to assume that the text can mean
anything just because it can mean many things.

Perhaps the image of advocacy, from the field of law, can shed light
on the situation of juggling and judging multiple contextual readings.
Perhaps we interpreters are like attorneys defending our clients (our
contextual readings), always dedicated to our own clients' best interests. One obvious advantage of this metaphor is that it makes room
for areas of expertise; if one wanted to argue an interpretive case
concerning the relative value of λεπτά, one would surely retain Swete
as a consultant. Another useful application of the metaphor is this:
just as attorneys have limited free choice of their clients (specialty,
location, financial needs or desires dictate accepting some clients;
others may be assigned by the court system), so many interpreters
select the context or contexts on which they focus neither at random
nor with perfect freedom and fully conscious deliberation (I doubt
that the feeling of being 'drawn' by one's approach—or one's text—is
rare). In addition, the image of advocacy suggests the strength of the
bond between an interpreter and his or her contextual reading. But
the legal analogy breaks down in the end. Scholarly debates, although
sometimes heated, are not basically adversarial situations. To suggest
that one contextual focus or one contextual reading could be adjudi-
cated 'innocent' and another 'guilty' assumes not only an acknowledged judge and jury of interpretation but also a standard that all are

55. James R. Kincaid, 'Coherent Readers, Incoherent Texts', *Critical Inquiry* 3
(1977), pp. 781-802; the quotation is from p. 783.
56. Kincaid, 'Coherent Readers', p. 783.
57. Kincaid, 'Coherent Readers', pp. 789-90.

sworn to uphold: *the* (right, best, whatever) context. In fact, it may make more sense to conceive of the text as the client of all its interpreters, in which case our common advocacy defuses our adversarial relations. Thus the advocacy image is inadequate.

A second image that might provide direction as we struggle to interrelate multiple contexts of multiple readings is neither as concrete nor as striking as the first, but it may prove more useful. It is the image of complication. Jonathan Z. Smith has asserted that the 'historian's task is to complicate, not to clarify'.[58] Perhaps the same might be said not only of the task of the interpreter but of that of the text as well. Texts, at least 'good' texts, 'classic' texts, including most biblical texts, 'complicate' readings of themselves. Thus interpreters of such texts take up their task from the text itself: to 'complicate', not to 'clarify', interpretation. The process of 'complication' requires dialogue, listening as well as speaking. As Dominick LaCapra has observed: 'The point here is to do everything in one's power not to avoid argument but to make argument as informed, vital, and undogmatically open to counterargument as possible', although 'the process of gaining perspective on our own interpretations does not exclude the attempt to arrive at an interpretation we are willing to defend'.[59]

LaCapra's words (argument, counterargument, defend) return us to the other image, advocacy, which, despite its final limitations, is not without useful application. I am willing to *defend* my reading of the poor widow's story in multiple narrative contexts as more revealing of the text's depth and power than Wright's reading of it in its most immediate narrative context. But I am also willing to appreciate how Wright's reading *complicates* numerous other readings that I am, it is true, less able to appreciate because they seem to import a context in which the poor widow serves as an exemplum for a stewardship campaign. Poor widow, indeed; poor woman to be so trivialized by being placed on the wrong pedestal!

But poor readers, indeed, are we, if we cannot deal with a wealth of readings as 'complications' of each other because of our own need to 'clarify'. Not that all readings are equal. Some are richer, some are poorer. But many are worth more than two λεπτά, and the dynamic *process* of reading and of reading readings may be for some of us worth a 'whole life'.

58. Jonathan Z. Smith, *Map Is Not Territory: Studies in the History of Religions* (Leiden: E.J. Brill, 1978), p. 129.

59. Dominick LaCapra, *Rethinking Intellectual History: Text, Contexts, Language* (Ithaca, NY: Cornell University Press, 1983), pp. 38, 45.

RENOWNED FAR AND WIDE: THE WOMEN WHO ANOINTED ODYSSEUS AND JESUS

Dennis R. MacDonald

The story of an unnamed woman anointing Jesus in anticipation of his death has become one of the most famous Gospel stories involving a woman. The earliest telling appears in Mark, followed closely by Matthew, though Luke and John tell their own versions, often considered independent of Mark. The prevailing wisdom is that these tales issue from an actual event in the life of Jesus, but apparently no commentator has noticed the remarkable similarities between Mark's tale and another famous story, the so-called *Niptra* (washing) of Odysseus's feet by his nurse Eurycleia. The parallels between the two accounts are not casual, incidental, or superficial.

I will argue that the earliest evangelist wanted his or her readers to see the similarities and differences between the stories and appreciate the anointing of Jesus as more profound than that of Odysseus, or, more precisely, to view the woman's recognition that Jesus would die as more perspicuous than Eurycleia's recognition of Odysseus's identity. This appreciation of the woman's insight comes at a cost: it calls into question her historicity. I propose that the historicity of the scene was irrelevant to Mark. Furthermore, if the earliest evangelist did indeed create this episode in imitation of the *Odyssey*, all other Gospel accounts would seem to issue from Mark and not from independent tradition of a historical event.

After 20 years away at the Trojan War and on his odyssey home, Odysseus could not reveal his identity when he returned for fear of Penelope's suitors, over one hundred of them. Athena disguised him as a beggar so he could test the loyalties of his family and slaves. To those who were faithful he revealed himself; from those who were perfidious he kept his identity a secret until he could slay them. Two characters, however, recognized him on their own: his dog Argos and his nurse, Eurycleia. As a boy the hero had suffered a wound on his thigh from a boar's tusk that became a distinctive scar. It was this scar that would give him away.

Odysseus, still in disguise, met privately with Penelope to reassure her that her husband soon would return. In gratitude for his kindness, she commanded her maidservants to 'bathe him well / and rub him down with oil'.[1] Odysseus replied that he eschewed such extravagance and would not let her maidens touch him, unless there was an old slave who had suffered as much as he had. 'I wouldn't mind if *she* would touch my feet'.[2] Odysseus was thinking of his old nurse, Eurycleia, who would not mock his poverty like the younger women might.

Penelope, impressed by the stranger's preference for the austere, commanded Eurycleia to wash his feet. As the nurse approached, she lamented the sufferings of her long-lost master and expressed her compassion also for the sufferings of the old beggar before her. 'I will wash your feet, / both for my own dear queen and for you yourself — / your sorrows wring my heart'.[3]

> The old woman took up a burnished basin
> she used for washing feet and poured in bowls
> of fresh cold water before she stirred in hot.
> Odysseus, sitting full in the firelight, suddenly
> swerved round to the dark, gripped by a quick misgiving —
> soon as she touched him she might spot the scar!
> The truth would all come out.
>   Bending closer
> she started to bathe her master...then,
> in a flash, she knew the scar...
>   That scar —
> as the old nurse cradles his leg and her hands passed down
> she felt it, knew it, suddenly let his foot fall —
> down it dropped in the basin — the bronze clanged,
> tipping over, spilling water across the floor.
> Joy and torment gripped her heart at once,
> tears rushed to her eyes — voice choked in her throat
> she reached for Odysseus' chin and whispered quickly,
> 'Yes, yes! you are *Odysseus* — oh dear boy —
> I couldn't know you before...
> not till I touched the body of my king!'[4]

Eurycleia wanted to tell Penelope of Odysseus's return, but he insisted she tell no one. The hero and his old nurse then discussed how to punish the unfaithful servants. The *Niptra* ends with Eurycleia finishing

---

1.   *Odyssey* 19.320 (Fagles 367–68). Fagles' line numbers are from Homer, *The Odyssey* (trans. R. Fagles; New York: Viking, 1996).

2.   *Odyssey* 19.348 (Fagles 397).

3.   *Odyssey*, 19.350–52 (Fagles 398–401), 353–58, 376–78 (Fagles 426–28).

4.   *Odyssey* 19.385–93, 467–75 (Fagles 437–45, 528–38).

the job she had started, including an anointing. '[T]he old woman went off through the hall to bring water for his feet, for all the first was spilled. And when she had washed him, and anointed him richly with oil, Odysseus again drew his chair nearer to the fire to warm himself, and hid the scar with his rags'.[5]

The *Niptra* is an important and memorable moment in the epic and often found expression in Greek art.[6] Furthermore, Eurycleia's recognition of Odysseus from his scar became a popular target of imitation. A fascinating case in point comes from the tragedians, who placed Orestes in a situation much like Odysseus. Orestes wished to return home to avenge the murder of his father, Agamemnon, but had to do so in disguise to avoid detection. The tragedians used a variety of signs to alert Electra that her brother had returned: a lock of hair, a footprint, a garment Electra had woven for Orestes, Agamemnon's seal and a scar.[7] Electra thus plays a role similar to Eurycleia in the epic. Aristotle evaluated the signs of recognition in several tragedies, includeing some that no longer exist, and judged Odysseus's scar one of the most successful in ancient literature.[8]

Odysseus's scar also is recognizable in Greek prose. Achilles Tatius had his protagonist-narrator describe adventures much like Odysseus's. As proof of his valor in battle he 'showed them the scar' from a wound he suffered 'on the thigh'.[9] The novelist Heliodorus portrayed two lovers discussing the signs of recognition they would use if they should be separated. The heroine displayed her father's ring, while the hero showed 'a scar upon his knee that he got hunting a boar'.[10]

---

5.   *Odyssey*, 19.496-98, 503-507. The washing and anointing of Odysseus here have an analog in *Odyssey* Bk 4, where Helen, still in Troy, recognized Odysseus in disguise. She washed and anointed him, and swore 'a mighty oath not to make him known among the Trojans as Odysseus before he reached the swift ships' (4.244-56).

6.   See 'Eurykleia', *LIMC*, IV, pp. 101-103 (items 5, 8, 9, 17); 'Eumaeus', *LIMC*, IV, p. 59 (item 19); 'Odysseus', *LIMC*, VI, pp. 943-83 (item 214, p. 966). Graphic depictions of the footwashing informed Christian depictions of footwashings in the Gospels: the woman who washed Jesus' feet in Lk. 7.36-50 and Jn 12.1-8 (both of which redact Mark's story of the anointing of Jesus' head) and Jesus' washing of the disciples feet in Jn 13.20 (Hildegard Giess, *Die Darstellung der Fusswaschung Christi in den Kunstwerken des 4.–12. Jahrhunderts* [Rome: Herder, 1962]).

7.   See Aeschylus, *Libation Bearers* 167-232; Sophocles, *Electra* 885-1223; and Euripides, *Electra* 509-46.

8.   *Poetics* 16 (1454b-55a). See Nicholas F. Richardson, 'Recognition Scenes in the *Odyssey* and Ancient Literary Criticism', *Papers of the Liverpool Latin Seminar* 4 (1983), pp. 219-35.

9.   *Clitopon and Leucippe* 8.5.1-2.

10.   *Aethiopica* 5.5.

The recognitions of Jesus from his wounds in Lk. 24.39-43 and Jn 20.27-28 fall into this same tradition. It is no accident that the anonymous poet who recast the Gospel of John into dactylic hexameters used the Homeric word οὐλή when referring to Jesus' wounds of recognition.[11]

Mark, too, may have imitated Eurycleia's recognition in Peter's so-called confession at Caesarea Philippi. Jesus had done his best to keep his identify as the Son of God a secret lest his opponents slay him. His plan worked, for the disciples told him that people variously took him to be 'John the Baptist; and others, Elijah; and still others, one of the prophets'. Peter, however, recognized him: 'You are the Messiah'. And Jesus 'sternly ordered them not to tell anyone about him' (Mk 8.28-30). Similarly, Eurycleia told the beggar, 'you are Odysseus', and he grabbed her throat and said, 'Nurse, you want to kill me?... [Q]uiet! not a word to anyone in the house'.[12]

Even closer parallels with the epic appear in the story of the woman who anointed Jesus while he was dining at the home of Simon the leper: '[A] woman came with an alabaster jar of very costly ointment of nard, and she broke open the jar and poured the ointment on his head' (Mk 14.3). Unlike Eurycleia, this woman did not wash and anoint the feet of the guest; she 'poured down' a lavish amount of nard over his head. This transform anticipates Jesus' interpretation of her action as an anointing for his burial. She apparently recognized the one thing about Jesus that most eluded the disciples, the necessity of Jesus' death. Eurycleia, one may recall, lamented the sufferings of her master when she agreed to wash the beggar's feet. Both Homer and Mark emphasized the value of the oil: Eurycleia 'anointed him richly with oil'; the woman at Bethany anointed Jesus with 'very costly ointment of nard', which initiated the complaint of extravagance. The very excessiveness of the woman's action points to her anticipation of his death, for this was no ordinary act of hospitality; it resembles an extraordinary expression of grief for a departed loved one. Jesus' statement to the disciples suggests the woman knew he would not long be with them: 'You will not always have me with you'. The evangelist enhances the extravagance of the woman's action by having her break the alabaster jar to release the oil. It may be more than coincidence that Eurycleia, when she recognized the beggar to be Odysseus, dropped the brass water basin to the ground, spilling its contents, like the woman's breaking of the jar to anoint Jesus.

---

11. Ps.-Nonnos, *Paraphrase of the Gospel of John* 20.127.
12. *Odyssey* 19.474, 482, 486 (Fagles 536, 545, 550).

The parallels between the *Niptra* and Jesus' anointing are striking. In both, a woman anointed a stranger as an act of hospitality while he sat in the home of his host. The epic contrasts this hospitality with the hostility of the suitors and the treacherous servants. Mark contrasted the woman with the authorities, who sought to kill Jesus, with Judas, who would betray him, and with the disciples generally, who objected to this costly show of affection. In the epic and the Gospel, a woman either spilled a bowl or broke a jar. Both women made recognitions: Eurycleia recognized that the beggar was her lord or king; the woman in Mark recognized what others did not, that Jesus soon would die. Odysseus discussed with Eurycleia the treachery of those servants who had sided with the suitors;[13] immediately after the anointing at Bethany, Mark says,

> Then Judas Iscariot, who was one of the twelve, went to the chief priests in order to betray him to them. When they heard it, they were greatly pleased, and promised to give him money. So he began to look for an opportunity to betray him (Mk 14.10-11).

Even if one were to grant the parallels between these two stories, one might object that recognitions are common in antiquity and thus attribute the similarities to the general form of recognition stories and not to imitation of the epic. Several details of the story, however, suggest *mimesis*. The passage immediately preceding speaks of Jesus' parousia or so-called second coming, with obvious Odyssean imagery: 'It is like a man going on a journey, when he leaves home and puts his slaves in charge, each with his work, and commands the doorkeeper to be on the watch. Therefore, keep awake—for you do not know when the master of the house will come'.[14] The vigilance for Odysseus's servants for his return is a dominating concern of the epic. Those who remained faithful and hopeful were rewarded, while those who were treacherous were executed.[15]

---

13. *Odyssey* 19.491–502.

14. Already in Q one finds master–servant parables, some of which may have come from the historical Jesus (Q 12.35–38 and 42–46; 19.12–27; see also 12.39–40). The early church allegorized such parables to refer to Jesus' absence and return at the Parousia.

15. *Odyssey* 21.207–16 and 22.462–77. Compare the following:

Odyssey 19.313, Neither *shall Odysseus* any longer *come home* (οὔτε Ὀδυσεὺς ἔτι οἶκον ἐλεύσεται).

Mk 13.35, [Y]ou do not know when *the master of the house will come* (οὐκ οἴδατε γὰρ πότε ὁ κύριος τῆς οἰκίας ἔρχεται).

Jesus uttered this warning about the unpredictability of his return to his four most intimate companions: Peter, Andrew, James and John. The washing of Odysseus's feet similarly follows his predictions of his own return to Penelope. The following similarities surely cannot be explained from oral tradition. Here one finds firm evidence of literary imitation.

For the first time in the epic, Odysseus and Penelope found themselves alone in the same room. She offered him a seat so that 'the stranger may sit down and tell his tale'. Then she peppered him with questions, testing to see if he actually had seen her husband alive. Odysseus accurately told her how her husband dressed and correctly identified the herald who had accompanied him on his journey. Penelope 'recognized the sure signs (σήματ') that Odysseus told her'. Odysseus continued, then, to comfort her by predicting that her husband was 'near at hand'.[16]

According to Mark, Jesus sat on the Mount of Olives where his four closest associates questioned him, asking for a sign (σημεῖον) concerning the completion of 'all these things'.

Odyssey 19.102–5	Mk 13.3-4
Then the much-enduring, noble Odysseus *sat down* (καθέζετ') *upon* it [a chair],	When he *was sitting* (καθημένου) *on* the Mount of Olives, opposite the temple,
and wise Penelope spoke first, and said: [Penelope and Odysseus were alone.] 'Stranger, this question shall I myself ask you first. *Who are you* among men, *and from where*? Where is your city, and where your parents?'	Peter, James, John, and Andrew asked him privately, 'Tell us, *when will this be, and what will be the sign* that all these things are about to be accomplished?'

The content of Jesus' answer to the disciples' question, 13.5-27, obviously reflects the evangelist's redaction of traditional materials into his own distinctive perspective on the Jewish War and the eschaton; even so, like Odysseus's prophecies to Penelope, Jesus speaks in the third person about his own return.[17]

Closer parallels with the epic resume at v. 28. Odysseus told Penelope that her husband was consulting the prophetic oak of Zeus at Dodona about how he should return. Priests at the site interpreted the rustling of the leaves, or the location of doves in its branches, or the gurgling of the adjacent stream, or the clanging of bronze pots

16. *Odyssey* 19.95–307.
17. Mk 13.21-37. Jesus' third-person predictions of the return of the Son of Man had already been established in pre-Markan tradition; e.g. Q 12.8, 40; 17.26, 30.

A Feminist Companion to Mark

suspended from its limbs. Later texts attributed the tree itself—and even its lumber—with articulate speech. Whatever the teratalogical technology, ancients thought the oak spoke for Zeus. Jesus told the disciples that they, too, should consult a prophetic tree, not an oak but a fig.

Odyssey 19.296–307 (cf. 14.327–30)	Mk 13.28–33
Odysseus…had gone to Dodona to hear the will of Zeus from *the high-crested oak* of the god, namely how he might return to his own native land after so long an absence, whether openly or in secret.	From *the fig tree* learn its lesson: as soon as its branch becomes tender and puts forth its leaves you know that summer is near.
Thus, as I tell you, he is safe, and will soon come; he is very near, and not long will he now be far from his friends and his native land. Even so, *I will give you an oath.* Be Zeus my witness first, highest and best of gods, and the hearth of flawless Odysseus to which I have come, that in very truth	*So also you,* when you see these things taking place, you know that *he is near at the very gates* (ἐπὶ θύραις).[18]
all these things shall be brought to pass (τάδε πάντα τελείεται; cf. 309: ἔπος τετελεσμένον εἴη),	*Truly I tell you,*
even as I tell you. *In the course of this very month shall Odysseus come* here, between the waning of this moon and the waxing of the next.	*this generation will not pass away until all these things have taken place* (ταῦτα πάντα γένηται; cf. 13.4: ταῦτα συντελεῖσθαι πάντα). Heaven and earth will pass away but *my words will not pass away…* Beware, keep alert; for you do not know when *the time will come*. (Cf. 13.24: 'the moon will not give its light'.)

In both columns a tree provides information concerning the return of the hero. In both, the speaker, referring to himself in the third person, comforts his intimate audience with the promise that the liberator is near ('he is very near'; 'he is near') and provides assurance with an oath ('Be Zeus my witness'; 'Truly I tell you'). In both, the heroes speak of the fulfillment of 'all things' (τάδε πάντα; ταῦτα πάντα) just as they had promised ('even as I tell you'; 'my words will not pass away'). Odysseus would return 'in the course of this very month'; Jesus would return before the passing of 'this generation'. Furthermore, Jesus predicted that at his return the sky would be dark (cf. Isa. 13.10; 34.4), which also has a parallel in Odysseus's speech to Penelope: 'In the course of this very month shall Odysseus come here, between the waning of this moon and the waxing of the next'; in other

18. Cf. *Odyssey* 1.255–56, where Athena says, 'Would that he might come now and take his stand at the outer gate (ἐν πρώτῃσι θύρῃσι) of the house'.

words, when the moon is invisible.[19] Similarly, people will see 'the Son of Man coming' when 'the moon will not give its light'.

Jesus then likens his return to that of a man who went on a journey, gave responsibility for his affairs to his servants, and would return unexpectedly with rewards and punishments, like Odysseus. The next narrative tells of the anointing by the unnamed woman. The immediate juxtaposition of privately offered prophecies immediately before women anoint the heroes surely is no accident.

Furthermore, the earliest evangelist provides a clue that the woman who anointed Jesus was a Christianized Eurycleia. Jesus praised the woman by saying, 'Wherever the good news is proclaimed in the whole world, what she has done will be told in remembrance of her', yet Mark does not even give her a name. Some interpreters think the name did not survive the selective and androcentric memory of the early church. Be that as it may, no name would have been more fitting for her than Eurycleia, which means 'far-flung glory'. The significance of this name did not escape the notice of a scholiast: 'Eurycleia (Εὐρύκλεια), she who had far-flung (εὐρύ) and great fame (κλέος), the daughter of Ops, "looked upon from all sides"; "Ops" is the eye'.[20] The remarkable relevance of the name Eurycleia to the woman who anoints Jesus surely is no accident. It is a flag to view her as one who would receive her due fame, like Eurycleia.

But Mark was no slave to Homer. He presented this woman with powers of perception not available to Odysseus's nurse. Characteristic of most imitations of Eurycleia's recognition is the use of a sign—a scar, a lock of hair, a footprint, a garment, a seal. The woman in Mark had the benefit of no such sign, yet she recognized Jesus must die. In this respect she is like blind Bartimaeus, who recognized Jesus without a sign, in contrast to the disciples who did not understand though Jesus had told them clearly and repeatedly that he must suffer and die. Eurycleia enjoyed 'far-flung renown' for having recognized Odysseus from his scar, but her renown pales to that of the woman who recognized that Jesus must die and accordingly anointed him: 'Wherever the good news is proclaimed in the whole world, what she has done will be told in remembrance of her'. She will be εὐρύκλεια.

19. Cf. *Odyssey* 14.160–64.
20. Scholion to *Odyssey* 1.429. See also *Odyssey* 3.83, κλέος εὐρύ.

MAKING JESUS*

Marianne Sawicki

Just as the grooming of the Messiah (Mk 14.3-9) begins the ending of
Mark's Gospel, so Mark's *writing* of that story was itself the crucial
turning point in the rhetorical practices of an independent christological tradition. Specifically, Mark's text was the beginning of the
end for women's catechesis as a principal designer of the figure of
Jesus. Leaving aside the question of the narrative function of the
anointing at Bethany *within* the Gospel text, this paper inquires instead
into the 'before' and 'after' of the Markan pericope.

Thus, the intention here is to provide methods and materials for
historical reconstruction and then to sketch how it might be begun.
Before Mark wrote, what components of this story were available in
the Jesus traditions? Should we assume that a single event lies behind
the anointing story? If so, did it happen as recounted, and was the
woman still living when Mark wrote? Or was 'she' a composite of
many who cumulatively renovated the memory of Jesus? Before
Mark's text, who was telling this story, and where? Or if the story is a
Markan invention, then what social conventions was he invoking?
After Mark wrote, how did it happen that three other versions of the
story soon came to be written? How do we account for the discrepan-
cies of detail? Did Matthew or Luke simply rewrite a text? Or has a
creative oral transmission continued alongside and independent of the
Markan version? What rhetorical and cultural pressures transformed

*   This article is a lightly edited version of a paper titled 'Making the Best of
Jesus' that I presented at the annual meeting of the Society of Biblical Literature in
1992 and posted on the IOUDAIOS listserver in the summer of that year. My thanks
to Brandon Scott, Vernon K. Robbins, and Kathleen E. Corley, members of the
panel who first discussed this work. The 1992 paper expanded upon portions of
my manuscript 'Making Jesus', which was sent to the publisher in August 1992 but
published some years later as *Seeing the Lord: Resurrection and Early Christian
Practices* (Minneapolis: Fortress Press, 1994). Thus, I have now given the paper the
title originally intended for the book, whose principal arguments and evidences it
presents.

the stories? What issues were being negotiated, and what struggles were staged upon the battleground of these texts?[1]

'Before' and 'after' questions like these will be framed but not settled in this paper, which is arranged in four sections. First comes a methodological note concerning the adoption of anthropological constructs for biblical studies. Second, I present comparative cultural data from secular Greek literature and from the archaeological record. Third, I present comparative data from Jewish literary sources — Greek, Hebrew and Aramaic. Finally, I propose tentative reconstructions of the 'before' and the 'after': social configurations on either side of the Markan anointing story that are coherent with the comparative data.

1. On Borrowing from Anthropology's Toolbox

Comparative study in the social sciences begins with two more-or-less arbitrary determinations: of a category for comparison, and of a range of societies in which instantiations of that category will be sought. These two determinations effectively construct or produce the phenomena that are to be observed. For example, categories such as 'honor' or 'domestic space' often are invoked to describe social conventions (and it is tempting to apply these particular constructs to our story of the anointing at Bethany). Or again, one often reads that 'the Mediterranean area' is unified by its peoples' preoccupation with the negotiation of honor and shame. Such descriptions may indeed prove helpful — if we take due care to avoid the twin traps of circular definition and ethnocentric projection of our own presuppositions onto the ancient world. In this section I survey some relevant considerations ✓ raised in debates among anthropological theorists during the last decade or so.

1.   On expanding the synoptic approach to take oral practices into account, see Bruce Chilton, *Profiles of a Rabbi: Synoptic Opportunities in Reading About Jesus* (Atlanta: Scholars Press, 1989) and Vernon K. Robbins, *Jesus the Teacher: A Socio-Rhetorical Interpretation of Mark* (Minneapolis: Fortress Press, 2nd edn, 1992). For discussions of methodological issues in the recovery of information about women from classical Greek material and literary artifacts, see the introductory chapters of Christine Sourvinou-Inwood, *'Reading' Greek Culture: Texts and Images, Rituals and Myths* (Oxford: Clarendon Press, 1991), and Synnøve Des Bouvrie, *Women in Greek Tragedy: An Anthropological Approach* (Oslo: Norwegian University Press, 1990). An invaluable survey of the scholarship on women in antiquity is Gillian Clark, *Women in the Ancient World* (Oxford: Oxford University Press, 1989).

a. *Range of Comparison*

✓ The basic question here is how to demarcate, geographically and/or historically, some portion of humanity for study. The validity of our findings depends upon how rigorously this is done. 'The Mediterranean area' did not exist until constructed in the 1970s through the selection of certain cultural characteristics as significant.[2] 'Mediterranean', then, is anthropologists' shorthand designation for the constellation of characteristics that certain adjacent twentieth-century societies seem to have in common (when one overlooks ways in which they differ).

Proximity to the sea of the same name is not enough to make a society 'Mediterranean', as is evident from the exclusion of Balkan and Israeli societies from the generalizations that anthropologists make about what is 'Mediterranean'. Among anthropological theorists, it is an unsettled question whether so-called area studies are more likely to reinforce the ethnocentric biases of the investigators than to advance what has been recognized as the fundamental objective of comparative studies: a correlation between characteristics of particular communities and those of humanity in general.[3]

Before placing first-century Palestine within 'the Mediterranean', we should ask what grounds we have for believing that its culture resembled those to its west more than those to its east—with which, after all, it shared the Aramaic language in several dialects. Geography alone does not make the case. We cannot validly conclude that since Galilee and Judea lay along the coast of the Mediterranean Sea

---

2.   One can observe 'the Mediterranean' under construction in the literature: Julian Pitt-Rivers (ed.), *Mediterranean Countrymen: Essays in Social Anthropology of the Mediterranean* (Paris: Mouton, 1963); J.G. Péristiany (ed.), *Honour and Shame: The Values of Mediterranean Society* (London: Weidenfeld & Nicolson, 1965); Jane Schneider, 'Of Vigilance and Virgins', *Ethnology* 9 (1971), pp. 1-24; J. Davis, *People of the Mediterranean: An Essay in Comparative Social Anthropology* (London: Routledge & Kegan Paul, 1977); David D. Gilmore, 'Anthropology of the Mediterranean Area', *Annual Review of Anthropology* 11 (1982), pp. 175-205; and *idem* (ed.), *Honor and Shame and the Unity of the Mediterranean* (Washington, DC: American Anthropological Association, 1987).

3.   Michael Herzfeld, 'Honor and Shame: Problems in the Comparative Analysis of Moral Systems', *Man* 15 (1980), pp. 339-51; *idem*, 'The Horns of the Mediterraneanist Dilemma', *American Ethnologist* 11 (1984), pp. 439-54; *idem*, '"As in Your Own House": Hospitality, Ethnography, and the Stereotype of Mediterranean Society', in Gilmore (ed.), *Honor and Shame*, pp. 75-89; and Lila Abu-Lughod, 'Zones of Theory in the Anthropology of the Arab World', *Annual Review of Anthropology* 18 (1989), pp. 267-306, in different ways have criticized recent anthropology of 'the Mediterranean', in dialogue with its proponents, especially Gilmore.

and had complex cultural and economic relations with their western neighbors, therefore their cultures *must have* exhibited the very traits that we understand from having studied them in twentieth-century 'Mediterranean' societies. There may indeed be similarities, but let's not beg the question.

This brings up the temporal aspect of the problem of finding an appropriate scope for cultural comparison. How reliably does knowledge of the twentieth-century Mediterranean region illuminate the customs and beliefs of people who lived there some eighty generations ago? All things being equal, cultural patterns would tend to propagate themselves unchanged, owing to the inherently conservative nature of human socialization and because culture is an adaptation to the physical environment, which remains relatively unchanged over historical time. Yet all things have *not* been equal around the Mediterranean over the last two millennia. Arguably, two cultural forces— Islamic civilization and the agricultural and economic revolutions precipitated by capitalism—stand between the ancient world and the contemporary 'Mediterranean area' and count against any presupposition of undisturbed cultural continuity between then and now.

Therefore, caution is appropriate when we extract generalizations about 'the Mediterranean' from contemporary anthropological studies and apply them to first-century Palestine. The same goes for generalizations about 'the Greeks' and 'the Jews'. In antiquity, both groups were quite diverse (and of course they overlapped). Greek texts possibly relevant to the anointing story span some seven centuries (from classic drama of the late fifth century BCE through poems collected in the second century CE or later). The same expanse of centuries gives relevant artwork and other archaeological findings as well. The Jewish sources cover an even broader time span: Isaiah (eighth century BCE), the Septuagint (third and second centuries BCE), the Mishnah (second century CE) and the Talmuds (fourth and sixth centuries CE).

Obviously, it is necessary to weigh the relevance of the comparative data according to their temporal proximity to our anointing story. There is far too little information accessible for us to attempt a full ethnographic description. Moreover, the literary record quite likely reflects the biases and practices of the privileged, literate classes.[4] These caveats apply even to the Gospel stories themselves. For example, it is tempting to regard the details recorded in Mk 14.3-9 as observations

---

4. This is a threefold problem: the ancient authors were a cultural élite; the scribal transmitters of these texts (instead of others) were religiously élite; and we who read them today do so with culturally élite interests as well.

of a discrete instance of social behavior. They are not. As I will show, the cultural comparisons indicate that Mark's anointing story projects a composite of behaviors from several different social locations and times. The narrative superimposes them, but they can be distinguished by analysis.

b. *Categories of Comparison*
I have just argued that the Mediterranean as a cultural region, and antiquity as a unified and distinct period of human history, both are constructs whose validity rides upon their careful use. The same goes for the interpretive pairs 'honor/shame' and 'public/domestic'. The polarity of these concepts displays their common theoretical parentage in structuralism and also portends their complicity with theorizations of gender.

The public/domestic distinction, though commonly made in contemporary popular anthropology, recently has been challenged on both theoretical and empirical grounds. Its basic assumption is that all human societies both understand and intend a distinction between two spheres: a public realm where important affairs are transacted among members of different kin groups, and a domestic realm where inconsequential matters are taken care of, usually within a kin group. The realms are identified with physical spaces; different rules hold in each, and human activities neatly divide between them. Typically the public realm is characterized as free, open, conversational, politically and economically significant, and male. The domestic realm is unfree, hidden, silent, politically and economically insignificant (despite the etymological contradiction!), and female.

While Aristotle distinguished οἶκος from πόλις, it is Lévi-Strauss's conceptualization of 'nature versus culture' that is the modern antecedent of the construction of public space as a universally available category. The public realm supposedly is the realm of culture and creativity, while the domestic realm belongs to nature and necessity. Early feminist anthropology assumed that the subjection of women is a human universal, brought about by the confinement of women to the domestic realm because of exigencies of reproduction. The benchmark statement of this position was made by Michelle Rosaldo.[5]

_____

5.   See Michelle Z. Rosaldo, 'Woman, Culture, and Society: A Theoretical Overview', in Michelle Z. Rosaldo and Louise Lamphere (eds.), *O Woman, Culture, and Society* (Stanford, CA: Stanford University Press, 1974), and Sherry B. Ortner, 'Is Female to Male as Nature is to Culture?', in Rosaldo and Lamphere (eds.), *Women, Culture, and Society*, pp. 67-87. It is tempting to map the public/domestic

Theoretical criticism of the domestic/public conceptualization follows along familiar post-structuralist lines. It is pointed out that the ✓ binary pairing creates a value and a disvalue, reductively defines the latter in terms of the former, and tends to force the data to fit the categories of explanation. Rosaldo has taken these criticisms into account in a reconsideration of her earlier statement.[6] *Empirical* criticism of the domestic/public distinction is more devastating, coming as it does from field anthropologists who find that the construct cannot be used reliably to interpret their data.[7] For example, in the archaeological record one cannot reliably identify an excavated space as 'domestic' or 'public' on the basis of tools and furniture found in it. One must first know how an activity—spinning, calligraphy, butchering, winnowing—was understood, the scale of the activity, how it fit into marketing arrangements, and so forth. Whether the activities in question, and the spaces where they occurred, were more 'public' or more 'domestic' depended on other factors, including the gender and the kin status of the people doing them.[8] The putative association of female gender with domestic space appears particularly tenuous; we know that in contemporary traditional societies, the gender of a place can shift with the time of day and the season of the year.[9]

boundary onto the story of the anointing at Bethany. The meal would be in supposedly 'public' space—the ἀνδρών of a great house—where a woman should not go. But the ἀνδρών was by no means public like an ἀγορά; guests needed invitations. See the data about women at feasts that are introduced below.

6. Michelle Z. Rosaldo, 'The Use and Abuse of Anthropology: Reflections on Feminism and Cross-Cultural Understanding', *Signs* 5 (1980), pp. 389-417.

7. See, for example, Alison Wylie, 'Gender Theory and the Archaeological Record: Why Is There No Archaeology of Gender?', in Joan M. Gero and Margaret W. Conkey (eds.), *Engendering Archaeology: Women and Prehistory* (Oxford: Basil Blackwell, 1991), pp. 38-41; Ruth E. Tringham, 'Households with Faces: The Challenge of Gender in Prehistoric Architectural Remains', in Gero and Conkey (eds.), *Engendering Archaeology*, pp. 93-131; Louise Tilley, 'The Social and the Study of Women', *Comparative Studies in Society and History* 20 (1978), pp. 163-73; Mark S. Mosko, 'The Developmental Cycle among Public Groups', *Man* 24 (1989), pp. 470-84 (471).

8. On the relation between kinship and production, see Christine Ward Gailey, 'Evolutionary Perspectives in Gender Hierarchy', in Beth B. Hess and Myra Marx Ferree (eds.), *Analyzing Gender: A Handbook of Social Science Research* (Beverly Hills, CA: Sage, 1987); and Karen Sacks, *Sisters and Wives: The Past and Future of Sexual Equality* (Westport, CT: Greenwood Press, 1979); *eadem*, 'Toward a Unified Theory of Class, Race, and Gender', *American Ethnologist* 16 (1988), pp. 534-50.

9. For example, among the Kabyle of Northern Africa, men are abroad in the village at different hours in different seasons. At those times, only girls and old women go to the fountain or tend the chickens. See Pierre Bourdieu, *Outline of a*

Thus when ancient texts inform us that upper-class Greek homes had women's apartments where men *without* kin status did not go (the γυναικών), as well as men's dining rooms where women *with* kin status did not go (the ἀνδρών), it is best not to treat this as a manifestation of either a human universal, or even a cultural universal. It reflects merely a kinship custom of the tiny privileged class. Jewish village homes like those excavated in Capharnaum and Meiron, in Galilee, had nothing like that.[10]

The honor/shame distinction was constructed as a defining cultural characteristic for the contemporary Mediterranean region and subsequently has been used as a criterion to label societies as 'Mediterranean'. The first articulators of this construct were careful to preserve differences of nuance among cultures and among individuals within cultures.[11] What western anthropologists term 'honor' can differ drastically from place to place around the Mediterranean, yet these different kinds of honor seem always to correlate with aspects of male gender definition shared by researchers and informants — a coincidence noted with interest by feminist readers of the ethnographic record.

More recently the constructed and tentative character of the honor/shame distinction has been overlooked by some anthropologists and by several important interpreters in biblical studies.[12] This renders their work vulnerable to criticisms recently raised against the construct, criticisms that again are both theoretical and empirical. *Theoretically,* if

---

Theory of Practice (trans. Richard Nice; Cambridge: Cambridge University Press, 1977), pp. 159-63, 90-91. Gender itself is not a stable category, for in some societies it varies with age and with social class. At best, one could say that masculine gender in some societies, when combined with class status, entails the ability to carry 'public' space along with oneself, while female gender in some societies entails the ability to transform 'public' or 'wild' space into 'domestic' space.

10.   Compare the floor plans published by Susan Walker, 'Women and Housing in Classical Greece: The Archaelogical Evidence', in Averil Cameron and Amélie Kuhrt (eds.), *Images of Women in Antiquity* (Detroit, MI: Wayne State University Press, 1983), and Eric M. Meyers, James F. Strange and Carol L. Meyers (eds.), *Excavations at Ancient Meiron, Upper Galilee* (Cambridge, MA: American Schools of Oriental Research, 1981).

11.   Gilmore, 'Anthropology of the Mediterranean Area' and *Honor and Shame,* surveys the development of this construct.

12.   John Dominic Crossan, *The Historical Jesus: The Life of a Mediterranean Jewish Peasant* (San Francisco: HarperSanFrancisco, 1991), and J.H. Neyrey (ed.), *The Social World of Luke–Acts* (Peabody, MA: Hendrickson, 1991), both superb applications of social theory to the interpretation of Gospel materials, nevertheless too uncritically import Mediterranean area anthropology.

one must select a defining characteristic for 'the Mediterranean', then it should be some trait that is not equally or even more common in non-Mediterranean societies. Yet the honor/shame sensibility bears such a strong resemblance to Euro-American gender values that it either may be an ethnocentric projection or may simply select out values that the male researchers happened to hold in common with their informants. *Empirically*, the English terms 'honor and shame' are but a rough approximation of the native terms that they are meant to explain, and they apply in dissimilar situations. Perhaps it is only the poor translation of many different indigenous terms into one English word that has made 'honor' appear to be a Mediterranean universal. Michael Herzfeld proposes that 'hospitality' is a better name to classify the diverse practices observed.[13] Lila Abu-Lughod finds that while honor is exclusively linked to masculinity in the literature, with womanly shame as its mere foil, among Bedouin people within 'the Mediterranean area' both genders participate in a discourse of vulnerability as well as a discourse of honor.[14]

Thus the use of the honor/shame construct to interpret *contemporary* Mediterranean societies has become increasingly perilous. We must be doubly careful, then, if we apply it to the *ancient* world. 'Honor' often is simply a cipher for masculine gender, and so in many instances gender analysis may prove to be more productive than analysis in terms of honor and shame. Like gender, honor is not a quality or commodity that one can statically possess. It is always being wagered and waged: use it or lose it. Honor and gender are in constant negotiation. Pierre Bourdieu insightfully describes the fluid character of social exchanges and has taught social theorists to think in terms of *practices rather than qualities*.[15] Thus, if we borrow conceptual constructs like 'honor' and 'domestic space' from anthropology's toolbox, we must use them properly to insure valid conclusions. They are not monolithic structures; they are more like games presenting numerous options and whose rules we must discern.

Moreover, the Mediterranean of the first century was not one culture

13. Herzfeld, 'As in Your Own House'.

14. Abu-Lughod, 'Zones of Theory', uses Appadurai's term 'theoretical metonym' to criticize the way in which honor has become a gatekeeping concept that filters the discussion of Mediterranean cultures and defines the questions that can be asked of them. Other criticisms are taken from Herzfeld, 'Honor and Shame', 'Horns', and 'As in Your Own House'.

15. Pierre Bourdieu, 'The Sentiment of Honour in Kabyle Society', in Peristiany (ed.), *Honor and Shame*, pp. 191-241, and *idem*, *Outline of a Theory of Practice* (Cambridge: Cambridge University Press, 1977).

(much less 'the same' culture that is there to be studied today). It was a seething society of many cultures in creative contact and conflict. For such a situation, comparative study does not mean constructing a lowest common denominator; it means tracing out those lines of contact and conflict along cultural frontiers and describing the interactions that occur along them.[16] Where contemporary 'anthropology of the Mediterranean' is questing for regional homogeneity, we should be looking instead for fractures and fault lines. That is, we should attend to the interplay of distinctive Greek and Jewish elements, and at the same time we should be on the lookout for points of communication where one cultural configuration is taken up and resymbolized by another.

I read Mk 14.3-9 as a story in motion across cultural frontiers. Therefore in this section I have raised criticisms against the constructs of 'honor', 'public space', and 'the Mediterranean' in order to show why I find them rather unhelpful tools for understanding the anointing at Bethany.

2. *Greek Cultural Comparisons*

The Greek text projects a context for itself that is distinctively Hellenistic and upper class. While no comparable story survives elsewhere in Greek literature outside the Gospels, nevertheless several of the components are commonplace. Elements have been adapted from at least four cultural sub-routines: (a) an ἀλάβαστρον tableau, (b) dining customs, (c) showering with sweets by a matron, and (d) discourse of tombs and mourning. Let's take a look at each.

a. *An ἀλάβαστρον Tableau*
The ἀλάβαστρον was a little glass bottle containing perfumed balm. It had no base and no handles, but a wide lip allowed it to be suspended on a cord around the neck as an ornament. The examples from sixth-through fourth-century Athens that are pictured and discussed by Richter and Milne range in length from four to seven-and-one-eighth

---

16. In *Seeing the Lord*, I employ the metaphor of storm fronts to characterize the upheaval and improvization occurring in the societies in which the Jesus movements took shape. Vernon K. Robbins, 'The Reversed Contextualization of Psalm 22 in the Markan Crucifixion: A Socio-Rhetorical Analysis', in Frans Van Segbroek *et al.* (eds.), *The Four Gospels: Festshrift Frans Neirynck* (3 vols.; Leuven: Leuven University Press; Uitgeverij Peeters, 1992), II, pp. 1161-83, suggests that the centurion of Mk 15.39 is speaking a language of broken boundaries, evoking the many voices of Mediterranean culture.

inches.[17] Those made in Hellenistic times and found in Palestine are usually glass, according to Galling's *Biblisches Reallexikon*. A glass ἀλάβαστρον also is pictured in the *Dictionnaire des antiquités*. There was no lid. A little wad of recycled paper might be used as a stopper. *The Oxford Classical Dictionary* remarks: 'Dry ointments were also wrapped in papyrus; to serve this purpose was the final destination of many an ancient book.'

Μύρον is pleasant-smelling ointment. It is the usual generic word for perfume, and can also denote the scent of flowers or the flavoring in wine. Μύρον was an appropriate, almost stereotypical, gift between lovers. A pair of epigrams in the *Greek Anthology* (5.90-91), dated before 50 CE by Page[18] and thought by him to exemplify repartee at a συμπόσιον, illustrate the erotic and seductive connotation of μύρον:

Πέμπω σοι μύρον ἡδύ, μύρῳ τὸ μύρον θεραπεύων,
ὡς Βρομίῳ σπένδων νᾶμα τὸ τοῦ Βρομίου.
I (masc.) give you sweet ointment, buttering up perfume with perfume,
just as if pouring out a stream to Bacchus with what is Bacchus's.

Πέμπω σοὶ μύρον ἡδύ, μύρῳ παρέχων χάριν, οὐ σοι.
αὐτὲ γὰρ μυρίσαι καὶ τὸ μύρον δύνασαι.
I (masc.) give you sweet ointment, doing a favor to the ointment, not to
you; for you yourself (fem.) are able to perfume even perfume.

Because changing the gender of the participles would change the meter, each of these couplets must be said by a male speaker. If the second was meant to outdo the first, as Page believes, then we must imagine two guests vying for the attention of one ἑταίρα between courses in a banquet, when people perfumed one another. (See discussion below.) The juxtaposition of μύρισαι and δύνασαι in the second couplet is interesting in comparison with Mk 14.8.

Daubing oneself with scent was part of preparing for a social outing, and additional perfume could be provided to refresh guests between courses during a banquet.[19] Ointment also enhanced intimate relations between couples. Nard is probably spikenard, a vegetable oil from the spikenard plant imported from the Himalayas.

In classical Athens, the ἀλάβαστρον was associated with weddings

17. Gisela M.A. Richter and Marjorie J. Milne, *Shapes and Names of Athenian Vases* (New York: Metropolitan Museum of Art, 1935).

18. D.L. Page (ed.), *Further Greek Epigrams: Epigrams before A.D. 50 from the Greek Anthology and Other Sources* (Cambridge: Cambridge University Press, 1981), p. 320.

19. In *Deipnosophistae* 4, Athenaeus tells of the distribution of whole jars of ointment at the customary intervals during an especially extravagant wedding feast.

and with Aphrodite.[20] Its connubial connotation is explicit in the most famous ἀλάβαστρον scene in Greek literature, which occurs in Aristophanes's comedy *Lysistrata*. During a politically motivated sex strike, Myrrhina fends off her husband Kinesias's advances with one excuse after another, including an exit to purchase an ἀλάβαστρον of ointment. In exasperation Kinesias indicates that they already have an ἀλάβαστρον—his ψωλῆ, which he likens to an abandoned orphan who needs suckling by a nurse.

M.:	ἔπαιρε σαυτόν.	[937]
K.:	ἀλλ᾽ ἐπῆρται τοῦτό γε.	
M.:	βούλει μυρίσω σε;	
K.:	μὰ τὸν Ἀπόλλω μή μέ γε.	
M.:	νὴ τὴν Ἀφροδίτην, ἤν τε βούλῃ γ᾽ ἦς τε μή. (*M. exits*)	
K.:	εἴθ᾽ ἐκχυθείη τὸ μύρον, ὦ Ζεῦ δέσποτα. (*M. enters*)	[940]
M.:	πρότεινε δὴ τὴν χεῖρα κἀλείφου λαβών.	
K.:	Οὐχ ἡδὺ τὸ μύρον μὰ τὸν Ἀπόλλω τουτογί,	
	εἰ μὴ διατριπτικόν γε, κοὐκ ὄζον γάμων.	
M.:	τάλαιν᾽ ἐγώ, τὸ Ῥόδιον ἤνεγκον μύρον.	
K.:	ἀγαθόν· ἔα αὖτ᾽, ὦ δαιμονία.	
M.:	ληρεῖς ἔχων. (*M. exits*)	[945]
K.:	κάκιστ᾽ ἀπόλοιθ᾽ ὁ πρῶτος ἑψήσας μύρον. (*M. enters*)	
M.:	λαβὲ τόνδε τὸν ἀλάβαστρον.	
K.:	ἀλλ᾽ ἕτερον ἔχω.	
	ἀλλ᾽ ᾧζυρὰ κατάκεισο καὶ μή μοι φέρε μηδέν.	
M.:	προιήσω ταῦτα νὴ τὴν Ἄρτεμιν... (*M. exits*)	
K.:	οἴμοι τί πάθω; τίνα βινήσω,	
	τῆς καλλίστης πασῶν ψευσθείς;	[955]
	πῶς ταυτηνὶ παιδοτροφήσω;	
	ποῦ Κυναλώπηξ;	
	μίσθωσόν μοι τὴν τιτθήν.	

In vase art, particularly funerary ware, the ἀλάβαστρον appears as an emblem signifying a wife's domesticity and devotion to her husband's needs. The proper matron, with the ἀλάβαστρον as her identifying emblem, is conventionally depicted working her loom in her home.[21]

But a ἑταίρα might also wear the ἀλάβαστρον and use it to apply

20. Sourvinou-Inwood, '*Reading*', pp. 106-18, 154-55, presents numerous examples of vase illustrations in support of this interpretation.

21. Eva Keuls argues persuasively for this interpretation of a number of illustrations that she presents in *The Reign of the Phallus: Sexual Politics in Ancient Athens* (New York: Harper & Row, 1985). But see Dyfri Williams, 'Women on Athenian Vases: Problems of Interpretation', in Cameron and Kuhrt (eds.), *Images of Women in Antiquity*, pp. 92-106, for caveats.

perfume to clients both in private and at banquets.[22] In addition, illustrations survive of somewhat larger ἀλάβαστρα in use at a bath. Any part of the body could be perfumed, but especially the head. A young man ready for a social outing is stereotypically described as 'perfumed and wreathed' (μυρισάμενος καὶ στεφανωσάμενος): that is, his hair is dressed.[23] Wreaths can signal that one has taken on a special status; or, like scent, they can be simply a preparation for good times. Those wearing wreaths to show status included magistrates, athletes, and — quite significantly for us — men slaughtering animals in religious sacrifices.[24]

Ἀλάβαστρα were ornamental, but their contents were useful as well as pleasant. The contents here are characterized as πιστικῆς, which means 'persuasive'. The gender and case endings in Mk 14.3 are odd, so it's impossible to be sure precisely *what* was persuasive (much less how a vial or some balm could be so). Translators fudge the question and read 'pure' or 'genuine'. Both Stephanus and the authoritative lectionary of Liddell and Scott supply 'liquid' for πιστικός (forcing an unlikely connection to πίνω, 'drink') in the singular instance of the Gospels, for there are no other examples of that usage. Bultmann's contributions to the *TDNT* article 'πιστεύω' are philologically worthless because he has excluded from consideration any usages that did not *a priori* appear relevant to 'the' biblical notion of faith, as he conceived it; see his first footnote. My view is that we cannot understand πιστικός in Mark without considering how the word was used elsewhere. Πιστικός is a variant spelling of πειστικός.[25] Both come from the verb πείθω (active: 'persuade'; middle: 'comply, obey, trust in'), which also gives us πίστις, the New Testament term for faith. So the text implies that this anointing has something to do with belief.

---

22. Ἑταῖραι, 'companions', were women who made their living by sexual service to an élite clientele. They attended banquets and the συμπόσια or drinking bouts that followed. Keuls, *Reign of the Phallus*, presents ancient depictions of the sexual use and abuse of ἑταῖραι at συμπόσια.

23. See examples below in *Mourning and Burial*.

24. See Marcel Détienne and Jean-Pierre Vernant, *The Cuisine of Sacrifice among the Greeks* (trans. Paula Wissing; Chicago, IL: University of Chicago Press, 1986), pp. 122, 110-13, for the wreath as designating that ritual participant who will slaughter the sacrificial victim. It is interesting that Mark gets Jesus decked out correctly to make a bloody sacrifice by completing the μυρισάμενος καὶ στεφανωσάμενος pair at 15.17.

25. Depending on the version consulted, one can find both spellings in Plato; e.g., at *Gorgias* 455b4, πιστικός in the *TLG* database, but πειστικός in the Loeb edition. When Sextus Empiricus cites the *Gorgias* he fastidiously spells it πειστικός (see *Adversus Mathematicos* 2.2 and 5). But Plotinus uses πιστικός.

Belief was not universally esteemed by the Greeks. Plato, who deplores the rhetors, says that 'rhetoric is a producer of persuasion' (πειθοῦς δημιουργός ἐστιν ἡ ῥητορική). He distinguishes between 'having learned' (μεμαθηκέναι) and 'having been persuaded' (πεπιστευ-κέναι) in this sense: there can be a false belief (πίστις) but there cannot be false knowledge (ἐπιστήμη). Since belief and knowledge thus differ, and since both are effected by persuasion (πειθώ, as a noun), there must then be two kinds of persuasion. So Plato formulates a clarification: 'rhetoric...is a producer of persuasion for belief, not for instruction about right and wrong' (ἡ ῥητορική...πειθοῦς δημιουργός ἐστιν πιστευτικῆς, ἀλλ᾽ οὐ διδασκαλικῆς περὶ τὸ δίκαιόν τε καὶ ἄδικον). The rhetor is not διδασκαλικός, but merely πιστικός.[26]

Plato's argument was widely known and very influential in antiquity, even though it had little impact upon the teaching and practice of rhetoric in the γυμνάσια and beyond. Kinneavy, noting the involvement of Jews in the public affairs of Greco-Roman cities in Palestine, infers that rhetorical training must have been provided to equip them to participate in the πόλις as they did.[27] The presence of the technical vocabulary of rhetoric indicates that the Gospel texts stem from an élite sector of the Jesus movements who knew the lingo of the γυμνάσιον.

Even though women did not receive formal rhetorical instruction, they could well be characterized as πιστικαί by men who had. Πιο-τικῆς could be the literary trace of persuasive, convincing women's speech that had the major effect of inducing the πίστις of the christ-hood of Jesus. This term rests unstably in the construction of Mk 14.3 as we now have it: ἀλάβαστρον μύρου νάρδου πιστικῆς. Πιστικῆς agrees in gender with ἀλάβαστρον, which is attested as a feminine noun at this period. But in case it agrees with the genitive μύρου νάρδου. Rather than attribute this irregularity to Mark's grammatical

26. *Gorgias* 453a-455a. The material issue here is *marketing*: given the availability of both rhetors and philosophers in the educational marketplace, which should be hired for one's adolescent heir?

27. This training would have focused on πίστις as both the techniques of political and legal persuasion, and the conviction induced in listeners who were competent to appreciate such techniques. James L. Kinneavy, *Greek Rhetorical Origins of Christian Faith: An Inquiry* (New York: Oxford University Press, 1987), pp. 79-80. Kinneavy works from translations and secondary sources, which have given him the mistaken impression that γυμνασία and 'synagogue schools' in the first century were as accessible as high schools are in American society. Yet Kinneavy is correct in his basic thesis that πίστις and πιστεύω in the New Testament are borrowed from the vocabulary of Hellenistic rhetoric. Unfortunately, the adjective πιστικῆς at Mk 14.3 and Jn 12.3 escaped his notice.

ineptness, I am suggesting that, prior to the crafting of the anointing tableau, this adjective 'persuasive/faith-inducing' attached to women and their teaching.

Under the influence of gender stereotyping, 'persuasive' will drift toward 'seductive' in subsequent retellings (Lk. 7.36, 47), as the link to live verbal instruction is forgotten.[28] Traditionally in Judaism, as in Greek philosophy, instruction is better than mere persuasion. Something that is πιστικός should be treated with extreme caution. In the first century, if someone described Jesus and his group as teacher and learners (μαθητής), then literate people would certainly ask what kind of teaching was going on and whether it was producing knowledge or mere belief.[29] This question seems to have had a formative influence upon the evolution of the gospel genre.

b. *Reclining at Table*
This detail of the social setting locates the story by culture and class. To recline at meals in the Greco-Roman manner, one needs a large staff and a house big enough to set apart a room for formal dining with the furniture (couches and tables) required. Great houses had dining rooms where men of the kin group entertained their friends along with hired women. In classical times, dining rooms in houses were typically square and held seven or eleven couches arranged head-to-toe around the walls, leaving room for a door. Entertainment would consist in discussion, recitation, and song *within* the nearly closed circle of guests. Later, the Roman *triclinium* angled the diners elbow-to-elbow along three sides of a square table, and the sigma-couch or *stibadium* arranged them fan-wise in a semicircle within an apse that opened out onto a large hall. Thus, diners in the *triclinium* and especially the *stibadium* could be (and were) entertained by rhetors, poets, musicians, dancers, and others, who were not part of the reclining group. Some private dining halls had seven or more apses opening out onto a single large performance space.[30]

Dining was educational. It taught you who you were. In earlier

28. Compare the fate of the eloquent Beruriah's legend in rabbinic tradition. The medieval commentator Rashi hands on the slander that she committed sexual improprieties with one of the students, then killed herself in remorse. See Rashi on *Abod. Zar.* 18b.

29. Robbins, 'Reversed', shows how the Gospels portray Jesus as a teacher using the culturally available models.

30. See Katherine Dunbabin, '*Triclinium* and *Stibadium*', in William J. Slater (ed.), *Dining in a Classical Context* (Ann Arbor: University of Michigan, 1991), pp. 121-48.

times, banqueters found diversion in the antics of beggars who, in exchange for scraps, acted out the upper-class caricature of themselves.[31] In Roman times, a wealthy host would take the opportunity to humiliate the clients who, by his command, were reclining in low-prestige locations and receiving both verbal insults and poorer food.[32] Dinner could be followed by pantomime and theater; dinner itself *was* theater.[33] The συμπόσιον was the means of social memory and παιδεία; it was the principal venue for reciting the poetry in which virtue was defined and brave deeds were immortalized in memory.[34] Slaves did not recline to eat, and it is thought that men did not recline until they entered ἐφηβεία, about age 18. Kathleen Corley has shown that by the first century, kinswomen (wives and even daughters) might also appear at formal banquets.[35]

Greek women's *domestic* cooking duties were comparatively light.[36] In the Greco-Roman cities, meat came from temple sacrifices. Slaughtering, roasting and distribution of meat were the work of men. The term μάγειρος derives from μάχαιρα, 'knife', and it designates the man who butchers, roasts or boils, and carves meat.[37] Μάγειροι hired on to work fancy banquets; we would call them caterers. In addition,

31. Burkhard Fehr, 'Entertainers at the Symposion: The *Akletoi* in the Archaic Period', in Oswyn Murray (ed.), *Sympotica: A Symposium on the* Symposion (Oxford: Clarendon Press, 1990), pp. 185-95.

32. See John D'Arms, 'The Roman *Convivium* and the Idea of Equality', in Murray (ed.), *Sympotica*, pp. 308-20. The Lukan version of the anointing story presupposes readers' familiarity with this practice; see Lk. 7.44-46. This élite men's ritual of humiliation through food and drink compares with the élite women's custom of καταχύσματα.

33. Christopher Jones, 'Dinner Theater', in Slater (ed.), *Dining in a Classical Context*, pp. 185-98.

34. On memory as the function of the συμπόσιον see Wolfgang Rösler, 'Mnemosyne in the Symposion', in Murray (ed.), *Sympotica*, pp. 230-37. On the παιδεία of the συμπόσιον, see Manuela Tecusan, 'Logos-Sympotikos: Patterns of the Irrational in Philosophical Drinking: Plato Outside the Symposium', in Murray (ed.), *Sympotica*, pp. 238-60.

35. Kathleen E. Corley, *Private Women, Public Meals: Social Conflict in the Synoptic Tradition* (Peabody, MA: Hendrickson, 1993).

36. For example, see Brian Sparkes, 'The Greek Kitchen', *JHS* 82 (1962), pp. 121-37 and *idem*, 'Not Cooking, but Baking', *Greece and Rome* 28 (1981), pp. 172-78.

37. See Détienne and Vernant, *Cuisine of Sacrifice*, pp. 132-33. For the range of the occupation, see Guy Bertiaume, *Les roles du mageiros: Étude sur la boucherie, la cuisine et le sacrifice dans la Grèce ancienne* (Leiden: E.J. Brill, 1982). Curiously, the *abridged* LSJ derives μάγειρος from μάσσω, 'because the baking of bread was originally the chief business of the cook', but in light of the gender evidence the linguistic connection to μάχαιρα seems more likely.

the host also had to hire women called δημιουργοί to prepare the sweet desserts and bake the fancy cheesecakes, cookies, and honeyed fruit pies.[38] At a lavish banquet, apparently, guests removed their wreaths for heavy eating during the meat and poultry (or fish) courses. Then they cleansed their hands, refreshed themselves with perfume, and re-wreathed themselves. The dessert courses followed, before the serious drinking of the συμπόσιον began.

We know these details from Athenaeus, who complains about variations in this 'classical' order. He grumbles that at modern banquets (late first to early second century CE) μάγειροι serve you sweets when you are ready for meat, but then, after you have wreathed and perfumed yourself again, those darn women, the δημιουργοί, bring on meat pies and thrushes.[39] Male meat chefs and female pastry chefs receive equal notice. Crews of each had to be hired to pull off a really fine banquet. They are described as working briskly through the night to prepare the fancy foods.[40]

It should be remembered that sequestering of women was an upper-class luxury. Comparative studies of contemporary sex-segregating societies suggest that women's confinement may be periodic or may be related to the life cycle. The ancient Greeks restricted only women of childbearing age to the γυναικών; menopause brought freedom of movement.[41] In the houses of the well-to-do, both slave women and kinswomen stayed within the women's apartments; but in ordinary homes there was not space enough for physical segregation, and we

38. A second-declension noun, δημιουργός is feminine when preceded by the feminine article ἡ, as here. Compare ἡ παρθένος and ἡ θεός. The term δημιουργός derives from words meaning 'people's work'. It applies to members of a skilled artisan class, such as sculptors. In a culinary context it takes on the specialized meaning of 'confectioner'. Plato calls rhetoric the δημιουργός of belief; see *Gorgias* 453, discussed above.

39. This implies that one would expect the women chefs to be bringing in sweets to refresh the palate after the heavier courses. See *Deipnosophistae* 4.172, quoting Menander's plays (fourth–third century BCE) as witness to earlier customs.

40. *Deipnosophistae* 4.171-174. Athenaeus tells us that in a pilgrimage center like Delos, virtually the whole population of ordinary men and women worked in the catering trade and had names corresponding to their specialties. Collectively they were called ἐλεοδύται, 'table-dodgers', by men of Athenaeus's class, because of the way they earned their living. Athenaeus also tells of an old woman who worked as a food-taster to protect her master from poisoning, and of a woman supervisor of a common men's dining hall on Crete. Thus when we imagine an elegant ἀνδρών banquet room in a Greco-Roman city, we must imagine women at work there — but very few of them are ἑταῖραι.

41. See Robert Garland, *The Greek Way of Life: From Conception to Old Age* (Ithaca, NY: Cornell University Press, 1990), p. 243.

do not know what other forms the custom may have taken. Contemporary comparative anthropological studies indicate that secluded women still find many opportunities to visit one another to negotiate matters of economic and cultural importance. In ancient Greece, élite women's friendships are known to have begun among age-mates in the choirs and dancing schools for little girls, and continued lifelong.[42]

Education in music, dance and pantomime for girls paralleled boys' physical education in martial arts. The ideology supporting both was that one should take one's assigned place in society, interact harmoniously and stand fast against any challenge. Greek dance was public participation in civic religious festivals. It combined poetry, music, movement and gesture into multimedia depictions of events significant to the community and its cultural foundations.

The social function of the girls' chorus was education as well as religious observance—but *not* entertainment as we know it. Girls learned to speak and move gracefully and expressively. Some would pantomime while others recited or sang. We know that Jewish men and boys participated fully in the παιδεία of the γυμνάσια, even in the cities of Eretz Israel itself. There is every reason to believe that girls received the parallel education that the chorus system had to offer. At Hammat Tiberias beside the Sea of Galilee, there is a floor from a late-Roman-era synagogue, with a large circular mosaic depicting YHWH/ Helios inside the wheel of zodiac figures. It is perfectly suited to guide the steps of a chorus of chanting pre-teens as they presented historic tableaux and gracefully performed festival circle dances before their proud parents and relatives.

With early marriage, the bond between mother-in-law and daughter-in-law was particularly significant. In imperial cities, women's religious rituals and festivals, such as the Adonia and the Thesmophoria, also brought women together without the supervision of their male kin. Thus women's access to news and conversation did not depend upon attending συμποσία or reclining in the ἀνδρών.

c. Καταχύσματα

Mark's text says that the woman 'poured' the sweet ointment on Jesus' head (κατέχεεν αὐτοῦ τῆς κεφαλῆς). It does not use the expected verb, μυρίζω, to indicate that she rubbed, daubed or slathered him with it. (This verb will be used later in Jesus' interpretation of the pouring as anointing: μυρίσαι in v. 8.)[43] Yet in fact there was a custom

---

42. See Claude Calame, *Les choers de jeunes filles en Grèce archaique* (2 vols.; Roma: Edizioni del'Ateneo and Bizzari, 1977); Garland, *Greek Way of Life*, p. 193.

43. Another instance of καταχέω, μύρον, κεφαλή and στέφω used together

among the Greeks according to which a woman threw something sweet over someone else's head. The link between that custom and Mark's text is the verb καταχέω. Καταχύσματα (literally 'things dropped') means dessert food, sweet spicy treats, goodies. But the term also signifies the domestic ritual through which the senior wife would welcome a newcomer to her household. Standing before the hearth, the matron would toss a handful of sweets over the head of a new daughter-in-law or a slave newly purchased (that is, a slave of non-Greek ethnicity perhaps captured in war). This gesture asserted the matron's authority over the bride or slave,[44] and at the same time it promised to fulfill the responsibility of providing for the needs of the new member of the household.[45]

Aristophanes (fifth–fourth century BCE) uses the term καταχύσματα in a similar way. One of his characters, Karion's wife, wishes to present καταχύσματα, or 'welcoming gifts', when her husband brings the god Plutus ('Wealth') home to dinner.[46] This may look to us like the simple courtesy of a hostess; however, given the meaning of the custom, the wife is signaling her intent to place the wealth-giving god permanently in service in her household. In Athenaeus (c. 200 CE), however, καταχύσματα appears with a more generic sense, 'sprinklings', that is, condiments.[47] The word can also mean sauce or gravy. Yet this sort of pouring still signifies a seasoning, a change in status.

The custom of the καταχύσματα, 'shower', asserts the authority of the mature woman as head of her household. Interestingly, just as working-class women δημιουργοί were associated with sweet confections, so here it is dessert food that is used to assert the status of senior kinswoman and mistress of the house. The authority, wealth and largesse of élite women also could be expressed in municipal gifts

comes from the fourth century BCE. Plato, who objects to poets (i.e. playwrights) because of their mimetic versatility, writes that in an ideal city the people should banish a poet 'after having poured perfume on his head and wreathed him with wool'. See the *Republic* 398a: ...ἀποπέμποιμέν τε εἰς ἄλλην πόλιν μύρον κατὰ τῆς κεφαλῆς καταχέαντες καὶ ἐρίῳ στέψαντες...

44. Their status is remarkably alike, since both bride and slave are from outside the kin group and therefore owe their labor to the kin group but are denied the free use of the fruits of their own labor. The young wife gradually acquires kin status as she gives birth to heirs, while the slave may earn freedom in various ways, e.g., by bearing a slave child to take her place or by going into business to earn her purchase price.

45. Keuls, *Reign of the Phallus*, p. 6, misses the point of the ceremony when she says that a new bride was greeted with a shower of nuts.

46. The custom is dramatized in *Plutus* 764-801.

47. See *Deipnosophistae* 2.76.15, 9.61.10

together with public service or λειτουργία. Civic offices entailed benefactions. An important bequest to a city was to provide for the needs of the γυμνάσιον, especially olive oil. We know from inscriptions that women did indeed hold the office of γυμνασιάρχος and supply the oil needed for bathing and massaging the athletes.[48] The lady benefactors probably did not personally pour out the oil for the athletes, but their control of (olive) oil-producing estates is attested by their extravagant generosity.

It is often noted that the public civic role of élite women in the Roman period departs from the earlier custom whereby women remained unnoticed and unmentioned.[49] But perhaps this exception proves the rule. The Greco-Roman city, functioning as a vehicle of Hellenization and then of cultural and political control across the empire, was re-imagined as one large house.[50] A woman of the ruling class was therefore 'at home' wherever she went in the public buildings to administer her household, the πόλις. However, élite women of slightly lower rank still remained secluded and unnamed, at least until after death.

c. *Mourning and Burial*
The same unguent and the same term, 'anointing' (μύρισαι), are used whether the scent is for live bodies or corpses. Μύρον, even when applied for romance and luxury, inevitably reminded Greeks of death.

---

48. Mendora of the second-century CE Pisidian city of Sillyon reputedly supplied 220,000 denarii worth of oil for the γυμνάσιον, according to Riet Van Bremen, 'Women and Wealth', in Cameron and Kuhrt (eds.), *Images of Women in Antiquity*, pp. 223-82 (223), who documents women as γυμνασιάρχοι. Historians have speculated that such offices were merely honorary in the case of élite women, but it is not clear that they were any less so in the case of élite men. However, Mary R. Lefkowitz, 'Influential Women', in Cameron and Kuhrt (eds.), *Images of Women*, pp. 49-64, argues that women did not participate in the processes of government.

49. David Schaps, 'The Women Least Mentioned: Etiquette and Women's Names', *Classical Quarterly* 27 (1977), pp. 323-30, documents the fact that élite women's names do not appear in the recorded oratory that comes down to us, unless the intention was to insult their male relatives. However, kinswomen could be eulogized at their funerals. Roman women had no personal names of their own, but were called by the feminine forms of their fathers' names. See John E. Stambaugh, *The Ancient Roman City* (Baltimore, MD: The Johns Hopkins University Press, 1988), p. 98; cf. p. 94.

50. This is the thesis of Van Bremen, 'Women and Wealth'. Thus under the system of euergetism ('good-works-ism'), the élite woman's civic benefactions became καταχύσματα — goodies — by which she asserted her benevolent authority over the πόλις as her household and its people as her retainers.

The playboy lifestyle, signified by wreathing and perfuming oneself, is typically contrasted with the grave that inexorably will overtake it. This association is made in several epigrams that come down to us. Here are two examples from the *Greek Anthology* (11.19; 9.409):

11.19
καὶ στεφάνοις κεφαλὰς πυκασώμεθα, καὶ μυρίσωμεν
    αὐτούς, πρὶν τύμβοις ταῦτα φέρειν ἑτέρους.
νῦν ἐν ἐμοὶ πιέτω μέθυ τὸ πλέον ὀστέα τἀμά·
    νεκρὰ δὲ Δευκαλίων αὐτὰ κατακλυσάτω.

Let us cover over our heads with wreaths and let us anoint ourselves, before others carry such to our tombs. For my part, let the bones inside me drink their fill of wine, but let dead ones soak in Deukalion's stuff.

9.409
Εἰ τινα μὴ τέρπει λωτοῦ μέλος ἢ γλυκὺς ἦχος
    ψαλμῶν ἢ τριγέρων νεκτάρεος βρόμιος,
ἢ πεῦκαι, κοῦροι, στέφανοι, μύρα, λιτὰ δὲ δειπνῶν
    λαθροπόδας τρώκταις χερσὶ τίθησι τόκους.
οὗτος ἐμοὶ τέθνηκε · μεριμνήτην δὲ παρέρπω
    νεκρόν, ἐς ἀλλοτρίους φειδόμενον φάρυγας.

If someone doesn't enjoy...wreaths and perfume, but takes a frugal supper...to me such a one has died, and I cautiously tiptoe past the corpse who penny pinches into (i.e. for the sake of) the gullets of strangers.

This last comment bears comparison to the complaint against extravagance, and Jesus' retort, in Mk 14.4-8. Extravagant waste was a feature of funerary practices in the ancient world.

The resonance between anointing and death is amplified in Greek because μύρον and μυρίζω are related to the verb μύρω, 'ooze, trickle', which in the middle voice, μύρομαι, is a common verb meaning 'weep, shed tears'.[51] Women took part in Greek mourning rituals, both in funerals of individuals and in annual women's religious festivals such as 'mourning Adonis' in the Adonia. The Thesmophoria and the Adonia both were women's festivals that included days of mourning followed by celebrations of restored life. The Adonia commemorated Adonis, the young lover of Aphrodite, killed by a wild animal. His death and rebirth were associated with the vegetation cycle. It is thought that Adonis originally was a Babylonian deity, Tammuz. When the Greeks appropriated the story of 'Lord Tammuz', they mistook the Semitic honorific term *adon* for his proper name. From

51. Some of the forms are quite close. For the aorist infinitive: μύρασθαι is 'to weep', μυρίσαι is 'to anoint', and μυρίσασθαι is 'to anoint oneself'. For the aorist middle participle: μυράμενος is 'having wept', and μυρισάμενος is 'having been anointed'.

that same root comes the Hebrew word *Adonai*, 'my Lord'. The two divine names would have sounded startlingly similar to Hellenized Jews. A famous poem apparently written for the Adonia festival is Bion's 'Lament for Adonis'. It reads in part (in Gow's translation):

> No longer in the thickets, Cyprian, mourn (μύρεο) thy lord. No fit couch (στιβάς) for Adonis is a lonely bed of leaves. Adonis, a dead body now, should have thy bed, Cytherea. Fair (καλός) even in death is he...strew on him wreaths (στεφάνοισι) and flowers. Let all be with him, for when he died all the flowers withered too. Pour on him Syrian unguents, pour on him perfumes (μύροισιν); perish all perfumes (μύρα) since Adonis that was thy perfume (μύρον) has perished.

Both private and cultic mourning afforded women an opportunity to gather and socialize among themselves, to tell stories and to reinterpret events.

3. *Jewish Cultural Comparisons*

First-century Judaism was linguistically and culturally diverse, and our access to it depends upon sources that are notoriously difficult to date. This section surveys possible cultural parallels in the literature of Greek Judaism as well as Hebrew and Aramaic Judaism. As it turns out, these are less significant for our interests than the secular Greek comparisons.

a. *Greek Judaism*
The Jewish scholars associated with the Alexandrian intellectual community gave the world the Bible translations that come down to us in the Septuagint (third–second century BCE).[52] Often the diction of the Gospels suggests that their writers knew the Bible in its Greek version (rather than in Hebrew or from Targums). For Mk 14.3-9, the influence of the LXX is significant for one item of vocabulary: συντρίψασα, 'having smashed'. Συντρίβω was a favorite LXX choice to translate שׁבר. The term is theologically loaded to connote dramatic divine agency. This word does more than lend Mark's text a biblical resonance: it suggests that the woman's gesture enacts something divinely authorized.

Snapping off the neck was *not* the ordinary way of opening an

---

52. Philo (first century CE) represents that same continuing tradition. The literature of Alexandrian Judaism influenced all Hellenized Jews of the first century, including those in Palestine and Syria. Josephus in his own way also offers glimpses of the customs and imaginations of Greek Jews.

ἀλάβαστρον, despite a statement in the *TDNT* to the contrary.[53] This assumption is certainly incorrect. The neck would be the strongest part of a hand-blown bottle, and the body would crack first. If the bottle were four inches or less in length, one could not get enough leverage to snap it with a thumb placed on its neck, and one would not clamp down on a glass bottle with one's teeth for fear of cutting one's mouth. Furthermore, considering the distinctive shape of the bottle, if the neck and lip were destroyed then it could no longer be worn as a pendant. Bottles found in excavations are too beautiful to have been meant for breaking, and published finds of ἀλάβαστρα do not show this kind of break. Therefore I read the woman's crunching of her ἀλάβαστρον as a gesture contrived to come across as shocking and unusual, and I regard the resonance with LXX uses of συντρίβω quite deliberate and meaningful.

Should the anointing at Bethany be read against anointing stories recounted in the Older Testament, and sometimes paraphrased by Josephus? A comparison of vocabulary is indecisive. The usual LXX terms are χρίω for anointing and ἔλαιον for oil. For example, see Isa. 61.1-3 and 1 Sam. 16.13.[54] In 2 Kgs 9 the story of Jehu's takeover brings together the notions of anointing, pouring, throwing down and destroying, which also cluster together in Mk 14.3-9; unfortunately, however, the vocabulary does not match.[55] Thus we cannot confidently characterize Mk 14.3-9 as a rewrite of any anointing story in the LXX, much less as midrash.

Finally, is there a LXX background for the statement about the poor in Mk 14.7? Is this an allusion to Deut. 15.11?[56] Interestingly, the LXX

53. Michaelis's claim that 'this was certainly the usual way of opening flasks of oil with a long neck' is referenced to the article 'Alabaster' in Kurt Galling's 1937 *Biblisches Reallexikon* (Tübingen: J.C.B. Mohr). Galling, however, has simply generalized on the basis of our text, Mk 14.3! 'Es ist bezeichnend, dass im griechischen Sprachgebrauch jedes henkellose Salbgefäss gleich welchen Materials als Alabastron gilt. Übliche werden in hellenistische-römischer Zeit Glasfläschchen gewesen sein, die man zum Öffnen am Halse abbrach (vgl. Mc 14.3)' (cols. 12-13).

54. But Ps. 132.2 (LXX) (MT 133.2) has: ὡς μύρον ἐπὶ κεφαλῆς τὸ καταβαῖνον ἐπὶ πώγωνα. Below in section four I suggest that this terminology comes in handy for Mark.

55. The words used are κέχρικα, ἐπιχεεῖς/ἐπέχεεν, κυλίσατε/ἐκύλισαν and ἐξολεθρεύσεις. Κέχρικα, 'he anointed', comes from χρίω and – unlike the Markan μυρίζω or κατάχεω – is related to χριστός, 'christ'. Josephus, changing the prefix, has κατεχέεν for the LXX's ἐπέχεεν at 2 Kgs 9.6, but without corroboration this cannot be taken as a common oral paraphrase of the LXX. However, let us note in passing that this story ends with the downfall, literally, of the Gentile and religiously heterodox old woman Jezebel, whom dogs devour.

56. B.L. Mack, *A Myth of Innocence: Mark and Christian Origins* (Philadelphia:

has something different there: οὐ γὰρ μὴ ἐκλίπῃ ἐνδεὴς ἀπὸ τῆς γῆς [σου], 'for it shouldn't happen that the weak die out from your (sing.) land'. The diction is completely different in Mk 14.7, which makes a positive statement addressed to a plural 'you'. Thus v. 7 is not drawn directly from the Bible of the Greek Jesus people. Possibly it translates an argument previously mounted by a non-Hellenized constituency quoting directly from Torah or from the Targum.

b. *Hebrew and Aramaic Judaism*

In Torah and Prophets, anointing signifies divine choice and empowerment. However, as is often remarked, such anointing does not take place with perfume at a banquet through a woman and for burial. One relevant ethnographic detail worth noting in the Hebrew Prophets is that Isaiah (eighth century BCE) mentions women of Zion who wear ornamental perfume bottles בתי הנפש — and of course he disapproves (Isa. 3.20). Much later, the rabbis would associate this passage with the Hellenistic ἀλάβαστρον, although the LXX translators did not do so. Amos (also eighth century) knows the custom of reclining at feasts (6.4-6).

The Mishnah too is Hebrew literature, but it reflects the urbanized and Hellenized society of the second century CE, while incorporating some older traditions.[57] It does not give us an exact ethnographic match with the society of Jesus, that of Mark, or that of the women between them (although arguably it comes much closer than contemporary comparative studies of 'the Mediterranean'). The Mishnah is familiar with women's custom of wearing perfume bottles containing nard. The following appears in a discussion of things that may be carried outdoors on the Sabbath:

> A woman may not go out...with a perfume charm (כובלת) or with a spikenard-ointment flask (צלוחית של פלייטון). This is the view of R. Meir. But the sages permit a perfume charm or a spikenard-ointment flask.[58]

Moreover, the *tannaim* know that these flasks are *glass*. Their legislation about the purity of vessels treats ointment flasks in the section pertaining to glass containers and implements: 'A small flask (צלוחית)

Fortress Press, 1988), p. 97, suggests the allusion to Deut. 15.11. This works for the MT but not for the LXX, at least the version that comes down to us.

57. The Mishnah was edited in Sepphoris, an urban administrative center an hour's walk from Nazareth, about a century after the destruction of the Second Temple.

58. *Šab.* 6.3, from Philip Blackman's Hebrew/English edition (*Mishnayot* [6 vols.; London: Mishnah Press, 1955]). The Gemara for this passage is discussed below.

that has lost its mouth is [still] susceptive to uncleanness… [A flask] of balsamum ointment (פל יטיון) that has lost its mouth is unsusceptive to uncleanness, for [the jagged edge] will scratch the hand'.[59] In the prosperous urban milieu of the Mishnah's compilers, wives are entitled to receive an allowance for perfume. The amount is set at ten *denarii*, but we are not told whether that is supposed to be a weekly or yearly sum, or a one-time payment.[60] The sages also know of the custom of stoppering a flask of nard ointment with recycled paper (*M. Šab.* 8.2).

The Mishnah preserves information about burial customs that may have relevance to the story of the anointing at Bethany. Mishnah assumes the practice of *ossilegium*.[61] In the case of a criminal whose execution was ordered by the Sanhedrin (as Jesus' was, says Mark), the body was not released to the family immediately. The court took charge of the corpse (perhaps through a delegated member like Joseph of Arimathea?) and laid it in a tomb reserved for the purpose, to undergo decomposition without the family's observing the customary mourning rituals. Only after a year would the bones be released to

59. *Kel.* 30.4, from Blackman's edition. A translator's note supplies 'spikenard ointment' as an alternative for 'balsamum ointment'. Thus a broken ἀλάβαστρον was a ritually clean one. The Mishnah's concern over the purity of vessels reflects a practical problem that Jewish households encountered in a multicultural urban center. Vessels, especially crockery, purchased in a Jewish pot-works like those of Kfar Hanania or Shikhin were above suspicion, but often it was cheaper or just more convenient to buy pots of Gentile manufacture. Since breaking a container rendered it clean, the pious Jewish household custom was to knock a little chunk out of the rim of any jar bought in the city market, just to make sure. Arguably, the breaking of the ἀλάβαστρον is meant to render it clean before the ointment touches Jesus.

60. *Ket.* 6.4. Danby translates: 'The bridegroom undertakes to give her ten denars as pin money for every mina that she brings in', interpreting לקופה (literally 'for the basket') to refer to a sewing basket. But the Gemara (*Ket.* 66b) explains that this is a perfume basket, although the ruling applied to Jerusalem only. This may reflect a memory of Hellenized and worldly customs in Jerusalem; nevertheless the rabbis recall Isaiah's (eighth-century BCE) condemnations.

61. According to this practice, a corpse was laid upon a stone shelf in the family tomb for a year in order to allow the flesh to decompose. On the anniversary the bones—which had to have fallen apart by themselves—might be gathered into a small box, or simply piled on top of the bones of relatives. See L.Y. Rahmani, 'Ancient Jerusalem's Funerary Customs and Tombs', *BA* 44 (1981), pp. 171-77, 229-35; 45 (1982), pp. 43-53, 109-19. Meyers, Strange and Myers (eds.), *Excavations*, pp. 118-20, and Byron R. McCane, 'Let the Dead Bury Their Own Dead: Secondary Burial and Matt. 8.21-22', *HTR* 83 (1990), pp. 31-43. The Mishnah discusses laws applying to second burial as well as to the first.

the family for *ossilegium* burial in the normal way (*M. Sanh.* 6.5). Thus someone facing capital punishment would expect his body to be unavailable to his family for anointing after death. On the other hand, the Mishnah reflects concern over securing burial for corpses found abandoned. Burial is a timely need that can override virtually any other custom or law. Finally, Mishnah attempts to discourage displays of grief through extravagant waste while lamenting over a corpse.

With the Babylonian Talmud (compiled third–sixth century CE), we have reached a time and a cultural situation when the custom of wearing perfume flasks appears no longer to be current. Examining the Mishnaic text, the rabbis understand that pendant flasks would be permitted on the Sabbath because they were ornaments, not burdens. They see that such a flask would become a burden if it were empty, or if a woman removed it from around her neck to show it off or carry it in her hand. How likely was that to happen? they ask themselves—for if it were at all likely, then a woman should not be permitted to go out on the Sabbath wearing such a flask. They take a guess: any woman who wore one of those flasks must have had a problem with body odor! If the flask were meant to be a remedy for such an embarrassing condition, they reason, then the woman would have been quite unlikely to let it get empty or to take it off, much less hand it around to be admired by her friends.[62]

Some customs change, but not all. The Talmud lets us glimpse some cultural attitudes that may have remained unaltered since the first century, though we cannot be sure. For example, there is a curious disparagement of perfume sellers, no doubt because they traded directly with women. It counts as evidence of adultery if a man returns home to find the perfume peddler coming out of the door and the wife adjusting her panties.[63]

Another example of information in the Talmud that may (or may not) reflect cultural attitudes already current in the first century is the concern over hair care among both men and women. Wealthy houses retained their own hairdressers, while villages supported a men's hair-cutter and a women's stylist as well. Weekly trims seem not to have

---

62. *Šab.* 62a-b. The rabbis of the Talmud had to explain to their students what a perfume charm was. *And*, the rapt young scholars heard, in olden days the women of Jerusalem wore special shoes that *squirted perfume* at passers-by.

63. *Yeb.* 24b. The רכל was traditionally interpreted to be a perfume salesman. This scenario agrees with information gleaned from the text of Aristophanes cited above (which is about a thousand years older): women purchased perfume directly for themselves. It also puts an interesting spin on the suggestion at Mk 14.5 that the unguent poured over Jesus should instead have been sold.

been unusual, since there are detailed rules about whether one can get a haircut when a holy season coincides with a period of mourning. There is nostalgia for the distinctive haircut maintained by the high priest while the Temple still stood.[64] As from earliest times in Israelite religion, vows and mourning rituals involved cutting one's hair or not, shaving one's head or not. Thus there is an indication that hair-dressing was as much a preoccupation for Palestinian Jews as it is for us—if not more so.[65]

Rabbinic texts of uncertain date offer some final cultural comparisons. Women are permitted to prepare bodies of either sex for burial.[66] 'The washing of the dead (טהרה) begins with the hair, because human hair is associated with the thoughts'.[67] Women probably took part in burial societies to assist with ritual duties and the customs of hospitality during times of grief.[68] In Jerusalem today, elderly women have a ritual of passing around sweet herbs to let one another pronounce the blessing upon smelling something pleasant.[69]

---

64. The Talmud also recalls that in olden days, when kings were anointed the whole head was covered with oil applied in the shape of a wreath, while for priests the head was drenched in the shape of a 'Greek *kaph*', that is, a *chi*, the sign of a cross (*b. Hor.* 11b-12a; also *y. Hor.* 47c). Interestingly, Mark labels Jesus' cross with the sign reading 'king'. Kingly anointing was more frequent than priestly, since Aaron's descendants didn't need to be anointed again except as high priests. Davidic kings were anointed when their right of succession was in doubt.

65. The Mishnaic Hebrew word for a woman hairdresser, מגדלא, is pronounced *megaddela*, which is how a storyteller might designate someone who applied scent to someone else's hair. Stories associating Jesus with 'Miriam the hairdresser' were circulating at the same time as stories associating him with Miriam of Magdala, or Mary Magdalene. (See *Ḥag.* 4b; also *Šab.* 104b, where derogatory information about Jesus appears near a discussion of writing the divine name.) A traditional reading of Luke's Gospel attributes Jesus' anointing to Mary Magdalene, and in John's Gospel the anointing is done by Mary the sister of Martha—but both of these use their own hair on Jesus' feet. The name Miriam is also suggested by Greek μύρον/μυρίσαι/μύρομαι, just as Aristophanes names the character in his ἀλάβαστρον scene Myrrhina.

66. *Sem.* 12.10; however, Dov Zlotnick, *The Tractate 'Mourning' (Semahot)* (New Haven, CT: Yale University Press, 1966), argues for an early dating of this treatise.

67. '*Sifre Renanot*' to '*Ma'abar Yabbok*', cited in 'Hair', *The Jewish Encyclopedia* (12 vols.; New York: Funk & Wagnalls, 1903), VI, p. 158.

68. In the Talmud, a formal association for burial is mentioned in *Moed Qatan* 27b. See also the information on burial societies and '*chaburoth*' in *The Jewish Encyclopedia*.

69. Susan Starr Sered, *Women as Ritual Experts: The Religious Lives of Elderly Jewish Women in Jerusalem* (Oxford: Oxford University Press, 1992), pp. 3, 45.

4. *Proposal for Reconstructing the Story's Career*

The last two sections laid out a number of cultural comparisons to elements of Mk 14.3-9. Much more has turned up than I can adequately account for in the remaining space, so I offer just a tentative sketch to promote further discussion. The story as it stands in Mark is a hybrid, a mixture of several patterns. I see in it two major layers: an older motif of teaching, upon which a sacrifice motif has been overlaid. Each of these motifs is a cluster of several components. Each motif, taken by itself, is culturally coherent. However the mixture presented in Mk 14.3-9 is so symbolically garbled that, if it had taken place just as it is recorded, it would have made no sense to anyone at the time. The scrambling of the two constellations, whose elements previously formed integrated sets, comes to have some discrete meaning of its own only long after the sacrifice pattern has consolidated its assimilation of its antecedent, women's catechesis.

a. *Teaching*

The most striking impression given by the comparative data is one of matronly authority reinforced by economic and class status. The μύρον is originally a κατάχυσμα, a shower that seasons and redefines the status of its target. In Mark the μύρον reveals and enacts the christhood (anointedness) of Jesus at a point in the narrative when the christological characterization starts to escalate toward Calvary.[70] But behind the Markan μύρον is some older discourse in which the memory of Jesus was refashioned to match the specifications for a christ (who was not a self-immolating priest).

That christological, christogenic discourse was καταχύσματα, the gift of matrons. Its *Sitz im Leben* was the women's apartments within elegant homes of certain Hellenized Jews, where matrons met and mourned for Jesus and talked about him among themselves. This fits perfectly well with élite women's customs as known to us from secular sources (and would fit equally well with the religious customs of *chaburoth* and sisterhood burial societies). In other words, it was the γυναικών whose closed doors the Spirit first penetrated; the first sight of a risen Christ came through women's tears.[71]

---

70. For example, Mack, *Myth of Innocence*, pp. 269-87, suggests that the Markan passion narrative is designed to redefine or characterize Jesus in christological terms.

71. As Crossan, *Historical Jesus*, pp. 246, 376-79, has suggested, scripture verses about weeping and looking upon a pierced animal were vehicles of proto-christological reflection. Zech. 12.10 is the focal verse.

A | The disaster at Calvary becomes known

B | Hellenized Jewish women gather in a γυναικών to grieve over Jesus. They come to accept his death as meaningful and deliberate. They synthesize a coherent account of his identity.

C | This women's christological interpretation of Jesus' career and fate is presented to members of a συμπόσιον/חבורה. It is discussed and debated, and found to be convincing.

D | The consensus of that συμπόσιον/חבורה is expressed in a dramatic composition that portrays Jesus as agreeing to die, not withstanding the objections of his companions. In the play, Jesus pledges his fidelity by allowing the μύρον πίστικον to be poured over his head.

> The Messiah shouldn't die
> ─── BUT ───
> I must die because…?

E | This dramatization is presented for other συμπόσια/חבורות, and it succeeds in establishing the notion of Jesus as slain Messiah. But various objections now are raised against the women's role. In subsequent renditions, Jesus is given new lines to answer these objections.

F | The anointing stories, featuring various objections and replies, circulate orally in several versions beyond the συμπόσια/חבורה where originally performed. These versions are available to the writers of the Gospels:

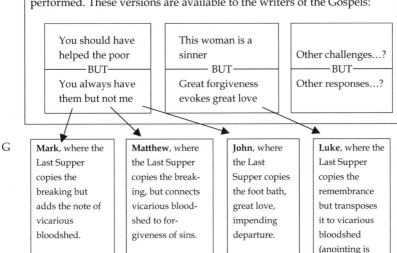

> You should have helped the poor
> ─── BUT ───
> You always have them but not me

> This woman is a sinner
> ─── BUT ───
> Great forgiveness evokes great love

> Other challenges…?
> ─── BUT ───
> Other responses…?

G | **Mark**, where the Last Supper copies the breaking but adds the note of vicarious bloodshed.

Matthew, where the Last Supper copies the breaking, but connects vicarious bloodshed to forgiveness of sins.

John, where the Last Supper copies the foot bath, great love, impending departure.

Luke, where the Last Supper copies the remembrance but transposes it to vicarious bloodshed (anointing is detached from crucifixion).

Mark's story commemorates the consternation that greeted this 'shower' when it was brought out of the γυναικών into the ἀνδρών and up to the table.

The Markan characterization of Jesus rides upon a prior redesign engineered by women who were both weepers and anointers. These women made something good out of Jesus. Mark has καλὸν ἔργον ἠργάσατο ἐν ἐμοί (v. 6). Ἐν plus the dative indicates the raw material out of which something was constructed and also the instrumentality through which it was accomplished. Ἐν ἐμοί here compares to the Pauline expression ἐν Χριστῷ. Mark means to say that something good was done with Jesus, and at the same time by means of Jesus.[72] Later Mark has ὃ ἔσχεν ἐποίησεν (v. 8), literally 'that which was happening, she made/produced/did'. The gist is not that 'she did what she could' but rather 'she made sense out of the situation'. The verb ποιέω describes creative, inventive work of any kind. It recalls the work of playwrights (οἱ ποιήται) or that of confectioners (αἱ δημιουργοί, who at a banquet scene like Mark's are lurking just out of sight). The creation that becomes the nucleus of the gospel message is 'her memory', μνημόσυνον αὐτῆς, the memory of Jesus that is attributable to her because she designed it. Mark says that what she has created (ὃ ἐποίησεν αὕτη) will be discussed wherever the gospel is announced. This women's *poietic* production is no less than the identification of Jesus as Christ in terms of his death.[73]

At first among themselves, and later more widely, these christifying women are teachers. Their catechesis is older than the so-called κήρυγμα both in content and in genre.[74] Their discussions confect belief. The μύρον is called πιστικῆς, connoting both faith and persuasion. This μύρον induces belief (πείθω/πίστις), as distinguished from learning (μανθάνω, ἐπιστήμη). The notion of 'something thrown' makes a startling connection between the Greek and Hebrew sensibilities: Greek καταχέω translates Hebrew ידד, and καταχύσμα translates

72. This is perfectly viable Greek. There is no warrant for assuming that Mark was groping around for the meaning that Matthew achieved: εἰς ἐμέ, 'to me' (accusative). Ἐν plus the dative indicates a personal means in Mt. 9.34 and parallels. The lexicon gives numerous examples of similar construction for impersonal media and means (including a wand in the magical papyri).

73. Crossan, *Historical Jesus*, p. 416, muses that Mk 14.9 may be an autograph.

74. Although the modern term 'catechism' and the patristic term 'catechesis' derive from the verb κατηχέω (not καταχέω), nevertheless between κατάχυσμα and κατήχυσμα there is only what Jacques Derrida, *Margins of Philosophy* (trans. Alan Bass; Chicago, IL: University of Chicago Press, 1982), pp. 1-27, calls *différance*. Forms of κατηχέω appear at Acts 18.25; Rom. 2.18; Gal. 6.6, for example.

תורה, 'instruction'. Thus the christ-making matrons' κατάχυσμα is identified with Torah.

Well in advance of Markan composition, then, there was a practice of women's constructive discussion among themselves, in which they grieved for Jesus and together re-remembered him (chart, stage B.) This was a rhetorical practice; it was πιστικός. In the midst of their gatherings was forged the distinctive understanding of christic identity that would supply the infrastructure for the Gospels. As yet, there was neither 'last supper' nor 'empty tomb'. The circle of matrons met to mourn the untimely death of a beloved young man and to cherish their recollections of him. Weeping women tried to find some sense in their bereavement. They comforted one another with assurances that the dear departed had been enfolded in divine care, and they framed expectations of reunion and vindication. Such behavior is culturally attested outside the Gospels, as we have seen—although no records survive of speech practices within the γυναικῶν.

This rhetoric of a dying Messiah passed *from* a small group of women *to* a small group of men, who discussed it in their συμπόσιον meetings (chart, stage C). Hellenized Jewish women were culturally both equipped for and inclined to choreography, as we have seen; this particular small group created a dramatic composition portraying Jesus as accepting the death of the Messiah (chart, stage D). That composition subsequently was performed for a few other συμπόσια, with adaptations (chart, stage E).[75] Dramatizations performed before συμπόσια subsequently were echoed in stories circulated beyond the συμπόσια (chart, stage F).

But in those stories, the συμπόσιον setting itself contributed the other major set of ingredients to the passion narrative: male dining, distribution of flesh to eat, a pledge to keep faith, and vicarious bloodshed. These cultural elements cohere in the Last Supper tableaux, which were inspired by the earlier dramatizations of the anointing and which feature mimetic re-presentations of various components of the latter: for example, the gesture of breaking, the foot bath, 'remembrance', forgiveness, great love, and the imminent departure of Jesus.

75. It is here (E) that I would place Mack's insightful argument that the two kinds of objections against the anointing found in the extant texts (G) were modifications of an earlier objection whose precise terms are a matter of conjecture (D). But where Mack assumes that the original objection was provoked by a gender transgression, I see it as responding to a shocking idea: the idea that it was meaningful and even necessary for Jesus to have died. I also disagree with Mack's assumption that the anointing happened before Calvary.

The Last Supper narratives, supported by ritual practices, finally overshadowed the older stories of anointing by a woman; one Gospel text detached the anointing from Jesus' death altogether (chart, stage G). Allusions to tortures and a rag lottery, first compiled by the grieving women, later entered the Gospel tradition as details in the passion narrative. The matrons' rhetoric had crystallized the selection and application of LXX passages to Jesus, but it did not continue very long. Yet the women's practice of reinterpreting Jesus with LXX imagery leaves us its trace in the 'event' of the anointing at Bethany.[76] The women's circle or *chaburah*, and their creative achievement, become condensed into the single unnamed woman with the ἀλάβαστρον and her singular deed.

b. *Sacrifice.*

Meanwhile, other constituencies were developing other Jesus materials, such as collections of sayings, miracle tales, and *halakhoth*. Burton Mack hypothesizes at least five 'Jesus movements' in contradistinction to a 'Christ cult'.[77] He correctly views Mark's compositional task as synthesizing a text that could pull their divergent traditions together—although not all strands of the tradition would survive the amalgamation.

The sacrifice motif in the passion may be the legacy of an earlier Christ cult. But whatever its origin, it is the keynote in the Markan orchestration, the fuel for his soteriology. Jesus cannot have died inadvertently (like poor Adonis, gored by a pig); the Christ has to sacrifice himself. He has to be a priest, so he needs a priestly anointing. To pull it off, Mark conscripts the figure of the 'pouring/teaching' woman, hangs an ἀλάβαστρον around her neck and thrusts her onstage to reveal at table Jesus' identity as death-destined Messiah. Mark's Jesus is anointed like proto-priest Aaron in LXX Ps. 133.2, with μύρον running down over his hair and beard. Jesus is portrayed as μάγειρος as well, passing out servings of (his own) flesh at table in 14.22 and receiving the victim-slayer's wreath in 15.17. These details make for the fusion of Greek and Jewish cultic traditions.

76. On practices and processes becoming events, see Crossan, *Historical Jesus,* pp. 331, 396. Historical reconstruction is theologically compatible with religious belief in divine agency working through Jesus' spirit abroad in this world after Calvary. The Gospels themselves are reconstructions of Jesus. As Crossan remarks (p. 426): 'If you cannot believe in something produced by reconstruction, you may have nothing left to believe in.'

77. Mack, *Myth of Innocence,* pp. 269-87.

Crossan has suggested that, before eucharists of bread and wine developed in Hellenistic house-churches, there had been outdoor meals of bread and fish shared among peasants, going back before Calvary.[78] Fish are fine for Aramaic-speaking peasants, but they cannot be used in Greek sacrifices.[79] So the ritual menu of the Christ cult is bread and wine, and now they are identified with the body and blood of the victim-sacrificer. To get the Jesus people to swallow this, Mark had to integrate it somehow with the strong tradition of teaching (not priestcraft) that was known to go back to Jesus' own practice before Calvary.

That integration was engineered through the ἀλάβαστρον at Bethany. Its μύρον is πίστικον because it is the distilled essence of a teaching program that had been burnishing the memory of Jesus with apt allusions to the LXX. Πιστικῆς in 14.3 suggests a boldly effective rhetorical practice and repertoire that perhaps already had made their way out of the γυναικῶν. Πίστις, 'faith', is also the term that denoted the loyalty of συμπόσιον companions to one another, as well as the daring deeds that they would pledge themselves to do in confirmation of that bond.[80] In Mark's story, the anointing amidst a συμπόσιον challenged Jesus to die for πίστις, and he accepted. The συμπόσιον was a social institution among whose principal functions were the maintenance of upper-class personal alliances and the memorializing of heroic deeds and virtues through poetic recitation.[81] The συμπόσιον was one of several types of formal banquets, and it involved lengthy discussion among a circle of intimates (ἑταῖροι) who reciprocated hospitality on a regular basis. Among élite Hellenized Jewish men the custom could easily have fused with that of the voluntary pious association or חבורה, but would have imported class exclusivity into the latter. If Jesus was a villager from Nazareth, it is quite unlikely

78. See Crossan, *Historical Jesus*, pp. 367, 398-404, who cites earlier work by Hiers and Kennedy (1976). Crossan observes that the description of Jesus serving the fish eucharist is gendered female.

79. Because, say the Greeks, except for tuna, fish do not bleed. See Detienne and Vernant, *Cuisine of Sacrifice*, p. 221 n. 8. Moreover, blood sacrifice was a male affair and fish reminded Greeks of female genitals. Meat-eating and manhood are closely associated today among mountain villagers on Crete described by Michael Herzfeld, *The Poetics of Manhood: Contest and Identity in a Cretan Mountain Village* (Princeton, NJ: Princeton University Press, 1985).

80. On πίστις as conspiratorial pledge or dare, see Murray, *Sympotica*, pp. 7, 153.

81. See Rösler, '*Mnemosyne*', pp. 230-37.

that he attended συμπόσια before Calvary. Nevertheless Mark's vocabulary associated the so-called anointing of Jesus with such a situation: reclining (κατακειμένου, v. 3), poietic performance (καλὸν ἔργον...ἐποίησεν, vv. 6-8), memory (μνημόσυνον, v. 9), pledging faith (πιστικῆς, v. 3), and intense discussion (ἀγανακτοῦντες, ἐνεβριμῶντο, λαληθήσεται, vv. 4, 5, 9).

This suggests a συμπόσιον where Jesus' death is the focus of the artistic performance and the conversation. A women's histrionic work has proposed to the symposiasts that Jesus dies obediently, faithfully, divinely and freely. The script with this reading of Jesus' death is no longer available to us. We do not know whether it was a pantomime (as the story suggests), a drama, an epigram or lyric, an epitaph, or another of the performance genres culturally attested for banquets in the Greco-Roman period. But we are given to understand that this interpretation of Jesus' stance toward his own death caused consternation amid the assembled company. There are divergent explanations of why. Luke mentions horror at the touch of a sinful woman; the other Gospels cite neglect of charitable obligations. This divergence indicates that the canonical accounts all branched off from an earlier story of the anointing. Mack suggests that an earlier challenge/ response pair has been displaced by different objections in Mark and Luke.[82] In my view, the underlying objection to the anointing was the disciples' protest that the Messiah should not have to die. That earlier story, I have suggested, was itself the precipitate of a prior practice of women's talking and teaching about Jesus in the years immediately following his death.

Mark subordinates the women's rhetorical practice and repertoire to blood sacrifice in the interest of investing Jesus' death with soteriological efficacy. The instruction (κατάχυσμα/תורה) now silently anoints the victim for his death. But bloody sacrifice is male-gendered for Greeks. When Jesus' death is turned into a sacrifice, for the first time it now seems wrong for women to have anything to do with figuring it out or grieving over his memory. Tearful matrons are banished from the banquet (though that was easier scripted than done, judging from Lk. 7.38).

The estrangement of women from the table is the price paid for the unification of the disparate Jesus constituencies behind the gospel

---

82. Burton L. Mack, 'The Anointing of Jesus: Elaboration within a Chreia', in Burton L. Mack and Vernon K. Robbins, *Patterns of Persuasion in the Gospels* (Sonoma, CA: Polebridge Press, 1989), pp. 85-106.

program. But ironically, it was—*and is*—the matrons' original chris-tological speculations that make belief in the sacrifice possible. Mark says as much.

c. *After Mark*

Mark dealt matrons' christological rhetoric a decisive blow when he cartooned it as a misdirected wifely gesture that, albeit unknowingly, detonated three more divine strokes: the broken loaf at 14.22, the broken body at 15.37 and the broken tomb at 16.4. Nevertheless, textualization of the practice seems not to have halted it immediately. There are indications, in the subsequent versions of the story (and in related stories),[83] that articulate women continued to demand a piece of the Jesus who, having been brought in from the hillsides and village hovels (as well as out from the women's salons), now reclined civilly in the house-churches.

One such indication is the dog-ification of the anointing woman in alternate versions of the story. It is the Greeks who give us the curious epithet 'bitch'. They perceive a natural affinity between women and dogs. Women are always hungry, they eat up a man's food, they yap incessantly and they poke their noses in where they don't belong. (They are faithful and devoted as well.[84]) Dog behaviors include feet-kissing, sniveling, slobbering, groveling, begging, brazenness, sneaki-ness and food-snatching. Dog hair gets all over anyone targeted for an exuberant display of canine affection. These elements of the Hellenis-tic bitch stereotype are like a discursive tide ripping the anointing woman away from Jesus' head and casting her up at his feet. Of course, by Hellenistic times, 'dogliness' also was attributed to a

83. Stories that should be read in comparison with Mk 14.3-9 include at least the following: other anointing stories (Mt. 26.6-13; Lk. 7.36-50; Jn 12.1-8); Mary and Martha (Lk. 10.38-42); the Syrophoenician woman (Mt. 15.21-28; Mk 7.24-30); and Lazarus stories (*Secret Mark* 1.1-13; Lk. 16.13-31; Jn 11.1-44).

84. Semonides captures the cultural stereotype in a seventh-century (?) poem; see Hugh Lloyd-Jones (trans.), *Females of the Species: Semonides on Women* (Park-ridge, NJ: Noyes Press, 1975). Aristophanes in *Lysistrata* 957 has Kinesias call his wife κυναλώπηξ, 'fox-bitch'. See also Jean-Pierre Vernant, 'At Man's Table: Hesiod's Foundation Myth of Sacrifice', in Detienne and Vernant (eds.), *The Cuisine of Sacrifice*, pp. 21-86 (59, 66-67). The affinity between dogs and women in Greek is abetted philologically. The verb for carrying and being pregnant, κύω, is related to κύων, 'dog'. Also in the group are κυνέω, 'kiss', and προσκυνέω, which means to drop down before something as if to kiss its feet. Forms of προσκυνέω appear in the LXX to indicate worship involving bodily prostration in the eastern fashion; Greeks for their part would think it unmanly to assume such a doglike foot-licking posture, even for a god.

philosophical tradition and proudly claimed by its adherents: the Cynics. So when rhetorical practice amplifies the dog-like qualities of a character in a story, suspicions arise: Have those bitches been acting up? Have they been snatching table food? Have they been chasing after Cynic philosophy? Whom are they pestering?...How?...And why?

These cultural notes must be considered in tracing the career of the anointing story beyond Mark's Gospel. It seems clear that synoptic study must include more than the four versions usually recognized as parallels.

WOMEN DISCIPLES OF JESUS (15.40-41; 15.47; 16.1)*

Hisako Kinukawa

I owe much to Elisabeth Schüssler Fiorenza's book *In Memory of Her* in formulating my feminist perspective for rereading biblical texts and reconstructing early Christian history. However, when she says in many places that Jesus called forth a discipleship of equals, I could not but ask whether a collaboration between men and women was ever realized even in Jesus' lifetime. It is needless to say that this call is Jesus' essential message, but in Mark's Gospel, at least, there is no explicit description of men and women disciples working together. The Markan narrative records individuals or a group of men or women separately, except on occasions when it refers to a family group or uses the generic expression 'the crowd'.

As I kept the question in my mind, I came to realize that the question is not just institutional but is rooted in my own experiences of being born, nurtured, educated, and living and struggling in a patriarchal society, even though Japanese society is said to have broken with patriarchal conventions in the course of its technological development. Men who have enjoyed their privileged relationship with women from generation to generation do not easily break with their androcentric mindset and accept a new praxis of egalitarian community life.

I fully agree with Schüssler Fiorenza that the discipleship of equals still needs to be discovered and realized by women and men today.[1] However, we also need to know how to do this, and she does not give detailed answers. In fact, it is comparatively easy for women who have been trodden down and neglected to accept equal treatment with men and behave as full members of the community. A negative evaluation by others usually lowers one's self-esteem and intimidates

* Originally published in Hisako Kinukawa, *Women and Jesus in Mark: A Japanese Feminist Perspective* (Maryknoll, NY: Orbis Books, 1994), pp. 90-106. Reprinted by permission, slightly revised.

1. E. Schüssler Fiorenza, *In Memory of Her: A Feminist Theological Reconstruction of Christian Origins* (New York: Crossroad, 1983), p. 154.

a person, but a positive evaluation is energizing. Women need motivation and encouragement to break out of their silence and invisibility
and not act as expected. However, it must also be remembered that
there are numerous women who, even under oppressive circumstances, find ways to overcome predicaments and live creatively.
They are not always passive and subservient to authority, nor do they
always yield to exploitation, especially in everyday life. They are
indomitable enough not to be completely tamed by the culture.

For men, on the other hand, the adjustment needed for them to
accept the 'equality from below' is even more difficult. As a result,
men tend to stick to the status quo or become more entrenched when
change threatens. I need to look for energy that will enable us to
accept each other as equals and to work together.

Women at Jesus' Death and Resurrection

When the passion narrative is nearly at an end, we meet the three
women who are introduced by name for the first time: Mary the
Magdalene, Mary the mother of James the younger and Joses, and
Salome (15.40). From the beginning of the Gospel to this place, all the
women are nameless except Herodias (6.14-29), who conspired to kill
John the Baptist, and Mary the mother of Jesus, who is mentioned in a
pejorative context (6.3). All the women are introduced in relation to
someone else: Simon's mother-in-law (1.29), Jesus' mother (3.31), Jesus'
sisters (3.32), Jairus's daughter (5.23), and one of the servant girls of
the high priest (14.66); or with some identifying modifiers: a woman
who suffered from hemorrhage (5.25), a Gentile woman, of Syrophoenician origin (7.26), a poor widow (12.42), and a woman with an
alabaster jar of very costly ointment of nard (14.3). The fact of women
being nameless may be expected because of the cultural bias of his
androcentric society that influenced Mark, and because of his intention to make the male disciples the main characters in his Gospel.
Winsome Munro goes further to say that women are intentionally
obscured and suppressed by Mark, even though there are actually
many active women in his Gospel.[2] The introduction of these three
named women seems very abrupt. They are first introduced at Jesus'
crucifixion and appear two more times, at Jesus' burial (15.47) and
Jesus' resurrection (16.1). It is hard to accept Munro's thesis that
women are not visible before 15.40 because they are 'embarrassing' or

---

2.   Winsome Munro, 'Women Disciples in Mark?', CBQ 44 (1982), pp. 225-41
(226).

'problematic',[3] while, after 15.40, though they are active as one might expect of disciples, Mark's androcentric view tends to suppress their appearance even there.[4]

A careful reading of the three references to women points up a subtle difference in the names. Most scholars take the second Mary at 15.40 (Mary the mother of James the younger and of Joses), 15.47 (Mary [the mother] of Joses) and 16.1 (Mary [the mother] of James) as the same person, with the inference that the modifiers in 15.47 and 16.1 are abbreviated versions of the reference in 15.40.[5] Some scholars take 'Mary the mother of James the younger and of Joses' as referring to two persons, 'Mary the wife of James the younger, and the mother of Joses'.[6] Thus four women are named.

Furthermore, Mary the mother of James the younger and of Joses may be identified with Jesus' mother, whose next eldest sons have been named James and Joses (6.3). If she were Jesus' mother, why does Mark not mention her that way? There seems to be a reason. Mark depicts Jesus' family as thinking that Jesus has gone out of his mind (3.21, 31). But if Jesus' mother and her sons and daughters have joined the community of faith after Jesus' death and resurrection, Mark might want to restore their honor in this indirect expression. Or he might be cautious about the tendency to heighten the status of Mary in his community. On the other hand, he may not be referring to Jesus' mother but be speaking of James the 'younger' to distinguish him from James, Jesus' brother.[7] Or the 'younger' could be a disparagement of Jesus' brother, who in a certain period dominated the Jerusalem church (Gal. 1.19; 2.12; 1 Cor. 9.5), to show that Jesus' family is not special (see also 3.31-35).

From consecutive references to these women in 15.47 and 16.1, in which names are inconsistent though overlapping, we may infer that 16.1-8 belongs to a resurrection narrative independent from the preceding section. Mark combines the two stories and uses 15.40 to adjust the difference between them.[8] At the same time, it is very important

3.   Munro, 'Women Disciples in Mark?', p. 235.

4.   Munro, 'Women Disciples in Mark?', p. 239.

5.   Munro, 'Women Disciples in Mark?', p. 226. Elizabeth Struthers Malbon, 'Fallible Followers: Women and Men in the Gospel of Mark', *Semeia* 28 (1983), pp. 29-48 (43). Fiorenza, *In Memory of Her*, p. 321.

6.   E. Schweizer, *Das Evangelium nach Markus* (Japanese edn; Tokyo: NTD, 1976), p. 486.

7.   Schweizer, *Das Evangelium*, pp. 486-87.

8.   Rudolph Bultmann, *History of the Synoptic Tradition* (trans. John Marsh; Oxford: Basil Blackwell, 1972), pp. 276, 284-85; Schweizer, *Das Evangelium*, pp. 486-87; S. Arai, *Iesu Kirisuto* (Tokyo: Kodansha, 1979), p. 337.

for the resurrection narrative to have these women see where Jesus was laid after his death at 15.47, because Mark must confirm through the women's witness that Jesus really died and was buried.

Mark has not referred to these women before in his Gospel narrative. What kind of relationship with Jesus these women have had is not mentioned. What kind of interactions with him they have experienced we cannot identify. Yet it is plausible to say that each must have had experiences similar to those recorded about the nameless women in Mark's Gospel. Mark only says that 'these used to follow and served him when he was in Galilee' and notes that there were 'many other women who had come up with him to Jerusalem'. At the end of Jesus' life, when the narrative is coming to a close, all these women appear as 'new actants', 'a remnant', and 'the lifeline of the discipleship narrative'.[9]

It is a dramatic reversal. Even the androcentrically 'biased' Mark has to record that when Jesus was arrested, 'all of them [male disciples] deserted him and fled. A certain young man was following him, wearing nothing but a linen cloth. They caught hold of him, but he left the linen cloth and ran off naked' (14.50-52). Then, while Jesus was being examined, 'Peter had followed him at a distance, right into the courtyard of the high priest' (14.54), and in spite of his promises he 'began to curse, and he swore an oath, "I do not know this man you are talking about"' (14.71). All the males forsook him when he was in the hands of the authorities. The story of Jesus' disciples seems to end disastrously.[10] 'The disciples of Jesus had their doctrine crossed out in a way which so threw them off course that they could only flee'.[11] Malbon claims that Mark's description there reveals the male disciples to be fallible.[12]

The Three Named Women as Disciples (15.40-41)

There are several characteristics of the women 'looking on from a distance' at the cross. There are three named women among many anonymous women who continued to follow and serve Jesus when he was in Galilee and who came up with Jesus to Jerusalem.

---

9.   F. Belo, *A Materialist Reading of the Gospel of Mark* (Maryknoll, NY: Orbis Books, 1981), p. 229; C. Myers, *Binding the Strong Man* (Maryknoll, NY: Orbis Books, 1988), p. 396.

10.   Robert C. Tannehill, 'Disciples in Mark: The Function of a Narrative Role', *JR* 57 (1977), pp. 386-405 (402-403).

11.   Schweizer, *Das Evangelium*, p. 490.

12.   Malbon, 'Fallible Followers', p. 32.

Does this mean that they are women disciples who form a nucleus of three within an inner circle of many women, as Peter, James and John do in relation to the Twelve (5.37; 9.2; 14.33)? While Mark says that Jesus personally and individually extended an invitation to Simon, Andrew, James, John, and Levi to follow him (1.16-20; 2.13), there is no woman who hears Jesus' personal invitation to follow within the Markan narrative.[13] It is not clear if Mark means the three women to correspond to the three male disciples. Munro argues that they are women 'disciples' but Mark intentionally obscured the fact.[14] Malbon uses the term 'followers' to depict these women characters.[15] Dewey asks why Jesus did not appoint any women among the Twelve, and says, 'Possibly, in order to proclaim his message so that it would be heard at all, Jesus had to make some accommodation to the standards of his own culture'.[16] This is plausible if we think of the difficulty people had even accepting Jesus' interacting with women and being followed by them.

But I would like to ask further whether Mark may have been affected by the structural system of the 'twelve apostles' in the church, which must have been on the way to becoming the establishment when he was writing. He seems to have criticized the disciples easily, because he felt them to be most important. I believe that his concerns for his community made him write this way. I must wonder how strictly and clearly the boundary of the circle of the Twelve was actually set during the days of Jesus, who rejected any hierarchical institution and tried to break down boundaries (2.15-16, 18-22, 23-27; 3.35; 9.34-35; 10.13-16, 42-45).

In any case, Mark portrays women with Jesus right from the beginning of Jesus' ministry to his death, but almost all of their interactions and conversations with Jesus are invisible.[17] We may rightly infer that Markan generic words indicating the wider circle of the followers, such as 'those who were around him' (4.10) and 'the crowd', must actually be meant to include both male and female.[18] But it is only

---

13. M. Selvidge, *Women, Cult, and Miracle Recital* (Lewisburg, PA: Bucknell University Press; London: Associated University Press, 1990), p. 105.

14. Munro, 'Women Disciples in Mark?', p. 231.

15. Malbon, 'Fallible Followers', p. 43.

16. Joanna Dewey, *Disciples of the Way* (New York: Woman's Division, Board of Global Ministries; United Methodist Church, 1976), p. 132.

17. Elisabeth Moltmann-Wendel, *A Land Flowing with Milk and Honey: Perspectives on Feminist Theology* (trans. John Bowden; New York: Crossroad, 1988), p. 109.

18. Fiorenza, *In Memory of Her*, p. 320.

women that have accompanied Jesus on the way to his death, risking their lives and safety. We may infer from the phrase 'and there were many others' that there must have been quite a number of women among the group of disciples.

In Mark the term 'disciples' is used 46 times. Sometimes it is used to designate just the Twelve (e.g., 9.31), but more frequently it is used to refer to Jesus' followers. Therefore a larger group than just the Twelve must be implied.[19]

'Looking Up'

In contrast to the male disciples, who try to deny Jesus' fate by fleeing and not facing up to reality, these women are looking up to Jesus on the cross (15.40) and watching his tomb at the burial (15.47). And further, they see that the stone of the tomb has been rolled back and they see a young man there (16.4-5). Women keep watching Jesus' most critical moments of crucifixion, burial and resurrection. Those moments are also the main points of the kerygma or tradition: 'Christ died for our sins in accordance with the scriptures, and he was buried, and he was raised on the third day in accordance with the scriptures' (1 Cor. 15.3-4). So women are the ones who do not lose sight of who Jesus was.[20] 'Watching' also symbolizes their expression of interest, concern, care and sorrow. Even though they cannot do a thing to reverse this crisis, their relationship to Jesus is not broken.

'From a Distance'

Opinions are divided on the meaning of the expression that the women are watching Jesus on the cross 'from a distance'. Fiorenza interprets it in a positive sense that characterizes them as Jesus' true relatives:

> That they are well aware of the danger of being arrested and executed as followers of a political insurrectionist crucified by the Romans is indicated in the remark.[21]

On the other hand, Munro, emphasizing the 'distance' that separates them from Jesus on the cross—in comparison with John's Gospel where they are close enough to converse with Jesus—questions whether the women take the place of the Twelve who have forsaken Jesus and fled. She concludes that Mark is not necessarily in favor of the women and they do not effectively replace the male disciples. Further, she says,

19. Fiorenza, *In Memory of Her*, pp. 49-50.
20. Fiorenza, *In Memory of Her*, pp. 319-22.
21. Fiorenza, *In Memory of Her*, p. 320.

The phrase ἀπὸ μακρόθεν has even stronger import if Mark intends an allusion to the innocent sufferer of the Psalm from whom friends, companions, and kinsfolk stand aloof and far off (Psalm 38:11; 88:8), which is quite explicit in Luke 23:49.[22]

Opposing Munro's interpretation, Marla J. Selvidge proposes an alternative reading of the text: 'women from afar watching' instead of 'women watching from afar'. Then the phrase only designates the place from which they originated, not the spatial and psychological distance between the women and Jesus on the cross.[23] This reading is attractive for confirming their closeness to Jesus, but it is unlikely. Malbon notes that the same expression is applied to Peter when he followed Jesus 'from a distance' as Jesus was arrested and taken to the high priest (14.53-54):

Presumably a stronger disciple and stronger followers would have drawn nearer to Jesus at these critical moments of trial and crucifixion. To be present at all is a mark of followership, but remaining at a distance is a mark of fallibility—for Peter and for the women.[24]

We cannot say for certain that Mark intends to apply the Psalms' image of the solitary, innocent sufferer to Jesus. It seems more probable that the phrase 'from afar' is parallel to Peter's case. Because 'from a distance' depicts Peter's spatial and psychological distance in remaining an onlooker and reveals his subconscious desire to act as if he were unrelated to Jesus, the same expression may also suggest the distance between the women and Jesus. At least we can say that Mark is not unreservedly praising the behavior of the women.

I suggest that women who are considered almost worthless in society have no need to flee from a dangerous place. Though they do not run the same risk of being seized as men might do, yet it is far more natural for them not to make their appearance in such a public place. They are used to being invisibly modest but are nonetheless ready to be with Jesus, who has given them a completely new and different self-image.

'Kept Following and Serving Jesus'
There are distinctive verbs that describe these women. Mark reports that 'they used to follow him and served him when he was in Galilee; there were many other women who had come up with him to

22. Fiorenza, *In Memory of Her*, p. 235.
23. Marla J. Selvidge, 'And Those Who Follow Feared (Mark 10:32)', *CBQ* 45 (1983), pp. 396-400 (399).
24. Malbon, 'Fallible Followers', p. 43.

Jerusalem' (15.41). Most scholars, seeing in the verbs 'follow' and 'serve' the key 'discipleship' themes described by Mark, recognize the women as model disciples.[25] The verbs used in the imperfect tense express their continual following of Jesus. The women's discipleship in Mark, specifically their 'following' and 'serving', can only be under-stood within his total description of what discipleship means. This kind of relationship created between women and a teacher, which has been engendered as a result of Jesus' ministry, is as far as we know distinctive to Jesus in first-century Palestine. All the rabbis are, of course, male, and since to be a disciple of a rabbi means to become a rabbi sometime, disciples are expected to be all male. The disciples go everywhere with their rabbi and learn all the details of the scriptural texts and the laws so that they may become experts in the traditions.[26] Jesus acts and teaches in completely different ways, even though he is considered a rabbi. Here is another instance of boundary-breaking by Jesus.

The women's discipleship in Mark, specifically their 'following' and 'serving', can only be understood within his total description of what discipleship means.

Mark's Threefold Teaching on Discipleship (8.34-38; 9.35-37; 10.42-45)

Structural Observation
Mark 8.31–10.45 contains the threefold teaching of Jesus on the role of the disciples. The teaching is carefully placed after the three passion predictions of Jesus (8.31; 9.31; 10.33-34), each of which is immediately followed by the disciples' negative response (8.32-33) or behavior con-trary to that of Jesus (9.33-34; 10.35-41).[27] The arrangement is decisive

---

25. Ched Myers, *Binding the Strong Man: A Political Reading of Mark's Story of Jesus* (New York: Orbis Books, 1988), p. 396; Fiorenza, *In Memory of Her*, p. 320; Dewey, *Disciples of the Way*, pp. 51, 132; Selvidge, *Women, Cult*, p. 107; Malbon, 'Fallible Followers', p. 40; and *idem*, 'Disciples/Crowds/Whoever: Markan Charac-ters and Readers', *NovT* 28.2 (1986), pp. 104-30 (109); G. Kittel, 'ἀκολουθέω', *TDNT*, I, p. 213; Leonard Swidler, *Biblical Affirmations of Women* (Philadelphia, PA: West-minster Press, 1979), pp. 194-95. Munro, referring to some scholars, says that these women are very rarely recognized as disciples. 'By and large their role goes unexplored and unexplained, while some interpret ἠκολούθουν in terms of διηκόνουν, understood to define their function as that of serving food and attending to domestic chores in general, or as rendering material support for Jesus' mission' ('Women Disciples in Mark?', p. 232).

26. Dewey, *Disciples of the Way*, p. 48. K.H. Rengstorf, 'μαθήτη', *TDNT*, IV, pp. 416-61.

27. Tannehill, 'The Disciples in Mark', p. 400; Werner H. Kelber, *The Kingdom in*

for the Markan redactional purpose. Teachings on discipleship are located following passion predictions and passion rejections, emphasizing 'passion' as the core of discipleship.

All three of Jesus' passion predictions follow the same literary pattern, which basically reflects the form of the kerygma of the early church. He predicts the suffering, crucifixion and resurrection of the Son of Man (8.31; 9.31; 10.33-34).

To call him Christ as Peter does in 8.29 may refer to the historical situation of the ministry of Jesus, but the terms used here reflect the christological vocabulary of the early church.[28] Peter's refusal to accept Jesus' political fate (8.32-33), the Twelve's argument over who is the greatest (9.32-34), and James and John's petition for the highest ranks (10.35-37) may all indicate that Mark's community does not comprehend who Jesus is and what Jesus wants of them. It is Mark's redactional intention to place the teaching on discipleship right after the prediction of the passion to stress the discrepancy between the way of Jesus and that of his followers. Mark is very conscious of the situation of the community of faith for which he writes his Gospel.

Mark makes us realize the necessity of such teaching as well as the fact that Jesus always goes before his disciples. Discipleship comes only as interaction with Jesus: there is no discipleship separate from his life.

The threefold repetition of the passion prediction, its rejection by the disciples and the teaching on discipleship is itself framed by healing-miracle stories of blind men who receive sight (8.22-26; 10.46-52). In no other place does Mark record two different stories of the healing of the same disability.[29] We may read the symbolic message of these two stories to be that to gain one's sight is one of the first steps for discipleship, but in order to gain one's sight one must get involved

Mark: A New Place and a New Time (Philadelphia:, Fortress Press, 1974), p. 67; Dewey, *Disciples of the Way*, p. 72; Fiorenza, *In Memory of Her*, p. 317; Myers, *Binding the Strong Man*, pp. 237, 405; Andrew T. Lincoln, 'The Promise and the Failure: Mark 16:7, 8', *JBL* 108.2 (1989), pp. 283, 300 (294).

28. Norman Perrin, *What Is Redaction Criticism?* (Philadelphia: Fortress Press), pp. 41-42. ' "Jesus" is the Lord addressing his church, "Peter" represents fallible believers who confess correctly yet go on to interpret their confession incorrectly, and the "multitude" is the whole church membership for whom the general teaching which follows is designed... It has the form of a story about the historical Jesus and his disciples but a purpose in terms of the risen Lord and his church. It represents Mark's understanding of what the risen Lord has to say to the church of his day.'

29. Dewey, *Disciples of the Way*, p. 72. Myers, *Binding the Strong Man*, p. 236.

with Jesus, as the nameless women already show. Therefore, 'immedi-ately he regained his sight and followed him on the way' (10.52).

'Follow Me' Means Taking on 'Shame' (8.34-38)

In the first section (8.34-38) of the threefold teaching on discipleship we read: 'He called the crowd with his disciples, and said to them, "If any want to become my followers, let them deny themselves and take up their cross and follow me"'. Malbon points out that this is 'a pivotal verse concerning disciples, the crowd, and followers',[30] in the sense that the invitation to follow Jesus is extended to anyone who wishes; therefore anyone can be a disciple. Though Malbon carefully uses 'follower', I would use both 'follower' and 'disciple' with the same meaning. Since this verse links the disciples and the crowd, Malbon argues against Ernst Best who makes a definite distinction between the crowd and the disciples.[31]

'Follow' is the key word. To follow Jesus means to deny oneself and take up one's own cross. One cannot follow without getting involved with Jesus, though the reaction shown by Peter after Jesus' first announcement of his passion (8.32) explains how easy it is just to make a confession that 'you are the Christ' (8.29) without knowing what it really means. To deny oneself means to renounce the pre-rogatives that create boundaries around oneself and keep one's life separate from the oppressed.

Crucifixion is the most painful and most shameful method of exe-cution that human beings have ever devised. Thus taking up one's cross means to become the shame of society, as Jesus does. It means that when we are in danger of being deprived of our honor we are challenged to face the situation. This seems to be the most serious challenge to face the privileged sector of the contemporary churches in Japan.

Nor should we neglect the fact that at the time of Mark's writing, Christians were already exposed to the danger of persecution by the Roman authorities. To be involved with Jesus is deeply and decisively related to taking the 'shame' of the society upon oneself. The verse, 'Those who are ashamed of me and my words in this adulterous and sinful generation, of them the Son of Man will also be ashamed when he comes in the glory of his Father with the holy angels' (8.38) also

---

30. Malbon, 'Disciples/Crowds/Whoever', pp. 109-10.
31. Malbon, 'Disciples/Crowds/Whoever', p. 110. See also Ernst Best, 'The Role of the Disciples in Mark', *NTS* 23 (1977), pp. 377-401 (377).

suggests this. Ched Myers explains such circumstances as 'a specific kind of political and community practice that takes the disciples/ reader into the deepest paradoxes of power'.[32] To follow Jesus is to choose between being ashamed of Jesus and his words for the honor of this world and being ashamed of the power of this world for the contrary honor of following Jesus. Once one encounters Jesus, one cannot escape from shame, which is the greatest humiliation reality in the 'culture of honor', because it means being excluded from the integrity of the holy. Thus, Jesus is demanding the most paradoxical decision from his followers.

Jesus' ministry, concentrated as it is on life-giving miracles and teachings, cannot be without interaction with those who need his life-giving ministry. The essence of this ministry lies in the restoration of those consigned to nonexistence to their wholeness as persons. For that purpose Jesus needs to break down the barriers that exclude the impure in order to preserve the integrity of the pure. In fact, these barriers have destroyed the wholeness of persons on both sides of the barrier. Therefore, Jesus' ministry cannot avoid the resistance and rejection that brings on his suffering, execution and death. Jesus' 'suffering is not an end itself, however, but is the outcome of Jesus' life-praxis of solidarity with the social and religious outcasts of his society'.[33]

To follow Jesus is to collapse the existing social framework and reverse the world of the 'pure' or the 'powerful'. Suffering and death will also be the outcome of this life-praxis. Fiorenza sees here Mark's crucial christological insight.[34] Jesus' teaching points to his suffering as a model for his followers. Jesus himself goes before them. His posture foreshadows the prediction announced in 14.28 and 16.7 that he is going before them to Galilee and they will see him there.

Thus discipleship is not the condition but the outcome of following Jesus.[35] With Malbon, we may say that 'discipleship is both open-ended and demanding; followership is neither exclusive nor easy'.[36]

---

32. Myers, *Binding the Strong Man*, p. 235.

33. Fiorenza, *In Memory of Her*, p. 317.

34. Fiorenza, *In Memory of Her*, p. 317.

35. I cannot agree with Dewey's interpretation on this point: 'Here, Jesus invites us all to follow him, but we must be willing to pay the cost. For the first saying goes on to list the conditions for following after Jesus; we must deny ourselves, take up our crosses and follow him' (*Discipleship of the Way*, p. 76).

36. Malbon, 'Disciples/Crowds/Whoever', p. 124.

'Serving' (9.35-37 and 10.42-45)
In chs. 9 and 10 of Mark, the skillfully designed composition of Jesus' teaching on discipleship deals with the issue of right leadership in the community of faith.

In each case the teachings are preceded by some manifestation of the Twelve's hunger for power or honor. In 9.33-34, the Twelve discuss who is the greatest among them, and in 10.35-41, James and John petition Jesus for the highest ranks and the other ten are incensed about the two. Jesus, responding to their hunger for power and status, discusses the true form of leadership in the community of faith. Thus Mark uncovers a major paradoxical contrast between the desire for power and domination-free service.

Jesus teaches them, 'Whoever wants to be first, must be last of all and servant of all' (9.35) and in 10.42-45, he puts the issue in direct contrast to the prevailing power structure.

> You know that among the Gentiles those whom they recognize as their rulers lord it over them, and their great ones are tyrants over them. But it is not so among you; but whoever wishes to become great among you must be your servant, and whoever wishes to be first among you must be slave to all. For the Son of Man came not to be served but to serve, and to give his life as a ransom for many.

As we read the three consecutive sections on discipleship, we see that the teaching becomes more detailed, the tension is heightened, the emphasis is pointed, and the climax becomes clear.

'Serve' is the key word. Jesus is now talking to those who feel it natural to be served and have never thought of serving others. In the last teaching, a statement about the Son of Man is added to show that Jesus himself stands at the opposite extreme from power by not being served. 'Being not served' means that the Son of Man is 'not one who holds such a position in the world as to have attendants—the servants of the rich and powerful'.[37]

The word 'serve' reminds Greek-speaking people of menial work with two basic meanings: first, to wait on table, an activity usually done by male servants; and second, to provide or care for, often in the sense of 'women's work', taking care of the home and bringing up

---

37. John N. Collins, *Diakonia: Re-interpreting the Ancient Sources* (Oxford: Oxford University Press, 1990), pp. 248, 252. He notes that 'to be served' is a 'comparatively rare passive', which is 'predicated directly of a person in a way that no other passive is' (p. 249). 'The passive belongs to the part of usage described as domestic and personal attendance; analysis of that usage has shown that, as in other areas of meaning, the verb looks to the activity rather than to the status of persons, who in this instance are "attendants"' (p. 252).

children. The word carries the general meaning to serve, especially in the sense of personal service rendered to someone by someone else.[38] People desired to be served, not to serve. They saw no freedom in serving others.[39] It is very interesting that Mark never uses the word 'serve' to describe the actions of the Twelve but only those of women and Jesus.[40] If Mark is thinking in an ordinary sense that 'serving' can only be applied to activities of the most despised or marginalized in society, he cannot apply the word to male disciples, even if Jesus teaches 'serving' as a content of discipleship. If Mark is thinking about how shocking Jesus' teaching of 'serving' is, he is commenting on how distant male disciples are from what Jesus wants them to be.

The word 'serve' is employed so as to present an extreme contrast with the dominant political structure, which seeks for more power at the expense of the subjugated. Jesus is very critical about the Twelve's aspirations to status and power. Actually the Twelve flee from Jesus when they realize that to follow him further is politically dangerous. In a patriarchal sociocultural order, we can see why the Twelve dare not pursue their following to the end. For them it is very hard not to want to seek honor. Their conservativeness vis-à-vis change is shown to contrast strongly with Jesus' sensitive perception and his freedom to crash through the barriers at key moments.

Here we see how Mark reflects the patriarchy of the age. But Mark rejects this alliance with the political and social system of patriarchy and demands that churches not compromise with the dominant trend of that time. Mark may be struggling over the true meaning of messianic politics.[41]

---

38. Hermann W. Beyer, 'διακονέω διακονία, διάκονος', *TDNT*, II, pp. 87, 82; Dewey, *Disciples of the Way*, p. 85; Luise Schottroff, 'Maria Magdalena und die Frauen am Grabe Jesu', *EvT* 42 (1982), pp. 3-25 (12): 'At meals in antiquity there were very strict hierarchical rules according to which the servant was the one who was lowest in the social scale, either the slave or the son or the daughter or the wife'. Quoted by Elisabeth Moltmann-Wendel, in her book *A Land Flowing with Milk and Honey: Perspectives on Feminist Theology* (trans. John Bowden; New York: Crossroad, 1982), who also says: 'In terms of social history this serving describes the situation of those whose situation is utterly inferior and who have to do the worst work' (p. 128). Collins argues that 'service at table' is not 'the so-called fundamental meaning of the words in either Christian or other literature but is one expression of the notion of go-between', which constitutes the root idea (*Diakonia*, pp. 249-50). The basic meaning of the word, according to his study, is 'doing messages and being another person's agent' (p. 194). But he also admits that it can occasionally mean menial service, as in some sayings of Jesus (p. 254).

39. Selvidge, *Women, Cult*, p. 102.

40. Selvidge, 'And Those Who Followed Feared', p. 398.

41. Myers, *Binding the Strong Man*, pp. 280, 236.

It is not clearly stated whom the Son of Man might be serving or what kind of service he proffers. John N. Collins notes that the second half of the verse, 'instead of clarifying the context for an understanding of "to serve", has tended to accentuate the word's singularity here because a theology of ransom would not seem to have a natural correlation with the idea of service, especially in a context that is basically ethical'.[42] The word 'serve' may indicate menial work, and 'servant' or 'slave' designate those who are considered property without human dignity. One could say that Jesus redefines the meaning of 'serving', culminating in suffering and death. The new definition may be more theological and severe, but it gives the absolute assurance of Jesus' solidarity with those who serve. Jesus' solidarity is expressed through giving his own life as a ransom for the benefit of many, thus going before those who choose to follow. If we take 'ransom' as a technical term for money paid to liberate slaves and make free citizens,[43] Jesus' life is virtually spent in bringing back to life those who are cast out of society by subjugation, marginalization, humiliation, objectivization, impurification, enslavement, and so on. For that purpose, he breaks down all sorts of artificial barriers essential for the dominant power to keep its exclusive integrity. Thus Jesus' life-giving ministry has to end in his losing his own life. We may say that Jesus' life is itself a new definition of 'serving', that is, to use one's life so that all human beings may share wholeness of life.

This following and serving is decided by one's own free will and is not fated or forced as we see in the slavery system. As Jesus' life evidences, life-giving discipleship cannot be without suffering in a patriarchal society. Therefore, we are invited to serve 'everyone', to practice 'life-giving' solidarity with the destitute. We see here the climax of Jesus' paradoxical teaching that the way of death is the way of life, that ultimate empowerment of 'serving' is found in struggling for 'life for all'.

Only when we reach this conclusion are we persuaded why Jesus had to use concepts that reflect the hierarchical structure of the serving and the served. To undermine the patriarchal, hierarchical mindset, Jesus needed to start by reversing their value system. Then Jesus redefined the concepts by giving his life on the cross. The cross symbolizes the absolute negation of oppressive power as well as full solidarity with the oppressed. Jesus had to die on the cross because the traditional division between the served and the serving was not

---

42. Collins, *Diakonia*, p. 249.
43. Fiorenza, *In Memory of Her*, p. 318; Dewey, *Disciples of the Way*, p. 94.

destroyed. The division was supported by all sorts of discriminations based on sex, race, handicap, and so on.

In contemporary churches in Japan, the division still exists. And so Jesus' teaching challenges us to overcome the oppressive situation. At the same time, I submit, we are challenged to redefine the concept of 'serving' once more so that we all may serve one another, even though we are different physically, sexually and racially.

Excursus: Simon's Mother-in-Law (1.29-31)

Here I will make an excursus on the story of Simon's mother-in-law in relation to one of the central themes of discipleship: 'serving'. The story is one of the first two miracle stories in Mark, both having taken place on the Sabbath day (1.21). Healings on the Sabbath always provoked major controversy between Jesus and the religious authorities (3.6). After an exorcism at the synagogue, Jesus leaves there immediately and enters the house of Simon and Andrew with James and John. Jesus' first four disciples, to whom he gave personal calls to 'follow' (1.16-20), are following him.

'Now Simon's mother-in-law was sick in bed with a fever, and they told him about her at once' (v. 30). They may tell Jesus of her fever to excuse her for being unable to entertain them. For the hosts (Simon and Andrew) or the inferiors (all four disciples), it is a shame not to be able to show proper hospitality to their honorable guest (Jesus). Therefore, the words of excuse come first. Luke misses this. Luke's view reflects a later time and either does not understand the excuse or does not want the disciples to give it. He responds that they request Jesus to heal her (4.38), while Matthew omits the whole statement and stresses Jesus' initiative as the miracle worker (8.14-15).

The story moves in an unexpected direction. 'Jesus came and took her by the hand and lifted her up. Then the fever left her'. Jesus goes straight to her and treats her with great care. He does not merely touch or tap her, but takes hold of her hand with his hands and raises her to her wholeness. The lifelike retelling of this encounter suggests that the event was unforgettable, and therefore the story could be very primitive. The encounter shows the impressive physical closeness Jesus has with the woman, expressing Jesus' deep concern for life. The verb 'lift' is the same verb used when Jairus's daughter was raised from her deathbed and in 16.6 when Jesus was resurrected. He devotes his life to healing the sick.

The story although short has stylistic features typical of miracle stories: (1) problem/crisis, (2) act, and (3) response. We can trace these features in this story as follows: (1) the woman is described as fever-ridden; (2) Jesus heals her by taking hold of her hand and the fever leaves her; and (3) she serves them.[44]

Antoinette Wire, who categorizes miracle stories using the theme of interactions as the organizing key, organizes them into four groups—the exorcism, the exposé, the provision and the demand—and classifies this as one of the demand stories, although she says this story is anomalous.[45] It is not certain whether the four meant to request healing for her, but they did play the role of interceding for her. There is, however, 'no intensifying of the demand to make a true demand story, possibly because the connection to Peter was sufficient reason for its telling'.[46] It is apparent that Matthew and Luke heighten the miraculous element in their stories.

We need to ask what Mark's redactional intention is here. Simon's mother-in-law, on being raised from her fever, 'served' them. Scholars point out that Mark carefully uses the imperfect tense for the verb 'serve' while he uses aorist verbs for the healing process.[47] The 'service' offered by Peter's mother-in-law is not momentary but lasting. Scholars vary on interpreting the meaning of the verb, because Mark does not elaborate on its content.[48]

44. Arai, *Iesu Kirisuto*, pp. 244-45. Bultmann, *History of the Synoptic Tradition*.

45. Antoinette C. Wire, 'The Structure of Gospel Miracle Stories and their Tellers', *Semeia* 11 (1978), pp. 83-103 (83-84).

46. Wire, 'Gospel Miracle Stories', p. 100.

47. Taylor, *St. Mark*, p. 180; Howard C. Kee, *Community of the New Age: Studies in Mark's Gospel* (Philadelphia: Westminster Press, 1977), p. 152.

48. It is very interesting to see Mark not explain what 'serving' really means in his Gospel. He only suggests for readers to learn from the story of Jesus' life and teaching. When Jesus taught his disciples what it means to be his disciples, he made it clear that he himself stood at the opposite extreme from those with power who only asked to be served. His life was devoted to serving those who were subjugated and marginalized in the society. Therefore 'serving' meant life-giving so that the destitute could recover the wholeness of their lives. When Mark writes that Peter's mother-in-law began serving them, he implies that she took her model of serving from Jesus' life and teaching. She might also even support Jesus and his followers by serving meals and providing other necessities, but her serving Jesus never meant what Jesus described as the powerful being served. The service of life-giving to the destitute could not help but result in being in conflict with the power. The cross symbolizes it. As Jesus had to pay the price for bringing the lives of the oppressed to their fullness, the life-giving serving itself implies suffering. Mark did not explicitly say this when Peter's mother-in-law began her serving, because he wants the readers to be enlightened as they read through his Gospel. It is very probable that Peter's mother-in-law was one of the women who stayed with Jesus as he went through the final suffering of crucifixion.

Vincent Taylor says, 'The serving at the evening meal is mentioned as the sign of the cure'.[49] Herman Waetjen goes a little further and says, 'She arises and spends the remainder of the day ministering to them and their needs. Certainly more than the preparation of a meal is implied here. Her service engenders serenity, joy, comfort, well-being, and communion for them all'.[50] He sees her gratitude as entailing the celebration of those who are present. Selvidge raises a question: 'Would the Markan writer preserve a story about Jesus healing a woman just for the purpose of fixing him dinner or demonstrating her "village hospitality"?'[51] Referring to the usages of the word in Mark, she reminds us of the connection with the central themes of discipleship in Mark, saying that the verb 'is central to the mission of Jesus and to those who claim to be followers of Jesus'. So, 'in this story the mother-in-law is carrying out the same mandate that Jesus requires of all followers. It does not necessarily have to be menial tasks'.[52] Howard C. Kee, also referring to the technical use of the word in Mark, says that 'she took care of their needs on a regular basis'.[53] On the other hand, Malbon raises the question of whether 'her service, her ministry, shares—and foreshadows—the theological connotations that the ministry of Mary Magdalene, Mary the mother of James and Joses, and Salome manifests later (15.41)'.[54]

If we read this story just as it is, it is possible to say both that she does serve an evening meal as an expression of her gratitude and that she carries out the praxis of discipleship. If the first interpretation is dominant in Mark's telling, it implies another instance of the hospitality expected from women. This interpretation supports the gender role ideology that has been accepted by the church.

The latter interpretation could be justified if we see that the story is located here to provide a hint that is to be developed later and to challenge the readers to think throughout the Gospel narrative. If so, it also explains why Mark does not elaborate its meaning here.

To clarify Mark's intention, I would like to refer to the story of Jesus calling his first four disciples (1.16-20). In the story we can see how Jesus calls male disciples. First, his calling is made verbally. Second, the calling is something that could replace their occupation. Third, the

49. Taylor, *St. Mark*, p. 180.

50. Herman C. Waetjen, *A Reordering of Power: A Socio-Political Reading of Mark's Gospel* (Minneapolis: Fortress Press, 1989), p. 83.

51. Selvidge, *Woman, Cult*, p. 399.

52. Selvidge, *Woman, Cult*, p. 398.

53. Kee, *Community of the New Age*, p. 152.

54. Malbon, 'Fallible Followers', p. 35.

first two followed him and the last two went after him. Both verbs imply one of the themes of discipleship: 'following'. Fourth, Jesus' calling coincides with forming a community of followers. It should be stressed that Jesus does not practice single-hook fishing of disciples.

Male disciples, responding to Jesus' words calling them to 'make them fish for people', started their praxis of following Jesus. Mark does not elaborate here what 'following' means. In this story, Mark simply foreshadows the first step in discipleship—'following'—thereby already introducing into the narrative the implicit possibility of their failure. The failure may be reflected in the fact that Mark never uses 'to serve' of male disciples. Disciples follow Jesus but do not go further. We can detect that Mark's criticism of the disciples is implicit from the beginning of the Gospel.

Reading together the stories of the calling of the four and the healing of Simon's mother-in-law, I wonder if Mark does not intentionally almost juxtapose the two stories and arrange the two important verbs explaining discipleship, one in each story. At the end of the Gospel, women are referred to as having continuously both followed and served (15.41). Apparently serving cannot be without following, but following can be without serving. If the true praxis of discipleship is found in both following and serving, while the male disciples follow, Simon's mother-in-law is the first to serve, and she keeps on serving. I see the significance of the imperfect tense of 'to serve' in this sense. It is noteworthy that her calling takes place through healing and physical contact, in contrast to the men, whose calling is only verbal. It is symbolic to see her raised by the life-giving Jesus to her wholeness and to start following him. The reciprocity of the giving of life and the response works vigorously here again. It entails the community of living interactions.

Therefore, I conclude that the verb 'serving' in this context plays a decisive role for the whole Gospel and implies far more than just serving a meal. In these small stories the Markan redactional intention concerning discipleship is beautifully carried out.

Women as True Disciples?

Many scholars try to evaluate how Mark dealt with disciples. Some interpret 'disciples' allegorically. Theodore Weeden, using a redaction-criticism method, concludes that the disciples represent Mark's historical opponents and therefore receive very negative treatment.[55] We

55. Theodore Weeden, 'The Heresy that Necessitated Mark's Gospel', *ZNW* 59 (1968), pp. 143-53.

find that adequate evidence is lacking to verify the existence and nature of such opponents. Ernst Best thinks the disciples represent the church and the crowd represents the unevangelized.[56] But it is not Mark's practice to draw such a distinctive line between the two groups, as we have already seen.

Some take a 'reader-response' approach. According to Robert C. Tannehill, the positive portrayals of the disciples are intended to get readers to identify themselves with the disciples and the negative depictions of them are meant to distance readers from the disciples' less acceptable behavior. The total idea is to lead the readers to a new self-understanding and repentance.[57]

Best interprets the disciples both positively and negatively, showing a dynamic interplay of faith and disbelief. The disciples fluctuate between success and failure.[58] John Schmidt sees the disciples' characterization as devastating in contrast with the women, who are viewed positively. 'Mark presents all of the inner group as male and as lacking the understanding appropriate to their position. They never are held up as models for Christian imitation'. But women, on the other hand, are depicted as positive models of discipleship. 'Women are presented as persons who really see who Jesus is and who act on that vision'.[59]

Munro, who uses an historical-critical approach, takes a negative attitude toward the disciples, although she thinks Mark also suppresses a more positive image of women because of the social, political, and cultural context in which he writes.[60]

Malbon suggests a composite view of looking at the different characters in the Gospel with positive and negative features. Discipleship is to be understood from both the failure and the success and from the tension between their success and failure.[61] 'The women characters supplement and complement the Markan portrayal of the disciples, together forming, as it were, a composite portrait of the fallible followers of Jesus'.[62]

56. Ernst Best, 'The Role of the Disciples in Mark', *NTS* 23 (1977), pp. 377-401 (377).

57. Tannehill, 'The Disciples in Mark', pp. 392-93.

58. Best, 'The Role of the Disciples', pp. 390-93.

59. John Schmidt, 'Women in Mark's Gospel: An Early Christian View of Women's Role', *The Bible Today* 19 (July 1981), pp. 228-33 (230-31).

60. Munro, 'Women Disciples in Mark?', pp. 234-35.

61. Malbon, 'Fallible Followers', p. 30.

62. Malbon, 'Fallible Followers', p. 33.

Having studied the verbs linked with discipleship, I conclude that the 'following' offered to everyone entails 'serving' in the sense of 'life-giving' suffering. 'Service to everybody' is inclusive and life-giving, while 'rule by power' is exclusive and not of any life-giving value in itself. In Mark, 'serving' is applied only to women, from the beginning of the story (1.31) to its end (15.41). So, returning to 15.40, we can only conclude that the women depicted by Mark are the true disciples of Jesus in the sense that they are ready for devoting themselves to 'life-giving' suffering. Thus, the women disciples keep challenging those who avoid joining the struggles of the oppressed. The women disciples continue to disturb churches that seek patriarchal honor and hierarchical authority. So it should be implied that the discipleship of 'following and serving' has the power to regenerate a true community of faith. Women and men are both asked to respond to the challenge of praxis so that we may become a church in its deepest sense.

SLAVES, SERVANTS AND PROSTITUTES:
GENDER AND SOCIAL CLASS IN MARK

Kathleen E. Corley

The Gospel evidence strongly suggests that Jesus had women disciples who traveled on the road with him as well as joined him for meals. This has become the consensus of several historical Jesus scholars. Others remain unconvinced.[1] There is one major early Gospel tradition which identifies by name the women traveling companions of Jesus, the Gospel of Mark. At least three of these women, Mary Magdalene, Mary the mother of James and Joses, and Salome, are described as having traveled with Jesus from the beginnings of his ministry in Galilee.

The Markan material also shows that the presence of women among Jesus' followers was a controversial characteristic of Jesus' movement. Mark records both that Jesus was accused of reclining at table with 'tax collectors and sinners' (Mk 2.14-17; see also Q [Lk. 7.34]) and that a group of women 'followed and served' Jesus throughout his ministry (Mk 15.40-41). The descriptions of these women suggest that at least Mary Magdalene and Salome came from the lower classes and were either working women, hired servants, slaves or runaway slaves, not wealthier women as Lk. 8.1-3 suggests.

Women Who Follow and Serve (Mark 15.40-41)

Discussions of women in Mark's narrative generally begin with Mk 15.40-41. This pericope connects women not only to Jesus' disciples, [2]

1. For example, E.P. Sanders, who doubts women traveled with Jesus, and if they did, it was only rarely. Women played primarily supporting roles in the movement. E.P. Sanders, *The Historical Figure of Jesus* (London: Penguin, 1993), p. 110.

2. Winsome Munro was the first to argue that Mark portrays these women as disciples, although he leaves mentioning them to the end of his story. See Winsome Munro, 'Women Disciples in Mark?', *CBQ* 44 (1982), pp. 225-41. Others argue that Mark positions the women at the end of the story as positive foils to the

but to meals with Jesus.[3] The lists of the women vary among Mk 15.40-41 (three women), 15.47 (two women), and 16.1 (three women). This suggests that some source may lie behind these stories, or perhaps separate pre-Markan traditions.[4] Certain scholars argue that Mark utilized an earlier Passion source and thus shares traditional material with the Gospel of John.[5] Most, however, argue that the reference to the women comes from the hand of the evangelist.[6]

unbelieving male disciples. See Mary Ann Beavis, 'Women as Models of Faith in Mark', *BTB* 18 (1988), pp. 3-9; Joanna Dewey, *Disciples on the Way: Mark on Discipleship* (Women's Division, Board of Global Ministries, UMC, 1976), pp. 123-37; *eadem*, 'The Gospel of Mark', in Elisabeth Schüssler Fiorenza (ed.), *Searching the Scriptures*, II (New York: Crossroad, 1994), pp. 470-509, esp. p. 506; Joseph A. Grassi, 'The Secret Heroine of Mark's Drama', *BTB* 18 (1988), pp. 10-15; Jane Kopas, 'Jesus and Women in Mark's Gospel', *Review for Religious* 44 (1985), pp. 912-20; Elizabeth Struthers Malbon, 'Fallible Followers: Women in the Gospel of Mark', *Semeia* 28 (1983), pp. 29-48; *eadem*, *Narrative Space*, pp. 35-37; Marla J. Schierling, 'Women as Leaders in the Markan Community', *Listening* 15 (1980), pp. 250-56; J.J. Schmidt, 'Women in Mark's Gospel: An Early Christian View of Women's Role', *Bible Today* 19 (1981), pp. 228-33; Marla Selvidge, 'And Those Who Followed Feared (Mk 10:32)', *CBQ* 45 (1983), pp. 396-400. Others concurring with this general appraisal of Mk 15.40-41 include Witherington, Moltmann-Wendel, Stagg, Swider and Fiorenza. Before Munro's article, the scholarly consensus was that the women in Mk 15.40-41 were not disciples, but present only for menial purposes. See, for example, Howard Clark Kee, *Community of the New Age: Studies in Mark's Gospel* (Philadelphia: Westminster Press, 1977), pp. 152ff. For a recent discussion, see Hisako Kinukawa, *Women and Jesus in Mark: A Japanese Feminist Perspective* (Maryknoll, NY: Orbis Books, 1994), pp. 90-106.

    3.   Corley, *Private Women, Public Meals: Social Conflict in the Synoptic Tradition* (Peabody, MA: Hendrickson, 1993), pp. 84-86.

    4.   So Rudolph Bultmann, *History of the Synoptic Tradition* (trans. J. Marsh; Oxford: Basil Blackwell; New York: Harper & Row, 2nd edn, 1968 [1963]), p. 276; Kinukawa, *Women and Jesus in Mark*, p. 92; Martin Dibelius, *From Tradition to Gospel* (Greenwood, SC: Attic Press, 1982), pp. 190-92; Frank J. Matera, *The Kingship of Jesus: Composition and Theology in Mark 15* (Chico, CA: Scholars Press, 1982), p. 51.

    5.   So Rudolf Bultmann, *Gospel of John: A Commentary* (Philadelphia, PA: Westminster Press, 1971), pp. 666-67. In his *History of the Synoptic Tradition*, he remarks that the reference to the women is patently unhistorical, both here and in Mk 15.47. The women are only mentioned because the men are not available (pp. 274-75). Some scholars argue that the reference is traditional, from a pre-Markan Passion account, and/or historical. See C.K. Barrett, *The Gospel According to John* (London: SPCK, 1978), p. 551; Raymond E. Brown, *The Death of the Messiah: A Commentary on the Passion Narratives in the Four Gospels*, II (New York: Doubleday, 1994), pp. 1194-96; Anton Dauer, *Passionsgeschichte im Johannesevangelium* (Munich: Kasel-Verlag, 1972), pp. 194-95; Gerd Lüdemann, *Resurrection of Jesus: History, Experience, Theology* (Minneapolis: Fortress Press, 1994), p. 160.

    6.   For a list of views, see Brown, *Death of the Messiah*, II, pp. 1516-17; Joel B.

The abruptness of Mk 15.40-41 supports the view that the reference to the women is pre-Markan. In neither John nor Mark do the women listed here play further important roles. Moreover, the lists of the women in both Gospels do show some correspondence (Mk 15.40; Jn 19.25). However, given that lists of two and, especially, three are common in folk narratives and oral storytelling,[7] the variations in Mark's Gospel may be accounted for on the basis of simple narrative style rather than pre-Markan texts.[8]

Like their male counterparts, the women form a subset of Jesus' followers with a triumvirate core (Peter, James and John/Mary Magdalene, Mary the Mother of James and Joses, Salome). Like the men, the women flee, show fear of epiphany, and do not do what they are told.[9] These women are said both to 'follow' (ἀκολουθέω) Jesus and to 'serve' (διακονέω) him, along with 'many others' (ἄλλαι πολλαί).[10] Thus, like the male disciples, at least three women followed Jesus while he was in Galilee and then to Jerusalem. In Mark the three named women are clearly distinguished from the 'many other women' (Mk 15.41b) who join Jesus for his final journey to Jerusalem. The many others are no doubt among those women who traveled to

Green, *Death of Jesus: Tradition and Interpretation in the Passion Narrative* (Tübingen: J.C.B. Mohr, 1988), p. 295. See also Adela Yarbro Collins, 'Composition of the Markan Passion Narrative', *Sewanee Theological Review* 36 (1992), pp. 57-77, esp. p. 76; *eadem, Beginning of the Gospel: Probings of Mark in Context* (Minneapolis: Fortress Press, 1992), pp. 116-17; John Dominic Crossan, *The Cross That Spoke: The Origins of the Passion Narrative* (San Francisco: Harper & Row, 1988), pp. 281-90; *idem, Who Killed Jesus? Exposing the Roots of Anti-Semitism in the Gospel Story of the Death of Jesus* (San Francisco: HarperSanFrancisco, 1995), p. 171; Matera, *Kingship of Jesus*, p. 52.

7.   Axel Olrik, 'Epic Laws of Folk Narrative', in Alan Dundes (ed.), *The Study of Folklore* (Engelwood Cliffs, NJ: Prentice–Hall, 1965), pp. 129-41, esp. pp. 133-34.

8.   Mark likes lists of two and three. See Matera, *Kingship of Jesus*, pp. 50-51.

9.   Malbon, 'Fallible Followers'. Also David Catchpole, 'The Fearful Silence of the Women at the Tomb: A Study in Markan Theology', *Journal of Theology for Southern Africa* 18 (1977), pp. 3-10; Grassi, 'Secret Heroine', p. 14; Kinukawa, *Women and Jesus in Mark*, p. 95; Munro, 'Women Disciples in Mark', pp. 230-311; Luise Schottroff, *Let the Oppressed Go Free: Feminist Perspectives on the New Testament* (Louisville, KY: Westminster/John Knox Press, 1983), p. 101; Selvidge, 'Those Who Followed Feared'; R. Tannehill, 'The Disciples in Mark: The Function of Mark', (Philadelphia: Fortress Press, 1985), p. 152; M.A. Tolbert, 'Mark', in Newsom and Ringe (eds.), *The Women's Bible Commentary*, pp. 263-74, esp. p. 273.

10.   Dewey, *Disciples on the Way*, p. 123ff.; Malbon, 'Fallible Followers', pp. 40ff.; Munro, 'Women Disciples', pp. 230ff. So also Kopas, 'Jesus and Women', pp. 912ff.; Schmitt, 'Women in Mark's Gospel', pp. 231-32; and Schierling, 'Women as Leaders', pp. 252ff.

Jerusalem for yearly festivals like the Passover.[11] However, the suggestion that crowds of women flocked with Jesus to Jerusalem may be an exaggeration.[12] Traditional evidence for the presence of even a few women among Jesus' entourage could have been perceived by Mark as a crowd. John records no such crowd of women (see Jn 19.25).

Mark's list of women is probably the earliest, and the source for Mt. 27.55-56, Lk. 8.1-3 and Jn 19.25. Matthew's list is most easily argued to be dependent on Mark's.[13] In fact, Matthew enhances the role of the women at the cross as disciples by moving forward Mark's reference to the large group of women (γυναῖκες πολλαί; Mt. 27.55, cf. Mk 15.41b), whose position he underscores with an emphatic αἵτινες in place of the Markan αἵ.[14] The lists of women in John and Luke often considered independent of Mark can also be argued as stemming from Mk 15.40-41. Gender analysis reveals it unlikely that John preserves an independent witness to the women at the crucifixion.[15] For example, in John's list of the women at the cross, Mary Magdalene is named last, rather than being in her usual primary position. This presupposes the Markan list and serves to weaken her importance (Jn 19.25; cf. 15.40, 47; 16.1). Further, the nearness of the women to the cross and the emphasis on Jesus' mother are often considered Johannine constructions, theologically motivated and historically implausible.[16] Next, John has apparently expanded a list of three women into four to correspond to the four soldiers (Jn 19.23).[17] And while John

11. Eduard Schweizer argues that Matthew limits even the three named women's travel to the final journey to Jerusalem. See his *Good News According to Matthew* (trans. D.E. Green; Atlanta: John Knox Press, 1975), p. 518. Gundry argues that Matthew's use of ἀπό (the women travel with Jesus 'from' Galilee), not ἐν ('in') Galilee (cf. Mk 15.41b; Mt. 27.55) does not limit their travel to the final journey, but emphasizes their accompanying Jesus to the cross. See Robert Gundry, *Matthew: A Commentary on His Literary and Theological Art* (Grand Rapids: Eerdmans, 1982), p. 578. So also E. Wainwright, *Towards a Feminist Critical Reading of the Gospel According to Matthew* (BZNW, 60; Berlin: W. de Gruyter, 1991), p. 297; Corley, *Private Women, Public Meals*, p. 172.

12. Against Kinukawa, *Women and Jesus*, p. 94.

13. Wainwright, *Towards a Feminist Reading*, p. 297.

14. Gundry, *Matthew*, p. 578; see also Wainwright, *Towards a Feminist Reading*, p. 294.

15. Kathleen E. Corley, 'Women and the Crucifixion and Burial of Jesus', *Forum* NS 1.1 (1998), pp. 209-10.

16. Corley, 'Crucifixion and Burial,' pp. 209-10.

17. See Richard Atwood, *Mary Magdalene in the New Testament Gospels and Early Tradition* (New York: Peter Lang, 1993), pp. 60-61; Barrett, *John*, pp. 551-52; P. Benoit, *The Passion and Resurrection of Jesus Christ* (New York: Herder & Herder,

clearly mentions Jesus' mother as traveling with Jesus and the other disciples (Jn 2.12), Mary Magdalene is conspicuous by her absence earlier in the narrative. This is a further indication that John wishes to limit the significance of Mary Magdalene.[18]

Luke 8.1-3 can also be argued to be redaction of Mk 15.40-41.[19] First, Luke omits any reference to the names of the women at the crucifixion scene proper, preferring to generalize the group of women gathered to view Jesus' death. Further, Luke adds a group of men to those witnessing the crucifixion: male dining companions (lit. 'friends', οἱ γνωστοί) join the group of (unnamed) women (Lk. 23.49).[20] In Luke these women are part of a larger group that includes men and women, but they are no longer part of a separate special group of women disciples. In fact, the key correspondence between Mk 1.17 and 15.41 that allows for the discipleship of the women in Mark all but disappears in Luke.[21]

The absence of the women's names in Lk. 23.49, combined with the use of διακονέω, 'to serve', in Lk. 8.1-3, makes it highly likely that Luke has split Mk 15.40-41 into two sections: Lk. 23.49, where a group of unnamed women 'follow' Jesus (συνακολουθέω) at a distance at the crucifixion; and Lk. 8.1-3, where a group of named women and 'many others' (ἕτεραι πολλαί, cf. Mk 15.41) join Jesus and the Twelve during their travels in the cities and villages of Galilee.[22] These women 'minister' or 'provide' (διακονέω) for not only Jesus (as in Mk 15.41), but also the Twelve out of their personal resources (ἐκ τῶν ὑπαρχόντων αὐταῖς).[23] Luke also includes a list of three women at the scene of the

1969), p. 189; Brown, *Death of the Messiah*, II, pp. 1014-15, 1018-19; Barnabas Lindars, *The Gospel of John* (London: Oliphants, 1972), p. 579; Ben Witherington, *Women in the Ministry of Jesus: A Study of Jesus' Attitudes to Women and their Roles as Reflected in His Earthly Life* (Cambridge: Cambridge University Press, 1984), p. 120.

18. Corley, 'Crucifixion and Burial', pp. 209-10.

19. See Corley, *Private Women, Public Meals*, pp. 110-19; Jane Schaberg, 'Luke', in Newsom and Ringe (eds.), *Woman's Bible Commentary*, pp. 275-92 (286); Turid Karlsen Seim, *The Double Message: Patterns of Gender in Luke–Acts* (Nashville: Abingdon Press, 1994), pp. 25-26, esp. p. 28; *idem*, 'The Gospel of Luke', in Elizabeth Schüssler Fiorenza (ed.), *Searching the Scriptures: A Feminist Commentary* (2 vols.; New York: Crossroad, 1993, 1994), II, pp. 728-62, esp. p. 734.

20. Corley, *Private Women, Public Meals*, pp. 111, 114.

21. J.A. Grassi, *Hidden Heroes of the Gospels: Female Counterparts of Jesus* (Collegeville, MN: Liturgical Press, 1989), pp. 85ff.

22. So also Seim, *Double Message*, p. 28.

23. The plural is well supported by the Alexandrian, Western and Caesarean text types. The singular αὐτῷ may reflect the influence of Mt. 13.4 and Mk 4.4 and a christocentric correction by Marcion. The editors of both the UBS and NA

empty tomb (Lk. 24.10) — Mary Magdalene, Mary (mother) of James and Joanna — but the occurrence of Mary (mother) of James shows Luke's reliance on Mk 16.1 at this point, not Mk 15.40-41.

In 8.1-3, Luke reworks Mk 15.40-41 rather than relies on special material. The services of the women are presented as acts of charity. The women are not table servants as in Mark, but more akin to Greco-Roman patronesses. Luke's shift serves to limit women's service (διακονέω) to charity, while restricting them from leadership roles (διακονία, 'service') reserved for men.[24] His narrative thus further reinforces a distinction between the women and the all male Twelve in 8.1-3.

One of these women, named Joanna, is described as being married to a steward of Herod's court. This does not indicate that she is an elite woman; she is rather a member of what would be called the retainer class. Retainers were dependent upon the aristocracy for their wealth,[25] and stewards of large households like that of Herod were commonly slaves or freedmen.[26] It is possible that Joanna could be the wife of a highly placed slave or freedman in Herod's court.[27] The name Chuza occurs in Nabatean and Syrian inscriptions in Aramaic as *Kuza*, which suggests an Aramean connection. Possibly Chuza, by means of his position at court, 'married up' by wedding a wealthier Hebrew

---

editions prefer the plural reading, and the editors of the UBS rate their decision with a {B}. See Bruce M. Metzger, *A Textual Commentary on the Greek New Testament* (London: United Bible Societies, 1971), p. 144; Corley, *Private Women, Public Meals*, p. 110, esp. n. 7; Schaberg, 'Luke', p. 287; Seim, *Double Message*, pp. 62-64; *idem*, 'Gospel of Luke', p. 739; Witherington, *Women in the Ministry*, p. 119.

24. Corley, *Private Women, Public Meals*, pp. 116-19; and now also see Seim, *Double Message*, pp. 85-88.

25. Kathleen Corley, 'Jesus' Table Practice: Dining with "Tax Collectors and Sinners", Including Women', in Eugene Lovering (ed.), *Society of Biblical Literature 1993 Seminar Papers* (Atlanta: Scholars Press, 1993), pp. 444-59, esp. pp. 452, 457.

26. On slavery in antiquity and the mixture of slaves and free among the classes most often represented in the New Testament, see Corley, *Private Women, Public Meals*, pp. 32-33 n. 46; for slave stewards, pp. 48-49 n. 128. For slave stewards/overseers in Palestine, see Gildas Hamel, *Poverty and Charity in Roman Palestine. First Three Centuries* (Berkeley: University of California Press, 1990), p. 152; see also especially Averil Cameron, 'Neither Male Nor Female', *Greece and Rome* 27 (1980), pp. 60-68.

27. Josephus records that slaves and freedmen were common in Herodian courts. See, e.g., *War* 1.33.9; E.E. Urbach, 'The Laws Regarding Slavery as a Source for Social History of the Period of the Second Temple, the Mishnah and the Talmud', in J.G. Weiss (ed.), *Papers of the Institute of Jewish Studies London* (Jerusalem: Magnes Press, 1964), I, pp. 1-94 (31).

free woman. Luke may thus intend for us to understand that the money Joanna contributes is her own.

This description of the women as philanthropists conforms to Luke's interest in portraying Jesus' group and the early church as a more highly placed movement. According to Luke even Jesus is no longer an artisan or carpenter, but spends much of his time lounging about with the rich.[28] Yet in Luke the Jesus movement and the early church are by no means upper class.[29] These named women are not in the category of the aristocracy, which means that their presence on the road with Jesus is not as scandalous as is usually supposed. Luke gives no indication that their presence is controversial or unusual,[30] in contrast to the clear overtones of scandal in the story about the sinful woman (Lk. 7.36-50).[31] The shift from the language of table service (in Mark) to that of charitable service (in Luke) also erases undertones of scandal present in Mk 15.40-41 that connects the women to meals, domestic service and the lower classes. This overall description of

28. See George Wesley Buchanan, 'Jesus and the Upper Class', *NovT* 7 (1964/65), pp. 195-209; Joel B. Green, 'Good News to Whom? Jesus and the "Poor" in the Gospel of Luke', in Joel B. Green and Max Turner (eds.), *Jesus of Nazareth: Lord and Christ. Essays on the Historical Jesus and New Testament Christology* (Grand Rapids: Eerdmans, 1994), pp. 59-74; E.A. Judge, 'The Early Christians as a Scholastic Community', *JRH* 1 (1960), pp. 4-15, esp. pp. 9-11.

29. See Richard Pervo, *Profit with Delight: The Literary Genre of the Acts of the Apostles* (Philadelphia: Fortress Press, 1987), pp. 40, 77ff., 106. See also Joseph Fitzmyer, *The Gospel According to Luke I–IX* (AB, 28; New York: Doubleday, 1981), p. 698; Carla Ricci, *Mary Magdalene and Many Others: Women Who Followed Jesus* (trans. Paul Burns; Minneapolis: Fortress Press, 1994), p. 155; Schaberg, 'Luke', p. 287; Schottroff, *Let the Oppressed*, pp. 65, 92, 131-36; Fiorenza, *In Memory of Her: A Feminist Theological Reconstruction of Christian Origins* (New York: Crossroad, 1985), p. 140; Seim, *Double Message*, p. 38; *idem*, 'Gospel of Luke', pp. 735, 741-42; Ben Witherington, 'On the Road with Mary Magdalene, Joanna, and Other Disciples—Luke 8.1-3', *ZNW* 70 (1979), pp. 243-48, esp. p. 246. Witherington considers this pericope to have historical value despite its Lukan compositional characteristics. See *Women in the Ministry*, p. 116. Luise Schottroff, *Lydia's Impatient Sisters: A Social History of Early Christianity* (trans. B. Rumscheidt and M. Rumscheidt; Louisville, KY: Westminster/John Knox Press, 1995), p. 210, argues that the women gave not only financial resources (which may have been limited), but love and physical labor.

30. Schaberg, 'Luke', p. 287; Seim, *Double Message*, pp. 38-39. See also Luise Schottroff, 'Women as Followers of Jesus in the New Testament: Exercise in Social-Historical Exegesis of the Bible', in N.K. Gottwald (ed.), *The Bible and Liberation: Politics and Social Hermeneutics* (Maryknoll, NY: Orbis Books, 1983), pp. 418-27, esp. p. 420. Against Witherington, *Women in the Ministry*, p. 117.

31. Corley, *Private Women, Public Meals*, pp. 121-30.

Jesus' women followers as able to support the movement financially (8.1-3) shows Luke's bias and is unlikely to be historical.

The only name common to Lk. 8.1-3 and Mk 15.40-41 is Mary Magdalene, which no doubt remained fixed in the tradition.[32] Joanna and Susanna should be seen as Luke's additions;[33] they may have been names of prominent women in his own community or chosen for literary reasons. Joanna, a Hebrew name, is attested for Hellenistic Palestine (at least eight times).[34] Outside of its use here and in the story of Susanna in the Apocrypha, the Hebrew name Susanna only occurs for Hellenistic Jewish women in two inscriptions from Italy.[35] Luke 8.1-3 thus provides little historical information about the actual names, status or situation of the women who followed Jesus. Of the two named women not found in Mark, Joanna is more likely to have been an historical follower. The inscriptional evidence renders the reality of Susanna unlikely.

In sum, Mark lists three women by name who were known to follow Jesus from Galilee, that is, from the very beginnings of his ministry: Mary Magdalene, Mary the mother of James and Joses, and Salome (15.40-41). The other women, if not Markan exaggeration, seem only to have journeyed with Jesus for his last visit to Jerusalem (15.41). Matthew lists Mary Magdalene, Mary the mother of James and Joseph, and the mother of the sons of Zebedee (Mt. 27.55-56). John expands this list into four, including Jesus' mother, Jesus' aunt, Mary (wife) of Clopas and Mary Magdalene.[36] At Mk 15.47 and 16.1, Mark varies the name of the second Mary by listing her as Mary (mother) of Joses and Mary (mother) of James respectively. Matthew simplifies this to 'the other Mary' (Mt. 27.62; 28.1).

---

32. So Schaberg, 'Luke', p. 286; see also Seim, *Double Message*, p. 32; *idem*, 'Gospel of Luke', pp. 734-35.

33. Seim, *Double Message*, p. 28.

34. Tal Ilan, 'Notes on the Distribution of Jewish Women's Names in Palestine in the Second Temple and Mishnaic Periods', *JJS* 40 (1989), pp. 186-200, esp. p. 195; *idem, Jewish Women in Greco-Roman Palestine: An Inquiry into Image and Status* (Texte und Studien zum Antiken Judentum, 44; Tübingen: J.C.B. Mohr, 1995), pp. 53-55; Günter Mayer, *Die jüdische Frau in der hellenistische römischen Antike* (Stuttgart: W. Kohlhammer, 1987), pp. 103-104.

35. Ilan, 'Notes on the Distribution', p. 199; Mayer, *Die jüdische Frau*, p. 110. The name Susanna in particular is highly unlikely to come from a Palestinian source as Witherington suggests in *Women in the Ministry*, p. 117.

36. Atwood, *Mary Magdalene*, pp. 60-61; Barrett, *John*, pp. 551-52; Benoit, *Passion and Resurrection*, p. 189; Brown, *Death of the Messiah*, II, pp. 1014-15, 1018-19; Lindars, *Gospel of John*, p. 579.

Despite these apparent similarities in the lists,[37] it is unwise to conflate the names.[38] Nearly 50 per cent of the women in Second Temple Palestine were named either Mary (Mariamme) or Salome.[39] These may have been popular names due to their association with the Hasmonean family: girls named Salome could have been named after Queen Salome (Shalomzion) Alexandra, girls named Mariamme or Mary after Mariamme, Herod's beloved wife. Similarly, the names of five early Hasmoneans (John, Simon, Judas, Eleazar, Jonathan) and their father Mattathias account for nearly 40 per cent of men's names during the same period.[40] This reinforces the likelihood that Mark preserves the earliest and best list in terms of reflecting the Palestinian situation of Jesus by naming two Marys and one Salome. Luke may plausibly provide us with a fourth, Joanna.

The Identity of the Women

About these women Mark tells us little. Mary Magdalene is the most fixed woman disciple of Jesus in the tradition. She is named consistently in all four canonical Gospels as well as in the Gospels of Peter, Thomas, Mary and numerous other non-canonical texts. In Gnostic literature Mary Magdalene is arguably Jesus' closest companion and an active participant in dialogues between the disciples and the spiritual Christ.[41]

Mary's name indicates that she came from Magdala, a village on the northwest shore of the Sea of Galilee, about three miles north of Tiberias. The identification of Mary by a particular location, rather than, as is more common, by her family, father or husband, puts emphasis on the character of that location.[42] Magdala was one of the better-known fishing towns along the Sea of Galilee; Josephus calls it Tarichea, from the Greek for 'salted fish'. Josephus also mentions that the city had a hippodrome, which indicates its Hellenistic character.[43]

37. For a convenient chart, see Brown, *Death of the Messiah*, II, p. 1016.

38. For cautionary remarks, see George R. Beasley-Murray, *John* (WBC; Waco, TX: Word Books, 1987), p. 349; Rudolf Schnackenburg, *The Gospel According to John*, III (New York: Crossroad, 1982), pp. 276-77.

39. The high incidence of these two names throughout our sources, including Josephus, the New Testament, Rabbinic literature and inscriptions, makes the chances of statistical error slim. See Ilan, 'Notes on the Distribution', pp. 191-92.

40. Ilan, 'Notes on the Distribution', p. 192.

41. See Susan Haskins, *Mary Magdalene: Myth and Metaphor* (New York: Harcourt Brace, 1993), pp. 3-57; Karen L. King, 'The Gospel of Mary Magdalene', in Fiorenza (ed.), *Searching the Scriptures*, II, pp. 601-34, esp. pp. 617-20.

42. So Seim, *Double Message*, pp. 34-35.

43. Josephus's description of Magdala as having forty thousand inhabitants

Mark's record that many of Jesus' first male followers came from the ranks of fishermen who worked along the Sea of Galilee (Mk 1.16-20) and that Mary Magdalene was with Jesus from his earliest travels in Galilee (15.40-41) suggests that Mary was a fisherwoman herself.[44] Thus, it is reasonable to conclude on the basis of Mary Magdalene's town of origin that she met Jesus along the Sea of Galilee as did Simon Peter, Andrew, James and John (Mk 1.14-20).[45]

Women among the working poor practiced many kinds of trades in antiquity: shopkeepers, butchers, innkeepers, weavers, waitresses, shoemakers, prostitutes, professional mourners, musicians, and fishers. In rural areas they managed farms with their husbands, engaged in a trade or ran inns in their homes; in towns and cities women shared the responsibility of managing small businesses.[46] Women rarely earned enough to secure financial independence; poorer families usually required the labor of all family members to survive. In times of economic hardship, women could be forced into prostitution (presumably even by trade or barter)[47] or to sell their children.

Household work was often divided on the basis of gender: women frequently handled the management of the household and children, including grinding, baking, washing, cooking and textile production; in rural areas men worked more often in the fields (cf. Lk. 17.34-35; Mt. 24.40-41). This distinction was not absolute, however, as rural women and children also worked in the fields.[48] The realities of life for lower-class women contributed to the elite perception and devaluation of their character and led to the stereotyping of lower-class women

and a fleet of hundreds of fishing boats is probably an exaggeration, but does indicate that Magdala was well known as a fishing town. See *War* 2.21.3-4; 3.10.1; Jack Finegan, *Archaeology of the New Testament* (Princeton, NJ: Princeton University Press, 1992), pp. 81-82; Ricci, *Mary Magdalene*, p. 130.

44. So also now Schottroff, *Lydia's Impatient Sisters*, p. 84.

45. Schottroff, *Lydia's Impatient Sisters*, p. 84.

46. See Corley, *Private Women, Public Meals*, p. 14, esp. n. 55. For the many occupations of working women in Palestine, see Ilan, *Jewish Women*, pp. 184-90. See also Schottroff, 'Women Followers', pp. 420-21; *eadem, Let the Oppressed*, pp. 88-90; Fiorenza, *In Memory of Her*, pp. 127-28. For more on fisherwomen in antiquity, see Schottroff, *Lydia's Impatient Sisters*, p. 83.

47. Sarah B. Pomeroy, *Goddesses, Whores, Wives, and Slaves: Women in Classical Antiquity* (New York: Schocken Books, 1975), pp. 199-202; Schottroff, *Lydia's Impatient Sisters*, pp. 93-97; Satoko Yamaguchi, 'Re-Visioning Martha and Mary: A Feminist Critical Reading of a Text in the Fourth Gospel' (DMin Thesis, Episcopal Divinity School, 1996), p. 85.

48. Schottroff, *Lydia's Impatient Sisters*, pp. 79-84; Yamaguchi, 'Re-Visioning Mary', p. 83.

as promiscuous, whether this reputation was realized in the form of prostitution or not.[49] The association of Jesus with working-class women combined with at least one more highly placed woman could further explain the tradition associating him with 'sinners/prostitutes' (Mt. 21.31-32). A woman like Joanna, despite her slightly elevated social position, would have easily been labeled a whore for associating with other women and men beneath her station.[50] However, Mark gives no indication that Mary Magdalene or any of the women around Jesus are prostitutes.

The longer ending of Mark records that Mary Magdalene was a former demoniac (Mk 16.9), a tradition that Luke also repeats (Lk. 8.2). Jesus was known for his attentions to those characterized as demon possessed, which suggests that certain women in his company were healed of various mental illnesses or madness (Q 11.20). Despite this common association, however, no Gospel narrative depicts Jesus casting an evil spirit out of Mary Magdalene or any other woman, although Luke records Paul's exorcising a spirit of fortune-telling from a slave girl (Acts 16.16-18). Mary Magdalene's association with demon possession serves to connect her to frequent tomb visitation and contact with spirits of the dead (necromancy). In Mark, this designation devalues her witness to the resurrection and functions to bar her from the ranks of the Twelve, as is the Gerasene demoniac (cf. Mk 5.1-15).[51] Given that possession by gods or spirits was associated with prophetic powers, any portrayal of Jesus' women followers as so possessed was probably dangerous. Because Jesus himself was also thought to be mad (Jn 8.48; Mk 3.20-21) and possessed by a demon—the prince of demons, Beelzebul (Mk 3.22)—the charge of demon possession places Mary Magdalene not in the category of the Twelve, but that of Jesus or even John the Baptist (Q 7.33). Men with such characteristics were labeled 'prophet'.[52] This charge strongly suggests that Mary could also be identified not just as a follower of Jesus, but as a prophet later demoted in an early Christian tradition that also demoted John.[53] Jesus, John and Mary would then have all exhibited similar

---

49. Corley, *Private Women, Public Meals*, pp. 48-52.

50. Corley, *Private Women, Public Meals*, pp. 89-93. On 'sinners' as members of lower-class service occupations, see I. Abrahams, 'Publicans and Sinners', in his *Studies in Pharisaism and the Gospels* (New York: Ktav, 1967), pp. 54-61, esp. p. 55; Fiorenza, *In Memory of Her*, p. 128; Joachim Jeremias, *Jerusalem in the Time of Jesus* (Philadelphia: Fortress Press, 1969), ch. 14.

51. On tomb visitation and women see Corley, 'Women and the Crucifixion', pp. 181-96.

52. See Corley, 'Women and the Crucifixion', for women and necromancy.

53. On Mary's status as prophet, see Karen King, 'Prophetic Power and

erratic behavior at an early point in their lives.[54] If she were a prophet similar to Jesus and John, Mary's words and sayings are either lost or incorporated into the Jesus tradition itself.

Of the other two women Mark names we know even less. Mark probably intends for us to understand Mary the mother of James and Joses to be the mother of Jesus (cf. Mk 6.3). According to Mk 6.3 Mary also had two other sons, Jude and Simon, and an unspecified number of (unnamed) daughters. If this is the case, then her presence at the crucifixion with Mary Magdalene and her subsequent desertion of the tomb would contribute not only to Mark's theme of the failure of the disciples, but the theme of the failure of Jesus' family as well.[55] The association of this Mary with Jesus' mother in Mk 6.3 would also in part explain John's placement of Jesus' mother both at the cross (Jn 19.25) and among Jesus' retinue (Jn 2.12). The Acts of the Apostles does attest Mary's presence among the disciples (Acts 1.14), as do several extra-canonical works.[56]

The only other early information concerning Jesus' mother in Mark is that her son bore her name, not his father's: Jesus is a 'carpenter (or 'artisan', τέκτων), the son of Mary' (Mk 6.3). Several manuscripts, including 𝔓[45], read: 'Is this not the son of a carpenter (τοῦ τέκτονος υἱός or τοῦ τέκτονος ὁ υἱός) and Mary?'[57] The intent of the question is to underscore the ordinariness of Jesus' origins. He is the son of well-known locals.[58] The identification of Jesus by his mother's name could

Women's Authority: The Case of the Gospel of Mary (Magdalene)', in Beverly M. Kienzle and Pamela J. Walker (eds.), *Women Preachers and Prophets Through Two Millennia of Christianity* (Berkeley: University of California Press, 1998), pp. 21-41.

54. See Sanders on Jesus' probable erratic behavior, *Historical Figure*, p. 151.

55. See John Dominic Crossan, 'Mark and the Relatives of Jesus', *NovT* 15 (1973), pp. 81-113, esp. 105-10; Kinukawa, *Women and Jesus*, p. 92; Winsome Munro, 'Women Disciples: Light from Secret Mark', *JFSR* 9 (1992), pp. 47-64 (57). Against Gundry, *Mark: A Commentary on His Apology for the Cross* (Grand Rapids: Eerdmans, 1993), p. 977; Witherington, *Women in the Ministry*, p. 92.

56. *Acts of Pilate*, in M.R. James (ed.), *The Apocryphal New Testament* (Oxford: Clarendon Press, 1953), pp. 116-17; *Coptic Assumption of the Virgin*, in James (ed.), *Apocryphal New Testament*, pp. 196-97; *Book of the Resurrection of Christ* by Bartholomew the Apostle, in James (ed.), *Apocryphal New Testament*, p. 151. See Munro, 'Secret Mark', p. 57, esp. n. 33; Witherington, *Women in the Ministry*, p. 121.

57. The Palestinian Syriac simply omits ὁ τέκτων. The UBS edition rates their decision with an {A}. This may reflect early concern about Jesus' humble vocation (Metzger, *Textual Commentary*, p. 88), but the early reading in 𝔓[45] remains problematic. See Witherington, *Women in the Ministry*, p. 88.

58. There is no evidence that Joseph is dead. For this view, see Raymond E. Brown *et al.*, *Mary in the New Testament* (New York: Paulist Press, 1978), p. 64.

imply that Mary was from a higher social class or status than her husband or simply reflect her own status in the early church. It was common in Second Temple Judaism for a man to be known by his mother's name when his mother was of a higher rank than his father (status in antiquity was a matter of birth, not necessarily wealth). This designation may in part explain Luke's connection of Mary to a priestly family (Lk. 1–2) as well as later legends suggesting that Mary came from the city of Sepphoris rather than poorer Nazareth.[59] It might also suggest that Jesus came from a socially mixed background, which was not uncommon among the ranks of slaves, freedmen and the free poor.[60]

It is thus less likely that the designation 'the son of Mary' suggests illegitimacy.[61] This is not to deny that a first-century illegitimacy tradition concerning Jesus arose (cf. *Gos. Thom.* 105; Jn 8.41; Mt. 1), but the designation 'son of Mary' in Mk 6.3 need not be connected to it.[62] The canonical infancy narratives (Mt. 1–2; Lk. 1–2), which contain later legendary material about Jesus' birth, provide little further historical information about Jesus' mother. Later infancy Gospels, such as the *Protevangelium of James* or *Pseudo-Matthew*, give even less.[63]

59. This tradition is recorded about 570 CE by the Pilgrim Piacenze in his *Travels*. See Richard A. Batey, *Jesus and the Forgotten City: New Light on Sepphoris and the Urban World of Jesus* (Grand Rapids, MI: Baker Books, 1991), p. 20.

60. Corley, *Private Women, Public Meals*, pp. 32-33 n. 46; 48-49, 59 n. 208. See especially Cameron, 'Neither Male Nor Female'.

61. See esp. Tal Ilan, '"Man Born of Woman..." Job 14.1: The Phenomenon of Men Bearing Matronymes at the time of Jesus', *NovT* 34 (1992), pp. 23-45; but also Brown, *Mary in the New Testament*, pp. 63-64; Harvey K. McArthur, 'Son of Mary', *NovT* 15 (1973), pp. 38-58. So also Amy-Jill Levine, 'Matthew', in Newsom and Ringe (eds.), *Woman's Bible Commentary*, pp. 252-62, esp. p. 253; *eadem, The Social and Ethnic Dimensions of Matthean Salvation History* (Lewiston, NY: Edwin Mellen Press, 1988), pp. 63-88, esp. p. 87. Against Jane Schaberg, *The Illegitimacy of Jesus: A Feminist Theological Interpretation of the Infancy Narratives* (New York: Harper & Row, 1987), pp. 160-64; Robert Funk, *Honest to Jesus: Jesus for a New Millennium* (San Francisco: HarperSanFrancisco, 1996), follows Schaberg (p. 288); see also Dewey, 'Gospel of Mark', p. 482; Witherington, *Women in the Ministry*, p. 88.

62. Matthew's infancy story is clearly concerned about Mary's reputation. See Corley, *Private Women, Public Meals*, pp. 147-52; Schaberg, *Illegitimacy*, pp. 36-41, 145-94. Dewey reads 'son of Mary' as an insult to Jesus and his mother ('Gospel of Mark', p. 482).

63. On the infancy Gospels *Proto-James* and *Pseudo-Matthew*, see Oscar Cullmann, 'Infancy Gospels: The Protevangelium of James', in E. Hennecke and W. Schneemelcher (eds.), *New Testament Apocrypha* (Philadelphia: Westminster Press, rev. edn, 1991), I, pp. 421-69; Ronald F. Hock, *The Infancy Gospels of James and Thomas* (Santa Rosa, CA: Polebridge Press, 1995); Jane Schaberg, 'The Infancy of

After Mary Magdalene, Salome is the most often-mentioned woman disciple of Jesus in early Christian literature. *The Secret Gospel of Mark* associates her with Jesus' family;[64] she appears in the *Gospel of Thomas* 61 on a dining couch with Jesus, and like Mary Magdalene she engages in dialogues with Jesus in extra-biblical sources, most notably in the *Gospel of the Egyptians* quoted by Clement of Alexandria.[65] In a 'Q-like' section of the *Manichaean Psalms*, Salome joins Mary Magdalene and other women in a group of wandering, ascetic itinerants.[66] Later stories which identify a Salome as Mary's midwife are no doubt legendary.[67]

It seems reasonable to conclude that two women named Salome and Mary Magdalene traveled with Jesus and were among his closest followers. They are joined by Jesus' mother. Mark's theme of enmity between Jesus and his family serves to discredit the role of women, and especially Jesus' mother, among the disciples.[68] This further suggests that Mark preserves a tradition about women disciples in 15.40-41 with which he is uncomfortable but cannot deny.[69] Mark underscores their discipleship by his use of 'follow' (ἀκολουθέω) and 'serve' (διακονέω). The two Marys and Salome follow and serve Jesus from the time of his early ministry in Galilee.

Service and Social Class
Behind this description of the women's discipleship lies an undercurrent of discomfort. This same description of discipleship likens the women's activity to that of slaves, hirelings or table servants. First, slaves or servant women would characteristically 'follow' (ἀκολουθέω) along behind their master, as would a female lover or sex slave.[70] A

Mary of Nazareth', in E.S. Fiorenza (ed.), *Searching the Scriptures: A Feminist Introduction* (2 vols.; New York: Crossroad, 1993, 1994), II, pp. 708-27, esp. p. 718.

64. Frag. 2 (III. 16). See Munro, 'Secret Mark'.

65. Clement of Alexandria, *Misc.* 3.45, 64, 66, 68, 91-97; *Excerpta ex Theodoti* 67.

66. *Manichaean Psalms* 191.21ff. and 194.19-22 in C.R.C. Allberry, *A Manichaean Psalmbook, Part 2* (Stuttgart: W. Kohlhammer, 1938). See Richard Bauckman, 'Salome the Sister of Jesus, Salome the Disciple of Jesus, and the Secret Gospel of Mark', *NovT* 33 (1991), pp. 245-75, esp. p. 263; Kathleen E. Corley, 'Salome', *ISBE*, IV, p. 286.

67. *Protevangelium of James* 20; Bauckman, 'Salome', pp. 249-53; Corley, 'Salome', p. 286; Cullman, 'Infancy Gospels', pp. 434-35; Schaberg, 'Infancy of Mary of Nazareth', p. 726; also C. Trautman, 'Salomè l'incrèdule: rècits d'une conversion', in *Ecritures et traditions dans la litèrature copte: Journée d'études coptes, Strasbourg, 28 mai 1982* (Cahiers de la bibliothèque copte 1; Louvain: Peeters, 1983), pp. 61-72.

68. See Crossan, 'Mark and the Relatives'; Munro, 'Secret Mark', pp. 56-58; Tolbert, 'Mark', p. 271.

69. So Munro, 'Women Disciples' and 'Secret Mark', p. 58.

70. G. Kittel, 'Ακολουθέω', *TDNT*, I, p. 10.

quote from Philostratus's *Life of Apollonius* (1.20) makes this image clear:

> And as they fared on into Mesopotamia, the tax-gatherers (τελῶνες) who presided over the Bridge led them to the registry and asked them what they were taking out of the country with them. And Apollonius replied: 'I am taking with me temperance, justice, virtue, continence, valor, discipline (σωφροσύνην, δικαιοσύνην, ἀρετήν, ἐγκράτειαν, ἀνδρείαν, ἄσκησιν).' And in this way he strung together a number of feminine nouns or names. The other, already scenting his own perquisites, said, 'You must then write down in the register these female slaves (τὰς δούλας)'. And Apollonius answered, 'Impossible, for they are not female slaves that I am taking with me, but ladies of quality (δεσποίνας)'.[71]

The tax collector's assumption is that a large number of women traveling with a man in this manner would be his slaves. Apollonius' response underscores that a man's traveling companions could stereotypically be characterized as slaves and therefore as unvirtuous women. His witty remark is nonsensical apart from this underlying connection between slave women and promiscuity. Thus, the women in Mk 15.40-41 could easily be mistaken by an ancient reader, not as disciples, but sexually available slaves. It cannot be ruled out that either Mary Magdalene or Salome is a servant, runaway slave or a hireling of Jesus or of his family, or a servant escort of his mother,[72] especially since ordinary travelers were rarely without at least one servant.[73] In fact, Mark is careful to distinguish between Jesus' women disciples and women like Herodias and her daughter, whom Mark portrays as a 'mother, madame and courtesan' offspring in a fictional scene laden with Greco-Roman banquet stereotypes.[74] This makes it improbable that the description of the women in Mk 15.40-41 is mere caricature.

Slave ownership and the use of domestic servants was common in Greco-Roman antiquity. Many peasant households owned at least one male/boy slave or maidservant, who was sexually available to all men in the household, as well as to visitors.[75] Like all slaves in antiquity,

71. F.C. Conybeare (trans.), *Philostratus: Life of Apollonius of Tyana* (LCL; Cambridge, MA: Heinemann, 1960).

72. So Gundry, *Mark*, p. 979; against Schottroff, *Lydia's Impatient Sisters*, p. 214.

73. Lionel Casson, *Travel in the Ancient World* (Baltimore, MD: The Johns Hopkins University Press, 1994), p. 76.

74. Corley, *Private Women, Public Meals*, pp. 93-95.

75. A.H.M. Jones, 'Slavery in the Ancient World', in *Slavery in Classical Antiquity* (Cambridge: W. Heffer & Sons, 1960), p. 1. For similar rabbinic statistics for Jewish

women slaves could be subjected to violence, rape and various forms of physical abuse.[76] Tasks assigned to slaves in either rural or urban households often followed along gender lines, but slave women could also serve as fieldhands, secretaries, household stewards, or managers.[77] They also worked in textile mills or other trades, or in brothels.[78] Finally slave women could engage in prostitution to earn extra money or their freedom. Slavery, poverty and high indebtedness among the lower classes were thus social realities linked in Greco-Roman antiquity.[79]

Although Jewish law put restrictions on the enslavement of other Jews, particularly Jewish males, Jewish families owned slaves as did

households, see E.E. Urbach, 'The Laws Regarding Slavery' as a source for Social History of the Period of the Second Temple, the Mishnah and the Talmud', in J.G. Weiss (ed.), *Papers of the Institute of Jewish Studies (London)*, I, (Jerusalem: Magnes Press, 1964), pp. 1-94 (32); Corley, *Private Women, Public Meals*, pp. 48-49. Against Seim, *Double Message*, p. 61.

76. See for example Seneca, *de Ira* 3.27.3; K.R. Bradley, *Slaves and Masters in the Roman Empire: A Study in Social Control* (New York: Oxford University Press, 1984), pp. 113-37. For a slave contract insuring the right of the new master to the physical punishment of the ten-year-old slave girl named Abaskantis, see S.R. Llewelyn and R.A. Kearsley, 'The Sale of a Slave Girl: The New Testament Attitude to Slavery', in *New Documents Illustrating Early Christianity*, VI (Macquarie University, Australia: Ancient History Documentary Research Centre, 1992), pp. 48-55, esp. p. 50. On young boy slaves, see Corley, *Private Women, Public Meals*, pp. 48-52.

77. Corley, *Private Women, Public Meals*, p. 15; Pomeroy, *Goddesses*, pp. 191-92; Schottroff, *Let the Oppressed*, p. 89; Yamaguchi, 'Re-Visioning Martha', p. 86. Yamaguchi notes Judith's appointment of a woman slave to manage her estate (Jdt. 8.10).

78. Corley, *Private Women, Public Meals*, pp. 48-52; Pomeroy, *Goddesses*, pp. 191-92; Schottroff, *Let the Oppressed*, p. 89; Yamaguchi, 'Re-visioning Martha', pp. 85-86.

79. John Dominic Crossan, *Historical Jesus: The Life of a Mediterranean Jewish Peasant* (San Francisco: HarperSanFrancisco, 1991), pp. 293-95; David Daube, *Roman Law: Linguistic, Social and Philosophical Aspects* (Edinburgh: Edinburgh University Press, 1969), pp. 92-94; Richard A. Horsley, *Jesus and the Spiral of Violence* (San Francisco: HarperSanFrancisco, 1987), pp. 232-33; Martin Goodman, 'The First Jewish Revolt: Social Conflict and the Problem of Debt', *JJS* 33 (1982), pp. 417-27; John S. Kloppenborg, 'Alms, Debt and Divorce: Jesus' Ethics in Their Mediterranean Context', *Toronto Journal of Theology* 6 (1990), pp. 182-200, esp. pp. 192-93; see also Isaac Mendelsohn, *Slavery in the Ancient Near East* (New York: Oxford University Press, 1949), pp. 5-19; Orlando Patterson, *Slavery and Social Death: A Comparative Study* (Cambridge, MA: Harvard University Press, 1982), pp. 124-26; Schottroff, 'Women as Followers', p. 423; *idem*, *Let the Oppressed*, p. 97. See also Paul Veyne, 'Slavery', in Paul Veyne (ed.), *A History of Private Life: From Pagan Rome to Byzantium* (Cambridge, MA: Belknap Press of Harvard University Press, 1987), p. 55; W.L. Westermann, *The Slave Systems of Greek and Roman Antiquity* (Philadelphia: American Philosophical Society, 1933), pp. 120-39.

other Greco-Roman people: the cultural values governing relationships between Jewish masters and slaves are virtually indistinguishable from their Hellenistic counterparts.[80] The presence of slavery in Palestine, although contested for apologetic reasons, is widely accepted as a plausible assumption.[81] Foreign slaves were cheap and easily available, although there is no evidence for the widespread use of slaves even for agricultural purposes.[82] Slave labor was therefore utilized on a smaller scale in Palestine, and then mostly for domestic service, as in Egypt.[83] Jesus' parables clearly reflect the presence of not only day laborers and tenants in Palestinian society, but also slaves, who more often served as household stewards. The parables use terms like δοῦλος, 'slave' (Mt. 18.23; Lk. 14.17; Mt. 21.34/Lk. 20.10; cf. *Gos. Thom.* 65; Lk. 19.13/Mt. 25.14), οἰκονόμος, 'steward' (Lk. 16.1), as well as γεωργός, 'tenant' (Mt. 21.34/Lk. 20.10; cf. *Gos. Thom.* 65), ἐργάτης, 'worker' (Mt. 20.1), and μίσθιος, 'hired laborer' (Lk. 15.17).[84]

Jews in Second Temple Palestine did hire and buy household or

80. Dale B. Martin, 'Slavery and the Ancient Jewish Family', in Shaye J.D. Cohen (ed.), *The Jewish Family in Antiquity* (Atlanta: Scholars Press, 1993), pp. 113-29; Ilan, *Jewish Women*, pp. 205-11; Corley, *Private Women, Public Meals*, pp. 58-59; Y.A. Solodukho, 'Slavery in the Hebrew Society of Iraq and Syria in the Second Through Fifth Centuries A.D.', in J. Neusner (ed.), *Soviet Views of Talmudic Judaism* (Leiden: E.J. Brill, 1973), pp. 1-9. Patterson demonstrates that manumission rates in antiquity were unaffected by developments in philosophy or religious perspective. See his *Slavery and Social Death*, pp. 273-93.

81. The standard discussion is Urbach, 'Laws Regarding Slavery', pp. 1-94; see also Paul V.M. Flesher, *Oxen, Women or Citizens? Slaves in the System of the Mishnah* (Atlanta, GA: Scholars Press, 1988); Goodman, 'First Jewish Revolt', p. 423, esp. n. 40; N.P. Lemche, 'The Manumission of Slaves—the Fallow Year—the Sabbatical Year—the Jubal Year', *VT* 26 (1976), pp. 38-59; Solodukho, 'Slavery in the Hebrew Society'; Solomon Zeitlin, 'Slavery During the Second Commonwealth and the Tannaitic Period', in *Studies in the Early History of Judaism, History of Early Talmudic Law* (New York: Ktav, 1978), pp. 225-69; J.P.M. Van der Ploeg, 'Slavery in the Old Testament', *VTSup* 22 (1971), pp. 72-87; F.M. Heichelheim, *An Economic Survey of Ancient Rome: Roman Syria* (Baltimore: The John Hopkins University Press, 1938); Mendelsohn, *Slavery in the Ancient Near East, passim*; Carolyn Osiek, 'Slavery in the Second Testament World', *BTB* 22 (1992), pp. 174-79. Against Urbach, see Joseph H. Heinemann, 'The Status of the Jewish Labourer in Jewish Law and Society in the Tannaitic Period', *HUCA* 25 (1954), pp. 263-325, esp. pp. 268-69.

82. Goodman, 'First Jewish Revolt', p. 421, esp. n. 29.

83. Heichelheim, *Economic Survey of Ancient Rome*, pp. 164-65; Goodman, 'First Jewish Revolt', p. 425; William L. Westermann, *The Slave Systems of Greek and Roman Antiquity* (Philadelphia: American Philosophical Society, 1933), p. 124.

84. See Hamel, *Poverty and Charity*, p. 163 n. 91; Osiek, 'Slavery', p. 177.

agricultural servants, especially Gentile slaves.[85] Thus, slave women in Palestine could be Gentile women owned by Jewish families, Jewish women sold to non-Jews, or Jewish women owned by Jewish families.[86] Traditionally, Gentile slaves were rarely manumitted, a prejudice that is likely to have persisted throughout the first century.[87] When increases in manumission did occur during the Second Temple period, the motivation was often the financial benefit of the owner, not the well being of the slave.[88] Josephus does not distinguish between Jewish and non-Jewish slaves—both are δοῦλοι.[89]

During times of impoverishment and crop failure, the self-sale of men, their children, or perhaps even their wives, was not uncommon.[90] Enslavement as a punishment for theft was also practiced.[91] Despite the tendency in Palestine towards the forfeiture of land and property as a means of settling debt, debt slavery was a reality.[92] This reality is reflected in Mt. 18.23-35. When a slave is unable to pay a king (his

85. On the duties of wives that could be transferred to their women slaves, see Hamel, *Poverty and Charity*, p. 112. See also Veyne, 'Slavery', p. 55.

86. See arguments by Ilan, *Jewish Women*, pp. 207-11.

87. Westermann, *Slave Systems*, p. 125; Urbach, 'Laws Regarding Slavery', p. 55.

88. Urbach, 'Laws Regarding Slavery', p. 47. Patterson documents a similar, contemporaneous trend in the fluctuations in the Roman slave market (*Slavery and Social Death*, p. 247). For a further discussion of manumission trends in the Augustan age, see Corley, *Private Women, Public Meals*, pp. 58-59. Late second-century Jewish manumission documents from Lower Russia mirror Delphic manumissions. See Westermann, *Slave Systems*, p. 125.

89. John G. Gibbs and Louis H. Feldman, 'Josephus' Vocabulary for Slavery', *JQR* 76 (1986), pp. 281-310, esp. p. 293.

90. At times of impoverishment, the biblical regulations fell into disuse. See Urbach, 'Laws Regarding Slavery', pp. 11-17; Klaus Baltzer, 'Liberation for Debt Slavery after the Exile in Second Isaiah and Nehemiah', in Patrick D. Miller *et al.* (eds.), *Ancient Israelite Religion: Essays in Honor of Frank Moore Cross* (Philadelphia: Fortress Press, 1987), pp. 477-84, esp. p. 481.

91. Exod. 22.1. See Josephus, *Ant.* 3.12.3 (282) and discussion by Urbach, 'Laws Regarding Slavery', pp. 18-19.

92. Goodman, 'First Jewish Revolt', p. 423; Zeitlin, 'Slavery', pp. 193-97. On solutions for cancellation of debts in Roman Palestine, including slavery, see also Hamel, *Poverty and Charity*, pp. 159-63; Horsley, *Spiral of Violence*, pp. 232-33; on the sale of children see Veyne, 'Slavery', p. 55; on the sale of children by slavewomen for the purposes of earning manumission, see Corley, *Private Women, Public Meals*, pp. 50-51. For documentary evidence on debt slavery in this geographical area, see Fritz M. Heichelheim, *Roman Syria*, in Allan C. Johnson (ed.), *An Economic Survey of Ancient Rome* (6 vols.; Baltimore: The Johns Hopkins University Press, 1930), IV, pp. 166-67 (165); M.I. Rostovtzeff and C. Bradford Welles, 'A Parchment Contract of Loan from Dura-Europos on the Euphrates', in Austin Harmon (ed.), *Yale Classical Studies* (New Haven: Yale University Press, 1931), II, pp. 3-78, esp. p. 67.

master) what he owes him, the king orders the slave, his wife, his children and all his belongings to be sold to pay the man's debts.[93]

Not usually considered in this discussion is the failure of Exod. 21.7-11 to require the manumission of Jewish girls six years after enslavement, although Deuteronomic legislation extended this privilege to women and girls (Deut. 15.12-18); girls could also be sold into concubinage, that is, as slave wives.[94] Although there is minimal evidence for the sale of Jewish girls by their families,[95] it seems likely that young girls would be far more affected by debt slavery than were boys or adult men.[96] Later *halakhic* sources assume the existence of slave women in Jewish households, as well as discuss their duties and the problems arising from their sexual availability.[97] It seems doubtful that girls sold in this manner would have been liberated when they came of age,[98] although women were more often manumitted than men elsewhere in the Roman world.[99] If liberated, they would be less valuable as marriage partners, due to the stain of their sexual availability during enslavement, whether realized or not.[100]

93. Discussion by Zeitlin, 'Slavery', p. 196; Osiek, 'Slavery', p. 177.

94. On the 'slave-wife' see N. Avigad, 'Epitaph of a Royal Steward from a Siloam Village', *IEJ* 3 (1953), pp. 137-52, esp. p. 146 n. 18; *idem*, 'A Seal of a Slave-Wife (*Amah*)', *PEQ* 78 (1946), pp. 125-32; Louis M. Epstein, *Marriage Laws in the Bible and the Talmud* (Cambridge, MA: Harvard University Press, 1942), pp. 34-76; Ilan, *Jewish Women*, p. 205; A. Jepson, 'Amah und Schiphchah', *VT* 8 (1958), pp. 293-97; Mendelsohn, *Slavery in the Ancient Near East*, pp. 50-55; I. Mendelsohn, 'The Conditional Sale into Slavery of Free-born Daughters in Nuzi and the Law of Exodus 21.7-11', *JAOS* 55 (1935), pp. 190-95; Van der Ploeg, 'Slavery in the Old Testament', p. 75. On distinctions between Exod. 21.7-11 and Deut. 15.12-18, see Lemche, 'Manumission', p. 44 and N.P. Lemche, 'The "Hebrew Slave": Comments on the Slave Law Ex 21.2-11', *VT* 25 (1975), pp. 9-144, esp. pp. 139, 143; also Sara Japhet, 'The Laws of Manumission of Slaves and the Question of the Relationship Between the Collections of Laws in the Pentateuch', in Yitschak Avishur and Joshua Blau (eds.), *Studies in the Bible and the Near East Presented to Samuel E. Lowenstamm* (Jerusalem: E. Rubinstein's Publishing House, 1978), pp. 199-201.

95. Goodman, 'First Jewish Revolt', p. 423, esp. n. 40.

96. Horsley, *Spiral of Violence*, pp. 232-33; Ilan, *Jewish Women*, p. 206. On the duties of wives transferred to a woman's slaves, see *m. Ketub.* 55; *t. Ketub.* 5.4; *b. Ketub.* 30a; Hamel, *Poverty and Charity*, p. 112; Yamaguchi, 'Re-Visioning Martha', pp. 85-86.

97. Ilan, *Jewish Women*, pp. 203-11.

98. Upon her death, Judith frees a slavewoman (Jdt. 16.23). See Ilan, *Jewish Women*, p. 205.

99. Further discussion in Corley, *Private Women, Public Meals*, pp. 50-51; now also Llewelyn and Kearsley, 'Manumission in Thessaly and at Delphi', in *eadem*, *New Documents Illustrating Early Christianity*, VI, pp. 76-81.

100. See Ilan, *Jewish Women*, pp. 205-11; Horsley, *Spiral of Violence*, pp. 232-33.

Notably, Simon b. Gioras' entourage included his wife and her attendants as well as runaway slaves, and his proclamation of slave emancipation was combined with a call for the abolition of debt.[101] Women slaves, even young girls, could run away from their masters; ancient novels portray wealthier women running away with their slaves from their husbands.[102] Jesus' admonition concerning the forgiveness of debts (Q 11.4) would thus have had direct significance for the well-being of not only impoverished families generally, but for the well-being of children, especially girls, who were probably the ones most often sold into slavery as a means to cancel family debts[103] or even to raise money for the purchase of farm animals and other household goods.[104] Slaves too could both owe debts and have debts to forgive (see Mt. 18.23-34).

It thus seems reasonable to suggest that at least one or more of the women described as being in Jesus' service in Mk 15.40-41 is a runaway slave or servant. Mary the mother of James and Joses, Jesus' mother, is unlikely to be a slave or servant; Mary Magdalene seems to be known for a trade. Of the women mentioned in Mk 15.40-41, Salome is the more likely to be a slave or domestic servant, given that she is closely associated with Jesus' family, but not identified as a family member in the *Secret Gospel of Mark* (Frag. 2, 3.16). Mark identifies 'table service' as Salome's occupation, although if she were a slave or hired servant she probably performed other services in the family as well. She could be both a servant and a disciple.

This suggestion does not detract from Salome's significance in the tradition as one of Jesus' disciples, but enhances it. For example, in light of the reputation of a slave's sexual availability and the fact that

---

101. Josephus, *War* 4.508; see Goodman, *Ruling Class*, pp. 204, 207.

102. In Lucian's *Fugitivi*, a female Cynic leaves her husband and runs away with two slaves. See Corley, *Private Women, Public Meals*, p. 63 n. 230. See also a Greek contract (P. Turner 22, 142 CE, Pamphylia) that insures the buyer that the ten-year-old slave girl Abaskantis will not run away; Llewelyn and Kearsley, 'Sale of a Slave Girl', p. 48. For a Syriac sale contract (Dura Pg. 20, May 243 CE, Edessa) making the potential loss from the flight of a 28-year-old slave woman named Amath-Sin the problem of the new owner, see Heichelheim, *Roman Syria*, pp. 166-67. The flight of slaves was not uncommon in antiquity; the classic early Christian case is Onesimus.

103. Horsley, *Spiral of Violence*, pp. 232-33; Ilan, *Jewish Women*, p. 206. On peasant indebtedness as a background for Jesus' interest in debts, see also Kloppenborg, 'Alms, Debt and Divorce', pp. 192-93; Douglas E. Oakman, *Jesus and the Economic Questions of His Day* (Lewiston, NY: Edward Mellen Press, 1986), pp. 72-80.

104. Urbach, 'Laws Regarding Slavery', p. 17.

women could be forced into prostitution due to economic hardship or to earn their freedom, the probability that Jesus' group included slave women would explain the accusation in Q that Jesus associated with or reclined at table with 'sinners/prostitutes' (Mk 2.16; Q 7.28-29). This accusation against Jesus suggests that he is lowering himself by eating with those beneath his station. If authentic, it calls into question the identification of Jesus as a peasant, at least a destitute or homeless one. Mark 6.3 and the description of the women disciples in Mk 15.40-41 thus may imply that Jesus had family ties to both the poorer working classes and a social class that was above the working class, either by means of wealth or status of birth, or by means of his earned prestige as a teacher/prophet (i.e. his popularity).[105]

This analysis also reveals it to be less likely that Jesus' women followers included actual prostitutes, given that such language functions as a form of slander and caricature, and not social description (Mt. 21.31-32). Rather, the Hellenistic evidence suggests that whether the women described in Mk 15.40-41 were slaves, runaway slaves, working class women, single or married, they could be equally undeserving of such blanket accusations of sexual promiscuity and prostitution.[106] Such an insult would have been particularly demeaning to Jesus' mother. The subjection of his mother to negative gender stereotyping due to the mixed company of her son's friends could also explain the stain upon her character present in early Christian tradition apart from assuming that Jesus' birth was illegitimate (cf. *Gos. Thom.* 105, 'child of a whore', πόρνη). It may be concern for Greco-Roman propriety that leads Mark to have the women stand 'from afar' during the crucifixion proper,[107] although he is probably influenced by literary precursors as well.[108] These women are probably waiting to perform the burial tasks often assigned to women.[109]

The language of this passage also suggests the presence of these women at meals with Jesus. 'Serve' (διακονέω) calls to mind the image

---

105. So Buchanan, 'Jesus and the Upper Class', and esp. Judge, 'Early Christianity', pp. 9-11.

106. Kathleen Corley, 'Were the Women Around Jesus Prostitutes?', in David Lull (ed.), *Women in the Context of Greco-Roman Meals* (SBLSP; Atlanta: Scholars Press, 1989), pp. 487-521 (521); *eadem*, *Private Women, Public Meals*, pp. 48-52. I am in essential agreement with Horsley, *Spiral of Violence*, p. 223. Against Schottroff, *Let the Oppressed*, p. 97; Luise Schottroff and Wolfgang Stegemann, *Jesus and the Hope of the Poor* (trans. M.J. O'Connell; Maryknoll, NY: Orbis Books, 1986), pp. 15-16; Fiorenza, *In Memory of Her*, pp. 121-22; *eadem*, *Jesus*, pp. 93-94.

107. Corley, *Private Women, Public Meals*, p. 86.

108. Corley, 'Women and the Crucifixion', pp. 196-202.

109. Corley, 'Women and the Crucifixion', pp. 181-96.

of women who serve Jesus at table, a task often assigned to household servants or slaves, or if there were no servants, to women or children in a household.[110] In large banquets of the wealthy, such table service was usually provided by handsome young male slaves.[111] In Mark, it is only women and angels who serve Jesus himself (Mk 1.29-31; 14.3-9), and even the angels are no doubt meant to serve Jesus by bringing him food at the end of his fast (Mk 1.13).[112] Mk 15.40-41 can thus be read as indicating that these women were present with Jesus for meals, at least as table servants. In combination with the tradition that Jesus ate with 'tax collectors and sinners' (Mk 2.17), we might conclude that the women joined Jesus for meals.

The convergence of the lower-class images of slavery, table service and sexuality in Mk 15.40-41 would not have been lost on audiences familiar with Greco-Roman meal protocol. In spite of these associations, Mark incorporates this description of the women into his larger theme of discipleship.[113] It is these overtones of scandal and the association of these women with the lower classes that Luke erases by raising the social rank of the women and characterizing their service as only philanthropy (Lk. 8.1-3).

Mark's depiction of these women disciples may reflect his Gospel's origin somewhere in the Western Empire, where the social mobility of women was more accepted than in the Greek East, although most

110. Corley, *Private Women, Public Meals*, pp. 48-49; Seim, *Double Message*, p. 61. For διακονέω as the household work of women and slaves, see Schottroff, *Lydia's Impatient Sisters*, p. 83, but also cautionary remarks on p. 206.

111. See Corley, *Private Women, Public Meals*, pp. 48-49, 106-107 n. 117. John H. D'Arms, 'Slaves at Roman Convivia', in W.J. Slater (ed.), *Dining in a Classical Context* (Ann Arbor: University of Michigan Press, 1991), pp. 171-83.

112. Marvin Meyer suggests that should the fragments of the *Secret Gospel of Mark* which feature the νεανίσκος, the 'young man', be considered part of the original version of Mark's Gospel, then Mark would be depicting an ideal male disciple at the garden and tomb (Mk 14.51-52; 16.5-6) similar to John's 'Beloved Disciple'. 'The Youth in the Secret Gospel of Mark', *Semeia* 49 (1990), pp. 129-53; *idem*, 'The Youth in Secret Mark and the Beloved Disciple in John', in James E. Goehring *et al.* (eds.), *Gospel Origins and Christian Beginnings: In Honor of James M. Robinson* (Sonoma, CA: Polebridge Press, 1990), pp. 94-105. In comparison to the youth, the women disciples also fall short, since they flee and tell no one about the resurrection ('The Youth in the Secret Gospel', p. 147). See also Munro, 'Secret Mark', p. 51. Since young men did serve meals, the youth could also be likened to the ideal διάκονος who serves at table in Mk 10.43-45. See Corley, *Private Women, Public Meals*, pp. 106-107 n. 117.

113. Corley, *Private Women, Public Meals*, pp. 84-86; Schottroff, *Lydia's Impatient Sisters*, p. 214.

scholars place the composition in Syria.[114] Further, although the presence of women at meals with men and frequent travel was controversial for elite women, travel by women of most social classes was not. In spite of the Greco-Roman ideal that women remain secluded in the home, even before the building of Roman roads it was not uncommon for women to travel with their husbands, particularly to religious festivals or sacred sites. Women could also travel long distances with servants to meet their husbands elsewhere. Women also obviously traveled *as* servants as well or simply became runaway slaves.[115] Only wealthy women lived more secluded lives; the rest of population probably couldn't afford to keep women idle and in the home.[116] There is little evidence directly from Palestine that women were kept in seclusion in women's quarters; the limited evidence applies only to the upper classes.[117] The travel of some unmarried women and younger virgins, however, may have been more restricted. The practice of debt slavery makes it difficult to imagine that girls sold in this manner would have had limited mobility due to the domestic services they would render their masters.[118]

Some ancient governments did have an interest in restricting the travel of women, especially prostitutes. These restrictions were enforced by the charging of exorbitant fares or taxation for travel services. Presumably, if women or their husbands could pay the fares charged by ship captains, they could board ships as passengers as well. Men were charged higher fares than their own for their wives,

114. See Corley, *Private Women, Public Meals*, pp. 24-79. For the Syrian provenance, see Helmut Koester, *Ancient Christian Gospels: Their History and Development* (London: SCM Press; Philadelphia, PA: Trinity Press International, 1990), pp. 288-92.

115. Casson, *Travel*, pp. 75-77, 82, 128, Pl. 6, 147, 160, 176-77. On runaway slave girls in ancient novels and documents, see Corley, *Private Women, Public Meals*, p. 63 n. 230; Heichelheim, *Economic Survey of Ancient Rome*, p. 167.

116. Ilan, *Jewish Women*, pp. 128-29, 132-34, 176-84; Ilan corrects Jeremias's assumption (*Jerusalem*, pp. 361-62) that Egyptian Jewish sources are necessarily applicable to Palestine. For secluded wealthy women and virgins see 3 *Macc.* 1.18-20; 2 Macc. 3.19; Ecclus. 26.10; 42.11-12. See also Schottroff, 'Women Followers', pp. 420-21; *eadem, Let the Oppressed*, pp. 88-90; Fiorenza, *In Memory of Her*, pp. 127-28.

117. Ilan, *Jewish Women*, pp. 132-34.

118. Horsley, *Spiral of Violence*, pp. 246-49. But see the conclusions of Llewelyn and Kearsley that *P. Ups. Frid.* 7 grants a slave woman her freedom of movement. This would imply that she would not automatically have such freedom. The interpretation of this text is disputed. See Llewelyn and Kearsley, 'He gives authority to his slaves, to each his work...' in *idem, New Documents Illustrating Early Christianity*, pp. 60-63, esp. 62.

but these fares were not nearly so high as those charged for prostitutes.[119] Such policy probably affected unescorted women, regardless of their true vocation, although even men rarely traveled alone. Ordinary travelers usually took along at least one servant.[120] Elite married women known for too-frequent holiday trips to seaside resorts or well-known spas could be characterized as pleasure-seeking courtesans or sexually loose. Such holidays were seen as occasions for adulterous liaisons.[121] Poorer women could in turn make money by renting rooms to these travelers.[122]

The many women mentioned in the Pauline letters as traveling either as missionaries or as the result of imperial edicts (Acts 18.2) should not be considered out of the ordinary for their time or social class. Rather, Paul's letters give additional evidence for the general mobility of women like Junia, Priscilla or even Phoebe. Paul himself shows no discomfort with the fact that women he knows travel long distances or that the apostles from Palestine are known to take a sister/wife on their journeys. In fact, he asserts their right to do so (1 Cor. 9.5). He even uses Phoebe, whom he calls his 'patroness', as a courier (Rom. 16.1-2).[123] Although it may be unwise to assume that Paul's information concerning the Jerusalem church is applicable to the Palestinian situation more generally, on the whole the evidence suggests that women did travel, to religious festivals, to engage in trade, to convey messages.[124] Mark's description of the women on the road with Jesus (Mk 15.40-41) is therefore quite explicable despite the undertones of scandal.

Mark 15.40-41 is even more probable if two of the women are associated with either Jesus' family (his mother and/or Salome) or the families of the other male disciples (cf. Mt. 27.56). Only Mary Magdalene seems to be unconnected to Jesus or the other disciples by familial ties; she may well be connected to the group by means of her trade, in the same way that Priscilla shared a trade with Paul.

---

119. This also implies that prostitutes could be expected to meet these higher fares. See Casson, *Travel*, p. 154.

120. Casson, *Travel*, p. 76.

121. Casson, *Travel*, pp. 142-44. For ample ancient references, see p. 346.

122. Casson, *Travel*, pp. 87-90.

123. On women missionaries, see Mary Rose D'Angelo, 'Women Partners in the New Testyament', *JFSR* 6 (1990), pp. 65-86; Schottroff, 'Women as Followers', pp. 424-26; Fiorenza, *In Memory of Her*, pp. 168-75.

124. Kathleen Corley, 'The Egalitarian Jesus: A Christian Myth of Origins', *Forum*, NS, 1.2 (1998), pp. 291-325.

Marriage and Social Class

It is difficult to determine the marital status of the women in Mk 15.40-41. No husbands are mentioned for Salome or Mary Magdalene, which may indicate either that they were not married[125] or that they were divorced. It is also possible that they simply left their husbands and children for a freer life. Salome, if a runaway slave or hired domestic servant, may have been single; there were difficulties involved in the marriage of women formerly enslaved or in domestic service due the stain of assumed sexual activity, although later sources record marriages of manumitted slave women to their masters or to others.[126] Mary Magdalene, if an ordinary working woman, could easily have been married, even perhaps involved in a business with her husband or family members. Mary (the mother) of James and Joses was probably married or divorced, given that she has sons.[127] If she is Jesus' mother, which seems likely on the basis of Mk 6.3, it is likely that she was married, and either of a higher social class or simply better known than her husband, who remains unnamed. She also could have been divorced or separated. Matthew and Luke independently attest that Mary was married to a man named Joseph (Lk. 2.4; Mt. 1.16), although there is no evidence that he joined Jesus on the road. It is thus just as possible that Mary left Joseph as it is that he was dead. There is no evidence in Lk. 8.1-3 that Joanna's husband or children are with her, but among the women she is most able to leave her family behind with servants to care for them. Hence the potential cost of the often-romanticized desertion of families and children to follow a prophet like Jesus by mothers, but especially fathers, should not be overlooked.[128]

The lack of references to husbands in Mk 15.40-41 is frequently taken as a sign that early Christian women were celibate and eschewed marriage.[129] This is unlikely. It is Matthew, not Mark, who offers the

---

125. Ilan, *Jewish Women*, p. 64; Ross Shepard Kraemer, *Her Share of the Blessings: Women's Religions Among Pagans, Jews, and Christians in the Greco-Roman World* (New York: Oxford University Press, 1992), pp. 133-34, 144; Schottroff, 'Women as Followers', p. 421. Also David C. Sim, 'The Women Followers of Jesus: The Implications of Luke 8.1-3', *HeyJ* 30 (1989), pp. 51-62, esp. p. 60.

126. The marriage of a former slave woman to her master would mirror the practices of other Greco-Roman people. See Corley, *Private Women, Public Meals*, pp. 49-50.

127. Ilan, *Jewish Women*, p. 64.

128. See David C. Sim, 'What about the Wives and Children of the Disciples?: The Cost of Discipleship from Another Perspective', *HeyJ* 35 (1994), pp. 373-90.

129. Discussion by Ilan, *Jewish Women*, pp. 62-65; see also Kraemer, *Her Share of*

harsh statement about becoming eunuchs for the Kingdom (Mt. 19.1-12). Mark records the full divorce prohibition without exception and so reinforces the value of marriage for both women and men (Mk 10.2-12). In spite of the oft-mentioned lack of fathers in Jesus' true family in Mark (3.31-35),[130] given the reinforcement and even strengthening of the importance of marriage in Mk 10.2-12, Mark's lack of interest in 'fathers' is unlikely to be related to a repudiation of marriage or a sign of an anti-patriarchal ethic.[131] The emphasis on the title of 'father' for God is not directly associated with the description of the true family as consisting of mothers and children, but no fathers (Mk 3.31-35; 10.29-31).[132] Finally, given the tendency of the Gospels to neglect personal details about even key individuals, it is also quite possible that Salome and Mary Magdalene were indeed married like most ancient Jewish women, and that Mark did not find details about their marital status to be of much importance.[133]

Jesus, Tax Collectors and Sinners in Mark (Mark 2.14-17)

In Mark 2 Jesus reclines at table with Levi the tax collector and a group of his friends.[134] The call to Levi has long been considered a Markan composition; Mack has suggested that Mark expands an earlier *chreia* by creating the scene.[135] The pun implied by the verb

the Blessings, pp. 133-34; Mary-Rose D'Angelo, 'Re-Membering Jesus: Women, Prophecy, and Resistance in the Memory of the Early Churches', *Horizon* 19 (1992), pp. 199-218 (215-16).

130. See for example, Dewey, 'Gospel of Mark', pp. 478-79; Horsley, *Spiral of Violence*, pp. 232-44; Fiorenza, *In Memory of Her*, pp. 145-47.

131. Nor Jesus'. So Mary Rose D'Angelo, 'Abba and "Father": Imperial Theology and the Jesus Traditions', *JBL* 111 (1992), pp. 611-30 (162); *eadem*, 'Theology in Mark and Q: Abba and "Father" in Contact', *HTR* 85 (1992), pp. 149-74. Against Marcus Borg, *Meeting Jesus Again for the First Time* (San Francisco: HarperSanFrancisco, 1994), p. 57; Crossan, *Historical Jesus*, pp. 301-302; Kloppenborg, 'Alms, Debt and Divorce'; Schottroff, *Let the Oppressed*, pp. 95-97; Fiorenza, *In Memory of Her*, pp. 143-45.

132. So D'Angelo, 'Abba and Father', pp. 629-30, and 'Theology in Mark and Q', p. 162.

133. Ilan, *Jewish Women*, p. 64; Schottroff, 'Women as Followers', pp. 418-27.

134. See Corley, *Private Women, Public Meals*, pp. 89-93, for many of the following remarks.

135. Mack, *Myth of Innocence*, p. 183. Mack and Vernon Robbins argue that behind the composition of Gospel narratives is a practice of '*chreia* elaboration' in which short pithy statements were elaborated into larger narratives. See B.L. Mack and V.K. Robbins, *Patterns of Persuasion in the Gospels* (Sonoma, CA: Polebridge Press, 1989). Markan composition of this section was noticed long ago: Bultmann,

καλέω, 'to invite', could indicate that in a pre-Markan form the saying pictured Jesus as the host rather than the guest.[136] Mark portrays Jesus as engaging in the kind of behavior of which the Pharisees accuse him: 'Why does he eat (ἐσθίω)[137] with tax-collectors and sinners?' (τελωνῶν καὶ ἁμαρτωλῶν, Mk 2.16). This swipe at Jesus' table etiquette also occurs in Q (7.34). In Q the association of Jesus' behavior with banquet revelry is clear: Jesus is called a 'wine-bibber' (οἰνοπότης) and a 'glutton' (φάγος). The accusation that he reclined at table with 'tax collectors and sinners' recalls typical slander against those known for dining with promiscuous women at public banquets. Tax collectors were stereotypically connected to slave trafficking and brothel keeping; 'sinners' were connected to the lower classes and prostitutes.[138] Mark, however, connects Jesus' meal to his own themes of calling and discipleship.[139]

It is notable that both Luke and Matthew interpret the phrase 'tax collectors and sinners' found in Mark and Q to include women. Luke describes a woman as an example of a 'sinner' (Lk. 7.36-50) and for this reason is hesitant to portray Jesus as clearly reclining with 'tax collectors and sinners'. This indicates Luke's care to conform his narrative to standards of Greco-Roman propriety as well as ancient literary conventions.[140] In Matthew the phrase 'tax collectors and sinners' even more explicitly includes women, in that Matthew retains the parallel construction of 'tax collectors and prostitutes', which I argue preserves Q (Q 7.29; Mt. 21.31).[141] Matthew also expands the guest list of the eucharistic feasts of the feeding narratives to include both women and children and strengthens the characterization of the women as disciples at the end of his Gospel (Mt. 27.55-56). Thus Luke and Matthew's narratives reflect the ramifications of the picture evoked in both Mk 2.16 and Q 7.34.

History, pp. 47-48; W.O. Walker, 'Jesus and the Tax-Collectors', *JBL* 97 (1978), pp. 221-38; Dennis E. Smith, 'The Historical Jesus at the Table', in David Lull (ed.), *Society of Biblical Literature 1998 Seminar Papers* (Atlanta: Scholars Press, 1989), pp. 475-76.

136. Bultmann, *History*, pp. 47-48; Smith, 'Jesus at Table', p. 476.

137. The addition of καὶ πίνει, 'and drink', to Mk 2.16 probably reflects the influence of Lk. 5.30. The editors of the UBS rate their decision to omit with a {B}. See Metzger, *Textual Commentary*, p. 78.

138. Corley, *Private Women, Public Meals*, pp. 89-93.

139. So Smith, 'Jesus at Table', p. 476.

140. Corley, *Private Women, Public Meals*, pp. 108-46.

141. Kathleen Corley, *Women and the Historical Jesus* (San Francisco, CA: Polebridge Press, forthcoming).

In Mark 2 the traditional slander is transformed into a narrative involving a later church conflict with the Pharisees over a more developed notion of ritual purity in the context of meals. It seems unlikely that Jesus himself would have been in conflict with Pharisees over purity and table fellowship. The general purity regulations that governed all Jews did not necessarily affect everyday, communal or celebratory meals, but the Temple.[142] Despite Mark's statement that 'all the Jews' were concerned about the washing of hands (Mk 7.6-9), only the *haberim*, 'associates', were strict about infusing priestly rules into the everyday handling of foodstuffs. Not only are the *haberim* not easily equated with the 'Pharisees', but they were no doubt a very small minority within Judaism before 70 CE.[143] Thus it remains doubt-ful that the concern of Jesus' contemporaries for his table practice reflects disputes over purity regulations.

In light of the Hellenistic evidence, the original accusation against Jesus functions as a form of slander and reflects not an interest in purity but in propriety. This would be far more indicative of the concerns of Jesus' real day-to-day opponents, who would have been local leaders from the ranks of wealthy landowners, old prominent families, government officials and priests and scribes. A few Pharisees could have numbered among these groups in Galilee during Jesus' lifetime but are not be equated with them.[144] The possibility that Jesus

142. S.J.D. Cohen, 'Menstruants and the Sacred in Judaism and Christianity', in S.B. Pomeroy (ed.), *Women's History and Ancient History* (Chapel Hill, NC: University of North Carolina Press, 1991), pp. 273-99 (278-79); E.P. Sanders, 'Jesus and the Sinners', *JSNT* 19 (1983), pp. 5-36, esp. p. 13.

143. Anthony J. Saldarini, *Pharisees, Scribes and Sadducees in Palestinian Society: A Sociological Approach* (Wilmington, DE: Michael Glazier, 1988), pp. 216-20; Sanders, 'Jesus and the Sinners', pp. 14-15; E.P. Sanders, *Jesus and Judaism* (Philadelphia: Fortress Press, 1985), pp. 176-99; Günter Stemberger, *Jewish Contemporaries of Jesus: Pharisees, Sadducees, Essenes* (trans. Allan W. Mahnke; Philadelphia: Fortress Press, 1995), pp. 41, 47-48, 75-82, 83-84. Jacob Neusner holds that the New Testament portrayal of the Pharisees as being concerned with ritual purity, tithes, and sab-bath observance accurately reflects the Pharisaic program of the first century. See *From Politics to Piety: The Emergence of Pharisaic Judaism* (Engelwood Cliffs, NJ: Prentice–Hall, 1973); *idem*, *The Pharisees: Rabbinic Perspectives* (Hoboken, NJ: Ktav, 1985); *idem*, 'Two Pictures of the Pharisees: Philosophical Circle or Eating Club', *ATR* 64 (1982), pp. 525-38.

144. Anthony J. Saldarini, 'The Social Class of the Pharisees in Mark', in J. Neus-ner *et al.* (eds.), *The Social World of Formative Christianity and Judaism: Essays in Tribute to Howard Clark Kee* (Philadelphia: Fortress Press, 1988), pp. 69-77, esp. p. 71; *idem*, 'Political and Social Roles of the Pharisees and Scribes in Galilee', in David J. Lull (ed.), *Society of Biblical Literature 1988 Seminar Papers* (Atlanta: Scholars Press, 1988), pp. 200-209.

came from a social class a step higher than that of many of his followers would make concern for his behavior on the part of the local leadership more explicable. The accusation that Jesus 'eats with tax collectors and sinners' makes better sense if his social standing is somehow above some of those he joins for meals.[145] Thus, the concern over Jesus' dining habits could indeed reflect a conflict over his challenge to Greco-Roman class structures, as Marcus Borg and John Dominic Crossan suggest,[146] although probably not a conflict over purity. Unless Jesus failed to cleanse himself before entering the Temple, it is hard to imagine that even local or rural priests would have objected to his dining habits or accused him of abrogating Jewish purity regulations.[147]

What these early traditions do suggest, however, is that Jesus was perceived as challenging Greco-Roman privileges and ideals of status on behalf of others by means of his actions. This increases the likelihood that although Jesus was probably from the ranks of the peasantry, he could not have come from the lowest ranks of that class, but from a level able to show resistance to authority on behalf of those beneath his station. Resistance by means of overt action is a common tactic among the lower classes.[148]

One could argue on the basis of Mk 2.15-17, which preserves the accusation that Jesus ate with 'tax collectors and sinners', and Mk 15.40-41, which names Jewish women from the lower classes as Jesus' disciples, that the mixed social constituency of Jesus' meals suggested by the parable of the feast (Q 14.16-24; *Gos. Thom.* 64) included household slaves, hirelings, runaway slaves, debt slaves and/or day

145. Dennis E. Smith, 'Table Fellowship and the Historical Jesus', in Luken Bormann *et al.* (eds.), *Religious Propaganda and Missionary Competition in the New Testament World: Essays Honoring Dieter Georgi* (Leiden: E.J. Brill, 1994), pp. 160-61.

146. I.e., concerns over purity may not have mediated the concerns over class. Marcus Borg connects purity issues to class issues. See *Jesus a New Vision*, pp. 157-60, and especially Borg, *Meeting Jesus*, pp. 46-68. Crossan also connects Jesus' open commensality to a rejection of social boundaries created by Jewish purity regulations (*Historical Jesus*, pp. 322-24). However, purity does not correspond to social class. See Paula Fredriksen, 'Did Jesus Oppose the Purity Laws?', *BR* 11.3 (June 1995), pp. 18-25; 42-47 (23). Against Hamel, *Poverty and Charity*, pp. 82-93.

147. There is no evidence that Jesus did not observe basic purity regulations regarding the Temple or food. See Fredriksen, 'Did Jesus Oppose the Purity Laws?', pp. 42-43. Against Borg, *Meeting Jesus*, pp. 46-68; Crossan, *Historical Jesus*, p. 355.

148. See James C. Scott, *Domination and the Arts of Resistance: Hidden Transcripts* (New Haven: Yale University Press, 1990); *idem*, *Weapons of the Weak: Everyday Forms of Peasant Resistance* (New Haven: Yale University Press, 1985).

laborers, among them women.[149] The image in the parable of the returning master is also notable, given that it contains an inversion of the master/slave roles at table (Lk. 12.35-38; cf. also Mk 10.42-45; Jn 13.1-16). The inclusion of servants, especially slaves, at meals was considered particularly controversial among the elite, since inviting a slave to recline for a meal was an informal means of manumission (*per mansam*).[150] Only a few Hellenistic philosophers advocated such an innovative table ethic.[151] Such a mixture of the free poor, freed, and slaves was relatively common in social situations, communal meals, and clubs.[152] Jesus' challenge to Greco-Roman ideals of rank in the parable of the feast, although not a direct challenge to notions of gender, could have had significance for women among the lower classes as well as men, albeit a secondary one.[153] This means that Jesus here shows an interest in class inequity, but not gender inequity.

Women Disciples and the Gospel of Mark: Some Conclusions

That Jesus dined and traveled with women named Mary Magdalene, Salome, Joanna, and his mother is very plausible. Despite of the fact that the Gospels themselves show knowledge that Jesus' association with women was controversial, this association pervades the early layers of the Gospel tradition and is therefore difficult to explain except as one aspect of Jesus' movement that is historically reliable. This suggests that Jesus earned social criticism from his contemporaries in

149.	So also Fiorenza, *In Memory of Her*, pp. 122-25, 127-28, 135-36.

150.	Corley, *Private Women, Public Meals*, p. 100, esp. n. 82. On manumission of slaves *per mansam*, see Thomas Wiedemann, *Greek and Roman Slavery* (Baltimore: The Johns Hopkins University Press, 1981), pp. 233-36. The most popular form of manumission was by will, when the slave was freed upon the death of his or her master. See A.M. Duff, *Freedmen in the Early Roman Empire* (New York: Barnes & Noble, 1958), pp. 21-25.

151.	See Seneca, *Ep.* 47 and discussion in Corley, *Private Women, Public Meals*, p. 100 n. 82; see also *Ps.-Heraclitus* 9.5. I am indebted to David Seeley for this second reference.

152.	See Cameron, 'Neither Male Nor Female'; Corley, *Private Women, Public Meals*, pp. 31-33, esp. n. 46; Fiorenza, *In Memory of Her*, pp. 179-82.

153.	So Crossan, *Historical Jesus*, pp. 261-64, 335. See also Corley, 'Jesus' Table Practice'; Fiorenza, *Miriam's Child*, pp. 93-94. Against Smith, 'Historical Jesus at Table', pp. 480-86; *eadem*, 'Table Fellowship and the Historical Jesus', pp. 143-48, 161-62; *eadem*, 'Table Fellowship as a Literary Motif in the Gospel of Luke', *JBL* 106 (1987), pp. 613-38, esp. pp. 636-38, who argues against the authenticity of the claims of dining with sinners/prostitutes. See Corley, *Women and the Historical Jesus*, for further discussion.

part because of his association with women, especially women as representatives of the working classes and the free poor. Early traditions linking women disciples to Jesus' meals strongly suggest that the 'Last Supper' narratives that limit his intimate circle to men are later literary creations that cast Jesus' meals with his disciples as all male *symposia*, or 'drinking parties', following Greco-Roman literary conventions.

That at least a few women traveled with Jesus, especially Mary Magdalene, Jesus' mother Mary, and a woman named Salome, also seems plausible, particularly since most non-elite women, particularly working women from the class of peasants, day laborers and slaves would not have been restricted in their travel as has been previously assumed. It is unlikely, however, that all of the women around Jesus were wealthy and able to support the movement financially as Luke records, given the tendency of Luke to increase the social status of Jesus' movement overall. Of the women mentioned in Luke, Joanna is more likely to have been a real woman who followed Jesus.

It is less likely that the women around Jesus were actual prostitutes, although women from the lower classes could be forced into prostitution or debt slavery at various times in their life due to economic hardship, and wealthier women could be branded whores for freer social behavior. The accusation that Jesus dined with 'tax collectors and sinners/prostitutes' thus functions as a form of slander against Jesus and his companions and remains suggestive of a socially mixed group that included slaves, runaway slaves and/or day laborers, as well as the freeborn poor, and, of course, women.

THE FAILURE OF THE WOMEN WHO FOLLOWED JESUS
IN THE GOSPEL OF MARK

Victoria Phillips

Introduction

Feminist critics are committed to producing liberating interpretations for women who have been marginalized and oppressed by patriarchal and androcentric Christian traditions. One important feminist strategy has been affirming women's exemplary discipleship.[1] As necessary as this strategy is, it has often been accompanied by a blind spot toward Mark's report about the women's behavior at Jesus' tomb on the third day. For example, discussions of women's discipleship are frequently based on Lk. 8.1-3 or Mk 15.40-41 without reference to 16.1-8.[2] This combination of texts permits feminists to emphasize that women as well as men are Jesus' disciples and even to claim that women are better or more faithful disciples than their male counterparts.

Since the women who go to the tomb on the third day are silenced by fear, feminist critics have begun to surrender the claim that women are more faithful disciples than men. To account for the women's shift from courageous to fearful disciples, feminists have adopted uncritically an explanation developed by traditional Markan scholars.[3] As Joanna Dewey states it, 'Mark presents the women remaining faithful after the men have deserted Jesus… But then the storyteller presents

---

1. Marla J. Schierling, 'Women as Leaders in the Marcan Community', *Listening* 15 (1980), pp. 250-56; Elisabeth Moltmann-Wendel, *The Women around Jesus: Reflections on Authentic Personhood* (London: SCM Press, 1982); Jane Kopas, 'Jesus and Women in Mark's Gospel', *Review for Religious* 44 (1985), pp. 912-20; Mary Ann Beavis, 'Models of Faith', pp. 3-9; Joseph A. Grassi, 'Secret Heroine of Mark's Drama', *BTB* 18 (1988), pp. 9-14.

2. Janice Nunnally-Cox, *Feminist Foremothers: Women of the Bible* (New York: Seabury, 1981), pp. 99-117; C. Ricci, *Mary Magdalene*, p. 62; Verna Dozier and James R. Adams, *Sisters and Brothers: Reclaiming a Biblical Idea of Community* (Cambridge, MA: Cowley, 1993), pp. 27-28.

3. See especially Malbon, 'Fallible Followers', pp. 29-48.

the women failing in their turn'.[4] Just as the men's failures at disciple-ship instruct the reader in the nature of true discipleship, so too does the women's. This interpretation needs to be evaluated from a critical feminist perspective.[5]

Interpreting the women's failure along with the men's failure as a teaching about discipleship expresses important feminist commit-ments. One of these commitments is recognizing that women are dis-ciples; in this way the androcentric split between 'the disciples' and 'the women' is overcome. Another feminist commitment is undoing the myth of women's intrinsic superiority or inferiority to men. Reading the Gospel of Mark as a text that shows that men and women are sometimes faithful followers, sometimes not, disrupts generaliza-tions based on gender as an essential trait.

Despite its strengths, this reading is seriously compromised. Failing to deliver a message is not comparable to deserting one's teacher after promising one's loyalty, as did the Twelve when Jesus informed them they would abandon him (14.28-31). The Twelve are in a relationship with Jesus; the women interact with a stranger. The Twelve make a pledge to which they can be held accountable; the women at the tomb never even speak to the young man. The young man presumes he can order the women to carry a message that he believes the other dis-ciples must hear. The women have no connection to the young man and no reason to assume they must obey him.[6] The women cannot be

4.   Dewey, 'The Gospel of Mark', p. 506.

5.   Norman Perrin was an early proponent of this view (*The Resurrection According to Matthew, Mark and Luke* [Philadelphia: Fortress Press, 1977], p. 30). Robert Tannehill developed a detailed treatment of it in terms of literary criticism that remains influential ('Disciples in Mark', pp. 386-405). Larry W. Hurtado gives an informative discussion of this reading and its history ('Following Jesus in the Gospel of Mark—and Beyond', in R.N. Longenecker (ed.), *Patterns of Discipleship in the New Testament* (Grand Rapids: Eerdmans, 1996), pp. 9-29.

6.   The text identifies him as νεανίσκος. Scholars have three reasons for deeming the young man an angel: he is wearing white; he repeats what Jesus said at 14.28; and the use of νεανίσκος for the divine messengers in 2 Macc. 3.26, 33, 34. The color of the robe is connected with Jesus' raiment during his transfiguration. It is whiter than any earthly bleach can make it (8.3). The young man's robe is not described as unusually white, so the parallel is not warranted. The 'young man' in 2 Macc. 3 is described as unusually tall and beautiful, and as having extraordinary strength. These attributes set the young man apart from ordinary young men. Scholars tried to make the color of the young man's robe carry the same weight, but it does not. The use of word νεανίσκος alone is not sufficient to make the parallel. If the young man is an angel, then he can repeat what Jesus said because he is a messenger of God. If the young man is not an angel, then scholars wonder

faulted for not obeying someone who has no claim on their obedience. Thus, their failure is not one of 'disobedience'.[7] Finally, the women's silence from fear does not prevent the disciples who abandoned Jesus from receiving information they need.[8] The Twelve heard from Jesus directly that he would go before them into Galilee (14.28). If they forget what Jesus said, or if they don't credit it, the women's failure to deliver the message does not exculpate those disciples' lack of memory or trust.[9]

Finally, interpreting the women's silence as a failure comparable to the men's cannot account for the women's failure as anything other than fallible human nature. From a liberation perspective, appeals to human nature are suspect, because any account of 'human nature' is likely to serve the interests of dominant social groups and to conceal the social and political structures that benefit the dominant groups.[10] Feminists have not contested that women fail or that they have been silenced by fear. Rather, they contest long-standing explanations for women's failures, such as women's lesser capacity for reason and morality,[11] and they explore instead how social structures perpetuate,

---

how he can know what Jesus said at 14.28. Scholars have regularly acknowledged that the only other use of 'young man' in the Gospel of Mark is in 14.51-52, but most have been reluctant to identify the young man at the tomb with this young man. After exploring the typical interpretations, I do. Even if the young man is an angel, the women might not recognize him as such, which means they still have to make a judgment about the best way to behave toward him.

7.   For examples of the argument that they are disobedient, see Thomas Boomershine, 'Mark 16:8 and the Apostolic Commission', *JBL* 100 (1981), pp. 225-39, and Andrew T. Lincoln, 'The Promise and the Failure: Mark 16:7, 8', *JBL* 108 (1989), pp. 283-300.

8.   See T.J. Weeden, *Mark*; W.H. Kelber, *The Oral and the Written Gospel*, pp. 103-104.

9.   Even if the women did deliver the message, as numerous scholars assert, there is no reason to assume that the Twelve will heed them. In the Gospel of Matthew, the eleven do listen to the women; at least crediting what they say is implied by the eleven's journeying to Galilee (Mt. 28.8, 16); in the Gospel of Luke the disciples (specifically the 'eleven and the rest') do not credit them (24.11).

10.   For an overview of feminist theological critiques of 'human nature' see Ann O'Hara Graff, 'The Struggle to Name Women's Experience', in *eadem* (ed.), *In the Embrace of God: Feminist Approaches to Theological Anthropology* (Maryknoll, NY: Orbis Books, 1995), pp. 71-89. For an account of theological anthropology from a specific social location, see in the same volume María Pilar Aquino, 'Including Women's Experience: A Latina Feminist Perspective', pp. 51-70.

11.   Nancy Tuana, *The Less Noble Sex: Scientific, Religious, and Philosophical Conceptions of Woman's Nature* (Bloomington: Indiana University Press, 1993).

if not foster, women's failures.[12] Thus, a liberating reading of the women's failure will investigate how social structures among the disciples contribute to the women's silence from fear. My aim is not to excuse or even to exonerate the three women who were silenced from fear, but to understand them.

A key step in constructing my interpretation is refining the use of gender as a category of analysis with respect to Jesus' followers. Early feminist criticism stressed gender as the main category of analysis in order to expose androcentric bias in terms like 'disciples' and to give female characters visibility.[13] Over the past decade, women of color, among others, have challenged the use of gender as a category in isolation from other variables of social location, such as ethnicity, class, or status.[14] Such feminist work has prompted me to explore the consequences of the creation of the Twelve, a gendered group that also has certain privileges, and on the women who followed Jesus, a gendered group that does not have those privileges. The women's silence from fear expresses the shock of discovering the consequences of their marginalization within the fellowship.

Jesus entrusts to the Twelve information that affects all the disciples, namely his relationship with them after he rises from the dead. The Twelve heard from Jesus directly that he would go before them into Galilee (14.28). The implication for the Twelve, at least, is that their association with Jesus continues after his resurrection. For the women

12. During the 1970s, the slogan 'the personal is political' was used to express feminist realization that gender was a social construct. For two different approaches to investigating how social structures contribute to women's failures, see Joan Wallach Scott, *Gender and the Politics of History* (New York: Columbia University Press, 1988); and Dorothy E. Smith, *The Everyday World as Problematic: A Feminist Sociology* (Evanstown, IL: Northeastern University Press, 1987). From a psychological perspective see Jean Baker Miller, *Toward a New Psychology of Women* (Boston, MA: Beacon Press, 1976), pp. 1-26 and 115-24.

13. For example, see Letty Russell (ed.), *The Liberating Word: A Guide to Non-Sexist Interpretation of the Bible* (Philadelphia: Westminster Press, 1976), and Elisabeth Schüssler Fiorenza, ' "You Are Not to Be Called Father": Early Christian History in a Feminist Perspective', *Cross Currents* 29 (1979), pp. 301-23.

14. Audre Lorde, 'Age, Race, Class, and Sex: Women Redefining Difference', in *idem* (ed.), *Sister Outsider: Essays and Speeches* (Trumansburg, NY: Crossing Press, 1984), pp. 114-23; bell hooks, *Feminist Theory from Margin to Center* (Boston, MA: South End, 1984); Elisabeth Schüssler Fiorenza, 'To Speak in Public: A Feminist Political Hermeneutics', in *eadem*, *But She Said: Feminist Practices of Biblical Interpretation* (Boston, MA: Beacon Press, 1992), pp. 102-32; Barbara H. Geller Nathanson, 'Toward A Multicultural Ecumenical History of Women in the First Century/ies C.E.', in Elisabeth Schüssler Fiorenza (ed.), *Searching the Scriptures: A Feminist Introduction* (New York: Crossroad, 1993), pp. 272-89.

who followed Jesus the implications are less clear and more distressing. In discovering that Jesus told the Twelve that he would go before
them after he was risen, the women confront their marginalization.
They will be disturbed, they will wonder why Jesus did not tell them,
and they will fear that they have been abandoned. Surely the women
who have followed him since Galilee (15.40-41) would want to and
have a right to follow back there. Finding out that one's discipleship
may no longer be needed or wanted could induce fear strong enough
to silence both desire and capacity to report or to challenge that
exclusion.

Gender, Privilege and Discipleship

A fundamental insight of feminist biblical criticism is that Jesus
included women among his followers, and that therefore the androcentric term 'disciple' is not limited by gender to men.[15] Feminists
conceded that the Twelve were an all-male group,[16] and largely, especially in scholarship on the Gospel of Mark, lost interest in them.[17] My
reading of the ending revisits the Twelve and considers the impact of
its formation on the women who followed Jesus. For one, the ending
of the Gospel links the Twelve with the three women who came to the
tomb. They are charged with taking a message to the Twelve (16.7),
because the young man recognizes that the women are members of
the same fellowship.[18] For another, Mark's Gospel does not explicitly
differentiate women disciples as a class from the male disciples;
regarding the women among the disciples as a distinct class is an
effect of feminist interest in women's discipleship in Mark's narra-

15. Elisabeth Schüssler Fiorenza, *In Memory of Her: A Feminist Theological Reconstruction of Christian Origins* (New York: Crossroad, 1985), pp. 41-52.

16. For a classic analysis of the Twelve, see Elisabeth Schüssler Fiorenza, 'The
Twelve', in L. Swidler and A. Swidler (eds.), *Women Priests: A Catholic Commentary
on the Vatican Declaration* (Mahweh, NJ: Paulist Press, 1977), pp. 114-22.

17. Winsome Munro discusses the Twelve in some detail ('Women Disciples in
Mark?', *CBQ* 44 [1982], pp. 228-29, 235-39), but subsequent feminist scholarship
that critiques Munro does not; e.g., Malbon alternates among discussing individual
male disciples, such as Peter, the disciples, and the 12 disciples, in 'Fallible Followers', *passim*. Mary Rose D'Angelo discusses the Twelve briefly in order to debunk
the traditional view of the women who followed as 'a sort of ladies' auxiliary'
('Reconstructing "Real" Women in Gospel Literature', in R.S. Kraemer and M.R.
D'Angelo [eds.], *Women and Christian Origins* [New York: Oxford University Press,
1999], pp. 113-14).

18. He acknowledges their status as followers when he asserts that they have
come seeking 'Jesus of Nazareth who was crucified' (16.6).

tive.[19] Rather, Mark differentiates disciples in terms of those chosen for the role and privileges of the Twelve and those who are not. To elucidate these points, I will first demonstrate that Mark does not differentiate the disciples by gender by discussing discipleship and gender roles. Following Joan Wallach Scott, I treat gender as 'social relations between the sexes and a signifier of power'.[20] Analyzing a text for perceived differences between the sexes is a matter of looking at what a text says about the difference between men and women in the context of their various social relationships, in this case in terms of their identities as disciples. Then I will discuss how Mark differentiates the disciples by privilege.

Some of Jesus' teachings about discipleship seem to transcend gender. For example, a key hallmark of Jesus' teaching about discipleship in the Gospel of Mark is willingness to suffer for the sake of the cross (8.34-35). Anyone who desires to follow Jesus is called to accept this potential sacrifice; there is little evidence that men or women are more willing to sacrifice their lives for what they believe. Disciples are to enter the kingdom of God as a little child (10.13-16); they are not to cause simple believers to lose their faith (9.42). The declaration that defilement arises from the human heart and not from foodstuffs applies to both men and women (7.14-20).

Some aspects of discipleship may be more difficult for persons of one gender or another to accept. For example, Jesus teaches that disciples must serve one another. Luise Schottroff has explored the resistance men of the first century might feel on being asked to serve at table.[21] Women who customarily bring food to the table may not feel the same resistance, nor might slaves.[22] However, upper-class women,

19. Mark's androcentric perspective keeps women's presence among the fellowship invisible until they emerge at 15.40-41 as explicit characters in the text. Their emergence after the Twelve desert and Peter denies Jesus, and their continued presence until the ending of the Gospel raise the question of their significance as a subset within the disciples.

20. *Gender and the Politics of History* (New York: Columbia University Press, 1988), p. 42.

21. Luise Schottroff, *Lydia's Impatient Sisters: A Social History of Early Christianity* (trans. B. Rumscheidt and M. Rumscheidt; Louisville, KY: Westminster/John Knox Press, 1995), pp. 204-23.

22. Luise Schottroff argues that for poor men and women, including slaves, the problem of men's rule over women was not the primary oppression but rather their social status and economic condition ('Women as Disciples in New Testament Times', in *eadem, Let the Oppressed Go Free: Feminist Perspectives on the New Testament* (Louisville, KY: Westminster/John Knox Press, 1993), pp. 80-130. Thus they might experience being served or serving in turn as empowering. For a more detailed

who have been accustomed to service by slaves, may also be challenged by Jesus' emphasis on service.

Mark's Jesus does use gendered terms to refer to members of his
fellowship when he refers to them as family. Rejecting his natal family,
Jesus declares that those who do the will of God 'are my mother,
sister, and brother' (3.35). Using family terms connotes relationships
and responsibilities among the fellowship, a theme that is underscored
whenever Jesus rebukes the Twelve for inappropriately expressing
their privilege (10.41-45). Even so, Jesus does not offer explicit teachings to differentiate male disciples from female disciples, or 'brothers'
from 'sisters'. That is to say, Jesus does not differentiate between male
and female disciples in terms of clothing, seating and ritual practices.
From the lack of explicit discussion about gendered differences
between disciples we can infer that Mark regarded discipleship as an
inclusive category for men and women.

Contrasting with this inclusive notion of discipleship is the creation
of the Twelve. Jesus institutes the Twelve as a subgroup within the
fellowship and distinguishes them with special roles, experiences and
information, which I will discuss below. By creating a select group,
the Twelve, and giving it distinctive activities, attention and instruction, he marginalizes the rest of the disciples, male and female, to
various degrees on different occasions. Although Jesus does not state
explicitly that gender is a significant factor in the selection of the
Twelve, he chooses only men. Nor does he—or Mark—give any
explanation why a limited number of men within the fellowship,
rather than all of them, should be charged with the three functions
that Jesus gives the Twelve: to be with him, to preach and to exorcize
demons (3.14-15). Thus, maleness is a prerequisite for the privilege of
being part of the Twelve. Maleness may even be a prerequisite for the
roles specified. The only other person whom Jesus bids preach is the
man freed from the Legion (5.19-20). As for exorcism, John objects to a
man casting out demons in Jesus' name, because he is not one of them
(9.38-41). Mark preserves no stories in which Jesus tells a woman to
preach or to practice exorcism. Unlike any male disciples not selected
to number among the Twelve, who may feel solidarity with those
men chosen,[23] female disciples are marginalized by their gender.

---

theoretical argument that gender is a class-indicator see Elizabeth V. Spelman,
Inessential Woman: Problems of Exclusion in Feminist Thought (Boston, MA: Beacon
Press, 1988), pp. 37-56.

23. Whether the remaining male disciples feel solidarity or resentment is not
addressed in the Gospel of Mark. The members of the Twelve are jealous of their

The Twelve have some privileged roles, experiences and informa-tion.[24] I will not discuss every instance of their privileges. Since my overall purpose is show how the privileges of the Twelve impact the women who go to the tomb in 16.1-8, I will focus on material that bears on their encounter with the young man at the tomb. The most important link between the Twelve and the women at the tomb is given in 16.7, when the young man repeats what Jesus said to the Twelve at 14.28 before he was arrested. Scholars agree that Mark created the connection between 14.28 and 16.7. Thus it is of signal importance for interpreting the ending.

Jesus holds the Last Supper with the Twelve (14.17). At this meal, he tells them several things. First, one of the Twelve will betray him. Second, to his repeated claim that he will rise on the third day, he adds that he will go before them into Galilee (14.28). Apparently Jesus extends the privileges of the Twelve to include a relationship with them, at least, after his rising from the dead. In commenting on his death and resurrection, Jesus has not mentioned any kind of relation-ship with his followers. At 9.1 to his disciples and to the crowd he asserted that some of those present would see the kingdom of God come in power. Jesus tells the high priest that he will see the Son of Man seated at the right hand of God, coming in clouds of glory (14.62). These comments indicate that Jesus expects to be vindicated and soon, but they do not imply a role or the presence of his followers. Jesus asserts that his followers will have 'eternal life in the age to come' (10.20), which indicates a future for all who follow Jesus, but how they will relate to Jesus in the age to come is not specified.

However, James and John want to sit on Jesus' right and left when he comes into his glory (10.42). This request suggests that they believe they will either be ruling with the vindicated Jesus or that they will be honored guests at the messianic banquet. Although these are mere hints — that is, Mark's Jesus gives no details about the eschatological function of the Twelve — they suggest that as far as Jesus is concerned, the Twelve will be with him in some role related to the end-time. In

---

status vis-à-vis each other; see Mk 10.35-41, which reports that 'the ten' (οἱ δέκα, Mk 10.41) resent James and John asking for further privileges.

24. Privileged experiences for the Twelve as a whole include: their mission (6.7-12, 30-33), being rebuked for their pride (9.33-36), the Last Supper (14.17-32), waiting with Jesus in Gethsemane (14.32-41), and deserting Jesus at his arrest (14.43-50). Privileged experiences for a subset of the Twelve include witnessing the healing of Jairus's daughter (5.37-43), seeing Jesus transfigured (9.2-9) and being instructed about the last days (ch. 13).

this respect they are privileged over the rest of the disciples, male and female.

Not only do they have a future, promised relationship of some kind, they know about it from Jesus directly. That is, they have privileged access to information. Jesus made public announcements about his passion, death and resurrection. He asserted that he would rise on the third day. He said nothing about what followers should do, other than to pick up their crosses and follow him. He does not ask them to witness his death, only to imitate it. Whatever actions the women who followed Jesus take, they take based on what they know, which is not the whole story. When they go to the tomb on the third day, they learn what the Twelve know, and the women have to decide the implications for themselves.

The Women Who Were Silenced by Fear

In order to understand why the women who go to the tomb might be overcome with fear as a result of their encounter with the young man, it is necessary to consider how they respond to what he says. He tells them why they have come (seeking Jesus of Nazareth, who was crucified), what they need to know (he is not here, he is risen, he has gone to Galilee), and what they should do about it (tell the disciples and Peter). Some scholars explain their reaction in terms of the mind's inability to grasp the meaning of the resurrection, thereby emphasizing the effect of learning that Jesus is risen.[25] Others place more weight on the exhortation to convey the message to the other disciples. The women respond fearfully to the command that they should speak in public, which means they must transgress typical cultural expectations that women should be silent in public settings.[26]

I focus on the women's response to information new to them (that Jesus has gone ahead to Galilee and that he told this to some, but not

25. For example, see José Cárdenas Pallares, *A Poor Man Called Jesus: Reflections on the Gospel according to Mark* (Maryknoll, NY: Orbis Books, 1986), pp. 124-28. For a similar conclusion but framed in feminist deconstructive terms, see Susan Lochrie Graham, 'Silent Voices: Women in the Gospel of Mark', *Semeia* 54 (1993), pp. 153-56.

26. Mary Cotes, 'Women, Silence and Fear (Mark 16:8)', in G.J. Brooke (ed.), *Women in the Biblical Tradition* (Studies in Women and Religion, 31; Lewiston, NY: Edwin Mellen Press, 1992), pp. 150-66. However, carrying a message to the other disciples in one's fellowship is not an instance of speaking in public. Given the metaphor of family that Jesus introduces at 3.35, the women's speaking would occur in a domestic context, the 'sisters' bringing their 'brothers' news. Thus, their fear-induced silence cannot be explained in terms of transgressing cultural expectation.

all, of the disciples) and to the messenger, a stranger to them. I place the stress on the information and the route by which the women learned it for four reasons. First, the women are part of the larger fellowship. Their story is interconnected with the others. Hence from whom they learn information, a fellow disciple or a stranger, has an impact in itself. Second, access to information is an important dimension of being privileged or being marginalized in social groups or institutions. Third, in keeping with a feminist commitment to understanding women as subjects, I do not imagine the women as accepting the young man's assertions without evaluating them in terms of their own judgment and perceptions. Fourth, the women came to the tomb, I suggest, seeking Jesus—the risen Jesus, not the body of Jesus, as is usually asserted. They expected to greet the risen Lord, not to discover that he had left them behind.

As disciples, the women traveled with Jesus and had many opportunities to listen to his preaching and teaching.[27] To them, as to the Twelve and the rest of the disciples, was given 'the mysteries of the kingdom of God' (4.11). They heard parables and their explanation. They witnessed various healings and miraculous feedings. They also had opportunities to hear Jesus predict his passion, death and resurrection, about which he spoke plainly (8.32). On the basis of this information, they may have decided to go to the tomb on the third day to see the risen Lord.[28]

Jesus made three predictions about his passion, death and rising (8.31-32; 9.30-32; 10.33-34). The first two of these were public (8.31-32; 9.30-32); the third time Jesus took the Twelve aside to talk to them (10.32). The women know this much: that after the third day, Jesus will rise from the dead. Jesus does not make any public announcement about where he will rise, nor where he will go after his resurrection. He informs only the Twelve about what he will do after having been raised—he will precede them into Galilee (14.28). Jesus imparts this information to the Twelve as they are walking with him to

---

27. The female disciples are not mentioned explicitly before 15.40. For arguments inferring their presence prior to that, see Dewey, 'The Gospel of Mark', *passim*.

28. I do not believe the women go to the tomb in mourning, nor that their function is, as D'Angelo proposes, to establish that Jesus is dead. The scene of the crucifixion is more than sufficient to establish the reality of Jesus' death. The text is ambiguous. According to 16.1, the women take τὰ ἀρώματα in order to anoint him (ἀλείψωσιν αὐτόν). Grant R. Osborne notes that the verb connotes messianic expectation; anointing for burial would use 'μυρίζω', but he dismisses as obvious that the women's motive in 16.1 'was of course hardly messianic' (*The Resurrection Narrative: A Redactional Study* [Grand Rapids: Baker Book House, 1984], p. 46).

Gethsemane after the Last Supper, a meal at which the women were not present.[29] Thus when three of the women from Jesus' company hear the young man assert that Jesus had told them that he would go to Galilee, they cannot verify this information themselves. However, they can verify that he never said anything like it to them. Nor did they ever hear Jesus indicate what his followers were to do about reconnecting with him after his resurrection. The decision to come to the tomb was theirs alone. Standing at the tomb, they can see that Jesus is gone. The Twelve were chosen 'to be with him' (3.14). The women were not. At the end of the Gospel, they are not with him. Rather than share the discovery that Jesus left them behind, 'they say nothing to anyone, because they were afraid'.

On this interpretation the young man plays a critical role, because he overcomes the gap in communication created when Jesus tells only the Twelve his plans for after he is risen. The young man is not one of the privileged Twelve but a follower who overheard Jesus instructing the Twelve at 14.28.[30] One might even suggest that Mark could be utilizing the young man to overcome the women's marginalization. By telling them what he overheard, he shares what had hitherto been information reserved for the privileged group. However his intervention is not effective, partly because of his approach, partly because of the women's reaction. He is peremptory, he gives orders, even though he has no clear relationship with the women. That is, he acts from male privilege, which creates no trust or relationship between him and the women that might lead to their acting on what he says.

---

29. I assert this is a literary conclusion, not a historical one. A close reading of the text reveals that Jesus sent two disciples ahead to prepare the meal (14.13) and that he and the Twelve arrived that evening (Καὶ ὀψίας γενομένης ἔρχεται μετὰ τῶν δώδεκα, 14.17). Unless one wishes to argue that the two disciples sent in advance were female, no women were present at the Last Supper. For a fuller examination of the issues involved in critically reading Mark's androcentric language, see my article, 'Full Disclosure: Toward a More Complete Characterization of the Women Who Followed Jesus in the Gospel of Mark', in Ingrid Rosa Kitzberger (ed.), *Transformative Encounters: Revisioning Jesus and Women* (Leiden: E.J. Brill, 1999), pp. 13-32.

30. Frank Kermode makes much of the anonymity of the young man (*The Genesis of Secrecy: On the Interpretation of Narrative* [Cambridge, MA: Harvard University Press, 1979], pp. 49-74). I treat the young man as 'an interested party' but not necessarily as a disciple. Throughout the Gospel Mark indicates that people other than the disciples and the Twelve associate with Jesus' fellowship; see, for example, 2.1, 10.32 and 10.52. The young man could be a member of the household at which Jesus ate the Last Supper; he could be someone who was curious about the crowd heading to Gethsemane and so followed them (14.43).

Conclusion

The Gospel closes with a portrait of communication thwarted. The women come to the tomb, seeking the risen Jesus. They do not know that Jesus would not be there but in Galilee, because they were not members of the group privileged to learn his plans. The young man, who overheard Jesus instructing the Twelve, passes the information along to the women, but does so in a manner that does not create a relationship. Jesus failed to consider the effects of his decisions on the women among his followers, the young man failed to establish a relationship with the women, and the women failed to confront the young man or even to report the incident to the other women who had accompanied them earlier.

What disturbs me is not that they are so afraid, because being abandoned by the fellowship to which one belongs is a fearful prospect. Furthermore, many women have been and are silenced from fear all the time — wives afraid to confront husbands who neglect them because the wives are economically dependent on their spouses; daughters who have been sexually abused but who fear they will not be believed and who mistakenly believe they are at fault; poor women who must conceal relationships rather than risk the loss of welfare payments; students who want to investigate women's history or literature who fear their advisors or professors will not take their work seriously; many other women in many disparate circumstances. Compassion is called for, and the end of Mark's Gospel is a rare New Testament text that presents women's failure with sympathy. More precisely, according to Thomas E. Boomershine, Mark invites readers to regard the women sympathetically even though they fail to communicate with other disciples, a failure that Mark condemns.[31]

Boomershine's argument rests on the norms of judgment and ethical action implicit in Mark's narrative technique and characterization of the women. The scene at the tomb is narrated in 'inside view, in which the narrator reports the internal thoughts or feelings' of the characters.[32] By providing an inside view, Mark induces the reader to identify with the women. The three emotional responses of the women ('fear', φόβος; 'astonishment', ἔκστασις; and 'trembling', τρόμος; 16.8) have positive ethical connotations throughout the Gospel.[33] The women's

31. Thomas E. Boomershine, 'Mark 16.8 and the Apostolic Commission', *JBL* 100 (1981), pp. 225-39.
32. Boomershine, 'Mark 16.18', p. 227.
33. Boomershine, 'Mark 16.8', p. 228.

flight and silence have strong negative connotations.[34] Thus, Mark presents a complex characterization of the women. Their emotions are understandable; their actions—flight and the decision to be silent— are wrong.[35]

I am disturbed and disappointed that they do not tell the other women with them about what happened at the tomb. I have difficulty being sympathetic at this point, because I value communication among women. Feminists have difficulty admitting that women do fail one another. Further work on the ending of Mark could provide a fruitful starting point for examining this issue. At the same time, I wonder about what they could say: 'We learned that Jesus left us behind?' Or, 'We learned that we should go to Galilee; could that be right?' Either would be a more constructive choice than remaining silent.

However, part of what it means to be oppressed, or to be over-whelmed, or to be marginalized is that one may lack the capacity to choose something other than silence. The effort by feminists to articulate how patriarchal culture silences women is testimony to power relations that are involved in acts of speaking. Emerging from a marginalized role into a visible role, as is the case with the women who go to the tomb, does not mean that one will be successful with-out further changes in consciousness. Liberation theologians as well as therapists who work with victims of sexual violence explain that a process of transforming consciousness is necessary.

Integral to that transformation is consciousness-raising. One route to consciousness-raising is the telling of stories. According to Beverly Wildung Harrison,

> Conscientization involves recognition that what we have experienced, in isolation and silence, as private pain is in fact a public, structural dynamic. *My* life is now perceived in a new way in light of *your* stories. Together we slowly re-vision our reality so that what appeared, origi-nally, to be an individual or personalized 'problem' or even a human 'failing', is exposed as a basic systemic pattern of injustice.[36]

Exploring the dynamics that silenced the women who followed Jesus is a way to contribute to such re-visioning.

34. Boomershine, 'Mark 16.8', p. 229.

35. I do not agree with Boomershine as to why their actions are wrong. He believes that the young man is an angel and that 'the women's silence is, therefore, the exact opposite of the angel's command... It is the most blatant form of disobedience to a divine commission' ('Mark 16.8', p. 229). As I explained earlier, I do not interpret the young man as an angel.

36. Beverly Wildung Harrison, 'Theological Reflection in the Struggle for Liberation: A Feminist Perspective', in Carol S. Robb (ed.), *Making the Connections: Essays in Feminist Social Ethics* (Boston, MA: Beacon Press, 1985), pp. 235-63 (243).

BIBLIOGRAPHY

Abrahams, I., 'Publicans and Sinners', in I. Abrahams, M.S. Enslin and H.M. Orlinsky (eds.), *Studies in Pharisaism and the Gospels* (New York: Ktav, 1967), pp. 54-61.

Abu-Lughod, L., 'Zones of Theory in the Anthropology of the Arab World', *Annual Review of Anthropology* 18 (1989), pp. 267-306.

Allberry, C.R.C., *A Manichaean Psalmbook, Part 2* (Manichäische Handschriften der Sammlung A. Chester Beatty, 2; Stuttgart: W. Kohlhammer, 1938).

Alwis, M. de, 'Motherhood as Space Protest: Women's Political Participation in Contemporary Sri Lanka', in Patricia Jeffrey and Amrita Basu (eds.), *Appropriating Gender: Women's Activism and Politicized Religion in South Asia* (New York: Routledge, 1998), pp. 185-201.

Anderson, J.C., 'Matthew: Gender and Reading', *Semeia* 28 (1983), pp. 3-27.

Anderson, J.C., and S.D. Moore (eds.), *Mark and Method: New Approaches in Biblical Studies* (Philadelphia: Fortress Press, 1992).

Aquino, M.P., 'Including Women's Experience: A Latina Feminist Perspective', in O'Hara Graff (ed.), *In the Embrace of God*, pp. 51-70.

Arai, S., *Iesu Kirisuto* (Tokyo: Kodansha, 1979).

Atwood, R., *Mary Magdalene in the New Testament Gospels and Early Tradition* (New York: Peter Lang, 1993).

Avigad, N., 'Epitaph of a Royal Steward from a Siloam Village', *IEJ* 3 (1953), pp. 137-52.

—'A Seal of a Slave-Wife (Amah)', *PEQ* 78 (1946), pp. 125-32.

Bagwe, A., *Of Woman Caste: The Experience of Gender in Rural India* (Atlantic Highlands, NJ: Zed Books, 1995).

Baltzer, K., 'Liberation for Debt Slavery After the Exile in Second Isaiah and Nehemiah', in P.D. Miller *et al.* (eds.), *Ancient Israelite Religion: Essays in Honor of Frank Moore Cross* (Philadelphia: Fortress Press, 1987), pp. 477-84.

Barrett, C.K., *The Gospel according to John* (London: SPCK, 1978).

Batey, R.A., *Jesus and the Forgotten City: New Light on Sepphoris and the Urban World of Jesus* (Grand Rapids: Baker Book House, 1991).

Bauckham, R., 'Salome the Sister of Jesus, Salome the Disciple of Jesus, and the Secret Gospel of Mark', *NovT* 33 (1991), pp. 245-75.

Beasley-Murray, G.R., *John* (WBC; Waco, TX: Word Books, 1987).

Beavis, M.A., 'Women as Models of Faith in Mark', *BTB* 18 (1988), pp. 3-9.

Belo, F., *A Materialist Reading of the Gospel of Mark* (Maryknoll, NY: Orbis Books, 1981).

Benoit, P., *The Passsion and Resurrection of Jesus Christ* (New York: Herder & Herder, 1969).

Berthiaume, G., *Les rôles du mágeiros: Étude sur la boucherie, la cuisine et le sacrifice dans la Grèce ancienne* (Leiden: E.J. Brill, 1982).

Best, E., *Following Jesus: Discipleship in the Gospel of Mark* (JSNTSup, 4; Sheffield: JSOT Press, 1981).

—'The Role of the Disciples in Mark', *NTS* 23 (1977), pp. 377-401.

Beyer, H.W., 'διακονέω, διακονία, διάκονος', *TDNT*, II, pp. 81-93.

Bible and Culture Collective, *The Postmodern Bible* (New Haven: Yale University Press, 1995).

Boomershine, T., 'Mark 16.8 and the Apostolic Commission', *JBL* 100 (1981), pp. 225-39.

Borg, M., *Meeting Jesus Again for the First Time: The Historical Jesus and the Heart of Contemporary Faith* (San Francisco: HarperSanFrancisco, 1994).

Boring, M.E., *The Gospel of Matthew* (NIB, 8; Nashville: Abingdon Press, 1995).

Bourdieu, P., *Outline of a Theory of Practice* (trans. Richard Nice; Cambridge: Cambridge University Press, 1977).

—'The Sentiment of Honour in Kabyle Society', in J.G. Peristiany (ed.), *Honor and Shame: The Values of Mediterranean Society* (trans. P. Sherrard; London: Weidenfeld & Nicolson, 1965).

Bradley, K.R., *Slaves and Masters in the Roman Empire: A Study in Social Control* (New York: Oxford University Press, 1984).

Brock, R. Nakashima, 'Dusting the Floor: A Hermeneutics of Wisdom', in Fiorenza (ed.), *Searching the Scriptures*, I, pp. 64-75.

—*Journeys by Heart: A Christology of Erotic Power* (New York: Crossroad, 1988).

Brooke, G.J. (ed.), *Women in the Biblical Tradition* (Studies in Women and Religion, 31; Lewiston, NY: Edwin Mellen Press, 1992).

Brooten, B., 'Jewish Women's History in the Roman Period: A Task for Christian Theology', *HTR* 79 (1986), pp. 22-30.

—*Women Leaders in the Ancient Synagogue: Inscriptional Evidence and Background Issues* (BJS, 36; Chico, CA: Scholars Press, 1982).

Brown, J.C., and R. Parker, 'For God So Loved the World?', in J.C. Brown and C.R. Bohn (eds.), *Christianity, Patriarchy, and Abuse* (New York: Pilgrim, 1989), pp. 1-30.

Brown, R.E., *The Death of the Messiah: A Commentary on the Passion Narratives in the Four Gospels* (2 vols.; New York: Doubleday, 1994).

Brown, R.E., *et al.* (eds.), *Mary in the New Testament* (New York: Paulist Press, 1978).

Buchanan, G.W., 'Jesus and the Upper Class', *NovT* 7 (1964/65), pp. 195-209.

Bultmann, R., *Gospel of John: A Commentary* (Philadelphia: Westminster Press, 1971).

—*History of the Synoptic Tradition* (trans. J. Marsh; Oxford: Basil Blackwell; New York: Harper & Row; 2nd edn, 1968 [1963]).

Calame, C., *Les choers de jeunes filles en Grece archaique* (2 vols.; Roma: Edizioni del'Ateneo and Bizzari, 1977).

Cameron, A., 'Neither Male Nor Female', *Greece and Rome* 27 (1980), pp. 60-68.

Cameron, A., and A. Kuhrt (eds.), *Images of women in Antiquity* (Detroit, MI: Wayne State University Press, 1983).

Camp, C., 'Feminist Theological Hermeneutics: Canon and Christian Identity', in Fiorenza (ed.), *Searching the Scriptures*, I, pp. 154-71.

Cantarella, E., *Pandora's Daughters: The Role and Status of Women in Greek and Roman Antiquity* (trans. M.B. Fant; Baltimore: The Johns Hopkins University Press, 1987).

Cardenal, E., *The Gospel in Solentiname*, II (trans. D.D. Walsh; Maryknoll, NY: Orbis Books, 1978).

Casson, L., *Travel in the Ancient World* (Baltimore: The Johns Hopkins University Press, 1994).

Catchpole, D., 'The Fearful Silence of the Women at the Tomb: A Study in Markan Theology', *Journal of Theology for Southern Africa* 18 (1977), pp. 3-10.

Chilton, B., *Profiles of a Rabbi: Synoptic Opportunities in Reading about Jesus* (Atlanta: Scholars Press, 1989).

Clark, G., *Women in the Ancient World* (Oxford: Oxford University Press, 1989).

Collins, A.Y., *The Beginning of the Gospel: Probings of Mark in Context* (Philadelphia: Fortress Press, 1992).

—'Composition of the Markan Passion Narrative', *Sewanee Theological Review* 36 (1992), pp. 57-77.

Collins, J.N., *Diakonia: Re-interpreting the Ancient Sources* (New York: Oxford University Press, 1990).

Cooper, M., 'Winsome Munro—1925–1994', *RSN* 9.3 (Sept. 1994), p. 24.

Corley, K.E., 'The Egalitarian Jesus: A Christian Myth of Origins', *Forum* NS 1, 2 (1998), pp. 291-325.

—'Jesus' Table Practice: Dining with "Tax Collectors and Sinners", Including Women', in Eugene Lovering (ed.), *SBL 1993 Seminar Papers* (Atlanta: Scholars Press, 1993).

—'A Place at the Table: Women and Meals in the Synoptic Gospels' (PhD dissertation, Claremont Graduate School, 1992).

—*Private Women, Public Meals: Social Conflict in the Synoptic Tradition* (Peabody, MA: Hendrickson, 1993).

—'Salome', *ISBE*, IV, p. 286.

—*Women and the Historical Jesus* (Sonoma, CA: Polebridge Press, forthcoming).

Cotes, M., 'Women, Silence and Fear (Mark 16:8)', in G.J. Brooke (ed.), *Women in the Biblical Tradition*, pp. 150-66.

Crossan, J.D., *The Cross that Spoke: The Origins of the Passion Narrative* (San Francisco: Harper & Row, 1988).

—*The Historical Jesus: The Life of a Mediterranean Jewish Peasant* (San Francisco: HarperSanFrancisco, 1991).

—'Mark and the Relatives of Jesus', *NovT* 15 (1973), pp. 81-113.

—*Who Killed Jesus? Exposing the Roots of Anti-Semitism in the Gospel Story of the Death of Jesus* (San Francisco: HarperSan Francisco, 1995).

Cullmann, O., 'Infancy Gospels: The Protevangelium of James', in E. Hennecke and W. Schneemelcher (eds.), *New Testament Apocrypha*, I (Philadelphia: Westminster Press, rev. edn, 1991), pp. 421-69.

D'Angelo, Mary-Rose, 'Abba and "Father": Imperial Theology and the Jesus Tradition', *JBL* 111 (1992), pp. 611-30.

—'Re-membering Jesus: Women, Prophecy, and Resistance in the Memory of the Early Churches', *Horizon* 19 (1992), pp. 199-218.

—'Theology in Mark and Q: Abba and "Father" in Context', *HTR* 85 (1992), pp. 149-74.

—'Gender and Power in the Gospel of Mark: The Daughter of Jairus and the Woman with the Flow of Blood', in J.C. Cavadini (ed.), *Miracles in Jewish and Christian Antiquity: Imagining Truth* (Notre Dame: University of Notre Dame Press, 1999).

—'Reconstructing "Real" Women in Gospel Literature', in R.S. Kraemer and M.R. D'Angelo (eds.), *Women and Christian Origins* (New York: Oxford University Press, 1999), pp. 105-28.

—'Remembering—Women Partners in the New Testament', *JFSR* 6 (1990), pp. 65-86.

D'Arms, J.H., 'The Roman *Convivium* and the Idea of Equality', in Murray (ed.), *Sympotica*, pp. 308-20.

—'Slaves at Roman Convivia', in Slater (ed.), *Dining in a Classical Context*, pp. 171-83.

Daube, D., *Roman Law: Linguistic, Social and Philosophical Aspects* (Edinburgh: Edinburgh University Press, 1969).

Dauer, A., *Passionsgeschichte im Johannesevangelium* (Munich: Kösel, 1972).

Davis, J., *People of the Mediterranean: An Essay in Comparative Social Anthropology* (London: Routledge & Kegan Paul, 1977).

De Alwis, M., 'Motherhood as Space Protest: Women's Political Participation in Contemporary Sri Lanka', in P. Jeffrey and A. Basu (eds.), *Appropriating Gender: Women's Activism and Politicized Religion in South Asia* (London: Routledge, 1998), pp. 185-201.

Derrida, J., *Margins of Philosophy* (trans. A. Bass; Chicago: University of Chicago Press, 1982).

Des Bouvrie, S., *Women in Greek Tragedy: An Anthropological Approach* (Oslo: Norwegian University Press, 1990).

Détienne, M., and J.-P. Vernant, *The Cuisine of Sacrifice among the Greeks* (trans. P. Wissing; Chicago: University of Chicago Press, 1986).

Dewey, J., *Disciples on the Way: Mark on Discipleship* (Women's Division, Board of Global Ministries, United Methodist Church, 1976).

—'The Gospel of Mark', in Fiorenza (ed.), *Searching the Scriptures*, II, pp. 470-509.

—'A Rejection of Sacrifice', *The Centerpoint* 1 *Voices* (May 1997), pp. 1-4.

—'The Gospel of Mark as Oral/Aural Event: Implications for Interpretation', in Malbon and McKnight (eds.), *New Literary Criticism*, pp. 145-63.

—'Women in the Synoptic Gospels: Seen but Not Heard?', *BTB* 27 (1997), pp. 53-60.

Dibelius, M., *From Tradition to Gospel* (New York: Charles Scribner's Sons, 1965; Greenwood, SC: Attic Press, 1982).

Donahue, J., *Are You the Christ?* (SBLDS, 10; Missoula, MT: Scholars Press, 1973).

Downing, F.G., 'The Women from Syrophoenicia', in Brooke (ed.), *Women in the Biblical Tradition*, pp. 129-49.

Dozier, V., and J.R. Adams, *Sisters and Brothers: Reclaiming a Biblical Idea of Community* (Cambridge, MA: Cowley, 1993).

Dunbabin, K., 'Triclinium and Stibadium', in Slater (ed.), *Dining in a Classical Context*, pp. 121-48.

Epstein, L.M., *Marriage Laws in the Bible and the Talmud* (Cambridge, MA: Harvard University Press, 1942).

Evans, C.A., 'Jesus' Action in the Temple: Cleansing or Portent of Destruction?', *CBQ* 51 (1989), pp. 237-70.

Fagles, R. (trans.), *The Odyssey/Homer* (trans. R. Fagles; New York: Viking, 1996).

Fander, M., 'Frauen in der Nachfolge Jesu: die Rolle der Frau im Markusevangelium', *EvT* 52 (1992), pp. 413-32.

Fatum, L., 'Gender Hermeneutics: The Effective History of Consciousness and the

Use of Social Gender in the Gospels', in M.A. Tolbert and F.F. Segovia (eds.), *Reading from This Place*, II (Minneapolis, MN: Fortress Press, 1995), pp. 157-68.

Fehr, B., 'Entertainers at the Symposion: The *Akletoi* in the Archaic Period', in Murray (ed.), *Sympotica*, pp. 185-95.

Fetterley, J., *The Resisting Reader: A Feminist Approach to American Fiction* (Blooming-ton: Indiana University Press, 1978).

Finegan, J., *Archaeology of the New Testament* (Princeton, NJ: Princeton University Press, 1992).

Fiorenza, E.S., *Bread Not Stone: The Challenge of Feminist Biblical Interpretation* (Boston, MA: Beacon Press, 1984).

—*But She Said* (Boston, MA: Beacon Press, 1992).

—*In Memory of Her: A Feminist Theological Reconstruction of Christian Origins* (New York: Crossroad, 1985).

—*Jesus: Miriam's Child, Sophia's Prophet: Critical Issues in Feminist Christology* (New York: Continuum, 1994).

—(ed.), *Searching the Scriptures: A Feminist Introduction* (2 vols.; New York: Cross-road, 1993, 1994).

—*Sharing Her Word: Feminist Biblical Interpretation in Context* (Boston, MA: Beacon Press, 1998).

—'The Twelve', in L. Swidler and A. Swidler (eds.), *Women Priests: A Catholic Commentary on the Vatican Declaration* (Mahwah, NJ: Paulist Press, 1977), pp. 114-22.

—'"You Are Not to Be Called Father": Early Christian History in a Feminist Perspective', *Cross Currents* 29 (1979), pp. 301-23.

Fitzmyer, J., *The Gospel According to Luke I–IX* (AB, 28; New York: Doubleday, 1981).

Flesher, P.V.M., *Oxen, Women or Citizens? Slaves in the System of the Mishnah* (Atlanta: Scholars Press, 1988).

Forster, E.M., *Aspects of the Novel* (repr.; New York: Harcourt, Brace & World, 1954 [1927]).

Fredriksen, P., 'Did Jesus Oppose the Purity Laws?', *BR* (June 1995), pp. 18-25, 42-47.

Funk, R.W., *Honest to Jesus: Jesus for a New Millennium* (San Francisco: HarperSan-Francisco, 1996).

Gailey, C.W., 'Evolutionary Perspectives in Gender Hierarchy', in B.B. Hess and M.M. Ferree (eds.), *Analyzing Gender: A Handbook of Social Science Research* (Beverly Hills, CA: Sage Publications, 1987).

Galling, K. (ed.), *Biblisches Reallexikon* (Tübingen: J.C.B. Mohr, 1937).

Garland, R., *The Greek Way of Life: From Conception to Old Age* (Ithaca, NY: Cornell University Press, 1990).

Gero, G., and M. Conkey (eds.), *Engendering Archaeology* (Oxford: Basil Blackwell, 1991).

Gibbs, J.G., and L.H. Feldman, 'Josephus' Vocabulary for Slavery', *JQR* 76 (1986), pp. 281-310.

Giess, H., *Die Darstellung der Fusswaschung Christi in den Kunstwerken des 4.–12. Jahrhunderts* (Rome: Casa Editrice Herder, 1962).

Gifford, C. DeSwarte, 'American Women and the Bible: The Nature of Woman as a Hermeneutical Issue', in A.Y. Collins (ed.), *Feminist Perspectives on Biblical Scholarship* (Chico, CA: Scholars Press, 1985), pp. 11-33.

Gilmore, D., 'Anthropology of the Mediterranean Area', *ARA* 11 (1982), pp. 175-205.

Gilmore, D. (ed.), *Honor and Shame and the Unity of the Mediterranean* (Washington, DC: American Anthropological Association, 1987).

Goodman, M., 'The First Jewish Revolt: Social Conflict and the Problem of Debt', *JJS* 33 (1982), pp. 417-27.

Gould, E.P., *The Gospel According to St. Mark* (ICC, 27; Edinburgh: T. & T. Clark, 1896).

Graff, A. O'Hara, 'The Struggle to Name Women's Experience', in *eadem* (ed.), *In the Embrace of God*, pp. 71-89.

—(ed.), *In the Embrace of God: Feminist Approaches to Theological Anthropology* (Maryknoll, NY: Orbis Books, 1995).

Graham, S.L., 'Silent Voices: Women in the Gospel of Mark', *Semeia* 54 (1993), pp. 153-56.

Grassi, J.A., 'The Secret Heroine of Mark's Drama', *BTB* 18 (1988), pp. 9-15.

—*Hidden Heroes of the Gospels: Female Counterparts of Jesus* (Collegeville, MN: Liturgical Press, 1989).

Green, J.B., *Death of Jesus: Tradition and Interpretation in the Passion Narrative* (Tübingen: J.C.B. Mohr, 1988).

—'Good News to Whom? Jesus and the "Poor" in the Gospel of Luke', in Green and Turner (eds.), *Jesus of Nazareth*, pp. 59-74.

Green, J.B., and M. Turner (eds.), *Jesus of Nazareth: Lord and Christ: Essays on the Historical Jesus and New Testament Christology* (Grand Rapids: Eerdmans, 1994).

Guardiola-Saenz, L.A., 'Borderless Women and Borderless Texts: A Cultural Reading of Matthew 15:21-28', *Semeia* 78 (1997), pp. 69-81.

Gundry, R., *Mark: A Commentary on His Apology for the Cross* (Grand Rapids: Eerdmans, 1993).

—*Matthew: A Commentary on His Literary and Theological Art* (Grand Rapids: Eerdmans, 1982).

Haenchen, E., *Der Weg Jesu: Eine Erklärung des Markusevangeliums und der kanonischen Parallelen* (Berlin: Alfred Töpelmann, 1968).

Hamel, G., *Poverty and Charity in Roman Palestine, First Three Centuries* (Berkeley: University of California Press, 1990).

Harrison, B.W., 'Theological Reflection in the Struggle for Liberation: A Feminist Perspective', in C.S. Robb (ed.), *Making the Connections: Essays in Feminist Social Ethics* (Boston, MA: Beacon Press, 1985).

Haskins, S., *Mary Magdalene: Myth and Metaphor* (New York: Harcourt Brace & Company, 1993).

Heichelheim, F.M., *An Economic Survey of Ancient Rome. IV. Roman Syria* (Baltimore: The Johns Hopkins University Press, 1938).

Heinemann, J.H., 'The Status of the Jewish Labourer in Jewish Law and Society in the Tannaitic Period', *HUCA* 25 (1954), pp. 263-325.

Herzfeld, M., 'As in Your Own House: Hospitality, Ethnography, and the Stereotype of Mediterranean Society', in Gilmore (ed.), *Honor and Shame*, pp. 75-89.

—'Honor and Shame: Problems in the Comparative Analysis of Moral Systems', *Man* 15 (1980), pp. 339-51.

— 'The Horns of the Mediterraneanist Dilemma', *American Ethnologist* 11 (1984), pp. 439-54.

— *The Poetics of Manhood: Contest and Identity in a Cretan Mountain Village* (Princeton, NJ: Princeton University Press, 1985).

Herzog, W.R., II, *Parables as Subversive Speech: Jesus as Pedagogue of the Oppressed* (Louisville, KY: Westminster/John Knox Press, 1994), pp. 53-73.

Hock, F.H., and E.N. O'Neil (eds.), *The Chreia in Ancient Rhetoric*, I (Atlanta: Scholars Press, 1986).

Hock, R.F., *The Infancy Gospels of James and Thomas* (Santa Rosa, CA: Polebridge Press, 1995).

Homer, *The Odyssey* (trans. R. Fagles; New York: Viking, 1996).

Hooker, Morna, *A Commentary on the Gospel According to St. Mark* (BNTC; London: A. & C. Black, 1991).

hooks, b., *Feminist Theory from Margin to Center* (Boston, MA: South End, 1984).

Horsley, R.A., *Jesus and the Spiral of Violence* (San Francisco: HarperSanFrancisco, 1987).

Hull, J.M., *Hellenistic Magic and the Synoptic Tradition* (Naperville, IL: SCM Press, 1974).

Hurtado, L.W., 'Following Jesus in the Gospel of Mark—and Beyond', in R.N. Longenecker (ed.), *Patterns of Discipleship in the New Testament* (Grand Rapids: Eerdmans, 1996), pp. 9-29.

Ilan, T., *Jewish Women in Greco-Roman Palestine: An Inquiry into Image and Status* (Texte und Studien zum Antiken Judentum, 44; Tübingen: J.C.B. Mohr, 1995).

— '"Man Born of Woman..." Job 14:1: The Phenomenon of Men Bearing Matronymes at the Time of Jesus', *NovT* 34 (1992), pp. 23-45.

— 'Notes on the Distribution of Jewish Women's Names in Palestine in the Second Temple and Mishnaic Periods', *JJS* 40 (1989), pp. 186-200.

James, M.R. (ed.), *The Apocryphal New Testament* (Oxford: Clarendon Press, 1953).

Japhet, S., 'The Laws of Manumission of Slaves and the Question of the Relationship between the Collections of Laws in the Pentateuch', in Y. Avishur and J. Blau (eds.), *Studies in the Bible and the Near East Presented to Samuel E. Lowenstamm* (Jerusalem: E. Rubinstein's Publishing House, 1978), pp. 199-201.

Jepson, A., 'Amah und Schiphchah', *VT* 8 (1958), pp. 293-97.

Jeremias, J., *Jerusalem in the Time of Jesus: An Investigation into Economic and Social Conditions during the New Testament Period* (trans. F.H. and C.H. Cave; Philadelphia: Fortress Press, 1969).

Jones, A.H.M., 'Slavery in the Ancient World', in idem (ed.), *Slavery in Classical Antiquity*.

— (ed.), *Slavery in Classical Antiquity* (Cambridge: W. Heffer & Sons, 1960).

Jones, C., 'Dinner Theater', in Slater (ed.), *Dining in a Classical Context*, pp. 185-98.

Judge, E.A., 'The Early Christians as a Scholastic Community', *JRH* 1 (1960), pp. 4-15.

Kee, H.C., *Community of the New Age: Studies in Mark's Gospel* (Philadelphia: Westminster Press, 1977).

Kelber, W.H., *The Kingdom in Mark: A New Place and a New Time* (Philadelphia: Fortress Press, 1974).

— *The Oral and the Written Gospel: The Hermeneutics of Speaking and Writing in the Synoptic Tradition, Mark, Paul, and Q* (Philadelphia: Fortress Press, 1983).

Kermode, F., *The Genesis of Secrecy* (Cambridge, MA: Harvard University Press, 1979).

Keuls, E., *The Reign of the Phallus: Sexual Politics in Ancient Athens* (New York: Harper & Row, 1985).

Kincaid, J.R., 'Coherent Readers, Incoherent Texts', *Critical Inquiry* 3 (1977), pp. 781-802.

King, K.L., 'Prophetic Power and Women's Authority: The Case of the Gospel of Mary (Magdalene)', in B.M. Kienzle and P.J. Walker (eds.), *Women Preachers and Prophets through Two Millennia of Christianity* (Berkeley: University of California Press, 1998), pp. 21-41.

—'The Gospel of Mary Magdalene', in Fiorenza (ed.), *Searching the Scriptures*, II, pp. 614-25.

Kinneavy, J.L., *Greek Rhetorical Origins of Christian Faith: An Inquiry* (New York: Oxford University Press, 1987).

Kinukawa, H., *Women and Jesus in Mark: A Japanese Feminist Perspective* (Maryknoll, NY: Orbis Books, 1994).

Kittel, G., ''Ἀκολουθέω', *TDNT*, I, p. 213.

Kitzberger, I.R. (ed.), *Transformative Encounters: Jesus and Women Re-viewed* (Leiden: E.J. Brill, 1999).

Kloppenborg, J.S., 'Alms, Debt and Divorce: Jesus' Ethics in Their Mediterranean Context', *Toronto Journal of Theology* 6 (1990), pp. 182-200.

Koester, H., *Ancient Christian Gospels: Their History and Development* (London: SCM Press; Philadelphia: Trinity Press International, 1990).

Kopas, J., 'Jesus and Women in Mark's Gospel', *Review for Religious* 44 (1985), pp. 912-20.

Kraemer, R.S., *Her Share of the Blessings: Women's Religions Among Pagans, Jews, and Christians in the Greco-Roman World* (New York: Oxford University Press, 1992).

Kraus, H.J., *Psalms 1–59* (trans. H.C. Oswald; Minneapolis: Augsburg, 1988).

Kwok, P., *Discovering the Bible in the Non-Biblical World* (Maryknoll, NY: Orbis Books, 1995).

LaCapra, D. *Rethinking Intellectual History: Texts, Contexts, Language* (Ithaca, NY: Cornell University Press, 1983).

Lefkowitz, M.R., 'Influential Women', in Cameron and Kuhrt (eds.), *Images of Women in Antiquity*, pp. 49-64.

Lefkowitz, M.R., and M.B. Fant, *Women's Life in Greece and Rome: A Source Book in Translation* (Baltimore: The Johns Hopkins University Press, 2nd edn, 1992).

Lemche, N.P., 'The "Hebrew Slave": Comments on the Slave Law Ex 21:2-11', *VT* 25 (1975), pp. 129-44.

—'The Manumission of Slaves—the Fallow Year—the Sabbatical Year—the Jubal Year', *VT* 26 (1976), pp. 38-59.

Levine, A.-J., 'Discharging Responsibility: Matthean Jesus, Biblical Law, and Hemorrhaging Woman', in D.R. Bauer and M.A. Powell (eds.), *Treasures New and Old: Contributions to Matthean Studies* (Atlanta: Scholars Press, 1996), pp. 379-97.

—'Matthew', in Newsom and Ringe (eds.), *The Women's Bible Commentary*, pp. 252-62.

—'Second Temple Judaism, Jesus and Women: Yeast of Eden', *BibInt* 2 (1994), pp. 8-33.

— *The Social and Ethnic Dimensions of Matthean Salvation History: 'Go Nowhere among the Gentiles' (Matt 10.5b)* (Studies in the Bible and Early Christianity, 14; Lewiston, NY: Edwin Mellen Press, 1988).

Liew, T.B., *Politics of Parousia: Reading Mark Inter(con)textually* (Political Interpretation Series: Leiden: E.J. Brill, 1999).

Lightfoot, R.H., *The Gospel Message of St. Mark* (Oxford: Clarendon Press, 1950).

Lincoln, A.T., 'The Promise and the Failure: Mark 16:7, 8', *JBL* 108 (1989), pp. 283-300.

Lindars, B., *The Gospel of John* (London: Oliphants, 1972).

Llewelyn, S.R., and R.A. Kearsley, 'The Sale of a Slave Girl: The New Testament Attitude to Slavery', in S.R. Llewelyn (ed.), *New Documents Illustrating Early Christianity*, VI (Macquarie University, Australia: Ancient History Documentary Research Centre, 1992).

Lloyd-Jones, H. (trans.), *Females of the Species: Semonides on Women* (Parkridge, NJ: Noyes Press, 1975).

Lorde, A., *Sister Outsider: Essays and Speeches* (Trumansburg, NY: Crossing Press, 1984).

Lüdemann, G., *The Resurrection of Jesus: History, Experience, Theology* (Minneapolis, MN: Fortress Press, 1994).

Mack, B.L., *A Myth of Innocence: Mark and Christian Origins* (Philadelphia: Fortress Press, 1988).

Mack, B.L., and V.K. Robbins, *Patterns of Persuasion in the Gospels* (Sonoma, CA: Polebridge Press, 1989).

Malbon, E.S., 'Disciples/Crowds/Whoever: Markan Characters and Readers', *NovT* 28.2 (1986), pp. 104-30.

—'Fallible Followers: Women in the Gospel of Mark', *Semeia* 28 (1983), pp. 29-48.

—'The Jewish Leaders in the Gospel of Mark: A Literary Study of Marcan Characterization', *JBL* 108 (1989), pp. 259-81.

—'Narrative Criticism: How Does the Story Mean?' in J.C. Anderson and Moore (eds.), *Mark and Method* (Minneapolis: Fortress Press, 1992), pp. 23-49.

— *Narrative Space and Mythic Meaning in Mark* (San Francisco: Harper & Row, 1986).

—'The Poor Widow in Mark and her Poor Rich Readers', *CBQ* 53.4 (1991), pp. 589-604.

Malbon, E.S., and E.V. McKnight (eds.), *New Literary Criticism and the New Testament* (JSNTSup, 109; Sheffield: Sheffield Academic Press, 1994), pp. 145-63.

Malina, B., '"Let Him Deny Himself" (Mark 8:34 & par): A Social Psychological Model of Self-Denial', *BTB* 24 (1994), pp. 106-19.

Malina, B., and R. Rohrbaugh, *Social Science Commentary on the Synoptic Gospels* (Minneapolis: Fortress Press, 1992).

Martin, D.B., 'Slavery and the Ancient Jewish Family', in S.J.D. Cohen (ed.), *The Jewish Family in Antiquity* (Atlanta: Scholars Press, 1993), pp. 113-29.

Matera, F.J., *The Kingship of Jesus: Composition and Theology in Mark 15* (Chico, CA: Scholars Press, 1982).

Mayer, G., *Die jüdische Frau in der hellenistisch-römischen Antike* (Stuttgart: W. Kohlhammer, 1987).

McArthur, H.K., 'Son of Mary', *NovTest* 15 (1973), pp. 38-58.

McCane, B.R., 'Let the Dead Bury Their Own Dead: Secondary Burial and Matt 8:21-22', *HTR* 83 (1990), pp. 31-43.

McClellan, T.L., 'Tyre', *HDB*, pp. 1101-1102.

Mendelsohn, I., 'The Conditional Sale into Slavery of Free-Born Daughters in Nuzi and the Law of Exodus 21:7-11', *JAOS* 55 (1935), pp. 190-95.

—*Slavery in the Ancient Near East* (New York: Oxford University Press, 1949).

Meyer, M., 'The Youth in the Secret Gospel of Mark', *Semeia* 49 (1990), pp. 129-53.

—'The Youth in Secret Mark and the Beloved Disciple in John', in J.E. Goehring *et al.* (eds.), *Gospel Origins and Christian Beginnings: In Honor of James M. Robinson* (Sonoma, CA: Polebridge Press, 1990), pp. 94-105.

Meyers, E.M., J.F. Strange and C.L. Meyers (eds.), *Excavations at Ancient Meiron, Upper Galilee* (Cambridge, MA: American Schools of Oriental Research, 1981).

Miller, J. Baker, *Toward a New Psychology of Women* (Boston, MA: Beacon Press, 1976).

Moltmann-Wendel, E., *A Land Flowing with Milk and Honey: Perspectives on Feminist Theology* (trans. J. Bowden; New York: Crossroad, 1988).

—*The Women Around Jesus: Reflections on Authentic Personhood* (London: SCM Press, 1982).

Mosko, M.S., 'The Developmental Cycle among Public Groups', *Man* 24 (1989), pp. 470-84.

Munro, W., 'Women Disciples in Mark?', *CBQ* 44 (1982), pp. 225-41.

—'Women Disciples: Light From Secret Mark', *JFSR* 9 (1992), pp. 47-64.

Murray, O. (ed.), *Sympotica: A Symposium on the Symposion* (Oxford: Clarendon Press, 1990).

Myers, C., *Binding the Strong Man: A Political Reading of Mark's Story of Jesus* (Maryknoll, NY: Orbis Books, 1988).

Nathanson, B.H. Geller, 'Toward A Multicultural Ecumenical History of Women in the First Century/ies C.E.', in Fiorenza (ed.), *Searching the Scriptures*, I, pp. 272-89.

Neusner, J., *From Politics to Piety: The Emergence of Pharisaic Judaism* (Englewood Cliffs, NJ: Prentice–Hall, 1973).

—*The Pharisees: Rabbinic Perspectives* (Hoboken, NJ: Ktav, 1985).

—'Two Pictures of the Pharisees: Philosophical Circle or Eating Club', *ATR* 64 (1982), pp. 525-38.

Newsom, C.A., and S.H. Ringe (eds.), *The Women's Bible Commentary* (Philadelphia: Westminster Press, 1992).

Neyrey, J.H., *The Social World of Luke–Acts* (Peabody, MA: Hendrickson, 1991).

Nineham, D.E., *The Gospel of St Mark* (Pelican New Testament Commentaries; Baltimore, MD: Penguin Books, 1978).

Nunnally-Cox, J., *Feminist Foremothers: Women of the Bible* (New York: Seabury, 1981), pp. 99-117.

Oakman, D.E., *Jesus and the Economic Questions of his Day* (Lewiston, NY: Edwin Mellen Press, 1986).

O'Day, G.R., 'Surprised by Faith: Jesus and the Canaanite Woman', *Listening: Journal of Religion and Culture* 24 (1989), pp. 290-301.

Olrik, A., 'Epic Laws of Folk Narrative', in A. Dundes (ed.), *The Study of Folklore* (Englewood Cliffs, NJ: Prentice–Hall, 1965).

Ortner, S.B., 'Is Female to Male as Nature Is to Culture?', in Rosaldo and Lamphere (eds.), *Women, Culture, and Society*, pp. 67-87.

Osborne, G.R., *The Resurrection Narratives: A Redactional Study* (Grand Rapids: Baker Book House, 1984).

Osiek, C., 'Slavery in the Second Testament World', *BTB* 22 (1992), pp. 174-79.

Osiek, C., and D.L. Balch, *Families in the New Testament World: Households and House Churches* (Louisville, KY: Westminster/John Knox Press, 1997).

Page, J.G. (ed.), *Further Greek Epigrams: Epigrams before A.D. 50 from the Greek Anthology and Other Sources* (Cambridge: Cambridge University Press, 1981).

Pallares, J.C., *A Poor Man Called Jesus: Reflections on the Gospel according to Mark* (Maryknoll, NY: Orbis Books, 1986).

Patterson, O., *Slavery and Social Death: A Comparative Study* (Cambridge, MA: Harvard University Press, 1982).

Perelberg, R.J., 'Equality, Asymmetry, and Diversity: On Conceptualization of Gender', in Perelberg and Miller (eds.), *Gender and Power and Families*, pp. 34-60.

Perelberg, R.J., and A.C. Miller (eds.), *Gender and Power and Families* (London: Routledge, 1990).

Peristiany, J.G., *Honor and Shame: The Values of Mediterranean Society* (London: Weidenfeld & Nicolson, 1965).

Perkinson, J., 'A Canaanitic Word in the Logos of Christ; or the Difference the Syro-Phoenician Woman Makes to Jesus', *Semeia* 75 (1996), pp. 61-85.

Perrin, N., *The New Testament: An Introduction* (New York: Harcourt Brace Jovanovich, 1974).

—*The Resurrection According to Matthew, Mark and Luke* (Philadelphia: Fortress Press, 1977).

—*What Is Redaction Criticism?* (Philadelphia: Fortress Press, 1969).

Pervo, R., *Profit with Delight: The Literary Genre of the Acts of the Apostles* (Philadelphia: Fortress Press, 1987).

Phillips, V., 'Full Disclosure: Toward a More Complete Characterization of the Women Who Followed Jesus in the Gospel of Mark', in Kitzberger (ed.), *Transformative Encounters*, pp. 13-32.

Pilch, J.J., '"Beat His Ribs While He is Young" (Sir 30:12): A Window on the Mediterranean World', *BTB* 23 (1993), pp. 101-13.

—'Understanding Biblical Healing: Selecting the Appropriate Model', *BTB* 18 (1988), pp. 60-66.

Pitt-Rivers, J., *Mediterranean Countrymen: Essays in Social Anthropology of the Mediterranean* (Paris: Mouton, 1963).

Pomeroy, S.B., *Goddesses, Whores, Wives and Slaves: Women in Classical Antiquity* (New York: Schocken Books, 1975).

—'Selected Bibliography on Women in Antiquity', in J. Peradotto and J.P. Sulivan (eds.), *Women in the Ancient World: The Arethusa Papers* (Albany, NY: State of New York University Press, 1984), pp. 315-72.

Rahmani, L.Y., 'Ancient Jerusalem's Funerary Customs and Tombs', *BA* 44 (1981), pp. 171-77, 229-53, 45 (1982), pp. 109-19.

Ray, D.K., *Deceiving the Devil: Atonement, Abuse, and Ransom* (Cleveland, OH: Pilgrim Press, 1998).

Rebera, R., 'Power in a Discipleship of Equals', in M. Kanyoro (ed.), *In Search of a*

Round Table: Gender, Theology and Church Leadership (Geneva: WCC Publications, 1997), pp. 82-90.

—'Recognizing and Naming Power', *In God's Image: Journal of Asian Women's Resource Centre for Culture and Theology* 17.1 (1998), pp. 38-42.

—'Understanding Power: Intellectual Elitism or Catalyst to Change', *In God's Image: Journal of Asian Women's Resource Centre for Culture and Theology* 17:3 (1998), pp. 2-4.

—'Women's Identity in Leadership', in *eadem* (ed.), *Affirming Difference*, pp. 77-95.

Rebera, R. (ed.), *Affirming Difference, Celebrating Wholeness, a Partnership of Equals* (Hong Kong: CCA, 1995).

Rengstorf, K.H., 'μαθητής', *TDNT*, IV, pp. 416-61.

Rhoads, D., and D. Michie, *Mark as Story: An Introduction to the Narrative of a Gospel* (Philadelphia: Fortress Press, 1982).

Rhoads, D.J., J. Dewey and D. Michie, *Mark as Story: An Introduction to the Narrative of a Gospel* (Philadelphia: Fortress Press, 2nd edn, 1999 [1982]).

Ricci, C., *Mary Magdalene and Many Others: Women Who Followed Jesus* (trans. P. Burns; Minneapolis: Fortress Press, 1994).

Richardson, N.F., 'Recognition Scenes in the *Odyssey* and Ancient Literary Criticism', *Papers of the Liverpool Latin Seminar* 4 (1983), pp. 219–35.

Richter, G.M.A., and M.J. Milne, *Shapes and Names of Athenian Vases* (New York: Metropolitan Museum of Art, 1935).

Ringe, S.H., 'A Gentile Woman's Story', in L.M. Russell (ed.), *Feminist Interpretation of the Bible* (Philadelphia: Westminster Press, 1985), pp. 65-72.

—*Jesus, Liberation, and the Biblical Jubilee: Images for Ethics and Christology* (Philadelphia: Fortress Press, 1985).

Ringe, S.H., and F.C. Tiffany, *Biblical Interpretation: A Road Map* (Nashville: Abingdon Press, 1996).

Robbins, V.K., *Jesus the Teacher: A Socio-Rhetorical Interpretation of Mark* (Minneapolis: Fortress Press, 1992).

—*Patterns of Persuasion in the Gospels* (Sonoma, CA: Polebridge Press, 1989).

—'The Reversed Contextualization of Psalm 22 in the Markan Crucifixion: A Socio-Rhetorical Analysis', in Frans Van Segbroek *et al.* (eds.), *The Four Gospels: Festschrift Frans Neirynck* (3 vols.; Leuven: Leuven University Press; Uitgeverij Peeters, 1992), II, pp. 1161-83.

Rohrbaugh, R. (ed.), *The Social Sciences and New Testament Interpretation* (Peabody, MA: Hendrickson, 1996).

Rosaldo, M.Z., 'The Use and Abuse of Anthropology: Reflections on Feminism and Cross-Cultural Understanding', *Signs* 5 (1980), pp. 389-417.

—'Woman, Culture, and Society: A Theoretical Overview', in Rosaldo and Lamphere (eds.), *Woman, Culture, and Society*, pp. 17-42.

Rosaldo, M.Z., and L. Lamphere (eds.), *Women, Culture and Society* (Stanford, CA: Stanford University Press, 1974).

Rosenblatt, M.E., 'Gender, Ethnicity, and Legal Considerations in the Haemorrhaging Woman's Story: Mark 5:25-34', in Kitzberger (ed.), *Transformative Encounters*, pp. 137-61.

Rösler, W., 'Mnemosyne in the Symposion', in Murray (ed.), *Sympotica*, pp. 230-37.

Rostovtzeff, M.I., and C.B. Welles, 'A Parchment Contract of Loan from Dura-

Europus on the Euphrates', in A. Harmon (ed.), *Yale Classical Studies*, II (New Haven: Yale University Press, 1931), pp. 3-78.

Russell, L., E.S. Fiorenza, S. Ringe and J. Dewey (eds.), *The Liberating Word: A Guide to Nonsexist Interpretation of the Bible* (Philadelphia: Westminster Press, 1976).

Sacks, K., *Sisters and Wives: The Past and Future of Sexual Equality* (Westport, CT: Greenwood Press, 1979).

— 'Toward a Unified Theory of Class, Race, and Gender', *American Ethnologist* 16 (1988), pp. 534-50.

Sakenfeld, K.D., and S.H. Ringe (eds.), *Reading the Bible as Women: Perspectives From Africa, Asia, and Latin America* (Semeia, 78; Atlanta: Scholars Press, 1997).

Saldarini, A.J., *Pharisees, Scribes and Sadducees in Palestinian Society: A Sociological Approach* (Wilmington, DE: Michael Glazier, 1988).

— 'Political and Social Roles of the Pharisees and Scribes in Galilee', in D.J. Lull (ed.), (SBLSP; Atlanta: Scholars Press, 1988), pp. 200-209.

— 'The Social Class of the Pharisees in Mark', in J. Neusner *et al.*, (eds.), *The Social World of Formative Christianity and Judaism: Essays in Tribute to Howard Clark Kee* (Philadelphia: Fortress Press, 1988), pp. 69-77.

Samartha, S.J., *One Christ, Many Religions: Toward a Revised Christology* (Maryknoll, NY: Orbis Books, 1991).

Sanders, E.P., *The Historical Figure of Jesus* (Harmondsworth: Penguin Books, 1993).

— 'Jesus and the Sinners', *JSNT* 19 (1983), pp. 5-36.

Schaberg, J., *The Illegitimacy of Jesus: A Feminist Theological Interpretation of the Infancy Narratives* (New York: Harper & Row, 1987).

— 'The Infancy of Mary of Nazareth', in Fiorenza, (ed.), *Searching the Scriptures*, II, pp. 708-27.

— 'Luke', in Newsom and Ringe (eds.), *The Women's Bible Commentary*.

Schaps, D., 'The Women Least Mentioned: Etiquette and Women's Names', *CQ* 27 (1977), pp. 323-30.

Schierling, M.J., 'Women as Leaders in the Markan Community', *Listening* 15 (1980), pp. 250-56.

Schmidt, J.J., 'Women in Mark's Gospel: An Early Christian View of Women's Role', *Bible Today* 19 (1981), pp. 228-33.

Schnackenburg, R., *The Gospel According to John*, III (New York: Crossroad, 1982).

Schneider, J., 'Of Vigilance and Virgins', *Ethnology* 9 (1971), pp. 1-24.

Schottroff, L., *Let the Oppressed Go Free: Feminist Perspectives on the New Testament* (Louisville, KY: Westminster/John Knox Press, 1993).

— *Lydia's Impatient Sisters: A Social History of Early Christianity* (trans. B. and M. Rumscheidt; Louisville, KY: Westminster/John Knox Press, 1995).

— 'Maria Magdalena und die Frauen am Grabe Jesu', *EvT* 42 (1982), pp. 3-25.

— 'Women as Followers of Jesus in New Testament Times: Exercise in Social-Historical Exegesis of the Bible', in N.K. Gottwald (ed.), *The Bible and Liberation: Politics and Social Hermeneutics* (Maryknoll, NY: Orbis Books, 1983), pp. 418-27.

Schottroff, L., and W. Stegemann, *Jesus the Hope of the Poor* (trans. M.J. O'Connell; Maryknoll, NY: Orbis Books, 1986).

Schweizer, E., *Das Evangelium nach Markus* (Japanese edn; Tokyo: NTD, 1976).

— *The Good News According to Matthew* (trans. D.E. Green; Atlanta: John Knox Press, 1975).

Scott, J.C., *Domination and the Arts of Resistance: Hidden Transcripts* (New Haven: Yale University Press, 1990).

—*Weapons of the Weak: Everyday Forms of Peasant Resistance* (New Haven: Yale University Press, 1985).

Scott, J.W., *Gender and the Politics of History* (New York: Columbia University Press, 1988).

Segovia, F.F., and M.A. Tolbert (eds.), *Reading from This Place*. I. *Social Location and Biblical Interpretation in the United States* (Minneapolis: Fortress Press, 1995).

—*Reading from This Place*. II. *Social Location and Biblical Perspective* (Minneapolis: Fortress Press, 1995).

Seim, T.K., *The Double Message: Patterns of Gender in Luke-Acts* (Nashville: Abingdon Press, 1994).

—'The Gospel of Luke', in Fiorenza (ed.), *Searching the Scriptures*, II, pp. 728-62.

Selvidge, M.J., 'And Those Who Followed Feared (Mk. 10:32)', *CBQ* 45 (1983), pp. 396-400.

—*Woman, Cult and Miracle Recital: A Redactional Critical Investigation of Mark 5:24-34* (Lewisburg, PA: Bucknell University Press, 1990).

Sered, S.S., *Women as Ritual Experts: The Religious Lives of Elderly Jewish Women in Jerusalem* (New York: Oxford University Press, 1992).

Sibeko, M., and B. Haddad, 'Reading the Bible "with" Women in Poor and Marginalized Communities in South Africa (Mark 5:21–6:1)', *Semeia* 78 (1997), pp. 83-92.

Sim, D.C., 'What about the Wives and Children of the Disciples?: The Cost of Discipleship from Another Perspective', *HeyJ* 35 (1994), pp. 373-90.

—'The Women Followers of Jesus: The Implications of Luke 8:1-3', *HeyJ* 30 (1989), pp. 51-62.

Simon, L., 'Le sou de la veuve: Marc 12/41-44', *ETR* 44 (1969), pp. 115-26.

Slater, W.J. (ed.), *Dining in a Classical Context* (Ann Arbor, MI: University of Michigan Press, 1991).

Smith, Dennis E., 'Table Fellowship and the Historical Jesus', in L. Bormann, *et al.* (eds.) *Religious Propaganda and Missionary Competition in the New Testament World: Essays Honoring Dieter Georgi* (Leiden: E.J. Brill, 1994).

—'The Historical Jesus at the Table', in David Lull (ed.) (SBLSP; Atlanta: Scholars Press, 1989), pp. 475-76.

—'Table Fellowship as a Literary Motif in the Gospel of Luke', *JBL* 106 (1987), pp. 613-38.

Smith, Dorothy E., *The Everyday World as Problematic: A Feminist Sociology* (Evanston, IL: Northeastern University Press, 1987).

Smith, J.Z., *Map is Not Territory: Studies in the History of Religions* (Leiden: E.J. Brill, 1978).

Solodukho, Y.A., 'Slavery in the Hebrew Society of Iraq and Syria in the Second through Fifth Centuries A.D.', in J. Neusner (ed.), *Soviet Views of Talmudic Judaism* (Leiden: E.J. Brill, 1973), pp. 1-9.

Sourvinou-Inwood, C., *'Reading' Greek Culture: Texts and images, Rituals and Myths* (Oxford: Clarendon Press, 1991).

Sparkes, B., 'The Greek Kitchen', *JHS* 82 (1962), pp. 121-37.

—'Not Cooking, But Baking', *Greece and Rome* 28 (1981), pp. 172-78.

Spelman, E.V., *Inessential Woman: Problems of Exclusion in Feminist Thought* (Boston, MA: Beacon Press, 1988).

Stambaugh, J.E., *The Ancient Roman City* (Baltimore: The Johns Hopkins University Press, 1988.)

Stemberger, G., *Jewish Contemporaries of Jesus: Pharisees, Sadducees, Essenes* (trans. A.W. Mahnke; Minneapolis: Fortress Press, 1995).

Stern, E. (ed.), *The New Encyclopedia of Archaeological Excavations in the Holy Land* (4 vols.; New York: Simon & Schuster, 1993).

Swete, H.B., *Commentary on Mark* (Grand Rapids: Kregel, 1977).

Swidler, L., *Biblical Affirmations of Women* (Philadelphia: Westminster Press, 1979).

Tannehill, R., 'The Disciples in Mark: The Function of a Narrative Role', in W. Telford (ed.), *The Interpretation of Mark* (Philadelphia: Fortress Press, 1985).

—'The Disciples in Mark: The Function of a Narrative Role', *JR* 57 (1977), pp. 386-405.

Taylor, V., *The Gospel According to St. Mark* (London: Macmillan, 1952).

—*The Gospel According to St. Mark* (London: Macmillan; New York: St. Martin's Press, 1966).

—*The Gospel According to St. Mark* (repr.; Grand Rapids: Baker Book House, 2nd edn, 1981).

Tecusan, M., 'Logos-Sympotikos: Patterns of the Irrational in Philosophical Drinking: Plato Outside the Symposium', in Murray (ed.), *Sympotica*, pp. 238-60.

Tetlow, E.M., *Women and Ministry in the New Testament: Called to Serve* (Lanham, MD: University Press of America, 1985).

Theissen, G., *The Gospels in Context: Social and Political History in the Synoptic Tradition* (trans. L.M. Maloney; Minneapolis: Fortress Press, 1991).

—*The Miracle Stories of the Early Christian Tradition* (trans. F. McDonagh; Philadelphia: Fortress Press, 1983).

Thurston, B.B., *The Widows: A Women's Ministry in the Early Church* (Minneapolis: Fortress Press, 1989).

Tiffany, F.C., and S.H. Ringe, *Biblical Interpretation: A Road Map* (Nashville: Abingdon Press, 1996).

Tilley, L., 'The Social and the Study of Women', *Comparative Studies in Society and History* 20 (1978), pp. 163-73.

Tolbert, M.A., 'Defining the Problem: The Bible and Feminist Hermeneutics', *Semeia* 28 (1983).

—'Mark', in Newsome and Ringe (eds.), *The Woman's Bible Commentary*, pp. 263-74.

—'Protestant Feminist Hermeneutics and the Bible: On the Horns of a Dilemma', in A. Bach (ed.), *The Pleasure of her Text: Feminist Readings of Biblical and Historical Texts* (Philadelphia: Trinity Press International, 1990), pp. 5-23.

—*Sowing The Gospel: Mark's World in Literary-Historical Perspective* (Minneapolis: Fortress Press, 1989).

Trautman, C., 'Salomè l'incrèdule: rècits d'une conversion', in *Ecritures et traditions dans la littèrature copte: Journée d'études coptes, Strasbourg, 29 mai 1982* (Cahiers de la bibliothèque copte, 1; Louvain: Peeters, 1983), pp. 61-72.

Tringham, R.E., 'Households with Faces: The Challenge of Gender in Prehistoric Architectural Remains', in Gero and Conkey (eds.), *Engendering Archaeology*, pp. 93-131.

Trocmé, E., 'Is There a Markan Christology?', in B. Lindars and S.S. Smalley (eds.), *Christ and the Spirit in the New Testament: Festschrift for Charles Francis Digby Moule* (Cambridge: Cambridge University Press, 1973), pp. 3-13.

Tuana, N., *The Less Noble Sex: Scientific, Religious, and Philosophical Conceptions of Woman's Nature* (Bloomington: Indiana University Press, 1993).

Urbach, E.E., 'The Laws Regarding Slavery as a Source for Social History of the Period of the Second Temple, the Mishnah and the Talmud', in J.G. Weiss (ed.), *Papers of the Institute of Jewish Studies (London)*, I (Jerusalem: Magnes Press, 1964), pp. 1-94.

Van Bremen, R., 'Women and Wealth', in Cameron and Kuhrt (eds.), *Images of Women in Antiquity*, pp. 223-42.

Van der Ploeg, J.P.M., 'Slavery in the Old Testament', VTSup 22 (1971), pp. 72-87.

Van Iersel, B., *Mark: A Reader-Response Commentary* (trans. W.H. Bisscheroux; JSNTSup, 164; Sheffield: Sheffield Academic Press, 1998).

Vernant, P., 'At Man's Table: Hesiod's Foundation Myth of Sacrifice', in M. Detienne and J.-P. Vernant, *The Cuisine of Sacrifice among the Greeks* (trans. P. Wissing; Chicago: University of Chicago Press, 1986), pp. 21-86.

Veyne, P. (ed.), *A History of Private Life: From Pagan Rome to Byzantium*, I (Cambridge, MA: Belknap Press, 1987).

Waetjen, H.C., *A Reordering of Power: A Sociopolitical Reading of Mark's Gospel* (Minneapolis: Fortress Press, 1989).

Wainwright, E., *Towards a Feminist Critical Reading of the Gospel According to Matthew* (BZNW, 60; Berlin: W. de Gruyter, 1991).

—'A Voice from the Margin: Reading Matthew 15:21-28 in an Australian Feminist Key', in Segovia and Tolbert (eds.), *Reading from this Place*, II, pp. 132-53.

Walker, S., 'Women and Housing in Classical Greece: The Archaelogical Evidence', in Cameron and Kuhrt (eds.), *Images of Women in Antiquity*, pp. 81-91.

Walker, W.O., 'Jesus and the Tax-Collectors', *JBL* 97 (1978), pp. 221-38.

Weeden, T., 'The Heresy That Necessitated Mark's Gospel', *ZNW* 59 (1968), pp. 143-53.

—*Mark: Traditions in Conflict* (Philadelphia: Fortress Press, 1971).

Westermann, W.L., *The Slave Systems of Greek and Roman Antiquity* (Philadelphia: American Philosophical Society, 1933).

Wilcox, M. '"Talitha Koum(i)" in Mark 5,41', in J. Delobel (ed.), *Logia* (BETL, 59; Leuven: Leuven University Press, 1982), pp. 469-76.

Williams, D., 'Women on Athenian Vases: Problems of Interpretation', in Cameron and Kuhrt (eds.), *Images of Women in Antiquity*, pp. 92-106.

Williams, D.S., 'Black Women's Surrogacy Experience and the Christian Notion of Redemption', in P.M. Cooey *et al.* (eds.), *After Patriarchy: Feminist Transformations of the World Religions* (Maryknoll, NY: Orbis Books, 1991), pp. 1-14.

Wire, A.C., 'The Structure of the Gospel Miracle Stories and Their Tellers', *Semeia* 11 (1978), pp. 83-113.

Witherington, B., 'On the Road with Mary Magdalene, Joanna, and Other Disciples—Luke 8.1-3', *ZNW* 70 (1979), pp. 243-48.

—*Women in the Ministry of Jesus: A Study of Jesus' Attitudes to Women and their Roles as Reflected in his Earthly Life* (SNTSMS, 51; Cambridge: Cambridge University Press, 1984).

Wright, A.G., 'The Widow's Mites: Praise or Lament? – A Matter of Context', *CBQ* 44 (1982), pp. 256-65.

Wylie, A., 'Gender Theory and the Archaeological Record: Why Is There No Archaeology of Gender?', in Gero and Conkey (eds.), *Engendering Archaelogy*, pp. 38-41.

Yamaguchi, S., 'Re-Visioning Martha and Mary: A Feminist Critical Reading of a Text in the Fourth Gospel' (DMin thesis, Episcopal Divinity School, 1996).

Zeitlin, S., 'Slavery during the Second Commonwealth and the Tannaitic Period', in *Studies in the Early History of Judaism, History of Early Talmudic Law* (New York: Ktav, 1978), pp. 225-69.

Zlotnick, D., *The Tractate 'Mourning' (Semahot): Regulations Relating to Death, Burial, and Mourning* (Yale Judaica Series, 27; New Haven: Yale University Press, 1966).

INDEXES

INDEX OF REFERENCES

OLD TESTAMENT

NEW TESTAMENT

INDEX OF AUTHORS